REACHING INNER CITY STUDENTS THROUGH THE POWER OF WRITING

Stephen O'Connor

SIMON & SCHUSTER

NEW YORK LONDON

TORONTO SYDNEY

TOKYO SINGAPORE

Will My

Name Be

Shouted

Out?

SIMON & SCHUSTER
ROCKEFELLER CENTER
1230 AVENUE OF THE AMERICAS
NEW YORK, NY 10020

SIMON & SCHUSTER AND COLOPHON ARE REGISTERED TRADEMARKS
OF SIMON & SCHUSTER INC.

DESIGNED BY BARBARA M. BACHMAN
MANUFACTURED IN THE UNITED STATES OF AMERICA

1   3   5   7   9   10   8   6   4   2

LIBRARY OF CONGRESS CATALOGING-IN-PUBLICATION DATA
O'CONNOR, STEPHEN.
WILL MY NAME BE SHOUTED OUT? : REACHING INNER CITY
STUDENTS THROUGH THE POWER OF WRITING /
STEPHEN O'CONNOR.
P.   CM.
1. ENGLISH LANGUAGE—COMPOSITION AND EXERCISES—STUDY AND
TEACHING (SECONDARY)—NEW YORK (N.Y.)—CASE STUDIES.
2. URBAN EDUCATION—NEW YORK (N.Y.)—CASE STUDIES.
3. JUNIOR HIGH SCHOOL STUDENTS—NEW YORK (N.Y.)—
ATTITUDES—CASE STUDIES. 4. JUNIOR HIGH SCHOOL STUDENTS—
NEW YORK (N.Y.)—SOCIAL CONDITIONS—CASE STUDIES. I. TITLE.
LB1631.036   1996
808'.042'0712—DC20   95-26536 CIP
ISBN 0-684-81186-3

THE PUBLISHERS GRATEFULLY ACKNOWLEDGE PERMISSION TO
REPRINT THE FOLLOWING PREVIOUSLY PUBLISHED MATERIAL:
HAIKU BY RYOTA, TRANSLATED BY KENNETH REXROTH, FROM *ONE
HUNDRED POEMS FROM THE JAPANESE;* REPRINTED BY PERMISSION OF
NEW DIRECTIONS PUBLISHING CORP.
"I AM NEW YORK CITY," FROM *COAGULATIONS: NEW AND SELECTED
POEMS* BY JAYNE CORTEZ. COPYRIGHT © 1983 BY JAYNE CORTEZ;
USED BY PERMISSION OF THUNDER'S MOUTH PRESS.

THIS BOOK IS DEDICATED TO:

Xia, Celeste, Yvette, Mayra, Ricky, Tarika, Shanequa, Diana, Hernan, Isaac, Cullen, Natalie, Yolanda, José, Arlene, Anna, Lily, Keisha, Tunisia, Chantell, Julie, and to all of my students at the Walt Whitman Academy;

TO:

Daniel Judah Sklar and Mayra Fernandez,
who constantly inspire me with their compassion and intelligence;

AND, FINALLY, TO:

John O'Connor and Alix Euwer, my first and best teachers;
Simon and Emma, for being so patient with their busy dad;
and most of all to Helen Benedict, my first editor and soul mate, who has given so much to this book, including the time to write it and live it;

WITH SPECIAL THANKS TO:

Pearl Wiener, Roberta Kirshbaum, Gil Turchin, Shelly Alpert, Kim Witherspoon, Bob Bender, Johanna Li, Katha Pollitt, Matt Sharpe, Jessica Sager, Erin Donovan, Siobhan Reagan, Elizabeth Shepard, Jenifer Polatsek, Fred Glover, Nancy Larson Shapiro, Elizabeth Fox, Simon Kilmurry, Jill Jackson, Ron and Pat Padgett, Gary Lenhart, Chris Edgar, Bruce Morrow, Geoffrey O'Connor, Chris Carras, Ted Haimes, Paul Attewell, Katherine Newman, Rob Cohen, Philip Graham, and Kenneth Koch.

Contents

When I die, will I be thought about?
Will my name be shouted out?

—From a poem written by Ian Moore, one of two boys killed
at Thomas Jefferson High School in Brooklyn,
on February 26, 1992.

Introduction

THIS IS THE STORY OF A GROUP OF NEW YORK CITY JUNIOR high school students with whom I worked closely over two school years. They inspired, infuriated, saddened, and surprised me with their talent, their courage, and their deep troubles. There were times when I cared about them almost as much as my own children and moments when we all felt that something miraculous had happened between us. But after two years they were graduated and went on to high school, to the rest of their lives, and I lost touch with them. I like to think that through the work we did together these students learned some truths about themselves and their world and that these truths helped them become happier, better people, but I will probably never know.

In many ways this is a story of limits—limits set by race, class, understanding, and strength; limits that lose none of their implacability even as they are transcended. Xia, Ricky, Yvette, Celeste, José, and all of their classmates at the Walt Whitman Academy were twelve, thirteen, and fourteen when I knew them, children on the verge of a very hard adulthood, children just about to enter what statistically would be the most dangerous time of their lives, the time when they would be most likely to become criminals or victims, when they would be most likely to make big mistakes that they might never outgrow.

These children were born at the start of the AIDS epidemic. During their toddler years, crack replaced heroin as the drug of choice in the ghetto, bringing with it a huge surge of gun deaths, especially among teenagers. Between 1985 and 1991, the number of teenagers murdered doubled nationally, while over almost the same period, murders committed by juveniles shot up 124 percent. The number of teenagers prosecuted in New York City for possession of a loaded firearm jumped from 103 in 1986 to 750 in 1992. Because crack addicted almost as many females as males, it dealt a terrible blow to an already fragile family structure. Between 1987 and 1991, the number of American children entering foster care rose by more than 50 percent. During these same years, one in four children was born into a single-parent household, and the same proportion were living in poverty. The adolescent pregnancy rate also continued its steady rise, with more teenagers having babies in the United States than in almost any other country in the developed world.

My students were both intimately acquainted with and oblivious to the social turmoil in which they lived. They were often terribly afraid of the prospects ahead of them and, at the very same time, convinced of their invulnerability, assured that in a decade's time they would be famous lawyers, doctors, rappers, or basketball players, with mansions in Beverly Hills and two BMWs in the garage. I have never had a student describe him- or herself as anything other than middle class, even though sociologists would label the vast majority of them working class or poor. While all of my students think of racism as one of the great evils of contemporary life, and while many of them tell stories of not being served in stores or of being assumed to be thieves simply because of their skin color, and even while many of them suffer from an extreme lack of confidence that is clearly a heritage of racism and slavery, I have never heard a student admit that racism might limit his or her particular opportunities in life to the slightest degree. Sometimes I admire my students' optimism and gumption. Sometimes I shake my head at their innocence—and at the terrifying and tragic experiences they report as if they were merely average events of a normal life.

I came to my students as a teacher, not a reporter. During the two years that are the subject of this book, however, I did keep a detailed diary. Initially it was just a forum for working out and evaluating my lessons. But as I became increasingly excited about my work, my diary entries became more and more extensive, often including transcriptions of classroom discussions and conversations with students or teachers. As I began to work more closely with individual students, my diary quite naturally came to focus on our interactions and my students' life stories.

I am telling their stories now because I think that they provide compelling insights into the true nature of the crisis in American schools and the cost to our country and to its children of our political leaders' ever more cynical abandonment of the poor and the working class. I want to tell these stories exactly as I experienced them. I don't want to hold back any of the important details. I want my reader to know that real children have thought, acted, suffered, and rejoiced just as I describe. This means telling things about my students that even some of their friends don't know. It also means placing them in categories in which they would never place themselves.

At the end of my story, some of my students will seem headed for miserable fates—fates that a couple, at least, will not even have begun to recognize. I don't think that anyone at age thirteen should feel that his or her destiny is sealed, and I hope that none of my students suffer the misery that seems to await them. But I would be lying if I did not represent the grave dangers faced by all of my students, even by the ones who seemed miraculously, heroically to be rising above their troubles.

So, to any student who recognizes herself or himself in this book, I am sorry if anything I say hurts you. I hope you know that I have faith in all of you, even if at times I have been very worried about you. And I hope you understand that with this book I am only trying to do what I said in class was the goal of all our writing, to make the world we live in a wiser, kinder, and better place.

While everything that I am about to describe happened, to the best of my knowledge, as I say it did, I have, out of a desire to protect the privacy of my students, left the location of the school vague, changed its name and the names of all the students and teachers. Also, except for those details that affect their social position (generally age, sex, and ethnicity), I have changed my students' physical descriptions. The only people whose names haven't been changed are the creative writing and drama teachers who were my colleagues at the junior high. It simply wouldn't have been fair for me to have taken the credit for what was very much a team effort.

All of the poems, stories, and plays are reproduced either from my teaching diary or from photocopies of the students' original work. Close to half of the conversations quoted in this book are also lifted straight from my teaching diary. An equal proportion are extrapolations from synopses of conversations in the diary. Only very rarely did I reconstruct conversations or scenes solely from my memory and knowledge of the people involved, and then only to make my narrative more true to the experiences it recounts. No significant details have been invented. There are no composite characters. Everything that matters in this book actually happened to real children.

PART ONE

Innocence and Guilt

1

I Wish My Life Will Be Good

WHEN I WALKED INTO MY FIRST CLASS AT P.S. 313 IN CENTRAL Harlem in February 1988, two boys were running across the tops of the desks. The one in the lead, trying to make too sharp a turn, knocked a desk over and sprawled onto the floor in front of the windows. His pursuer jumped on top of him. On the opposite side of the room, a group of girls were leaping after a bounding Superball. Against the back wall, a boy lay on the bookshelf, fast asleep in his winter jacket. More boys and girls sat on the radiators, playing with action figures, talking. Alone at the front of the room, beside the vacant teacher's desk, three girls huddled forlornly over their open textbooks.

I had been escorted to the classroom by Mrs. Flanagan, the school's Bronx Irish assistant principal, who had explained to me that this class had not had a regular teacher in five months. Their original teacher had fallen sick in September, and ever since, the students had been in the care of a series of substitutes. I was to be the writer in residence at P.S. 313—a "treat for the students" was what Mrs. Flanagan called me. My job was to teach creative writing to this class and three others once a week for twenty weeks.

Just at the moment that Mrs. Flanagan and I opened the door, the current substitute, a middle-aged African American man, had been flapping a newspaper in the air and pleading with the two boys to get down off the desks. Mrs. Flanagan strode past him as if he were merely another student. Taking a position at the front of the room, she shouted at the class: "You should be ashamed of yourselves! Is this any way for fourth-graders to behave? I was about to offer you the privilege of working with Mr. O'Connor, a fine writer who has come to this school to teach you how to write poetry—but maybe you don't deserve to have Mr. O'Connor! Maybe I should tell Mr. O'Connor to go to another class and keep you all upstairs for lunch today!"

She went on in this vein for another minute or two, eventually inducing the students to put away their toys and return to their desks—though neither she nor anyone else paid the slightest attention to the boy sleeping on the bookshelves. "You let me know how they behave," she instructed me as she left the classroom.

No sooner had the door closed behind her than the Superball resumed its crazy bounding, pursued by a good third of the class. I looked to the substitute for help, but he just shrugged as he rocked back in a chair by the door and lifted his newspaper. I was on my own.

I turned to the class and said, "Hey, listen, we're gonna have a whole lot of fun, but you've got to quiet down. All right? Just quiet down and we'll have a real good time! *I mean it!*"

I got one curious glance, a couple of mocking ones—and that was all. As far as most of the students were concerned, I might not even have existed. I made a few more attempts to gain control of the class and finally hunkered down with the three girls beside the vacant teacher's desk, thinking that they, at least, might welcome an escape into the pleasures of poetry.

They followed my instructions, but joylessly and without showing the slightest sign of the fresh, playful imagination I had always considered ubiquitous in children. The problem, I realized afterward, was that what they wanted was a rescuer, someone to quell the chaos that assailed them from every side. Sadly, I had already shown them that I was not their man.

In my next class, another fourth grade, the young white teacher bullied his solidly African American students into submission by bellowing at them constantly that they were rude, lazy, and stupid. Here too there were sleepers. One boy's eyes rolled when he spoke, and his words came out slurred, as if he were deeply drunk or drugged. Here too the joyless poetry and disappointment.

I was to take six students from my third class, a combined fifth-and-sixth grade, to the library for a special playwriting workshop. But when the teacher (another young white man) called off the names of the students he had selected, three of them (all girls) ran into the coat closets and pulled the doors shut. As the teacher attempted to drag the kicking and cursing students out of the closets, I protested: "Nobody has to come. It's entirely voluntary!"

"Don't worry," he said. "They're just playing. They really want to come."

As far as I could see, the only thing these girls wanted to do was humiliate their teacher—and they succeeded. Red faced and panting after a prolonged struggle, he finally told them they could stay in the closet all day as far as he cared. Then, turning to the three other students, who had been waiting patiently by the door, he said, "What are you doing here! Didn't I tell you to go down to the library!"

The three students (two girls and a boy) took his outburst with equanimity. As we walked down the hall, one of them explained to me that she wrote poems and plays at home, and I began to think that, at last, one of my classes might actually run according to my expectations. But no sooner had we taken our seats around one of the big library tables than we were interrupted by frantic shrieks from the playground. In an instant all three children had leapt up onto a bookshelf so that they could peer through the narrow strip of windows (air vents, really) running just below the ceiling. "Oh, look!" one of the students shouted. "A girl got bit by a dog! A girl got bit by a wild dog!" When I joined my students at the window I saw a little girl, maybe seven years old, writhing on the ground, blood all over her leg, and the loudmouthed teacher from my second class down on his knees, both hands in a stranglehold around the dog's throat, just below its snapping jaws.

THIS WAS THE FIRST DAY OF ONE OF MY EARLIEST RESIDENCIES with Teachers & Writers Collaborative, an organization that has been sending writers and other artists into New York City schools since 1967. I would like to say that it was the awful opening chapter to a success story, but that would be a sad overstatement, at least as far as the children at P.S. 313 are concerned. It is true that I never had another day quite as bad as this, in part because Mrs. Flanagan substituted a more controlled class for that first one. It is also true that I ultimately established solid relationships with several of the children who joined my playwriting workshop, and I discovered many beautiful images and insights in writing from students in all of my classes. One class would even cheer when I came into the room, and leap out of their chairs to hug me when I had to leave. But no matter how many victories I may have had, no matter how strong the poems in the photocopied anthology I put together at the residency's conclusion, there was simply too much wrong with the school and in the lives of my students for me ever to remember my time there without thinking of all the things I could and should have done better.

Although I didn't know it at the time, P.S. 313 had a reputation as one of the catastrophes of the New York City educational system. Every year its reading scores ranked second- or third-lowest of the city's more than 600 public elementary schools. Whenever I tell veteran teachers that I taught there, they raise their eyebrows and say things like, "That school is a nightmare! How could you stand it?"

The school had always been rough, but it became decidedly worse when its principal of twenty years died suddenly in 1985, three years before my residency. His successor didn't last a year. Thereafter P.S. 313 was run by a series of reluctant Board of Education bureaucrats who did little more than hide out in the principal's office, leaving management of the school to Mrs. Flanagan, the assistant principal. This power vacuum at the top meant that the teachers got no support. They felt utterly abandoned at the front of their classrooms, trying to do the impossible for their impossibly needy students. I have met several teachers who told me that they started their careers at P.S. 313 and got out as soon as they could. Indeed, I saw this pattern in action during my tenure. The only really good teacher I worked with there told me that she was leaving at the end of the year. She didn't have another job lined up, but she said she would go crazy if she had to come back.

Low teacher morale and a lack of administration made for only part of the problem—the smaller part. As in many other inner-city and rural schools, the most formidable enemies of education at P.S. 313 were the hopelessness and alienation induced by endemic poverty and a long history of racism.

Virtually all of the students were black, and the vast majority of them were poor. Many of my students were homeless, living in welfare hotels (a great shame, never to be mentioned in class). Most of them lived with only one adult, usually a mother or a grandmother. Most of them had to walk to school along streets of charred, gutted buildings or past stoops tenanted by nodding junkies and hyped-up crack addicts. All of them had seen gun and knife fights. Every day I heard another story about someone getting shot on the block or arrested. Many of my students had been threatened with guns or knives. And every single one of them had lost a brother, sister, mother, father, grandparent, or cousin to violence, drugs, or jail. The only sources of medical care for most of my students were hospital emergency rooms or overcrowded clinics, where they often waited hours to see a doctor and rarely saw the same doctor twice. The result was that many of them came to school with fevers, or oozing, untreated skin conditions, or in hypoglycemic stupors.

One day I came into a fourth-grade class to find one of my favorite students lying on a rug and moaning at the back of the room. When I asked the teacher what was the matter, she told me that the girl's father routinely abused her sexually and that she wasn't "feeling very well" that day, so was excused from class. Another time, when I had asked my students to write letters explaining life on earth to the children they would one day have, one of my very best writers, a bright, extremely sensitive fourth-grade boy, wrote, "Dear Son, The only thing you got to do is find yourself a good woman and bloody her face every day, 'cause that's the only thing women understand."

I couldn't give a writing assignment that didn't produce dozens of images or statements revealing the bleak experience and outlook of my students. Yes, they also wrote poems and stories in which they talked about how smart, strong, brave, and happy they were. But there was so much misery, so much anger, so much fear even in the happy compositions.

Just glancing over the anthology (which includes only the most *presentable* student works) and the few other pieces of writing I have preserved from that residency, I find the following:

I hear rats in the back yard. I hear them raggle in the garbage and look for food. I hear people scream and talking.

When I was coming home from school there was this man following me home. I was scared. But I got back to my building and he saw all the boys I know, he left.

When I was going to school I saw a fat man and I said, "Why don't you lose some weight?" And he said, "Mind your own business!" And I said, "Do not be eating bad meals, because . . ." And he said, "If you want me to get bad, I will."

I can stay in school, but I can't be so good.

A lady was walking down the street and a tree said, "Hey lady, I love you, baby. Give me a kiss." . . . I saw two trees and one of the trees was sitting in a chair and the other was saying, "I am bad, I am bad, you know. So leave me alone blue birds!"

Oh Maine blue gain don't kill me.

Letter to an Unborn Child

The best thing is art and the worst thing is crack, cause it will crack up your mind. But don't do crack. But my baby will not smoke no crack and my son will learn lots of things.

I can take a flame thrower and fry you to pork chops. I can take a rocket launcher and make it give you a hair cut. I can take an M-16 and kill you. But I can't be innocent. I can go to the zoo, but I can't live with the monkeys. I can go to Africa and dance with the people, but I can't leave. I can make my teeth turn into piano keys, but I can't eat with them. I can take a 45 and shoot you, but I got to go to jail.

One day I went over to the store and I saw a man sleeping outside. And when I come up he was awake. And his pants was rolled up past his knees. And then he was scratching his legs. And then I went home. And then when I came back he was drinking beer. I saw a fly on his leg. And he did not have his coat.

One day I wish I have money. I seen a bum. The lady was looking inside the garbage. I treated the lady to dinner. I gave the lady five dollars. I said, "What is you going to do with the five dollars?" She said, "I am going to go to Third Avenue to see if they got $1.99

shirts and some underclothes." I gave it to her. She left. She had rag bum clothes on. And she smell fishy.

I can tell you I hate you but I can't tell you I love you . . . I can die, but I can't live.

At the end of every class I would either ask the students to read aloud what they had written or, if they were too shy, read it myself. Several times during each reading session I would come across material like the above that would cry for a response entirely different from what I was expected or prepared to give. I wanted to ask my students: "Did that really happen?" "Do you really feel that way?" I wanted to console an individual child or the whole class, telling them: "No, you are not bad. Of course you are angry! You have a right to be angry! But the world is not all evil. You can escape the evil if you work hard, if you believe in yourself. You really can. You don't have to end up like these bums and crack addicts and scary men." Every now and then I would venture such a consolation, but invariably I would lose confidence in it halfway through; my words would start to sound naive, simpleminded, and even cruel—insofar as they implied that my overwhelmed students were not doing enough to help themselves. Every now and then I would take a student aside for two minutes of sympathy and a pat on the back, but I suspect that, by and large, I was the only one who slept better on account of such gestures.

The truth is that there was nothing I could do to solve my students' enormous problems, certainly not as a writing teacher and not even if, as I often fantasized, I could somehow adopt the most troubled of these children and bring them into my own home, my safe white world. So I sought refuge in my job description. I acted as if all the anger, hopelessness, and fear that throbbed beneath the surface of my students' writing was somehow irrelevant to the writing itself or of only aesthetic significance. I praised my students for their sharpest images and wisest insights and tried to convince them (and myself) that something of importance really did depend on William Carlos Williams's famous red wheelbarrow glazed with rainwater.

Despite this retreat to professionalism, or perhaps because of it, a feeling of grim helplessness would rise in my guts every day as I stood at the front of the classroom, a feeling only made worse because I would have to spend a large portion of every class haranguing the students, telling them they were rude, reminding them that they had each worked hard on their compositions and deserved to be listened to. Sometimes I would get as furious as that teacher who tried to drag the three girls out of the closets. When a girl in the hallway tried to disrupt my class by pounding on the locked door and shouting obscenities through the crack, I kept thinking that there had to be a better way to deal with her than by shouting back at her with all of her own rage and even some of her vocabulary, but I was helpless before my own anger and my own despair.

Every day when I was finished teaching I would burst out the front door of the school thinking: "Thank God that's over! Thank God I'm free! Thank God I wasn't born one of these kids!"

The same bright boy who advised his future son to bloody his woman's face wrote a piece that expresses so well the awful feeling that I and so many others—teachers, administrators, and students alike—felt at this school.

When I was a baby I used to have dreams about monsters in my back room and I used to get in my mother and father's room and hide by the dresser. I used to have these dreams most often. I be so scared and my mother and father and my brothers wouldn't be home. I just be watching TV and then I hear a funny noise. I be scared a lot of times. I be trying to go in the back room, but they scare me away. I'm mad that I had this dream and was so scared. I just wish that I wouldn't have these nightmares. I wish I will have beautiful dreams like I'm a baby with some other babies playing in the garden with lots of flowers. It is so nice to me when I have that dream. But I don't like the dream that I'm having . . . I'll be scared when I hear them funny noise and I see with my own eyes the ugly monsters. I wish my life will be good. I like doing good things, not bad things. I wish that it wasn't no monsters or nothing. I wish my life will be beautiful. I love being good, but I don't know why I am bad. I'm just bad because I see the things them monster be doing. I be scaring because I see what them monster be doing.

2

A Devil Eating the Glasses

DURING MY FINAL WEEK AT P.S. 313, NANCY LARSON SHAPIRO, the director of Teachers & Writers Collaborative, asked me if I would like to run the residency program at P.S. 227. I was so surprised that at first I was afraid to say yes. The residency at P.S. 227 was the longest-running, most extensive, and most innovative of all the Collaborative's programs—"our flagship," Nancy called it. I had been with T&W only a few months. Could Nancy really be offering so coveted a position?

Whereas most T&W writers visit a school only once a week for ten to twenty weeks, the writer in residence at P.S. 227 was not only a teacher but the director of a staff of up to six interns from Columbia University's graduate creative writing program. The residency at P.S. 227 had been established in 1971 and ran for most of the school year, serving every grade. Its first director had been Phillip Lopate, who made his years at the school the subject of *Being with Children,* one of the most influential books ever to come out of the Collaborative. Under Lopate's guidance (and during an era when, by today's standards, astronomical amounts of money flowed into both arts and educational programs), students at the school had staged a full-length production of Chekhov's *Uncle Vanya* at a local theater and had run a glossy literary magazine, a small press, and a radio station. Under Lopate's successor and my predecessor, Alan Ziegler, P.S. 227 students had, among many other celebrated accomplishments, written the script for an Emmy Award–winning CBS after-school special.

As a part of my training for Teachers & Writers, before being assigned any residencies of my own, I had observed Alan Ziegler at P.S. 227. Following him from class to class, listening in as he conferred with students and teachers, seeing how well liked he was and how integral the T&W program was to the school, I had been filled with a deep yearning for a job like his. It had seemed to me that there were no limits to what I could do in a school where I could spend so much time with the children, seeing them year after year, and where I would get so much support from the staff and parents. Thus, when Nancy told me that she needed a replacement for Alan, who was leaving P.S. 227 to head the creative writing division at Columbia's School of General Studies, the news seemed too good to be true.

I must confess that I felt some trepidation about whether I could live up to the standards set by Lopate and Ziegler. I was also concerned when Nancy told me that the Teachers & Writers program was expected to play a large role in making a success of the new junior high that the P.S. 227 principal was starting on the school's largely vacant third floor. Ever since joining the Collaborative, I had dreaded the day when I would be assigned to work with junior high school students, who were infamously uncooperative and self-absorbed. But if the P.S. 227 residency hadn't been challenging, I probably wouldn't have been interested. As soon as I understood that the job was really mine, I said I would take it. Nancy told me that I could think about it for a couple of days. But I told her I was sure. It was just the job I wanted.

On the first page of my first teaching diary on taking over the P.S. 227 residency, I wrote:

> I love this job. What I like most are the people I'm working with: savvy, slightly weary, committed, old-guard New York lefties. I've never been so involved in the community before. Through T&W I can make my craft matter in the real world, give it political and social importance, transcend writerly elitism and solitude.

The most interesting word in this passage is "make," at the beginning of the last sentence. I can still feel the subtle desperation with which I wrote it. In my mind it bore much of the meaning of "force," as if through my new job I was going to *force* writing to "matter," to have a "political and social importance" that I wasn't at all sure it could sustain. I was very happy as I made that first entry, but also worried that I was deceiving myself—that there was something fraudulent not only about teaching creative writing but about literature itself.

Such ambivalence is perhaps inescapable for any artist growing up in a country where the National Endowment for the Arts is widely thought of as welfare for perverts and snobs, but in my case it was very much a heritage of my time at P.S. 313, where the students' enormous problems often made the craft I was teaching them seem obscenely irrelevant. The day had come when I had at last burst out the front door of P.S. 313 and breathed a final sigh of relief, knowing I would never have to go back. But the moral and aesthetic challenges posed by my time at that school were not ones I could ever put behind me, certainly not at P.S. 227 or the Walt Whitman Academy, as the new junior high was to be called.

The blocks immediately surrounding the school were middle to upper-middle class, a neighborhood of lawyers, actors, scholars, and the occasional politician. These were the people I was working with during the first days of my residency. They were the ones who dominated the parents' association and who volunteered to work in classrooms and help out with special programs. White middle-class children like their own, however, were very much in the minority at the school. In the lower grades, the student body was about a third white, a third African American, a third Latino, with a smattering of Asians. After third grade, the white component dwindled until, in the Walt Whitman Academy, on average, only 4 out of the 132 seventh- and eighth-graders were non-Latino white. Everyone else was fairly equally divided between African Americans and Latinos.

Since the Walt Whitman Academy had no track record during my first years at the school, its students were mostly those who couldn't get into the district's more reputable junior high schools. Only a small portion of P.S. 227's sixth-grade students enrolled at Walt Whitman. "These kids are the dregs," one teacher told me as I was about to start my very first lesson at the school. "They've got no skills and big attitudes." While none of these students were anywhere near the dregs, they did tend to be much poorer than those at P.S. 227. As at P.S. 313, 90 percent of Walt Whitman students lived with only one adult, often a grandmother or aunt. Most of them weren't particularly interested in school. A few coasted through their days with the same listless or sullen expressions I had seen everywhere at P.S. 313, but none of them were about to climb up on the desks or shout obscenities from the hall, and none of them were so sick of life that all they could do was sleep. There were fights at the school, but usually not with weapons and never with guns. Not once during my seven years at Walt Whitman did I ever feel physically endangered by a student.

True to my initial reservations, however, it was in front of the Walt Whitman students that I most often felt a fraud. As in the lower grades, I would visit each of the junior high classes (two seventh and two eighth grades) once a week for forty-five minutes. With their regular language arts teacher present, I would spend the first ten minutes discussing a writing idea, then let the students write for twenty minutes. In striking contrast to the lower grades, however, there were many times when I would ask the class a question and not a single student would raise a hand, or when I'd make a joke only to be met with contemptuous silence. My students would write, often enthusiastically, but half the time all the bribes, threats, and cajolery I could muster were not enough to get them to come to the front of the classroom and read their compositions aloud. In most cases they would agree to the presentation of their works only if I read them aloud anonymously.

What I was dealing with here, largely, was normal adolescent self-consciousness, intensified by the fact that for these kids, out on the street, a failure to maintain a gruff, cool image could literally become a matter of life and death. But at the same time I was engaged in a very real struggle, if not with the shortcomings of literature itself, then with the way I was presenting it to my students.

I AM PRIMARILY A FICTION WRITER, BUT DURING MY FIRST THREE years at P.S. 227/Walt Whitman I taught my students mainly to write poetry, concentrating on the form or language of the poetry rather than its content. There was nothing particularly unusual about my approach. I had my own tricks, spiels, and writing ideas, but essentially I was only applying the standard writer-in-the-schools curriculum—a curriculum that had been fashioned largely by the earliest members of Teachers & Writers, especially by Kenneth Koch, whose books, *Wishes, Lies and Dreams* and *Rose, Where Did You Get That Red?* sparked a revolution in the way poetry was taught to schoolchildren during the 1970s. Koch's influence on me was particularly strong, since I had been his student as an undergraduate at Columbia. In fact, it was largely to do for other people what Kenneth Koch had done for me that I began to teach creative writing in the first place.

For the most part, Koch and the other pioneers of the writer-in-the-schools movement simply tried to inspire their students by showing them what they themselves found most fascinating about literature. Whatever their individual interests, however, these writers were inevitably influenced by their own education and by the literary fashions of their era. For much of this century, the hottest academic and avant garde theories have tended to separate literature from life, to discuss writing primarily as language and form, and, especially of late, to assert that language is incapable of representing "truth" or "reality." These ideas have played an important role in shaping the standard writer-in-the-schools curriculum, which emphasizes the freshness and originality of students' language rather than the accuracy or honesty of their observations, and which concentrates far more heavily on poetry than on fiction and drama.

Literary fashion alone, however, could never explain the enduring popularity of the language- and poetry-based curriculum. Perhaps the most important reason for its success is the simple fact that, despite the universal prejudice against poetry among American schoolchildren, it is the literary form that is closest to the verbal constructions (the insults, jokes, and even stories) they make every day on street corners and basketball courts. Snaps, an African American form of ritualized insult, even have the same reliance on imagery and the three-part structure with surprise ending as Japanese haiku—although obviously the two forms aim for very different effects. Compare these two famous haiku, for example, with the two snaps that follow them. (Snaps, an oral form, are almost never written down; I have broken them into lines to make their structure more clear.)

> In summer grass
> Lie warriors'
> Dreams.
> —Basho

> No one spoke,
> The host, the guest
> The white chrysanthemums.
> —Ryota

Your house is so small
you walk in the door
and fall out the window.

You're so fat
you jumped up in the air
and got stuck.

To borrow an old schoolyard witticism: All kids are poets even if they don't know it. Children may not have the education or intellectual sophistication necessary for the more intricate meditation of much adult poetry, but even before they come to school they are well trained to appreciate the punchy image, the apt metaphor. Writing assignments that play to this strength by asking children to focus on language or formal structures almost inevitably produce images, lines, and sometimes whole poems that are the envy of adult poets.

Here is a poem, for example, written by a second-grade boy. The assignment could hardly have been more simple. I asked the students each to imagine a thing—anything at all—then describe what was underneath that thing, and then what was underneath the second thing, and underneath the third, and so on, until the poem felt finished.

Underneath a ball there are glasses
  that are brown and blue.
Underneath the glasses there is a
  gold striped earring.
Underneath the earring there is a
  devil eating the glasses. The devil
  goes, "Hmm humm—Yummy!"
Underneath the devil there is a panther trying to eat the devil.
Underneath the panther there is a
  girl tiger and a boy lion. They're
  kissing.
Underneath the kiss there is a red
  heart.
Underneath the red heart there is a
  baby lion and baby tiger sleeping.

Underneath the sleep they are
dreaming of love.

This poem is typical of the best writing produced by the standard writer-in-the-schools curriculum. It is full of specific detail and surprises and moves with enviable freedom between incompatible categories—from the mundane to the demonic to the cuddly kitsch—while managing to make them feel all of a piece. This poem is also intriguing—at least to adult readers—because it appears to have a metaphorical content. Its seven-year-old author, who was one of the more troubled children in his class, seems to be struggling with the relationship between love and evil, or between kissing and devouring, and at the same time seems torn between the impulse to raise his fears and the impulse to bury them.

While his classmates, no doubt, were affected by the poem's odd imagery, probably none of them—including the young poet himself—could have explained what the images "meant" or have even comprehended how the poem might have a secondary "content." What is more, had my assignment focused on this content—had I asked the class to write about the relationship between kissing and devouring, for example—the best I could have hoped for would have been boring statements like, "You kiss with your mouth and you eat with your mouth"; while the most likely result would have been a classwide writer's block. It was by playing to my students' strengths, by asking them to think about a superficial structural device, that I made it possible for the class to produce several poems with lively surfaces and often, albeit unwittingly, with intriguing undercurrents.

The same lack of sophistication that makes it so difficult for children to write exciting poetry by consciously focusing on the poem's psychological, moral, or other content also makes it difficult for them to write compelling stories that are longer than anecdotes. Although children (reflecting the views of society as a whole) tend to think of fiction as the more natural literary form, it in fact requires the mastery of many more skills than the most basic forms of poetry. Some of these skills are merely technical: to write a short story a student must know how to write description and dialogue and how to integrate these elements into a narrative with conflict, rising action, and a climax. The most challenging skills, however, are those that derive from students' experience of life: fiction writers must have some comprehension of psychology and of how people can change over time; they must also be able to bear in mind multiple points of view and feel a measure of sympathy even for characters whose actions and opinions are antithetical to their own. Given that the mastery of such skills is extremely rare among adult writers, to say nothing of children, classes that produce even truly remarkable short stories generally don't seem to have written nearly as well as classes that produce only average poetry.

THE UNQUESTIONABLE EFFECTIVENESS OF THE LANGUAGE-AND-poetry-based creative writing curriculum initially made it difficult for me to see anything wrong with it—at least in regard to my own pedagogical objectives. Teachers loved the poems my students produced. So did parents—and so did I. During my first two years at P.S. 227/Walt Whitman, I organized a series of readings at which well-known adult writers (Paul Auster, Oscar Hijuelos, Terry McMillan, Mona Simpson, Lynne Sharon Schwartz, and Quincy Troupe, among others) read their works on the same stage as young authors from my program and from other T&W residencies. Often during the readings I would notice that, excellent as they were, the works of the adult writers would seem ponderous and obscure by comparison to the sprightly writing of the children. I remember listening to my students read and being filled with pride, largely for their sakes but also for the way their brilliance reflected on me. My students were glad of the loud, sustained applause they got after their readings, but I know that some of them didn't have the faintest idea what it was about. To an extent, they were like trained dogs who had just jumped through hoops. On some level they may even have felt tricked.

There are, of course, many children who have a real taste for language play. They love to see what happens when words and images are jumbled together in unusual combinations. I was one of these kids myself. But such children are in the minority. Many kids think that writing weird and/or funny poems (in which devils eat glasses, for example) is okay, but not especially interesting. And many others, particularly at junior high age, think it's just silly. It is easy to inflate oneself with all sorts of highbrow assumptions and simply dismiss these kids as Philistines, but I couldn't do that, largely because of that article of (perhaps bad) faith that I had registered on the first page of my teaching diary. I wanted to make writing matter, not just charm adults or conform to current literary fashion, but matter *to my students*. If I couldn't help them see the value of writing in their own lives, how could I be sure it had any value at all? More important, if the students themselves didn't think that writing mattered, they wouldn't be motivated to put any more effort into it than they needed just to get by. If they didn't put effort into their writing, they wouldn't improve, and if they didn't improve, not just at poetry but at all kinds of writing, then I was indeed a fraud, and in a sense, so was literature. In my diary entry I had also said I wanted to make writing have "political and social importance." If this was to happen, I couldn't teach just to my more middle-class students—the ones who tended to be most interested in language play—but also to the poorer and more troubled kids, the ones who didn't have time for anything that wasn't going to help them save their lives.

I WAS FINALLY DRIVEN TO REASSESS MY WAY OF TEACHING WRITING not by any single event but by a succession of tiny incidents: the common failure of students to understand what I thought was brilliant about the poems they had written for class, for example, or the frequency with which students, when it came time to assemble writing for the year-end anthology, would ignore their most lively and original pieces in favor of the more sentimental and ordinary.

As I became increasingly uncertain of the relevance of my curriculum, my first response was to employ the strategy favored by politicians when they discover that their constituencies want some real and radical change: I didn't do anything different—I just talked about what I was doing in a different way.

This new way of talking was the result of a number of teaching-diary entries in which I tried to figure out what ways of thinking and feeling were encouraged by my writing assignments and the poems they were based on. To my surprise, I found a striking coherence among what I had always thought of as largely independent aesthetic principles. It seemed to me that by encouraging my students to be playful, to experiment, to avoid clichés and stereotypes, to pay attention to their own feelings and experiences, to use specific details, and to write from specific points of view, I was encouraging them to explore and, ultimately, to celebrate their individuality. I was telling them that by being "different" they were, in a way, being more true to themselves, and that one of the main reasons their writing was good was that it reflected what was unique in their character.

Since it was clear to me that many of my students didn't think they had much cause to celebrate themselves, I thought that I had at last discovered what writing could give them that they really needed. The problem was that I don't think a single one of my students ever bought it. No matter how many times I said, "See, nobody else but you could have written this," or, "I've never read anything like this before—you've given me a new way of looking at the world," or, "Don't tell your readers what they already know; tell them what only you know"; no matter how vehemently I disparaged clichés and praised novel ways of writing or precise, honest observations, I don't think that a single one of my students took my proselytizing to heart. To them it was just more irrelevant teacher stuff, more of that naive enthusiasm for which poets are always made fun of in popular culture. It is, of course, always hard to tell what is going on inside the heads of adolescents, whose habitual expression of sulky indifference is often nothing more than a self-protective pose. Let me put it this way, I never saw the slightest sign that all of my chatter about the value of the individual made those kids who already had a taste for poetry like it any better or that it made those who couldn't care less about writing any more interested.

What I did notice, however, was that certain of my assignments that had a more thematic (or content-based) focus often got good writing out of a broader range of students than those that were primarily about language or style. Those assignments had to have a very clear structure. I couldn't just tell my students, "Write about fear." Rather, I would say, "Tell me what you hear and see when you lie in bed at night," or, "List all the things that you think about when your mother has left you alone." One of my most surefire assignments helped students write about their ambivalence regarding power, freedom, and dependence by placing them in a specific—if fantastic—situation: "Tell me about the day you came home from school and found that your parents had shrunk down to the size of Barbie and Ken dolls." (The tiny parents in these stories are often thrown out windows, washed down the drain, given to the cat to play with, or subjected to other acts of equally breathtaking violence—though almost all the stories end with the child's happiness at the parents' restoration to normal size.)

By far my most successful content-oriented assignment began with my reading aloud a couple of monologues from August Wilson's play *Fences,* in which the play's troubling protagonist, Troy Maxon, tells how his father's abuse drove him away from home and into a life of crime that culminated in a murder conviction. In prison Troy began playing baseball and, on his release, joined a team in the Negro leagues, becoming a star.

When I first decided to read these monologues to my students I was worried that they were too rough and that my inability to do an African American accent would make them seem laughable. But to the contrary, my fifth-, seventh-, and eighth-grade students graciously overlooked my lack of expertise as an actor and were absolutely fascinated by every aspect of Troy's story: his father's violence, his own criminal violence, his life in jail, and the Negro leagues (which, to my surprise, only about a third of the students had ever heard of). When it came time to write, the students in every class simply bent their heads over their papers, and for long minutes there was no sound except for the scratching of pencils and pens. I had never seen anything like it.

My assignment was intentionally open ended—"Write a monologue in which a parent tells his or her life story to a child"—but Wilson's play exerted such a powerful influence over my students that virtually every one of them wrote about some form of physical or sexual abuse of children or about crime and punishment. What pleased and surprised me was how detailed and authentic these pieces were. One especially bright eighth-grade girl did nothing for the rest of the year but write a series of monologues about a black girl's relationship with her alcoholic father. I was particularly impressed by how well she rendered the motives and point of view of the father, by no means portraying him as a simple villain. The aspect of this assignment that most excited me, however, was that virtually everybody participated. Kids who had never written a word in class filled whole pages, a couple with truly powerful and authentic voices. None of these pieces would inspire envy in an adult fiction writer, but they did show that, properly motivated, my students could write far better fiction than I had ever suspected, especially when (as with monologues) their narratives were broken into short chunks.

The *Fences* assignment had its greatest success with my Walt Whitman Academy students, who, not surprisingly, seemed most interested in dealing with the hard facts and dilemmas suggested by Maxon's monologue. Thus it was that, at the start of the 1991–92 school year—my fourth at the school and Teachers & Writers' twentieth—I decided I would do nothing but fiction writing with my two seventh-grade classes (the two eighth grades were being taught by Columbia interns that year). By making this choice I was reversing one of the principles that had previously guided all of my curriculum choices. I was having my students focus on what they found hardest rather than what they did best. My thought was that the very fact that fiction required a sophisticated understanding of human character was precisely the reason to teach it. I didn't want my students only to be good writers, after all, but also to be good and happy people. It seemed to me that the ability to understand different people's needs and viewpoints was not only a requirement of good fiction but the foundation of moral thinking and a skill essential to virtually every aspect of my students' personal lives and careers. And I could think of no better way to encourage the development of this ability than to require my students to use it.

This time my new way of talking about what I was doing actually changed the way I taught, and most important, it ultimately allowed me to come to a much deeper understanding of my students and to develop a much more mutually enlightening and supportive relationship with them.

A Technical Note

DURING THE 1991–92 SCHOOL YEAR THE TEACHERS & WRITERS program at P.S. 227/Walt Whitman Academy suffered the first of a series of substantial budget cuts that have progressively diminished its scope over the last few years. My salary was paid primarily with arts funds allocated to the school by the local Board of Education's district office. The Columbia MFA student interns, however, were paid by the Urban Corps, a sixties-era job-training program. At the start of the 1991–92 school year, city budget difficulties caused the Urban Corps to cut the number of internships it funded at the school from six to only two. This meant that for the first time in Teachers & Writers' twenty-year history at P.S. 227/Walt Whitman, writers were not able to work with the students of every teacher who requested their services. It also meant that I couldn't train the Columbia interns as extensively as I had in the past. Fortunately, that year I was able to hire two particularly talented and dedicated interns, Matt Sharpe and Elizabeth Shepard, both fiction writers.

The three of us taught a total of seventeen different classes, visiting them each once a week, on Thursdays or Fridays, from October to May. I personally taught six of those classes (team-teaching one of them with Elizabeth) and had a total of more than 180 students. On Fridays we were joined by my colleague from Teachers & Writers, the playwright Daniel Judah Sklar, who taught three playwriting classes and ran the after-school Walt Whitman Academy Drama Club. The principal of P.S. 227/Walt Whitman was Fran Kaplan, but I worked most closely with Rachel Suarez, the director of the Walt Whitman Academy, and Joan Gold, the seventh- and eighth-grade language arts teacher.

PART TWO

On This Day a Poor Boy Died

3

New York and Bensonhurst

THE FIRST ASSIGNMENT I GIVE ANY NEW CLASS HAS TO BE EASY, fun, and guaranteed to produce exciting writing, just as a comedian's first joke has to be one of his best. A flopped first assignment, especially in junior high, could mean weeks of battling groans, glazed eyes, and my own plunging ego. So, despite my enthusiasm for my new fiction unit, I started my year by giving my seventh-grade students one of my most reliable poetry assignments, but one that would pave the way for writing monologues, which in turn would lead to writing dialogues and, finally, the blending of dialogue and description in full-fledged stories.

I began by telling my students that I had chosen this assignment as a means of getting to know them but that, since I was a creative writing teacher, I didn't want to get to know them in the usual way: I didn't want to hear how old they were, what they did on their summer vacation, what they hoped to be when they grew up. What I wanted was to find out how crazy they could be. I told them that every writer had to be a little crazy and that some of the deepest truths were told through the wildest lies. Then I said that I was going to read a poem—Jayne Cortez's "I Am New York City"—that sounded like the kind of thing a crazy person might shout on a street corner. "Listen to how she seems to get herself all mixed up with the city," I said. "She writes this poem as if she thinks she *is* the city." The poem begins:

i am new york city
here is my brain of hot sauce
my tobacco teeth my
    mattress of bedbug tongue
legs apart   hand on chin
    war on the roof   insults
pointed fingers   pushcarts
my contraceptives all

look at my pelvis blushing

i am new york city of blood
police and fried pies
i rub my docks red with grenadine
and jelly madness in a flow of tokay
my huge skull of pigeons
my seance of peeping toms . . .

The kids seemed to like the poem. There was no restlessness as I read. When I had finished, I asked what Cortez could mean by "brain of hot sauce" and at first got no response. But when I asked if the poem could have been written by someone with a brain of hot sauce, there was laughter. "Maybe she's really talking about the kind of craziness you need to be a poet," I said. "And maybe she thinks the city is full of that kind of craziness." I pointed out how she talked about different parts of her body as if they were things you might see in the city and that this was not the postcard New York: there were no Statues of Liberty, no Empire State Buildings. This was New York as you see it from the sidewalks. I asked what feeling about the city the poem gave us. No answer. So then I asked: "Does the New York in this poem seem like a happy place?" Shaken heads, a few nos. "Does it seem like a clean place?" No. "A boring place?" No. "A place that can be a little weird?" Yes. "A little scary?" Yes. "An exciting place?" Yes.

Then I got to the writing idea: "I want you to think about a place that is important to you, that you've liked or visited or even just dreamed about. Then I want you to write a poem in which you talk as if you *are* that place. Do what Jayne Cortez did. Talk about parts of your body as if they are things that you can find in the place you are writing about. Use lots of details."

It was as I walked around the room to look over shoulders at what the kids were writing and to help out those who were having a hard time, that I first noticed two students with whom I would soon begin to work very closely.

RICKY ORTIZ SAT AT THE VERY BACK OF THE CLASS, WHERE THE troublemakers were always put. He was a big, bony kid with beefsteak hands, very light skin, and large, serious brown eyes. When I walked up to him he was leaning back in his chair picking at the calluses on his palm, his legs kicked out in front of him in a clear posture of defiance. As I approached his desk I saw that the page in front of him was blank and that his pen was in his pocket. Preparing myself for surly dismissal, I asked, "Having trouble getting started?"

"No," he answered, frowning as he glanced at me.

"Then how come you haven't written anything?"

"I'm finished." He flipped over his spiral notebook, and sure enough, there was a short poem in it. When I asked if I could read it, he said, "Sure," and leaned slightly to one side so that I could pick up the notebook myself.

The Arcade

I am the arcade
with my blinking lights
and my bing bong tilt.
I am Mario
with my dark brown hair.
I am Ultra Beast
with my wolf-like legs
and my furry face.
I am all of the games,
for I am the Arcade!*

I told him that I loved the sound of "with my blinking lights / and my bing bong tilt," that it really had the feel of Jayne Cortez's poem, but that his ending was boring, that the poem would be more exciting if he

---

*Except where otherwise noted, all student work is reproduced exactly as it was written, with spelling and grammar unaltered.

could describe himself as other things at the arcade, maybe not just other games but the things going on around the games, the crowds, the lighting, the noises. Ricky looked me straight in the eyes as I talked. There was such an intensity, such a stillness in his gaze. He seemed to be listening carefully to everything I told him, and said, "Okay, thanks," as I got up to move on to the next student. I returned to his desk later in the class to see what he had added to his poem, but he hadn't touched it. "Sorry," he said, turning his hands palms-up as if his failure to write had been merely a matter of fate. I decided not to push it. "That's okay," I said. "You've made a good start."

Xia Sanchez sat at a cluster of desks at the front of the room. She was a tall, square, spunky girl with amazing hazel eyes that looked almost gold in contrast to her dark skin. She showed me her poem happily:

> New York City oh what a
> beautiful place. There is crime every-
> where even when you turn your face.
> The hot dogs of New York are as hot as
> steam, so hot that it'll make you scream.
> But as you scream you feel the
> heat cool down Way down my
> throat until there's no way out.
> You know why, thats me New York City.

This was a typical first-session poem, in which the need to make the rhyme limited the poet's imagination and made her grammar even more awkward than it might already have been. I pointed out to Xia that she hadn't spoken as if she *were* New York until the very end of her poem, where she also stopped trying to rhyme. "I like that part best," I said, "because it has the strongest feeling. Usually its easier for beginning poets to say what they really mean when they don't try to rhyme. Why don't you do this poem over without rhyme and see what happens?"

I could see that Xia was disappointed by my reaction, but she didn't sulk or mouth off to me as many students would when I ventured to criticize their work. She simply listened attentively, without objection, until I mentioned that in poems the rhyming word generally came at the end of the line, not in the middle.

"Oh, I know," Xia said. "I write a lot of poems. Look"—she picked her backpack up from the floor—"I've got my poetry book right here." After a good few minutes of zipping and unzipping and searching through the chaotic interior of her tightly stuffed pack, she pulled out a bright red imitation leather account book/calendar, which, as it turned out, had only one poem in it. "I'm just getting started," she said as she handed me the book to read.

Secret Love

My secret love comes by my window
to say hello or just to giggle
under the moon shining about our heads
we laugh and hug until the night ends
No one will stop us from doing it again
No one will 'cause our love will never
        end.

The End

This poem was sappy, of course, but also charming as an artifact of adolescent sexual development. While it was technically much more proficient than Xia's New York poem, I suspected it was at least partly plagiarized—the first two lines in particular sounded very familiar. I had had compulsively plagiarizing students before—all of them eager to please, even ambitious, but with very low self-esteem. I didn't want to insult Xia with a false accusation, but if I complimented her for work she hadn't done, that would only further depress her self-esteem and make her more likely to plagiarize again. In the end I simply told her that her poem was "nice" and that I was eager to see her revision of her New York poem. I never really expected that she would get around to redoing the poem, so I was surprised when, toward the end of the class, she handed me the following:

I am New York. I am the
chimnees that puffs out smoke
into the air I am the earth
quakes that rips trough the ground
under the houses all around
I am a building being torchered

by a crane banging and banging
until I'm all gone. I am New York
a very unpeaceful place.
<u>The End</u>

At the same cluster of desks with Xia was a tiny, twig-thin girl named Clara Ritos. I'd known Clara since she was in fourth grade. (Now in its fourth year of existence, the Walt Whitman Academy was drawing more and more of its students from P.S. 227.) Clara was shy and a giggler. Half the time when my eyes fell on her in the midst of class she'd be giggling helplessly, often when no one else at her table seemed to find anything to laugh at. The rest of the time she'd be staring morosely down into the crooks of her folded arms.

When the writing session was finished, I told the class that anyone who would like me to read his or her piece aloud should give it to me. I would shuffle the pieces up and read them anonymously, so that no-body could tell who had written what (this was the only sure way I had found of getting past my students' self-consciousness). Xia and Ricky handed me their pieces, as did several other students, including Clara. I had not had a chance to look at Clara's poem, so had not formed any judgment of it before I read it aloud.

I am a tree
that's being picked on.
I am a tree,
my heart is being split in half.
I am a tree
that's being cut into pieces.
People use me for fire
to keep them warm,
and use me to make
tables and chairs.
I am a wooden floor
that's being stepped on
and scraped so hard
that I can feel it
in my heart.

This was the best thing Clara had ever written. She hadn't talked about being a place, but she had given herself over to metaphor more completely than anyone else in the class. I had nearly gotten tears in my eyes as I read, "my heart is being split in half," and, "I am a wooden floor / that's being stepped on / and scraped so hard / that I can feel it / in my heart." When I had finished, Joan Gold, the Walt Whitman Academy language arts teacher, who was always in the room with me, looked up from her newspaper and said, "Who wrote that?"—a question that was echoed all around the classroom.

"Well," I said, taking care not to let my gaze stray in Clara's direction for more than an instant, "does the author want to stand up and take credit?" I saw Clara's head dip down as if she were going to cry. And then, with her head still dipped down, she slowly got to her feet and the whole class applauded her.

THAT WAS THE HIGH POINT OF MY FIRST MONTH TEACHING. I introduced my fiction unit the following week by asking my students to tell me all the things one had to do to tell a good lie: "Tell it with a straight face," one student suggested. "Make it sound real," said another.

These were both excellent points, but the latter needed clarification. "How can you make a lie sound real?" I asked.

The same student raised her hand: "By telling something that could really happen."

"That's right," I said. "You don't want your lie to be too crazy. Suppose you didn't do your homework. You don't want to tell your teacher: 'I was just sitting down to do it when aliens beamed me out the window.' But also, you don't want to use a cliché—that is, a story the teacher has heard ten thousand times: 'My little brother tore up my homework.'"

I had been delivering lectures about clichés for years, but never before had I been able to make their evils so self-evident. All my talk about being original or avoiding "borrowed" or "tired" language not only had never made much of an impression on my students but had often left me wondering if I had just been trying to cram my own taste for the unconventional down their throats. But from their responses during our discussion, it was clear that my students had no trouble understanding how many of the elements that were necessary for good fiction—not just originality, but a discrete use of detail and a thorough understanding of the psychology of both characters and audience—were also needed to tell good lies. I was very happy as we talked and would have been well pleased with the whole session if the students hadn't gone on to produce such lackluster writing. The writing idea was that each student would tell two stories, one true, one false, and the class would guess which was which. But the lies that weren't boring were fabulously unbelievable.

The next week we worked on "voice." I read my students an angry monologue from Ntozake Shange's verse play *for colored girls who have considered suicide/when the rainbow is enuf.* Then I asked them to choose an emotion and write a monologue in which the speaker was feeling that emotion. "We should be able to tell what the emotion is," I explained, "not only by what is said but by the way it is said, because people speak differently when they have different feelings." Once again the writing was boring, perhaps because Shange's monologue lost some of its power outside the context of the play.

For the next class meeting, which happened to fall on Halloween, I chose a text I knew the kids would be gripped by, Poe's "Tell-Tale Heart." I read it aloud, taking care to emphasize the manic urgency of the narrator's voice. When I finished the last lines ("I admit the deed!—tear up the planks!—here, here!—it is the beating of his hideous heart!"), I slammed the book down on the table in front of me, drawing a gasp from every student in the class. We had a good discussion about the narrator's voice and about how Poe created it, but once more the writing was disappointing: just a bunch of horror story clichés.

It wasn't looking good for my fiction unit. As always, a few students wrote beautifully, but most were just going through the motions, filling up pages merely because I had told them to. The problem, as I saw it, was that I had presented them with the tools to write fiction but hadn't given them any compelling reason to use them.

Then one Sunday morning about a month and a half into the term, I was reading the *New York Times Book Review* over breakfast when I came across a review of *For the Color of His Skin* by John DeSantis, a book about the murder of Yusuf Hawkins in Bensonhurst. As the review described it, the chain of events that led to Hawkins's death began when Gina Feliciano invited sixteen-year-old Keith Mondello to her seventeenth birthday party. Mondello asked her if she was inviting any "niggers and spics," and when she answered yes, he told her that there was going to be "trouble." Feliciano countered that her black and Latino friends were going to "get" him. Ostensibly fearing for his life, Mondello organized a gang of about forty bat- and knife-wielding young men, who gathered in front of Feliciano's building on the night of her party. Hawkins and two friends had the bad luck to turn a corner and walk right into the middle of the crowd. They didn't know Feliciano and had only come to Bensonhurst to look at a used car they had seen advertised in the newspaper. The reviewer then went on to quote the following dialogue from DeSantis's book:

> "What are you niggers doing here?" somebody shouted.
> "We're looking for an address," one of the blacks replied, holding out the advertisement. A couple of whites in front quickly realized that these were not the blacks they were after . . . Keith [Mondello] looked at [Charlie] Stressler, and shook his head. "I ain't gonna hit them," he said. "These are babies. They're kids. These aren't them."
> "I ain't gonna hit them either," Stressler said, and turned to leave as an excited John Vento ran up and the larger crowd pressed closer.
> "Is this them? Is this them?" Vento asked, and drew back his arm, preparing to hit Hawkins.
> A short figure, dressed all in white—Joey Fama—stepped forward, holding his gun in his right hand. "To hell with beating them up! I'm gonna shoot the nigger!" he reportedly said.
> James Patino hollered "No!" But it was too late.
> When Hawkins fell to the sidewalk, . . . he was clutching part of a Snickers bar he had been eating.

My first reaction to this passage came from my heart: like most people, I suppose, I had tended to feel that Hawkins's murder had been somehow inevitable, dictated not so much by fate as by the poisonous forces of racial hatred and urban violence. But this passage showed that there had been randomness in the midst of the inevitability—that, had it not been for the sudden intrusion of Fama, an emotionally disturbed young man with a hand-washing obsession and low-level Mafia connections, Hawkins might well have gone his way having suffered nothing more than one of the countless high-testosterone confrontations that go on every hour of the day in every big city. This thin sliver of randomness—of hope—only made Hawkins's death seem more tragic.

Because I am a writing teacher, however, my next reaction was to try to imagine how I could employ such a dramatic passage in the classroom. Initially I thought of using it merely as a sample dialogue that would both intrigue my students and make clear the correspondence between reality and the constructed events of fiction. Then all at once it occurred to me (the moment has a mystical radiance in my memory) that I could have my students spend several weeks exploring the tragic incidents at Bensonhurst by writing monologues and dialogues as they might have been spoken by all the people involved. Perhaps, if the students wrote well enough, I could even weave their work into a play that they could perform. But at the very least I might get an interesting collection of pieces to put on the Teachers & Writers bulletin board in the school's main hallway.

I went straight from my breakfast table to my computer, where I typed into my teaching diary the idea for what I was already calling the Bensonhurst Project. I knew right away that this was the answer to all my student motivation problems. The elements of racism, violence, and teenage sexuality (Gina Feliciano, called a "slut" and a "crackhead" by neighbors, apparently had a crush on Keith Mondello) would be irresistibly fascinating to my students. The tools of fiction and drama would fit perfectly into their own attempts to understand and reach a judgment about this social and moral tangle. My chief worry was that my students, all but two of them African American or Latino, would be so angry at Mondello and his gang that they would resent being asked to write from their points of view. This worry stemmed from one of my many misconceptions about my students that this project would reveal to me.

I WAS EAGER TO GET GOING ON THE PROJECT BUT REALIZED THAT I would need at least four classes in a row to maintain the coherence and momentum necessary for its success. Unfortunately, the Thanksgiving holidays were only a week away. Then, after only one week back in the classroom, I was scheduled to take a paternity leave to help my wife with our new baby, who was due the first week of December. I wasn't going to have even two classes in a row until after New Year's. This was a frustrating state of affairs, but I decided to use the extra time to refine my presentation.

I returned to the school after the Christmas vacation in love with my new daughter, but cotton-brained from a month of twice-nightly feedings, only to be greeted with a new frustration. The Walt Whitman Academy was considering changing the length of its class periods from forty-five minutes to seventy minutes—an excellent idea, I thought; I relished the chance to spend an extra twenty-five minutes with my students; forty-five minute periods had never seemed long enough. But if the change were made, the schedule would have to be so drastically reorganized that there was no guarantee that I would have any of my old classes.

I tried to find out when the new schedule would be put into effect. Nobody knew. Rachel Suarez, the director of Walt Whitman, told me that several of the teachers were opposed to the change and that they were all going to thrash it out at the teachers meeting the following Wednesday. I called her at home Wednesday night only to find that nothing had changed. Rachel and her allies still hadn't overcome the other teachers' objections to imposing the new schedule, let alone decided when they were going to start it. Realizing that in true public school fashion, this process could go on for months and result in nothing, I decided to take my chances and start the Bensonhurst Project the following morning.

I SAW BOTH SEVENTH-GRADE CLASSES IN A ROW ON THURSDAY mornings during one of their five weekly sessions with their language arts teacher, Joan Gold. Joan was a veteran teacher in her mid-fifties, slender and always elegantly dressed in creams and grays, with radiant auburn hair that swept back from her forehead, skirted her shoulders, and arced along the line of her jaw. Her refined appearance and gentle voice masked a will that was as sharp and uncompromising as a machete. She could silence a room of out-of-control students merely by walking in the door with her fists on her hips. Some students claimed to hate her, calling her mean, but others, more often girls, loved her. Occasionally she would bring in her own daughter's clothes or those of her friends' children for girls whose poverty meant they had to come to school in the same dress day after day. I had taught in Joan's classes for three years, and we had developed a firm mutual respect and an effective working partnership: I ran the class, but she was always there to back me up. Essentially this meant that I got to play good cop to her bad, a role that suited my tastes perfectly and for which I was always grateful to her.

As the students in my first seventh grade were filing into the classroom, I wrote FICTION = LIES on the blackboard. Once everyone had taken a seat, I asked them what this equation meant. (We had discussed it at least twice before, but with junior high students I never counted on anything sticking.) There was a long moment of silence before a boy named Dakwan raised his hand and said, "It means they're stories that are not true." Deciding this was good enough, I turned to the board and added a third word to the equation, so that it now read: FICTION = LIES = TRUTH.

"All right . . ." I turned back to the class. "How can we make sense of this? How is it possible that we can get the truth from something that's not true?"

A boy named Ike raised his hand: "Even if it's a lie, it tells us about the way people really do react to different things."

"That's right!" I exclaimed, astonished to get such a good answer so quickly. "When you read fiction you read about people saying, doing, thinking, and feeling things. If it's good fiction, if the story is really well written, then the characters do all those things just the way people do in real life, which means it's telling you the truth about the way some people talk and think and behave." I looked out over the class to see if this had sunk in. I saw the usual assortment of attentive and inattentive heads, some turned toward me, some lying down on the desks.

"What other sorts of truth can you get from lies?"

A girl named Odella raised her hand. "You get lies that tell the truth."

This was a more normal response to this sort of question. I accepted it: "Yes, but how do those lies give you the truth? What about a science fiction story or a fairy tale in which people do all kinds of things they never do in real life? What kind of truth do you get from those stories?"

Another student raised her hand and shyly recapitulated what Ike had already said. I called on a girl named Bernice, an excellent writer who always understood the drift of my discussions well ahead of her classmates but rarely talked in class. It had long been one of my ambitions to get

Bernice to speak her mind more readily, on the idea that it would make the classes more stimulating for her and for everybody. But today Bernice just shrugged, annoyed at me for having suddenly thrust her to the center of the class's attention. I had to go this one on my own.

"Stories can also tell larger truths that have nothing to do with how realistic they are," I said. "A story about dragons, for example, might tell you that to be a hero you must be brave and generous. If you think that heroes really should be brave and generous, you will say that the story contains a truth. If the story's hero is vicious and greedy, then you will say that the story is not true, that it is telling us something false or wrong about the way things are."

Dakwan sighed and shifted in his seat. Maria was passing a note to Irena. In the back of the room, Danny was laughing at something Armando had just whispered. I wasn't sure if anyone had heard a word I said. If I didn't move on to something more dramatic, I would lose the class. Pulling a wad of photocopied handouts from my briefcase, I said, "We're going to be telling both kinds of truth in the writing we do over the next couple of weeks." Although I was planning for this project to last at least a month, I didn't want the students to be intimidated by its magnitude right at the start. I also wanted an easy escape in case it flopped.

While the handouts were being passed around, I asked the students if any of them remembered the murder of Yusuf Hawkins, which had occurred about a year and a half earlier. Not a single hand was raised. "You must remember," I said. "It was in the newspapers and on TV for months. Yusuf Hawkins was a black teenager who was murdered by this white gang in Bensonhurst, Brooklyn."

"No, he wasn't," said Tiara, an extremely bright but angry girl who hadn't let her exile to the back of the room stop her from leading her classmates in their ongoing war against the teachers. "He was shot by a cop."

"No, not Yusuf Hawkins . . ." As I tried to remember the details of a recent case in which a black child had indeed been shot by a cop, I was interrupted by Malika, a bright though normally quiet girl.

"Yusuf was shot by a white cop," Malika pronounced with assurance. "I went to a demonstration about it."

"It wasn't Yusuf Hawkins," I began.

"Yes, it was."

"It was somebody else," I said, wishing I could remember the details of the other shooting. Was this the beginning of the racial antagonism I had worried might ruin the project? I held up the handout. "Let's all read this together and we'll find out what happened to Yusuf Hawkins."

"He got shot by a white cop," Malika insisted.

"This is stupid," pronounced Tiara, flinging the handout onto her desk. But when I started to read aloud, she picked it up again and read silently along with the rest of her class.

"Gina Feliciano turned seventeen that night," I began and knew instantly that I had the attention of everyone in the class. They weren't all reading along with me, but they were completely quiet. When I got to the part where Keith Mondello told Gina Feliciano that there would be "trouble" if she invited "niggers and spics" to her party, one of the girls said, "Ooh, that's nasty!" I interrupted myself to say, "I wasn't sure if I should use those words in class, but I decided that if we're going to talk about racism, you should know what these people really said and really thought." I resumed reading, and when I got to a description of Joey Fama's white suit and silver-plated .38-caliber pistol, I heard a murmur of approval pass through my audience, particularly the male portion of it.

On finishing the reading, I decided that the best way to hold the class's attention was to launch right into controversy: "All right, now that you've heard the basic facts of the story, who do you think was most to blame for Hawkins's death?" While everyone involved in the slaying (except for Hawkins and his friends, of course) bore some measure of guilt, I assumed that the class discussion would focus on whether it was Keith Mondello, the organizer of the gang, who was most guilty or Joey Fama, the one who actually shot Hawkins. To my astonishment, the first person to respond to my question, a small boy named Joseph, said, "He shouldn't have gone there."

"You mean Hawkins?" I asked. When Joseph answered, "Yeah," I started to say that Hawkins was completely innocent, that he had a perfect right to buy a car in whatever neighborhood he chose, but I was interrupted by Bernice: "What's he going out there for when he knows all those white boys is gonna get him?"

"But he didn't know," I protested. "He was just going to an address listed in an ad for a used car."

"He shouldn't have gone out there," Joseph reiterated and was seconded by "yeah's" and nods from around the room.

"He can go anywhere he damn wants!" Tiara said from the back of the room, and she too was seconded by "yeah's" and nods.

"Okay!" I said happily, seeing a pedagogical opportunity. "We've already got some disagreement here. We've got two different points of view. Some of the people involved in the murder will agree with Joseph and Bernice, some of them will agree with Tiara. Your job when you start to write will be to chose one of those people and write from his or her point of view . . . But let's get some other points of view first. Who else is to blame for Hawkins's death?"

A boy named Fernando raised his hand. "Gina Feliciano."

Once again I was surprised but tried not to show it. I asked Fernando to explain why he thought Feliciano was to blame.

"Because she started it."

"Really? How?"

Fernando just shrugged. Maria, the girl sitting next to him, said: "It's her fault, 'cause if she hadn't of said that to Keith, none of that would have happened."

"You mean when she told him her friends were going to 'get' him?" I asked.

Maria and Fernando both nodded. Other kids in the class expressed their approval.

"But she did that only after he had threatened her," I said. "Mondello told her there was going to be 'trouble'—that was a threat."

"But still, *she* started it," Maria insisted. "If she hadn't of started it, none of it would have happened."

I was perplexed by Maria's intransigence on this point and puzzled by the fact that no one had yet mentioned the two boys who seemed most obviously to bear the blame. But what astonished me the most was when Dameon interrupted my reiteration that since Mondello had made the first threat, *he* had "started it."

"She shouldn't have invited those people," said Dameon.

Dameon was a very dark-skinned African American. My incredulity showed on my face when I asked him, "Which people?"

Dameon answered with obvious discomfort. "Those people she invited to her party . . . Her friends."

"And who were her friends?"

Dameon shrugged. "Black people. And Hispanics."

I turned and looked at the class, which was solidly black and Hispanic, and asked them all as well as Dameon in particular: "But shouldn't Gina

Feliciano have had the right to invite anyone she wanted to her party?" No one responded. I continued, giving more of my own opinion than I had intended to: "Keith Mondello was the racist. He threatened her *because* he was a racist. All she was doing was inviting the people she liked to her party. She wasn't a racist."

"She was a crackhead," said Maria.

I was amazed that no one was rising to the defense of Feliciano or to attack Mondello and Fama. I decided to hold a vote, chiefly to see what the silent members of the class were thinking. Roughly twelve out of thirty-three students thought Gina Feliciano started the dispute that led to Yusuf Hawkins's death; five, including Malika and Tiara, thought Keith Mondello started it; and the remaining sixteen never bothered to raise their hands. (I held a similar vote in my second seventh-grade class and the proportions were roughly the same.)

My first thought was that the rampant sexism of so many of my students was causing them to cast Gina Feliciano in the role of evil temptress, even though there were no facts to support such an interpretation. Later on, as I turned over the discussion in my mind, and especially as I read the writing the students produced that day, I realized that they were far more realistic and far less idealistic than I had expected them to be. They were indeed outraged by the racism of Mondello, Fama, and the other members of the gang, but more when they considered it in the abstract than when they thought about the specifics of the situation. When they imagined themselves on the streets of Bensonhurst that August night, many of my students saw Yusuf Hawkins as foolish, if not entirely blameworthy, for having gone into a neighborhood he should have known was full of white bigots. Gina Feliciano was stupid at best, but perhaps also provocative for inviting a bigot like Mondello to her party when she should have known how he would respond. The fact that she had been rumored to be a crack addict further cast doubt on her position, since my students knew full well that crack addicts are not to be trusted.

As for Keith Mondello, he was just "watching his back" by organizing the gang to protect himself, a perfectly acceptable activity. To a certain extent, even his racial antagonism was acceptable, at least among some Latinos, as simple realism in a city where hostility between groups is a given. One Latino boy wrote, "I like Mondello the most because he didn't let people threaten him. He stood up for his rights." Another Latino boy, this one in the second of my two seventh-grade classes, expressed some of the conflicting impulses that were felt by many of my students:

It was messed up what happen to Yusuf it was a sad day for every one just like what happen with JFK everyone was sad and quiet but the world didn't end yet but not everyone is going to die sooner or later I hope I live to the age 77 getting back to Usus Mondello I like him because he was the one who organize all this. James Patino he try to stick up for Uusus because that was his friend

This piece is interesting both for its blend of sentimentality and sad fatalism and for its sloppiness. Its author, Danny, was far from the most intelligent student in the class, but he was not nearly as unintelligent as this piece might make him seem. He was very popular among his peers and the following year wrote a series of quite clever raps. The piece was sloppy primarily because schoolwork and the kind of distinctions it called for were fundamentally unimportant to Danny. His sloppiness, however, left him particularly exposed. I was especially struck by the fact that, although he professed to admire Mondello, he had partially blended him with his victim by giving him a name sounding like "Yusuf." His admiration for Patino was equally double edged, since Patino stuck up both for Mondello, by being part of the gang, and for Hawkins, by shouting "No!" when Fama pushed through the crowd with his gun.

There was a lot that was likable about Danny. He spent much of his time in school wearing the bored, faintly menacing expression of a street dog but could break into a bigmouthed grin that was as infectious as a toddler's. He was greedy for approval, from his peers primarily, but also from teachers. Whenever I praised one of his raps, a surprised, happy expression came onto his face. In the midst of his indifference, a part of him really wanted to do well in school, just as a part of him could not bear the violence he admired in Mondello. His admiration was nonetheless genuine, and Danny himself could be violent in an instant. He was one of those kids who, quite cannily, had decided that school had nothing to offer him, that if he was going to make it in any sense of the term it would be according to the rules of the streets, even if a part of him despised those rules.

Despite the initially puzzling failure of the class to construe Keith Mondello's character and guilt as I had expected, I was extremely happy with the seriousness of their participation in the discussion and was already convinced that this project would turn out to be just as exciting and worthwhile as I had hoped.

Only in my second seventh-grade class did someone finally get around to suggesting that Joey Fama bore the largest guilt, since he had actually shot Hawkins. While we were discussing Fama's hand-washing obsession and the strange fact that he wore a white suit to murder Hawkins, a boy named Lavaun made the fascinating suggestion that maybe Fama wore white because he hated dirt and that he wanted to kill blacks because he thought they were dirty. The whole class was struck by the poetic simplicity of this analysis, and it ended up influencing many of the students in their writing.

The class was also struck by an exchange I had with another student. Many of the students in my first class had written expository essays about the characters rather than monologues spoken by them, so I decided to make sure that this class knew precisely what I was asking for. "I want your characters to sound as if they are really speaking to us," I said. "Have them talk the way they really would. I mean it; they can use any word that you think kids like that would really use."

James raised his hand, grinning because he thought he had caught me out at something: "You said you want them to talk the way they would really talk, but you don't really want us to—"

"I want them to have the accents that they would really have, and I want them to use *all* the words they would really use."

"But you don't really mean—"

"Yes, I do! Curses. Four-letter words. Anything. As long as it's realistic. As long as it sounds like the truth. All I want is the truth." The whole class exchanged gasps and openmouthed grins at this new freedom. It was clear that many of them did not know how far to go with it, but they were all curious to try it out.

Usually about half the class dawdled and chattered before getting down to writing. Not this time. The room was uncommonly quiet, almost every kid scribbling away. Even the kids who were stumped didn't talk, and when I came by their desks they seemed eager for my help. Unfortunately, after the class had been writing for only about five minutes, a fire drill bell sounded. I was furious—although my anger was mitigated by the fact that as soon as the bell sounded, a disappointed groan rose from all around the room. "Don't worry," I told the class. "You'll be able to finish next week. We'll spend the whole class writing."

When I looked in the writing folders after class, I was thrilled by what I saw. Virtually every student had written something. And while many, despite my instructions, had still written expository essays rather than monologues, every student who had put pen to paper had made an earnest attempt to understand and express his or her understanding of a character through writing. The most impressive piece was by Sasha Ortiz—Ricky Ortiz's sister. (Ricky was a year older but had been held back.) Sasha was one of the students who picked up on Lavaun's remark about Joey Fama's hatred of dirt.

My name is "Joey Fama" I'm real CLEAN GUY! I can't STAND Dirt! I was hit by some dirty car when I was 3 and got brain damage. I always wash my hands and where white clothes. I don't like anything that has anything to do with dirt! I hate the smell, the color, the feeling and even the look of dirt! I killed this guy named "Yusuf". I had a right to kill Yusuf! He's ugly, a baby and worst of all he's BLACK! Anyway, whats the use of him being alive? He's a baby! He's walking in the street with two ugly niggers, looking for some address! Hey, he's better off in Heaven! In Heaven he does not have to worry about anything or get killed ever again! Anyway, there is always a time to dye. But now Yusuf does not have to wait that long.

This was the longest piece of writing Sasha had ever produced in my class. She was a strange girl, big, bony, and meat-handed like her brother, but with smaller, suspicious eyes. All of her speech came in eruptions, like bubbles rising through thick soup; jokes, questions, observations in class—everything she said came out like the irritable expostulations of someone who believes she is despised but who is damned if she is going to keep quiet.

What impressed me about this first piece of hers was its voice. Unlike most of her classmates, she had stepped directly into the character of Joey Fama—almost uncannily so. It seemed to me that Fama could easily have written a piece just like this, with all its leaps of logic and its often babyish nastiness. What I wondered was how much of this vivid voice was a product of art and how much was a reflection of her own true character. Sasha and Ricky called themselves Puerto Rican, but their mother was half Irish and half Italian. Ricky's skin was light but with a definite olive cast. Sasha's blue eyes and pale freckled face seemed to have come straight from Ireland. She was the only kid in the class who really looked white. I hoped this monologue didn't reflect her own true feelings about race. I also worried about how the other students would react to what she had written. Where would *they* draw the line between art and life? It was perhaps because of this anxiety that, as I handed Sasha her writing folder at the start of the next class, I said, "Great job. Are you going to try doing someone else today?"

"Nope!" she said, shaking her head smugly. "I'm sticking with Fama."

Sasha was one of the very few students with any enthusiasm for the Bensonhurst Project that particular day. Joan Gold, the junior high language arts teacher, was sick, and no matter how exciting the students might have found the project the previous week, there was no way they could resist exerting their freedom in the absence of so ferocious a disciplinarian. With my first seventh grade I had started out making good-natured jokes about the level of chaos and had ended with loud threats, which accomplished little apart from keeping the kids in their seats. Not more than half a dozen students got a complete sentence down on paper—not a pattern I wanted to repeat with my next class.

While the second seventh grade filed into the room—already excited, having heard about Joan's absence—I went across the hall to the office of Rachel Suarez, the director of Walt Whitman Academy, because I had to make a quick phone call. When I came back, all the students were still on their feet and the substitute was calling out good-naturedly, "All right, everybody. Time to settle down." Nobody paid him the slightest attention. It was my turn to be the bad cop.

I dropped my briefcase loudly onto a desk at the front of the room and called out, "Let's go, everybody, in your seats! We've got a lot of work to do today, and I don't want to waste any time." The uncharacteristic harshness of my voice got the students' attention, and soon they were all sitting down, although not before I had threatened to send a couple of them to Ms. Suarez.

They were sitting, but they were not in their own seats. Joan had arranged the seating so that the students were separated from friends with whom they were most likely to get disruptive. The seating arrangement was the first thing to go on substitute days. I looked around the room at half a dozen expectant, barely repressed smiles. The students were waiting to see what I would do. The truth was that, since I had only the vaguest idea where most of them were supposed to sit, any effort I made to get them back to their normal places would only have made me look like a fool and wasted half the class in pointless argument, so I decided just to leap into my lesson.

"We're going to continue with our Bensonhurst Project today—" A moan rose from somewhere at the back of the room. "Hey!" I called out. "What're you moaning about? You guys were doing great work last week. I want to give you a chance to finish." No more moans, though I wouldn't exactly have called the class attentive.

Once again I wanted to make clear to my students that they should write monologues, not essays. Despite all my talk about voice and natural speech, many of the students had not figured out that they were to write as if they *were* the characters at Bensonhurst telling their own stories. I thought these students might find it easier if I got them thinking both about how the characters might feel about the events they had participated in and about why they might want to tell their stories.

"Who knows what the word 'justified' means?" I asked. For a long moment there was no answer, then a boy raised his hand.

"Arrested," he said. "Put in jail."

"No," I answered. "But I can see why you say that. It does have to do with justice. Who knows? Who can tell me what 'justified' really means?" Nobody spoke. And the longer I waited for an answer, the closer I came to losing the fragile discipline I had attained. I decided to try another question: "Let me put it this way: do you think people intentionally do things that they *know* are wrong?" Still no answer. "Well, I don't," I said. "I don't think that anyone ever does anything they know deep in their hearts is wrong." I didn't believe anything of the kind, but I hoped that by pretending I did I would provoke a response—which I got: a couple of mocking laughs and a "No way!"

I turned to one of the boys who had laughed. "All right, give me an example of someone who does wrong when he knows he is wrong."

The boy hesitated a long while, not sure whether it was cool to cooperate with me, then said, "A mugger."

"All right. That's good. A mugger knows he is doing something wrong, or at least he knows he is breaking the law. But don't you think he's got some idea in his head of why it is okay for him to break the law? Maybe he thinks that he's some kind of Robin Hood and that it's right for him to take money from rich people. Maybe he's a junkie and he thinks that it's okay because he needs his heroin so badly and there's no other way to get the money. Isn't that so? Don't people usually have some idea that the thing they are doing, no matter how wrong it may be, is somehow right, or at least okay?—Isn't that so, James?" I turned to a boy who had been laughing behind me. "Don't you feel that it is somehow all right to talk during class when you've got a substitute?"

I had been ignoring all the chatter and goofing that had been building up during my discussion, but now it was beginning to get out of hand. Since my joke didn't seem to have much effect, apart from embarrassing James, I had to threaten the students with Ms. Suarez again.

When at last I had diminished the distractions in the room sufficiently, I continued: "Anyhow . . . what James or the mugger felt was 'justified.' You feel justified when you come up with some idea about why whatever you may have done is really right. Now, as we know, everyone involved in the murder of Yusuf Hawkins did something wrong—except for Yusuf Hawkins and his friends, of course. But they *all* felt *justified,* at least at the time."

The class was getting noisy again. I was coming to my most important point, but I wasn't sure if more than five kids were listening to me. Once again I issued a few loud threats, then said: "I'm almost done. Just listen to this: Your job as writers is to get into the minds of these characters and try to figure out how they felt justified doing the awful things they did. If you can do that, then you will really understand their points of view. You will really understand who they are."

A tall, good-looking boy named Isaac Moreno—another student with whom I would soon begin to work closely—raised his hand. "When're we going to write?"

Isaac didn't want to write. He just wanted me to stop talking, but I took him at his word. "Right now."

Once I had given the students their writing folders, which I took home to write comments in after every class, I went over to Danny, the boy who had written that he admired "Uusus Mondello" for organizing the gang. I told him I liked what he had written but that I would like him to try to write as if he were Keith Mondello telling what happened.

"But this *is* what I think," Danny said.

"I know that, but I want you to tell me what Keith Mondello thinks."

"But I don't know him."

"That doesn't matter. Just pretend." I could see that what I was saying didn't make any sense to Danny, so I decided to illustrate: "You could do it like this, 'My name is Keith Mondello. You probably read about me in the newspaper. Well, all of that was fucking lies. Don't you believe anything you read in the newspapers. I'll tell you what really happened.' And then you just write it down. Have Keith tell us the real story."

All the time I was talking there was a half smile on Danny's face. He was enjoying the novelty of hearing a teacher use four-letter words, but I think he was also engaged by the situation I had set up for him. I walked away from his desk feeling pleased, but when I came back to him later, I saw no sign that he had even lifted his pen.

He was not alone by any means. Only Sasha sat quietly at her desk, filling pages with her loopy scrawl for the whole period. Despite her promise, she didn't write any more about Fama. Instead she just skipped a line and went on:

My name is Yusuf Hawkins I am lookin for an address with my two friends. I finally saved up enough money for this used car! Well, now I am in BEnsonhurst with my friends and all of a sudden I see a whole bunch of white people standing with bats and other dangerous weapons. So I continue walking. So as I was saying I saved enough money for my car. It was hard saving up money. I had to run errands for my mom for about 3 weeks! And I had to watch my little sister and brother and some other stuff. "those people look mean" I said to my friend. So I'm at the right address for my car. And then somebody shouted "Is it them? Is it them?" Is it who? What did I do? Then somebody said "I ain't gonna kill them." Thats when I started to panic. I did not know what to do. Then this guy that was all in white clothes just comes and says "the hell with beating him up, I'm gonna shoot the nigger" then boom!!————— (1 day later Yusuf becomes a ghost after his death.) I knew it they killed me!! For absoultely no reason! Why?! Why?! WHY!!! I did not do anything! I hope that ugly ass that killed me get arrested along with all of those white people. Only if I could come alive again maybe that kid will get some dicipline!! All I was doing was walking in the street with my friends!

I was very pleased when I came across Sasha's piece in her folder, in part because (without making too fine a point of the aesthetic merits of the piece) it proved that she was an artist and not a racist, but also because it vindicated what had been a very depressing day.

Most of my students had added absolutely nothing to what they had written the week before. A few had filled a page with swearwords. But Sasha had shown that it was possible for one writer to imagine the point of view not just of one character but of two and make them both seem credible—a fact that many of the other students, and not just Danny, were having trouble grasping. I was also pleased by Sasha's piece because I knew that next week, if I read it aloud to the class together with a few other of the better pieces, especially if I read them in something close to a chronological order, the kids would see very clearly a point I had been trying to make to them since the beginning of the year: that if you develop your characters by presenting in detail their thoughts, feelings, words, and actions, the result is much more powerful than if you merely summarize what happened. In other words: "Show, don't tell."

Here are a few of the other pieces I wanted to read with Sasha's. The first is by Xia Sanchez, the dark-skinned girl with light hazel eyes who kept her poems in a red account book/calendar.

One Summer
Night in Bensonhurst

Hello my name is Russell Gibbons and I was one of the people who were in the gang. I was scared man, I didn't know what to do. I was scared that if I didn't join the group that they might kill me because I was black. Boy you don't know how scared I was. It was kind of embarrassing being the only black guy in the group but it didn't matter because I didn't want to die. I was kind of shock because Joey Fama shot Hawkins. I didn't think he was really gonna shoot him, I thought he was gonna try to bluff them you know get them scared. But when that bullet hit hawkins I stood frozen there in the croud, Well, I'm never gonna forget this night bye.

Russell Gibbons fascinated me. As the only black member of the white gang and the one who collected the baseball bats that many of the gang members were carrying, I thought that he might have particularly strong and complicated feelings about Hawkins's murder, his own role in it, and about the relations of blacks and whites generally. Were a play to emerge from this work, I could imagine Russell Gibbons becoming almost as important a figure as Hawkins. In his conflict between loyalty to his friends and loyalty to his race, I saw the potential for a truly tragic figure. To my disappointment, however, almost none of the sixty-six students in my two classes wrote about Gibbons, perhaps because his situation was just too complicated. Those who did write about Gibbons, as we see in Xia's piece, apparently could conceive of only one motive for his involvement with the gang: fear. No one seemed able to imagine that he might have had a real friendship with at least some members of the gang—which is intriguing when you consider that many students had professed to admire Mondello themselves. Perhaps these students were put off by the degree of humiliation and obsequiousness that friendship with members of this bigoted community would entail.

It is interesting that Xia didn't even mention that Gibbons collected the baseball bats. She also had difficulty focusing on the one motive she did give Gibbons. After having him tell twice how scared he was, she had him talk about his situation as if it were merely embarrassing. Xia herself seemed to feel that she had not done her best work here. At the bottom of the page she wrote me a note that amounted to an excuse for the piece's insufficiency: "Dear Steve, I was going to do joey fama but I didn't know what to write so I did something else o.k."

I decided to read this piece to the class despite my misgivings about it, because I wanted to call attention to Gibbons and because it would be instructive to my students to think about the ways in which this piece failed. I knew Xia well enough by this time to know that she could take a bit of criticism, especially if her piece could remain anonymous. She hardly ever participated in class discussions but wrote with great seriousness and sensitivity, even if her use of language was generally a bit rough. I had come to like and respect her a great deal.

Joey Fama was by far the most popular monologue subject, partly, I think, because he was the most comprehensible of the characters. He was the living cliché of a white bigot, even down to his white suit and his silver gun. Also, he was a bit crazy, which made him fun to write about and provided a simple explanation for any of his actions. And finally, while the state of his mind was, if anything, probably more distasteful than Russell Gibbons's, there was a major difference: Joey Fama was a man of action and, within the narrowest definition of the word, strong. Russell Gibbons, on the other hand, was weak. As I had already found out, weakness was more offensive to many of my students than racism and, in a certain sense, than murder. Here is a piece by Isaac Moreno.

> There was a crowed in front of too Black kids. I was walking like know one could stop me. I was lean and mean and matching I had my white shoes and suit. there was a crowed infront of me. but that didn't stop me. I got to the crowed and I was redy to push people out of my why. But they move out of my why. Because I am the man in POWER.

The next piece, also about Fama, was written by Ricky Ortiz, who like his sister had picked up on Fama's mania for cleanliness. Although Ricky's punctuation makes this confusing to read, he heard Fama's voice (or voices) clearly in his mind and could give an eerily convincing reading of this.

Joey Fama

> My name is Joey Fama why did I kill that kid cause they told me to and a cop called out who's them the voice in my head What did they say the voice said they said he was dirty and to kill him cause he would have gotten my hands dirty and—and—and I d-d-didn't I have to tell him don't worry I have to tell him so shut up j-j-just shut up. So what are you saying the cop said I didn't wanted to get my hands dirty.

Interestingly, although Fama was the most popular subject for monologues, only one African American student wrote from his point of view, a broad-shouldered and tall dark-skinned boy named Chris Wood, who looked tough but was really sweet and gentle. His Joey Fama is a benign character who wants to kill himself after shooting Hawkins but decides that that would hurt his mother, so instead he says: "I can not life with this guilt so I will turn my self in. I did it you no what my friends felt the same way as me. Look at them now here they come just like me I figure now they are turning they self in." The year after his graduation, Chris was stabbed by a gang from a rival junior high when he tried to stop them from ripping the earrings out of two girls' ears.

Most of the African American kids in the two classes wrote about Yusuf Hawkins.

Yussef Hawkins

I finally got enough money to save up on a used car. Thats what I want. So my friends and I went to a place to look at a use car. As we were walking about 40 or 50 white boys started surrounding us I was scared. They started to call us niggers I didn't want to say anthing next thing you know my friends ran away I was alone. Then I saw a black guy with the whites. A girl started yelling out the window no thats not him. They said so we are going to kill him anyway. Some of the white guys left that was scared they didn't want to go to jail. But some asshole came up and shot me I was on the floor trying to breath but I couldn't. If I was alive I will kill that dame Bastard. Shot him until his body parts fall off. And after I am finish I will burne his head and stick it in a pile of shit And while he is in hell I hope he remember this dame day.

In many ways this piece is typical of the seventh-graders' presentation of Yusuf Hawkins. His voice is much less distinct than any of the other characters'. He seems to go through his confrontation with the gang almost in his sleep. This monologue is somewhat exceptional in that Hawkins says he is "scared." In most of the other Hawkins monologues, he just recites all the terrible things that happened to him in an anesthetized voice, at least until he has been killed. Then, in many of the pieces, as in the above, his voice suddenly becomes vivid and strong as he expresses his anger and plots revenge. Once again I saw that my students had difficulty writing about weakness and passivity but had no trouble writing about anger, revenge, and action.

Gina Feliciano was an attractive subject for kids of all races. Despite all our discussion and all my proselytizing, in virtually every Gina Feliciano monologue she blames herself for what happened. Sometimes, as in this case, you can read her sense of guilt as merely a part of her trauma, but that was not usually the case.

My Point of view
On one Summer
Night in Bensonhurst

Gina Feliciano

It seem's that nobody likes me so I had to find some friends. It not my fault I have black friend's. I Don't look at Peoples Skin I look at their Personalitys. There my only friends Why Should I dispise them Their the only one's who understands me So what if their Spanish and Black. Those Boys have a big problem. The don't like anybody but their own color. That's why they'll never have any real friend's. I don't understand the reason Why People think I'm a crack addick. The reason why they don't like me is Becuse I get along with other people or Different Races. It was my fault in a way I should have never said that my black friends were gonna Beat them up. Im just another mixed up girl growing up in Brooklyn.

I WAS WELL AWARE OF THE LIMITATIONS OF MY STUDENTS' WRITING, which are in part generic: as I have already mentioned, children's fiction virtually never attains that sparkling freshness that often makes their poetry the envy of adult writers. But the fact remains that, with all of their limitations, the Bensonhurst monologues were vastly more interesting, powerful, and well imagined than any other group of stories produced by Walt Whitman seventh-graders. Heretofore, when asked to write fiction, the boys would generally produce either accounts in sportscasterese of tense moments in basketball games or endless, pointless video game stories in which indistinguishable "good" and "evil" robotic louts zapped and clobbered one another until their author lost interest in them. The girls, who generally found inspiration in a much wider range of subjects than the boys, nevertheless tended to write fifth-rate imitations of *Beverly Hills 90210* that, no less than the boys' stories, were all but impossible for anyone except their authors to pay attention to.

When I read many of the pieces quoted above and a couple of others at the third meeting of each of my seventh grades, nobody had any trouble paying attention. The students were astonished by their own talent and shocked by the power of the story that collectively they had told. In both classes, Joan Gold and the students demanded to know who had written several of the pieces (the authors would rise from their chairs or raise their hands with shy, proud grins), and one class applauded when I had finished reading.

While the students were still under the spell of their own success, I told them that I wanted them to finish the pieces they had already started. I also said that I would like more Russell Gibbons monologues and monologues for Yusuf Hawkins that contained more of what he was thinking and feeling while confronting the white gang. The kids in both classes went to work eagerly and wrote hard for the remainder of the period. I had never had such broad, enthusiastic participation in any of my assignments. On a normal good day, somewhat more than half the class would do the assignment, and maybe a handful would write well. But during the Bensonhurst Project, especially after the students had listened to me read their writing, almost everybody participated, and half the class produced its best writing ever.

Another reason why I was thrilled by the project was that, perhaps for the first time ever, it was clear to me that this writing really did "matter," that it really did have "political and social importance." When I had finished reading their monologues aloud, I told my students: "I am so proud of you. You are doing a fabulous job at discovering the truth behind the cold facts of this story. You are making the true ugliness and tragedy of what happened at Bensonhurst terribly real. You are making it live. You are making me understand not only how horrible these events were but, perhaps more important, why they happened. Only if we understand why such events happen can we learn to prevent them."

It was wonderful to talk this way. Never before had I been able to hook writing, the writing my students were *doing,* to the great mission of literature and, really, of all artistic and intellectual disciplines: to help us *experience and understand* life as completely as possible so that our lives can be richer and we can, through the wisdom we gain and share, make the world a better, saner place to live.

There was one other benefit of the Bensonhurst Project that I wasn't quite aware of at first but that in the end excited me perhaps most of all—it was allowing me to get to know my students more intimately than I ever had before. When I had first thought up the project, I hadn't realized how close the world my students lived in—and perhaps dreaded—was to the world of confrontation, violence, and death that they were writing about. By putting on the voices of other people, they were dealing with their own worst fears and experiences more honestly (for the most part) than they would have had they been avowedly writing about themselves. The immediacy of the subject matter made not only for powerful writing but also for heartfelt discussion, especially when I would crouch beside a student's desk to talk about a piece of his or her work.

The project was also changing the way my students saw me. Before, I had been a showman, an odd sort of comedian, who once a week gave the students a good time, if only by providing low-pressure relief from their normal schoolwork. Students liked me, but comparatively few of them took me seriously. Then, by bringing the raw events at Bensonhurst into the classroom and by constantly emphasizing that I wanted to hear the truth even when it consisted of normally forbidden language or sentiments, I had broken down some of the standards of classroom decorum and won the trust and respect of many of my students. Although I am sure that there were plenty who still thought me naive and "white bread," they nonetheless felt they could be honest with me and write about things that really mattered to them. Several students began to write about subjects other than Bensonhurst. One girl wrote about her mother's suicide and how she herself wanted to die (I made copies of her writing for the school guidance counselor). Many children wrote about their problems with girlfriends, boyfriends, parents, and teachers. One boy used his Teachers & Writers folder as a confessional journal, in which he wrote detailed accounts of the severe beatings he and his older brother had received from their father and about how those beatings had affected him and his whole family.

THE DAY AFTER THOSE WONDERFUL CLASSES, DURING WHICH I read my students' work aloud, I went to work a bit early so that I could stop off at Rachel Suarez's office to brag to her about how well the Bensonhurst Project was going. As soon as I walked in her door she said, "Oh, Steve, I was going to come looking for you. We finally worked out the new schedule." She handed me her clipboard and, just as I had feared, the seventh grades would be meeting at a time when I couldn't see them.

"How long before this goes into effect?" I asked, hoping that I might be able to meet twice with my classes next week, rather than once, and bring the project at least close to a conclusion.

"On Monday," she said.

It was Friday. The Bensonhurst Project was over.

4

Do You Know How Death Feels?

I TOOK A COPY OF THE NEW WALT WHITMAN ACADEMY SCHEDULE with me to my first class but didn't have time to look at it carefully until a couple of periods later, when I had a break. Getting myself a cup of tea at a deli across the street from the school, I went up to the writing room, an old dressing room behind the auditorium where my staff and I held weekly meetings and saw small groups of students, and where I went whenever I wanted to escape the din of children's shouts and teachers' bellows that constantly echoed along every inch of the school's gray-tiled hallways.

A closer examination of the new schedule only confirmed my first impression. In order to continue seeing the seventh grades, I would have to switch four of my other classes, which wouldn't have been possible given how tight schedules were at the school. But if I started seeing the eighth grades, who were now with Joan at almost the same time Thursday mornings as the seventh grades had been, I would only have to switch one of my P.S. 227 classes. With similarly minor changes, I could arrange for each of the Columbia MFA student interns, Matt Sharpe and Elizabeth Shepard, to take over one of the seventh-grade classes.

Having found what seemed the perfect solution, I began to get excited. I felt bad about abandoning the seventh-graders in the middle of the project, but at the same time I thought that, with the benefit of experience, I could probably make a much more stimulating presentation of the Bensonhurst material to the eighth grades and thereby get some much stronger writing. I was also excited about the new seventy-minute periods, which would give the students twenty-five more minutes per session in which to develop their ideas without interruption. But the schedule change also brought me new anxiety, which was largely the result of developments outside the school.

As I have already mentioned, this school year, 1991–92, was Teachers & Writers Collaborative's twentieth at P.S. 227. Phillip Lopate, Alan Ziegler, and I had decided to mark the anniversary with a celebration to which we would invite all the writers, teachers, students, and parents who had been involved in the program. The celebration would include exhibits of the best work from the last twenty years. Phillip and Alan would also briefly reminisce about their years as directors of the program. I would be host and MC, but my work at the school would be represented primarily by a performance of the play that I would edit together from the Bensonhurst work.

I had made these plans in the first flush of my enthusiasm for the project. But now that I was having to start it all over again with the eighth grades, I began to wonder if my plans had been a bit rash. The celebration was to be held on Friday, May 6. Casting and rehearsing the play would take eight weeks. With vacations taken into account, this left only five class meetings for writing the play—just enough time so long as Joan Gold was never absent or there were no class trips, assemblies, or other unforeseen events that would preempt my teaching. The pressure on me was increased by the fact that 1991–92 was also the twenty-fifth anniversary of Teachers & Writers Collaborative itself. When T&W director Nancy Shapiro heard about the party Phillip, Alan, and I were planning, she decided to make it the kickoff event of the Collaborative's own weeklong celebration. I was pleased and honored by her decision, but it meant that to a certain extent the Bensonhurst play would be representing not only my work but the work of all current members of the Collaborative—and not only to P.S. 227/Walt Whitman alumni but possibly even to the press.

My anxiety about the play was eased immensely by the presence at the school of Daniel Judah Sklar. Daniel is a playwright, the author of

Playmaking: Children Writing & Performing Their Own Plays, and has had many years experience helping children write and perform plays with Teachers & Writers and the 52nd Street Project, a theater workshop for children. Daniel had filled in for me at P.S. 227/Walt Whitman the previous year, when I had taken a semester off to accompany my family to Berkeley, where my wife was a visiting professor. He had done such a great job that I had invited him to come back to the school, teach a few drama classes, and continue to run the after-school Walt Whitman Academy T&W Drama Club, which he had started during my sabbatical.

Although I had often had students write monologues and dialogues during my four years with Teachers & Writers, I had never directed a student play and had never performed in a play myself. I am not sure I would ever have had the courage to put on the Bensonhurst play had not Daniel agreed to help me direct it. It was not only Daniel's experience that put me at ease; it was also his manner. Daniel is one of those rare teachers who can hold a whole class's attention by speaking softly. He is extremely clear, fair, and firm, but he leads by being unassuming, by letting the children feel free to follow their creative impulses, by being encouraging and not judgmental. When I would start to voice my worries about whether the students could master the play in time for the celebration, Daniel would just hold up his hand and say in a velvety tenor: "Look, Steve, we'll do what we can. But the kids will come through. You'll see. They always do." I put my trust in Daniel's skill and experience, and he did not give me one moment of disappointment.

MY FIRST DAY WITH THE EIGHTH GRADES WENT EXCEPTIONALLY well. Some of the students had already heard about the Bensonhurst Project and were eager to participate. I began by handing out and reading my plot summary: "Gina Feliciano turned seventeen that night . . ." Once again I instantly had the students' full attention; and once again they were eager to blame Gina Feliciano for stirring up the trouble that led to Hawkins's death and were just as unimpressed as the seventh grades had been by my assertion that Keith Mondello had been the first to issue a threat.

When it came time to write, I tried to preempt some of the misunderstandings that had weakened the seventh-graders' earliest efforts by telling the students that they should not only think about their chosen character's point of view and about how their character would justify his or her actions, but also try to imagine how that character felt at each separate moment during that tragic summer night. My main intention in giving these instructions was to get a Yusuf Hawkins with a more lively and distinct voice—and that is just what I got. Whether it was due to my more precise instructions or just because the students were a year older, I can't say for sure, but the various Yusuf Hawkinses that came out of the eighth grade had far more memorable voices. Here is my favorite.

Yusuf H.

I was mad happy when I got my license yesterdy. I was even happier when my cousin showed me the newspaper ad. Money that car looked mad dope, and it was just $3,000 bucks too. I'd been saving up for three months, as soon as I got some of my friends went to get the car, it was somewhere out in Bensonhurst, I've never been out that way but my moms told me how to find my way around. I was out lookin' for the place in the ad for an hour or two, it was getting dark out, when we saw guys up ahead they had bats and shit. When I saw that they was headin' our way I was about to be outty out in a second they was around us, they started talkin' shit like "What you niggers doin' here" and shit like that. I held out the ad one of them said somethin' about us not bein' somebody or somethin' like that, when one of the punks in the bunch stepped up like he was gonna hit me or somethin', I was about to pop that motherfucker in the head, when someone whit a shiny .38 said somethin' about not hittin' me and then blew me inna head, I felt somethin' movin' in my head then I tasted some chocolate in my mouth.

Asa Taylor, the boy who wrote this, was very intelligent and had grown up in a more middle-class family than most of his classmates. He was also a stunningly talented artist, but he almost never wrote. This was by far the longest piece he had given me in the three years he had been my student, which was certainly one of the main reasons why I was so thrilled by it. I loved the slangy enthusiasm he gave Hawkins at the beginning, making him cool but also sweet—a distinct character.

Nevertheless, Asa, like all of the other students, was unable to render Hawkins's fear, except by having him declare that he wanted to run ("be outty out") and by the sudden evaporation of his enthusiasm. Such understatement, commonly used by professional writers to render terrifying situations, works very well here, making the confrontation seem nothing but a series of senseless threats and gestures that Hawkins never fully comprehends. The understatement is especially effective when Asa renders Hawkins's final disorientation by having him give the same weight to the utterly unprecedented and sinister sensation of motion in his head and the tragically ordinary and childish taste of chocolate.

A girl named Angela Cordero also portrayed Yusuf Hawkins's death as a moment of incomprehension. Her piece concludes:

> Then all of a sudden This guy come to me dressed all in white and with a bright silver gun. So he pulled the gun out, when I saw that I froze. He started screaming I'm gonna kill him. They all started screaming, "no don't do it, it's not him, it's not him." He shot at me. I felt nothing. I saw blood falling to the ground, it was then that I realized it was my own. Quickly I didn't think of anger I thought peace and my family. it was also then when I realized how much I loved them. If only I would have been able to say good by. all I want to say is . . .
>
> "DON'T WORRY I'LL BE BACK."

Again, there was no fear in Angela's piece. When Hawkins is shot he says, "I felt nothing." Angela ends her piece with a promise of resurrection, and indeed, promises of resurrection and often of revenge were common ways for students to deal with (and soften) Hawkins's death. Angela revealed the nature of her feelings about deaths like Hawkins's more completely than most of her classmates through an extraordinary piece that she had written for Matt Sharpe, the Columbia intern who had taught her Teachers & Writers class before the schedule change. As she handed me both papers at the end of class, she tapped the second and said, "I want you to read this. It's sort of the same thing as what we were talking about."

Do you know how death feels? Do you know what the pain feels like? The ripping and slow tering of your heart, stomach and soul. Well I've gone threw that. You don't know how it is, until you've experienced it, Most of you haven't and I hope you don't. Let me explain. It was a day I'll never forget. I don't live in the greatest block. there are always gangs fighting, screaming, shootting; Boolets, Boolets that have killed many unfortunat people. I went downstairs to get some grosieris with my best friend, 9 years we've been together I never thought this could happen That day she became another victim of a boolet - One of thows unfortunat people. why? She droped to the ground and me to my nees. I picked her head up and said "Don't worry. Please someone call an ambulanse, hang on"!! Blood was all over the ground it got all over me I didn't care. She looked up and laughed and said "don't worry I'll be o.k. I'm going to high school. I'v made it this far and nothing's going to stop me." I didn't know less than a minuet later she'd be dead. She died in my arms. I didn't get to say good by I didn't get to say good by. She died and that day a part of my heart died too. good by I said but she didn't hear me She was dead. that day my best friend became yet another statistic.

I read this piece while Angela waited beside me, and when I was finished I had no idea what to say to her. I was shocked, also embarrassed. No student had ever confessed so grim an experience to me before, and in such detail. At first all that came into my head to say, absurdly, was that this was one of the most effectively written pieces I had ever gotten from a student. Finally my jaw came unstuck: "Angela, this must have been so horrible for you!"

"Yeah . . . Well . . ." She smiled and didn't say anything else.

"I hope Bensonhurst won't be too hard for you to write about. You don't have to do it if you don't want to."

"Nah. That's all right." Then she reached out and tapped her paper. "Actually she wasn't my best friend. I just put that in because it sounded better."

AT OUR REGULAR STAFF MEETING THE FRIDAY BEFORE STARTING the new schedule, the Columbia interns, Matt Sharpe and Elizabeth Shepard, and I discussed the classes we were exchanging (they were each taking over one of my seventh grades, while I got an eighth grade from each of them). Matt contributed the most fascinating item to the discussion: a girl in my first eighth grade (Asa Taylor and Angela Cordero were in the second) had gotten pregnant around Halloween and, as of the start of Christmas vacation, had been resisting the urgings of her mother and friends to get an abortion. The girl's name was Yvette Santoro. I didn't know her. She was not one of the children who had matriculated from P.S. 227. "You'll have no trouble recognizing her," Matt said. "She's incredibly beautiful."

Matt was right. I spotted Yvette Santoro instantly on my first day in the class, both by her beauty, which lived up to Matt's description, and her seriousness. I was pretty sure—correctly, as it turns out—that she was no longer pregnant. Yvette was small and very thin and wouldn't easily have been able to conceal a baby past the first trimester. She had the face of an actress, coffee-and-cream skin, full lips, and long wavy hair, hennaed to a copper brown, that poured out of a topknot like an unraveled silk rope. She sat in the front row of the class and seemed to listen to Joan Gold and myself with an extraordinary concentration. I had heard that her boyfriend was twenty-six—almost twice her age— and indeed she gave the impression of someone who had prematurely learned the follies of her young generation.

I was very curious to see what her writing was like but wasn't able to make my way over to her desk until nearly the end of class. Happy at my attention, she scribbled a last sentence and handed me her paper.

—Gina is it true you dropped out of High School?

—Im yes I did dropped out of High School because I was in to much pressure going to school going out with friends so I chose what I wanted to do so I dropped out.

—Gina is it true you a crack addict. Why?

—Yes is true I am a crack addict and why because I think it Get's me off my problems and I think is cool.

—Gina about that night why you told Keith Mandello that those Niggers and Spics were coming to your party and that they were coming to beat him up?

—Well I told him that becouse he got me on my nurve becouse I like him and he doesn't so I told him that those guys were coming to beat him up So he could get mad. but I didnt know that he was going to get his friends and wait for those guys. but the bad part is that I didn't know that guys were coming into the Neighborhood. at that time and that day.

—now that everything pass dont you fell guilty?

—NO becouse it didn't happen to me.

—You should fell sorry because it happen to an innocent kid that had nothing to do with your problem and you little stupid lie that became a tragidy now what do you think?

—I still think the same way that am glad it didn't happen to me.

Reading that composition now, I see that it contains all sorts of hints about what was going on in Yvette's life, especially the passage about dropping out of school because of social pressure. But at the time I was mainly struck by how poorly written it was. Her apparent concentration had led me to expect much better.

One point that particularly intrigued me, however, was Gina's idea that she needn't feel guilty about what had happened, since it hadn't happened to her. This seemed an astute dramatic insight. I could easily imagine that the real Gina Feliciano might have felt this way. But it also got me wondering—as I had with Sasha Ortiz's racist Joey Fama monologue—where the boundary between life and art lay in Yvette's work. Was Gina's pronouncement truly the product of Yvette's aesthetic, psychological, and moral perspicacity, or did Yvette herself tend to feel remorse only for actions that had caused her personal harm? She did have the interlocutor condemn the pronouncement in forceful—if somewhat confused—terms, but the very confusion of that condemnation and of the rest of the dialogue only gave me more reason to suspect that Gina's pronouncement sprang not from Yvette's clarity of vision but from her fundamental fogginess about the nature of guilt. My suspicions about Yvette were not derived only from her work, however, but also from school gossip, which treated her as a tragic but serious delinquent—which is to say that I was perhaps prejudging Yvette in the same way my students did Gina Feliciano.

"What do you think about what Gina says here?" I asked, pointing to the last line of her piece—the one she had finished as I approached her desk.

Yvette shrugged. "I don't know."

"Do you think she was right to feel this way?"

Yvette seemed shocked by my question: "No! Of course not!"

Embarrassed, I tried to shift the implication of my comment: "I think it's the most interesting part of your piece. It's surprising but believable. I think Gina really comes alive there."

Yvette smiled broadly. "Yeah. That's what I thought. I wasn't liking what I was writing. But then I wrote that part and I started liking it."

VALENTINE'S DAY WAS COMING UP AND I WANTED TO DO A bulletin board of love stories and poems. I gave a love poem assignment to my fourth- and fifth-grade classes but was precluded from doing the same with the eighth grade by the Bensonhurst Project. I remembered, however, that when Matt Sharpe had been teaching Yvette's class, he had asked the students to write about first meeting somebody and had told them, as an example, the story of when he met his girlfriend. Thinking this assignment might have yielded a love story or two, I searched through my eighth-grade folders and found the following piece by Yvette.

Michelle is a beutyful eighteen year old girl who fall in love with this guy named Kevin. once she is taking a bath in the river naked he comes along just to pick up some fruit for his father and when he look he sees this butyful girl taking a bath in the river he almost faints. But she doesn't see him until she turns over and sees this gorjus guy looking at her. so she was so surprized that at the same time she felt as if she was in Heaven. Then, imedeitly, she reached her senses. She stated cursing at Kevin because he was looking at her. so then he finish picking fruits for his father and he ran away. She was sad because she thought she might never see him again. Two months later she was in the park sitting in the grass just thinking about the guy that stol her heart but then she felt this shadow of someone that the Sun reflected. Suddenly she turn over and saw this gorjous guy that was looking at her two months ago. He said hi to her she said hi back They star at each other. Suddenly he grab her and kiss her passionately they grab each other tight as if they would never let go she was so Happy that she couldn't beleve what was happening to her. Suddenly he stoped kissing her and told her I love you very much she said I love you too! Then he asked her if she wanted to go out with him she said yes and they liv happily ever after.

What struck me when I first read this piece was that, much as it revealed an acquaintance with sexual passion, it was the work of a much sweeter and more innocent girl than the Yvette of school gossip. I felt bad when I finished this piece, partly because it made me see how I had been prejudiced against Yvette, but also because, little as I knew about her life then, I was pretty sure that such happy innocence would not last for long.

Yvette's best friend, Diana Delacruz, who also had a boyfriend in his mid-twenties, wrote a fine story that showed a similar mix of innocence and sexual experience but that was more true to the mundane details of their lives. It may even have been strictly autobiographical, since Diana's boyfriend was named Darrell.*

I remember the first time I met Darrell. I was on [. . .] Street and this guy named Frank came outside of Burger King. That's where they hang out. So Frank was rapping to my sister Rita. He was talking to her—like saying, What's your name? How old are you? What school do you go to? Well, then Frank, since he saw me all bored, he knocked on the window of Burger King and told Darrell to come out. First I was seeing him through the window. I really didn't like him because he had long hair . . . Not really, but it was quite long. So when he came outside to talk to me he was wearing his hat and he looked so cute. Oh, my Lord! If you had seen him you would have jumped up and down! I tried to control myself, but I couldn't. He started saying what's my name. I said Ana Michelle. He was like, I will just call you Michelle. Drop that Ana thing. So he started

---

* I no longer have the original of this piece. What follows is the corrected version that appeared on the T&W bulletin board. I have deleted the street name to preserve Diana's privacy.

rapping to me. Finally I said, Let's go, because my hands were beginning to get cold. I started to shiver and my head was pounding. He was like, You're not gonna give me your phone number? And he went inside Burger King, got a piece of paper and started to write his number and his beeper number. So I gave him my number. Then when I was about to turn around, he held my hand and said, You're not going to give me my good-bye kiss? So, I gave him and Frank a cheek kiss. So did my sister. Then, when we left, I couldn't stop talking about them.

I used both pieces in the Valentine's Day bulletin board, together with a funny surreal story by another eighth-grader about a couple who meet on a California cheese line.

THE NIGHT BEFORE MY NEXT MEETING WITH THE EIGHTH GRADES I got a cryptic message on my phone machine from Joan Gold, telling me that I should still come to school even though the eighth grades were going on a trip at nine-forty. I hadn't known about the trip and had been planning to come to school as normal. My interpretation of Joan's message was that I would only have time to see my first class, so I didn't bother to bring the folders for the second one, nor did I go to the school with great expectations. As good as my first sessions with the eighth grade may have been, I knew there was no way the students would be able to pay much attention to me on the morning of a trip—a fact I found very frustrating. I had planned only three more meetings with each class to finish writing the play. If I had to extend the writing phase of the project, that would mean taking rehearsal time away from the Drama Club.

When I walked into Joan's classroom, however, I discovered that things were worse than I had imagined. The trip—to a play downtown—was a "privilege," Joan informed me, not an "entitlement." Only those students who had done the best work were going. This would mean that half the students in my first class would be too excited to concentrate, while the other half, by definition the worse half, would be too angry. My second class, however, which would begin after all the "privileged" students had gone, would consist entirely of the rejectees, who almost certainly would not feel like working while their classmates were out having a good time. To make matters worse, I didn't have their folders, so that those who wanted to continue working on pieces they had started the previous week would either have to try to remember where they had left off or just give up and start anew. Both options, I was quite sure, would spark complaints. My one consolation was that this second class would be half its normal size, which would allow me to devote much more attention to individual students.

In my first class I decided to deal with the students' restlessness by cutting my presentation to a minimum and having the kids write for most of the period. That way, those students who could concentrate on their writing would be occupied and quiet and those who couldn't could be dealt with as they made noise.

This strategy proved surprisingly effective. I read the Bensonhurst fact sheet aloud again, gave the kids a few pointers about voice and the perspectives of the different characters, then set them to work. The class was far noisier than usual, but most of the kids got some writing done. The noise didn't really get out of control until the time the class would have had to stop anyway, so that the students could get their coats out of the closet and line up to leave.

As Joan was marshaling the privileged members of the class out of the room, she gave me the really bad news: since she was going along on the trip, and Walt Whitman would therefore be one teacher short, they had decided to combine the eighth-grade rejectees into one class for the day. Joan tried to soften the blow with flattery: "This means that the first eighth grade will miss math today, but we thought that it was more important that they get Teachers & Writers." It also meant that not only would this class of resentful children be slightly larger than a normal class and have no seating order, but half of them would already have sat through my presentation, while the other half would have no folders.

Brenda Brodsky, the math teacher whom my first class would have been seeing this period, came to fill Joan's shoes. Brenda was not nearly as effective a bad cop as Joan. She was a nice woman, but tired: worn out by nearly forty years in the classroom. Her virtue as a teacher derived from experience. She knew precisely how much and how little her students understood. She knew just what she wanted to teach and exactly how she wanted to teach it. She might never win converts among students who went brain-dead at the sight of a fraction, but she also would never confuse those willing to follow along with her lesson.

I opened my lesson by apologizing to the first class for having to re-peat myself and was promptly met by a round of groans led by a very bright but obstreperous girl named Taletha. "Listen," I said, "you guys from the first class already have your folders. Just keep writing; you don't have to pay attention to what I'm saying."

Taletha: "Oh, man—this is stupid!"

I ignored her and began to read the Bensonhurst fact sheet aloud as a way of focusing the class's attention. Enough students were interested that something approaching a normal calm settled over the room. But I hadn't even gotten halfway through the sheet when the classroom door slammed against the wall and the assistant principal bustled over to my side. Recognizing the distinct lack of welcome in my expression, she whispered to me, "This will only take thirty seconds. It's important! I have to make sure that these students know where they are going."

Naturally, this interruption took a good deal longer than thirty sec-onds since, no matter how many times the assistant principal repeated the schedule, there was always one kid who didn't understand it or an-other who had understood it the first time through but had become confused by the repetitions. After a good ten minutes of this, the major-ity of kids who had understood the schedule right off, or even before-hand, were utterly exasperated by their slower classmates and the assistant principal—and so was I.

When at last I was left alone again with my class, I had to spend a good two or three more minutes summoning people back from the wa-ter fountain, interrupting conversations, telling students that, no, they couldn't go to the bathroom; no, the checkerboards and Monopoly games had to stay in the closet. When I finally started up on the fact sheet again, having backtracked a bit so that the class could follow, I had not gone a sentence further into the unread portion when the fire alarm sounded. Defeated, I tossed the fact sheet into my briefcase and let Brenda supervise the class's exit from the room. No sooner had the students lined up along the closets than, with the alarm bell still sound-ing, the school secretary shouted over the intercom: "Ignore the bell! IGNORE THE BELL!" That was the whole announcement. We got no other explanation of what had happened. Groaning, the kids returned to their seats.

The class was a shambles. With only the dimmest hope of success, I pulled the fact sheet out of my briefcase and said, "Okay, here we go again."

Adan said: "Come on, why can't we just play games?"

"Yeah," said Taletha. "How come we have to work when everyone else gets to go on a trip?"

"Three reasons," I said, beginning to get angry. "First, this is school, and when you are in school you are supposed to learn. Second, because, if we are going to get this play done in time to perform it at the twentieth-anniversary party in May, we have to use every minute we have. And third, because *this is interesting*! You guys have been doing incredible writing, the best I've ever seen in all my years of teaching. When we are done we are going to have a very powerful play that will not only help people understand what happened at Bensonhurst but help them feel how tragic it was."

Some of the students were listening. Some of them really did want to write. I was sure that if I could just get through the fact sheet (which the kids needed to hear in order to remember the details of the story), at least some of them would settle down and produce good work.

Just as I was about to start reading again, Brenda Brodsky decided that dramatic action was needed. "All right everybody," she said. "Take your chairs and come up to the front of the room. I want to talk to you."

More groans, from throats and scraping chair legs. More chaos. More delay. I got myself a chair, sat next to Brenda, and waited to see what she would do. It did occur to me that, given the students' mood, talking to them in a circle might work better than shouting to them at their desks.

Brenda did not really want to talk to them, however. She wanted to scold them. After a good five minutes of haranguing them about how rude they had been, and how they didn't deserve to work with Teachers & Writers, and how they had been left behind because they were a bunch of troublemakers, who should therefore be on their best behavior, she told them to go back to their seats.

"No," I said. "I've got an idea. Everybody just stay where you are. I want to do something that I had planned to do later, after you had had time to really get to know, through your writing, what had happened at Bensonhurst. But since we're all gathered here, and since it looks like the fates are against our doing any writing today, I think we might as well do now what I had planned for later." I was purposely keeping the class in suspense, on the idea that the more I piqued their curiosity, the more likely they were to listen and the better my chances were of rescuing my lesson. This strategy had worked for only half the class, however. The other half had merely grown more and more restless. The time had come to tip my hand.

"What I want to do is talk about Bensonhurst a bit, get a larger perspective on what happened there, talk about what the murder of Yusuf Hawkins tells us about the whole of society." I paused, hoping to draw everyone's attention with silence, but a collection of black students (mostly girls), centered around Taletha, were gabbing and laughing together with such enthusiasm that they probably wouldn't have noticed if I had walked out the door. This bothered me because it was actually the African American students whose opinions I was most eager to hear. I raised my voice: "Does anyone here have any idea what social problems led to the death of Yusuf Hawkins?" No one ventured a suggestion. The only sound in the classroom was the gabbing around Taletha. I raised my voice a bit more. "It seems to me that two social problems contributed to the death of Yusuf Hawkins. One was violence, and the other racism."

The classroom quieted a bit. There was always a slight charge in the air when a white teacher talked about racism. I had climbed up onto a tightrope, and everyone was curious to see if I would fall—perhaps no one more than myself.

Racism is one of those topics that make idiots or fascists out of anyone who talks about them for too long, especially in the wrong company. Every now and then during my four years of teaching I had referred to racism, but only to express a thoroughly conventional disapproval, and never in a way that even allowed for a response from my students. There was no telling what could happen were such an incendiary issue—and the passion it evoked—let loose in the classroom. Despite this fear, or perhaps because of it, I had always had a deep longing to have a serious and honest discussion of race with my students—especially my black students. I would even say that having just such a cathartic exchange had been one of my main—though less conscious or rational—ambitions for my teaching career. These were hardly the most auspicious circumstances in which to commence so important a discussion, however. The chief danger, it seemed to me, was not so much that I would set off an explosion of racial fury as that this room of bored and resentful students would just yawn and laugh the whole topic off, thereby making it much harder to introduce later in the project. But it was too late to go back now. The topic had been introduced, my deep passions and anxieties were rising up in me, and my class, perhaps sensing my feelings, had at last become quiet.

"Where do we see racism in what happened at Bensonhurst?" I asked.

I started with such a simple question because I wanted us to be clear about the basic details of what had happened and I wanted all of the students to be able to participate. But perhaps the question was too simple. Only after I had asked it a second time did a couple of kids call out that Mondello was a racist. Then an earnest boy named Tarron said: "Joey Fama didn't give a damn who the nigger was, he was just going to shoot him."

I was impressed by the simplicity with which Tarron described Fama's motives, using the term "nigger," and thought that such frankness might make for a good discussion. But none of these responses to my question were exciting enough to hold the attention of Taletha's crowd. I decided to up the ante a bit by asking for an expression of emotion: "How does that racism make you feel?"

Yvette, who was sitting next to Tarron and whose expression matched his for earnestness, said, "It makes me feel angry and sad."

I was going to ask her to elaborate, but at that moment Taletha let out a loud hoot, unrelated, I think, to what Yvette had said.

"How does it make *you* feel, Taletha?" I called out.

"Hunh?"

"How does the racism of Mondello and Fama make you feel?"

"Me?" She laughed. "I want to shoot them muthafuckin' white boys!" Loud laughter and repetitions of her remark rose from the group around her, and slightly less enthusiastically from other parts of the room.

Taletha was testing me, which was fine. I was willing to go as far as she wanted. "All right," I said. "That's an interesting point, and it's bringing us around to the other social problem that affected what happened at Bensonhurst: violence. How many other people feel like this? How many others want to murder those white boys?"

To my surprise, only Taletha raised her hand, and even she only snapped it up and down, as if it were merely a joke.

"Come on," I said encouragingly. "It's natural that you would feel that way, that you would get so angry you would want to kill. But just because you feel that way doesn't mean you would actually do it or even that you think it would be right."

Still no hands went up. Finally Tarron lifted his hand. "I don't want to shoot them," he said. "It makes me angry. I don't like thinking that someone from your own race is getting killed. But I don't think you should kill them. I don't know what you should do. It makes me sad."

This was a wonderfully forthright and honest remark. But nobody heard it because the din around Taletha and elsewhere in the room had only risen since her proclamation.

I had Tarron repeat his remark in a louder voice. Then I said, "What do you think of that, Taletha?"

She just gave me a sassy "What?" so I ignored her.

"What about the rest of you?" I asked. "What do you think of what Tarron said?"

"What he say?" asked Austin, a dark-skinned Latino boy with a scarred face and a reputation for making trouble. Sad to say, in eight out of ten cases his reputation was well deserved. In this one, however, I thought he was being earnest. But Brenda Brodsky didn't. She told him to go to the back of the room. His indignation, echoed by his friends, only added to the din in the room and further delayed the discussion, in which, chaotic as it may have been, some important points were being made. I suspected that most kids felt exactly like Tarron, and I wanted to lead the conversation around to the point that by writing, and writing well, about the racism and violence, we were doing something to diminish them—not the *only* thing, but *something*.

I asked Tarron to repeat his remark one last time. Clearly sick of saying the same thing over and over, and worrying that he might be making a fool of himself in front of his classmates, he graciously agreed to make his wise and honest point once again. But no sooner had he begun to speak than the classroom door, in front of which he was sitting, opened and slammed against his chair.

That was it. Tarron was fed up. I was exhausted. While half a dozen students shifted their chairs to one side to let in two boys who had been to special ed, I decided to just send the whole class back to their desks to write. Probably nothing would come of it, but I simply couldn't talk anymore.

Just at this moment, Brenda leaned toward me and asked, "Can I say something?" Gratefully, I turned the class over to her, only to have my heart sink as she proclaimed: "I just want you to know that it isn't only black people who get hurt by this." She then went on to tell a truly awful story about her niece being stabbed by a black man when she was in college.

Much as I sympathized with Brenda and her niece, in the final analysis her story told the students nothing about racism that they didn't already know. It was just another of those "your race abused mine" accusations that have characterized too large a proportion of the dialogue between blacks and whites for far too long. I am sure that many students were affected by Brenda's story, just as she wanted them to be, but I am equally sure that they all understood the story's secret hostility, which could only confirm their worst ideas about white teachers.

When she had finished, I sent the students to their desks and, to my astonishment, got a couple of very interesting, though angry, pieces from them. The first was written by Ali Ahmed, a skinny, birdlike boy with big brown eyes, whose family came from Syria.

Grammer

Yusuf Hawkins—

My name is Yusuf Hawkins I was going to Bensonhurst to this white boy town I was going with my friends to check out my first ride it was a used one and I knew we werent going to get jumped but we did when these fuckin whiteboys steped to me and my friend fuckin calling us niggers and the pulled out a fuckin gun you he pulled that shit he better fuckin kill I said to myself, or else Im fuckin comeing back witt a Tek 9 and bustin 12 clips in that fuckin whiteys ass, so the fuck shot me I laid there with my snikers bar in my hand.

I was shocked by the intensity of the anger in this piece, since Ali had never written anything like this before and, quite frankly, looked too cute even to be able to conceive of such emotions. I attributed the anger to art and wrote at the top of his paper: "Ali—You've got a good voice here. I believe it. It sounds like Yusuf might have talked. But the piece would have been stronger, and would have had more <u>truth</u> in it, if you had used more details." (A couple of weeks later—as I shall describe in Chapter 6—Ali became involved in an event that has me wondering to this day about the connection between art and his anger.)

The second piece was written by Austin Gonzalez, the scar-faced boy whom Brenda had sent to the back of the class. I've done my best to render his bizarre, graffiti-influenced typography in print.

ONE SUMMER NIGHT IN BENSONHURST

BROOKLYN

WHAT!

JOEY FAMA—I'M 19 YEAR OLD JOEY FAMA
I don't kear about any body not even my self
I'm that type that if anybody gives me any
problems I would just have to use my 32-
caliber to color that motherfucker dead
Now I didn't really know my self that
good because like I said I'm crazy so
I might as well shoot my self in
the head. Bang

The End WHAT?

At the bottom of the page, after the "bang," Austin drew a picture of a pistol. Further down there were two gravestones, one with an arrow pointing to the name Joey Fama and another with an arrow pointing to the name Yusuf Hawkins. At the very bottom of the page the word "silver" was written in a drawing of a tiny banner.

I don't think that Austin was taking the assignment seriously when he wrote this. He was just stewing in his own indignation at having been sent to the back of the room, and the character of Fama happened to provide a convenient means of expressing his own bad feeling. I think he thought that I would hate what he had written. His conclusion—from "Now I didn't really know my self" to "shoot my self in the head"—essentially blows off my presentation of the assignment as a means for getting to *know* a character. Despite these intentions, what immediately struck me about this piece was how well it expressed, both in form and content, the workings of a sick mind like Fama's. The truth is that it made me worry a bit about Austin, but I also saw it as an opportunity to win him over. He was astonished when I not only read but praised his piece to the class—all the more so because, I think, he saw that my praise was not merely a pedagogical ploy. However unwittingly, he really had captured something of Fama, and so well that a few days afterward his piece was quoted when a *New York Times* reporter wrote about the class.

That's How Life Really Is

I DIDN'T LOOK THROUGH THE EIGHTH GRADE'S WRITING FOLDERS until the following Monday morning. It was a dank, bitter-cold day with a sky so dimmed by weighty gray clouds that I needed a lamp to read, even sitting next to the window. Between the weather and my lingering frustration after that day of the class trip, I had pretty low expectations as I pulled the students' writing into my lap, but within a very few minutes I began to realize that something quite wonderful was happening inside those folders. Whether out of inspiration or fury, these eighth-graders had produced such vivid and compelling voices that, time and again as I read, I felt I was getting authentic and surprising insights, if not into the specific events that had occurred at Bensonhurst, then certainly into the mix of fear, prejudice, and warped innocence that had made them possible.

Not only were there many fabulous individual monologues but, as with the seventh grade, the best pieces only gained power when read together. I was sure that when I finally read them out loud to the class (I had been postponing this moment until I had enough complete monologues), none of my students would have trouble understanding the virtues of thoroughly imagining specific events, points of view, motivation, and voice. In the past I had tried to encourage my students to write more completely imagined works, mainly by asking for more "details." I think many students came to hate that word. It was too abstract. It referred to too many different kinds of information and was based on a standard of good writing that they neither understood nor particularly cared about (and, of course, it also meant more work!). But that morning, when I wrote comments on their papers, I was able to ask them for truth. I wrote: "Your Joey Fama's voice sounds real, but I need more TRUTH. Have him tell me EVERYTHING that he DID in the minutes before he shot Yusuf Hawkins. Have him tell me EVERY-THING he THOUGHT and FELT. I need to know these things if I am going to understand the truth of how a young man can become a murderer." "Truth," of course, is a more complicated abstraction than "details," but it was not one my students had any trouble understanding or respecting.

Another virtue of the work I found in the folders that morning was that there were so many stunning contrasts between voices for the same character—for example, Asa Taylor's "mad happy" and Ali Ahmed's Tec 9–toting Yusuf Hawkins. Such contrasts would make it very easy to show students the difference between the truth that is simply a matter of more facts and the truth that is the creation of the artist.

I ALSO BECAME EXCITED ABOUT MY STUDENTS' WORK FOR REASONS less directly related to pedagogy. It was on that dim, dank morning that I first began to realize that this new vision my students were giving me of their lives and their city—my city, too—might be of interest to a far larger audience. I had been trying to think of angles to interest the media in the twentieth-anniversary celebration, and it occurred to me that the Bensonhurst Project might be just the thing.

I called a friend who worked for the *New York Times,* and he suggested that I talk to Douglas Martin, who was then writing the paper's "About New York" column. It took a couple of tries, but finally I got Martin on the phone. I told him that I thought the work my students were doing at the school was newsworthy because it addressed so many social issues simultaneously: these largely Latino and African American children were using writing to present a compelling vision of some of our nation's worst problems while at the same time helping themselves to rise above those problems. To my astonishment, Martin said, "Sounds great. When's your next class? I want to sit in on it."

I asked Martin to sit in on the second of my two eighth grades—the one with the more vocal and productive students, including Asa Taylor, Angela Cordero, and Austin Gonzalez. Although I hadn't realized it when I set up the date, this was the ideal session for Martin to have attended, since it was the first time the students would hear me read their Bensonhurst work aloud.

As with the seventh grade, these eighth-graders were astonished by the power of what they had written—only more so, since the eighth-grade work was so much better on average than the seventh. I repeated much of what I had said in previous classes and in my written comments about fiction as a means for helping people understand the truth of what happened at Bensonhurst, only this time my claims didn't sound like mere idealistic blather, since there at the back of the classroom was a representative of one of the nation's most important papers, eager to present the students' insights to millions of readers all over the world.

I was very impressed (and relieved!) at how diligently the students wrote during that class, finishing their monologues and starting dialogues. Only at the very end did some of them get up from their seats to look at the drawings *Times* artist Lynn Pauley had done of them. Unfortunately Martin's article appeared in the Saturday paper, which meant that, since most students saw the *Times* only when it was delivered daily to their classroom, many of them didn't get to read the article the day it came out. I made photocopies of it for every student in the eighth grade, however, and brought them to my next class.

I can't say for sure what effect Martin's visit to the classroom had on my students. Not one of them ever said anything about it to me—but that is not so unusual among adolescents. It is true that, right until the end of the year, the students in the second eighth grade—the one Martin had visited—produced more interesting work than their counterparts in the other class, but then, they always had. The effect of Martin's visit was most obvious on those students whose work had been quoted in the article—Austin Gonzalez in particular. Until he wrote his throwaway piece about Joey Fama ("I might as well shoot my self in the head. Bang"), Austin had done nothing but jot notes about how he hated Joan Gold or why he couldn't write—too sick, too tired, and so on. After the article, Austin wrote every day and by the end of the year was producing quite polished and moving pieces about playing football in the snow and about how much he loved his girlfriend.

I was interested in Martin's article because it gave me independent evidence that the project was having the effect I was aiming for. Angela Cordero, the girl who had written about her friend's death, told Martin that she liked the class because "you're able to like say what you usually wouldn't say." Asa Taylor, who produced the vivid, enthusiastic Hawkins ("I was mad happy when I got my license yesterday . . ."), clearly had been thinking about the conditions that had led to the violence in Bensonhurst. "If you changed one thing in your life," he told Martin, "you could turn into Joey Fama."

The article also contributed to a growing excitement about the project at the school. Rachel Suarez wanted me to link up with the social studies teacher so that the students could explore the social dimensions of the events at Bensonhurst in greater detail. I liked this idea, since it had become clear to me that if I was going to get this play written on time, I had to sacrifice giving my students that detailed understanding of the crime's socio-historical context that I had once thought was an intrinsic part of the project. Unfortunately, the social studies teacher and I never managed to get together—partly on account of our crowded schedules, but perhaps also out of some mutual turf anxiety. Rachel did have another idea that worked out wonderfully. She commissioned a muralist from LEAP (Learning Through an Expanded Arts Program) to help the eighth-graders paint a grim but beautiful mural about Bensonhurst that ultimately served as the backdrop of the play.

As I walked into Joan Gold's classroom the week after Douglas Martin's visit, she drew me aside and said in a terse whisper, "Listen, Steve, something terrible has happened, and I would like it if you could get the kids to write about it."

"What is it?"

"Susan Carmody got badly beaten up by two girls in the class last night. She's in the hospital."

"Is she all right?"

"She's got a concussion and some broken ribs. She may even have a punctured lung."

I had known Susan since she was a bright, willowy fourth-grader. She had always been one of the best writers in her grade, although in recent years she had been absent a great deal and had often seemed too depressed to write much when she was in school. The previous year, in this very classroom, which at that time had belonged to an inexperienced teacher who had no control over the students, I had come in to find Susan at the center of a crowd of jeering girls, one of whom had just spat on her winter coat. As I pushed into the crowd trying to find out what was going on, another girl handed Susan a crumpled-up photograph of Susan and her mother. Ripping the photograph out of the girl's hand, Susan cried out, "Oh, God! Why did you wreck it up like that?" then sank onto a chair, covered her face with the spat-on coat, and began to sob. I told all the girls to get back in their seats and brought Susan up to the teacher, who, to my outrage, had simply watched all this cruelty without saying a word. I don't think that Susan's difficulties were the result of conscious racism, but nevertheless, the fact that she was one of the two non-Latino whites in the eighth grade certainly contributed to her alienation from her classmates.

"Who did it?" I asked Joan.

"Bianca Chavez and Denise Sandoval."

Again I was shocked. Denise was stout and sulky, and I didn't know her very well. But Bianca was a sweet, bright girl, whom, like Susan, I had known since the fourth grade and who, also like Susan, had always been one of my best writers. I couldn't imagine her even getting into a fight, let alone breaking a girl's ribs and giving her a concussion. When I said as much to Joan, she laughed. "Oh, Bianca's got a mean temper!"

"So what's happening with them?"

"That's a crime all by itself! Since they didn't do it on school grounds or during school hours, Rachel says they can't be suspended. I think that's absurd! These girls have got to be taught that they can't get away with this sort of thing."

Sure enough, I looked around and there were Bianca and Denise, both with expressions of fragile defiance, sitting in their regular seats. No one was talking to them. But the conversation going on around them was plenty energetic enough. In fact, the noise level in the room had gotten dangerously loud while Joan and I were talking. I had to get my lesson started or I would never get control of the class. As I opened my briefcase to pull out the students' folders, Joan entered one last plea: "Please try to get the kids to write about this. They're really upset. They need to get it off their chests." I told her I would do what I could.

I WAS IN A BIND. FOR ONE THING, I COULDN'T IMAGINE HOW I could get the class to talk or write honestly about the beating with Bianca and Denise sitting right there in the class. Even to bring up the topic, however discreetly, would have put the girls on the spot and risked polarizing the class and damaging the atmosphere of frankness and mutual respect that I had worked hard to develop. These kids wrote for me because they thought I was on their side. Anything I said about the fight would have antagonized a portion of the class. I was also restricted by time. Thus far in the Bensonhurst Project, I had gotten plenty of good monologues but no dialogues. Without dialogues—that is, without scenes—there was no action and no play. This was the only day the class could work exclusively on dialogues. I didn't think I could sacrifice a minute of it.

All that said, Susan's beating was a serious matter, and one that eerily corresponded not only to the racial violence we had been writing about, but to a crime that had happened on the very same day: the murder at Thomas Jefferson High School in Brooklyn of two boys by one of their friends. Not to make some sort of connection between the three events seemed an obscene shirking of a pedagogical and a moral obligation. To further complicate matters, a documentary maker who had been intrigued by the *Times* article was observing the class that day, and I wanted whatever I did to be exemplary.

I called the class to order without having even the faintest idea what I was going to do. I decided to give myself some time by going ahead with the lesson I had planned. For reasons that I don't entirely understand, I was extraordinarily uneasy as I began to speak, more uneasy than I had been since I had first started teaching. My voice was shaking as I told the students about the photocopied *New York Times* article in their folder and as I introduced the documentary maker, Ted Haimes, mentioning that his presence in the classroom showed that their writing had already begun to have an effect on other people.

Just as I was introducing Haimes, Rachel came in and took Denise and Bianca away—easing my anxiety considerably. Out of my briefcase I pulled a copy of *New York Newsday* that I had picked up on my way to school and held it up so that the class could read the headline:

BANG!
> BANG!

BANG!
> . . . YOU'RE DEAD!

"Here is more proof of why it is important for us to write about and understand incidents of violence in our city," I said. "Does anyone here know what this headline is about?"

Yvette raised her hand: "Those boys that got shot."

"Where did they get shot."

"Brooklyn," said Taletha. "It's 'cause they don't got no metal detectors there. What they expect when they ain't got no metal detectors?"

"Should they expect kids to shoot each other?" I asked. "Are you saying that's what they *should* expect?"

"I'm not saying that's what they *should* expect," said Taletha. "I'm just saying if they had metal detectors that boy couldn't of got that gun into school, that's all."

"You're right, of course. But I think the question I was asking is an important one too. Is it right that we live in a world where we can expect kids to kill each other if we don't put up metal detectors?" The answer to this question was obvious, but I waited a moment just to let it sink in. Then I said, "If it isn't right, then shouldn't we try to do something to change it?"

I was about to go on to make the point that the work we were doing in the class was part of the struggle to change that world by making people more aware of the real causes and consequences of violence, when all at once it occurred to me that not only had the Bensonhurst project done little or nothing to inhibit Bianca and Denise in their violence, it may even have encouraged them by making such violence glamorous. Now I was really thrown off my stride. I went on to make a banal statement about how violence was terrible, and how we all suffer from it—this was as close as I got to fulfilling Joan's request—and then sought refuge in the familiar territory of the Bensonhurst Project.

"Today we're going to write dialogues," I said. "Most of you have written monologues for one or two of the people at Bensonhurst. All of you have heard me read monologues for the major characters. So you now have a pretty good idea of who they are, and why they did what they did, and how they feel about it. What I want you to do now is get those people talking to one another. Your challenge as writers is to remember what you know about each of the people in the dialogue as you write down what they say. Think about what they have done. Think about what they feel about themselves and the person they are talking to. What do they want? What do they fear? Think about all of these things for each of the characters in your dialogue. Try to make them all seem equally alive. But don't just have them talk about a baseball game or the price of cheese. Remember, we're writing a play. We've got to put only the most interesting conversations in it, the ones that best help us understand what happened in Bensonhurst."

I asked the class to suggest interesting and important conversations and wrote them on the board. The suggestions included the conversation during which Gina invited Keith to her party and they ended up threatening each other; Keith's subsequent conversations with those friends (and especially Joey Fama) whom he wanted to back him up; Joey's conversation with his mother after the murder; and (since so many kids had written about Yusuf Hawkins's afterlife) Yusuf Hawkins's conversation with his mother when he came back to her as a ghost.

The students went to work and produced some of the very best writing I had seen so far, and I began to breathe easier about whether I would have enough good material to weave together into a play.

Although I said nothing to either class regarding writing about what had happened to Susan, four girls—two from each class—wrote disguised versions of the incident. I'll quote the whole of Diana Delacruz's piece because it is typical of the other girls' pieces but has an intriguing ambivalence. Diana was Yvette's best friend. She wrote the long love story I have already quoted about first meeting a boy named Darrell at a Burger King.*

Characters

DIANA—DROP OUT.
PEDRO—DROP OUT.
ROSAL—BULLY
NAIMA—SCHOOL GIRL
TARIK—BUM & DROP OUT

* To protect Diana's privacy, I have deleted all references to location in this piece, as well as changed the characters' names.

narrator:

   Once opon a time, In [. . .] There was This gang and The name was Bitch and assholes with attitude and There was one name Diana they called her Di and Pedro was this cool guy and Rosal was the neiborhood Bully and none of the people in the group liked naima and Tarik was in Naima side so They never liked him either. So they all got Together to Beat the hell out of him. By the way this was in Burger king in [. . .].

Rosal: So when we gonna hit that little bitch, I dont like her.

Diana: Calm down Rosal. We have to plan it First.

Pedro: We gonna go to her school and wait for her at 3:00 And we gonna jump that bitch.

Part 2

Naima: Tarik walk me home because I am scared.

Tarik: all Right.

Rosal: okay there she is let's kill.

Diana: Rosal, Rosal take it easy girl. What's wronge with you.

Pedro: okay let's follow her up the Block then we jump them.

Narrator:

        okay so There all ready up the block.

Part 3

Rosal: runs and jumps on Naima's back.

Diana: Takes Tarik in ahead lock and punches Tarik in his bolls.

Pedro: Then takes Tarik by himself Then they finished and went to Burger King.

lAST PArt

Narrator: So they kept on doing it. Beating people up not only Naima and Tarik but they kept on doing it to other people. and that's how life really is, because I know people that are like that so watch your back I tell you from experience.

The main thing that struck me as I read this piece (apart from how much more poorly written it was than anything else Diana had ever done for me) was how riddled it was with self-hatred. Diana names one of the villains—a "Drop out"—after herself. Admittedly the fictional Diana is a moderating influence on Rosal (named after the girl sitting next to the real Diana), but only, it seems, because she is worried that Rosal's overeagerness will spoil their plans. Diana's own attack on Tarik is certainly vicious enough—although, perhaps, it is significant that she did not attack Naima, who was the character most like Susan Carmody.

The saddest part of Diana's play was the narrator's final speech, which I read as being, at least in part, a response to the feeble moralizing I had done in class. Diana thought that my disapproval of violence was naive and dangerous. Her narrator is telling me how "life really is" and to "watch (my) back." But at the same time the narrator's disapproval of Diana and her friends seems even more vehement than my own, since it comes from bitter personal experience. The cruelty of these people is no less real for being an inevitable part of life. The ultimate message of this piece is: although violence is indeed horrible, the only safe way to deal with it is not to reject it but to become violent yourself. I find this message especially sad when I superimpose it over the comparatively happy and innocent meeting with Darrell at this same Burger King. How can happiness or innocence endure in the midst of such fear, anger, and brutality?

The other thing that struck me about Diana's play and all the others that were inspired by Susan's beating was that, despite all the work the class had been doing trying to figure out the motives and the interpersonal dynamics that led to Yusuf Hawkins's murder, in these plays the violence had no source, no history. It was almost entirely arbitrary. In Diana's play the only reason for attacking Naima was that the "Bitch and assholes with attitude" gang didn't like her. No attempt was made to show why she was not likable or was in any way deserving of the beating she got.

In Rosal's play, the Susan character, the victim, is called "the neighborhood slut" in the dramatis personae. She flirts with "Pedro" who is married to "Diana" (the real "Pedro" was Bianca's boyfriend), but the flirtation and Diana's objection to it only seem to provide the ritualistic pretext for the violence, whose real source is much more mysterious. In yet another play, the cause of the fight is simply the fight itself. Sona hits Lola. When Lola is asked why Sona hit her, she says, "I don't know. She's crazy. She going to pay."

Certainly part of the reason these fights were motiveless was simply that the girls writing about them were impatient to get to the most exciting and important part of the story. But at the same time, as I pondered these narratives, I began to realize that, to a certain extent, they did accurately represent the genesis of the fights they recounted.

In a world where everyone constantly felt in danger, often from truly random acts of violence (muggings, rapes, drive-by shootings), my students had a natural incentive to demonstrate their strength or toughness, merely as a form of protection. The stronger they seemed, the less likely they were to get attacked. The result is that fights really would begin for no other reason than each participant's desire to prove his or her strength. A trivial infraction would occur, often one that is a traditional part of a prefight ritual: a flirtatious remark to a potential combatant's girl- or boyfriend, or just a sustained stare. The object of these infractions would either see an opportunity to prove his or her strength or fear that if he or she didn't take advantage of this opportunity, he or she would be thought weak and thence more in danger of challenges or attacks by other children seeking to establish a protective reputation for strength.

Interestingly, the boys never wrote about real or even realistic fights, but by reading the girls' accounts of real and imaginary fights I began to understand that the boys' causeless, pointless video game stories were more firmly anchored in their real lives than I had imagined. I also attained a deeper recognition of the nightmare world in which many of my students lived, one in which most violence was the result of a *fear* of violence.

I WASN'T TO FIND OUT THE REAL STORY OF SUSAN CARMODY'S beating until the following week, and when I did, I saw that as much as it inspired Diana and her classmates to write about the nearly pointless cruelty they hated and admired, this particular fight was more than just an occasion for proving strength, though that certainly played a role.

I heard the story from Rachel Suarez, who during this year had become my best ally and friend at the school. Rachel gives her life to the Walt Whitman Academy. I have never seen her when she isn't in full stride, hurrying to a parent conference, a teacher's meeting, or to handle some emergency. Even when she is at her desk, she is always doing several things at once: filling out forms for students while she is calling

up substitute teachers for the following day, helping a guidance counselor choose the best high schools to recommend to eighth graders
while putting a Band-Aid on a student's injured finger. Nights she is on
the phone to harried teachers, to troubled students or their parents. If
the students' families don't have phones (as many at Walt Whitman
don't), she goes to visit the families at their homes or jobs. She always
has a cold and always talks about how crazy her life is or how tired she
feels, but I have never seen anything slow her down, dim the enthusiasm in her bright chestnut-brown eyes, or diminish the deep compassion she feels for every student at the Walt Whitman Academy.

As Rachel explained it to me, Susan's home life began to fall apart
when she was in fifth grade. First her parents separated, then her
mother, who had a management position at a major corporation, lost
her job as a result of "downsizing" during the late 1980s. Susan's mother
eventually found another demanding job, which meant that Susan was
left at home alone afternoons and early evenings. Susan had never been
a popular girl, but as she became increasingly depressed over the state
of her family life, her position in the school hierarchy became even
more precarious. One of the ways Susan found to buoy up her status
among her classmates was to have girls and boys over for parties when
her mother wasn't home. Unfortunately, these parties seem to have resulted in Susan being labeled a "slut" in school gossip. Obscene graffiti
about her appeared in the girls' bathroom, and Denise was caught writing "Susan is a hoe [whore]" on Susan's locker.

The day before Valentine's Day, school let out at noon and Susan invited several girls, including Denise and Bianca, to her house. Bianca
brought along her wallet containing $20, with which she intended to
buy a gift for her boyfriend, Pedro. She left the wallet on Susan's dresser
and, when it was time to go, discovered that the wallet was missing. Although, according to Rachel, there was absolutely no substantiating evidence, and any of the other girls could just as easily have stolen the
wallet, Bianca accused Susan of the theft. Susan denied taking the
money and the girls left, although the theft continued to be a source of
arguments between Susan and Bianca, with the prevailing opinion at
the school being that Susan was guilty. Then, a couple of weeks later,
Bianca and Denise cornered Susan and beat her up.

Despite Joan Gold's fears, Rachel suspended Bianca and Denise for
five days, during which time they and Susan attended special mediation

sessions at the local police station. Rachel also borrowed an idea from the Bensonhurst Project by asking Bianca and Denise to write accounts of Susan's beating from their own and from Susan's points of view. Denise, whose folder was filled almost exclusively with I-hate-my-teacher notes, refused to do the assignment, but Bianca wrote several extremely detailed and thoughtful accounts.*

—What happened that night—

—That night I went to dry my clotes. I had set the dryer on for about 1 hour and a half. While it was drying me and Denise went to the store, we had went to [. . .] st. Well then we had saw Susan and I went to talk to her. I had asked her if she had found my wallet she said NO and that she wasn't going to give it to me either At that moment I didn't aks her to give me the money. So then she started to get her attitude with me rolling her eyes and stuff so I pulled her hair and I swong her to the ground

While she was on the ground I was punching her. Then Denise got on top of Susan to try to block me from hitting Susan but then I had punched Denise in the back of her ear by mistake so Denise got off and let us fight.

I was getting mad. At first it was because of the wallet but then I dont know what, It just got out of hand. I really dont know what happened to me because now when I go back at it I remember the begining but tords the end it's blank. All I know is that I was very angry. I do have a bad temper and Ive show it before but never this bad. After the fight when this man broke it up Susan was laying on the floor so I kicked her.

Well, then I had calmed down I saw Susans face it had blood clogs and black and blues and her nose was bloody. I was surprised because I didn't know I had done that, well I knew but I didn't know that I had been hurting her that bad. So me and denise had took her upstairs to clean her up. I didn't say a word to Susan what so ever, I couldn't even say sorry because I was speachless and surprised.

The End

* Once again, place names have been deleted.

What I think is especially interesting about this piece is Bianca's surprise at her own behavior. I don't believe that she claimed to have been surprised primarily as a means of minimizing responsibility, because, as I have said, she had always seemed a sweet and thoughtful girl to me. Also, the detail with which she relates what she did shows a desire to face her guilt and make a clean breast of it. In her accounts from Susan's point of view she portrays the attack as even more vicious than it appears in this version. She talks a lot about Susan's heavy bleeding and reveals that the last kick she delivered to Susan after the fight had broken up was not to the body but the face.

In a piece called "At the Hospital," Bianca writes the following from Susan's point of view: "When the doctor checked me they said I have a mile concussion. I was scared I couldn't even remember my phone number, I was throwing up and I was seeing double, my back was hurting a lot. I felt so bad. I had bruises all over my face."

She also wrote, again from Susan's point of view, about Susan's emotional response to the beating, focusing on a type of insecurity that I am sure many children at Walt Whitman Academy have experienced.

> The feeling of having my friends beat me up is a terrible, sad and scarey feeling. Its like your all confused because you dont know who are your real friend, If they just want to use you.
>
> Now a days you cant realy trust anybody expecially friends because your afraid they going to turn on you or something. With friends like mine who needs enemys. And then coming to school and having to see grafity on the bathrooms and on my locker is another thing saying I am a H——E, and other nasty things. that hurts me alot and then there's rumers. People spread alot of bad things about me and some of it is probably not true. And then putting all of this all together I have to put up with it every day.

In a composition entitled "What I am going to do," Bianca promised that she would inform Rachel if she heard that anyone was planning to beat up Susan or if she knew who was writing graffiti or spreading rumors about her. But Bianca also said that she did not want anyone to know what she was doing "expissily" Susan. As the year went on Bianca did in fact come to Susan's aid from time to time, most notably rushing to her side one day when she fell and twisted her ankle in the playground.

After the fight I looked through Susan's, Bianca's, and Denise's folders to see if I could find any more clues as to what other factors might have contributed to their animosity. Bianca's situation turned out to be surprisingly like Susan's. She had several pieces in her folder about a girl whose parents fought a lot and whose kind, sympathetic father was no longer living at home. And, like Susan, she had several pieces about fighting with her mother.

It was Denise who had the worst relationship with her mother, so bad that the previous year her mother tried to turn her over to the city's foster care system. Denise was a very bright girl, scoring above the ninety-eighth percentile on standardized reading and math tests, but was always getting into trouble at school. Although Denise's role in Susan's beating had been comparatively minor, she never said one word of apology—and thereby gained a reputation among her classmates for being tough. Denise's mother would never take responsibility for her, telling Rachel whenever she was called in for a conference, "I just can't control her! She's impossible!"

Denise wrote almost nothing for me for most of the school year, until long after the completion of the Bensonhurst Project, when I read the eighth grade Tillie Olson's story "I Stand Here Ironing" and asked them to write a story like Olson's, in which a parent describes the whole life of his or her child. For the first and only time that year Denise was inspired. Her composition was not only one of the best pieces of writing I got that year but showed a surprising understanding of the mother's point of view.

My daughter is very disrespectful. She yells back at me using dirty language. She doesn't listen to me. I tell her to do something she does the opposite. She goes and comes as she pleases. I try to talk to her but she doesn't listen. It's like it goes in one ear and comes out the other. If I tell her she cant go outside she just walks out the door. like who are you telling me what to do? She lies all the time. Everything she says is a lie. I've threaten to put her in a home. not because I want to but just to scare her. I thought maybe she'll be good so I wont put her away. But all it has done was got her worse. I don't know what to do. anymore. She's 13 and wants to be 20 yrs old. I have her go see a concelor once a week. so she'll have someone to talk to. she tells me she went but he calls me and tells me she hasn't. I went threw everything in the book I tried to talk to her. I tried to hit her but she hit me back. I tried everything but nothing seems to work. I'm scared for her and I don't know what to do.

I was thrilled and moved when I read this piece. I asked Denise if her own relationship with her mother was anything like the one she had described, but she denied it flatly. I told her I thought the daughter was getting shortchanged by this, that there must have been reasons for her behavior that her mother did not understand or know about. I said I thought it would be interesting if Denise could write another monologue from the daughter's point of view. She seemed to like that idea, but when I came back to her desk, she had written the following, still in the mother's voice:

But I guess most of it is my fault. I say this because I don't give her much attention. I don't hug her or tell her I love you like I used to. I don't talk to her unless I have something to complain about. I guess her friends give her more attention and so she listens to them more then me. Its not my fault. My Mom never huged me or told me she loved me or talked to me. So I don't do it to her. I know what its like to live in a house with your mother and have no communication with her because I've lived it myself. And it isn't a good feeling and thats how I think she feels. But I don't know what to do to change.

Although I didn't know it at the time, Denise was pregnant when she wrote this. That summer—as I would later hear from Rachel—Denise's mother tried once again to have her placed in the city's foster care program, but a judge, saying that it was unconscionable for a mother to abandon her pregnant thirteen-year-old, rejected the request. The baby, a girl, was born the following winter. Denise kept her. I don't know whether Denise continued to live with her mother. I only hope that her clear-sightedness about the nature of her own relationship with her mother enabled her to avoid recreating that relationship with her own daughter—but I can't be optimistic.

Here is the last piece of writing that Susan Carmody did for me. It was written the week after Denise wrote her monologue.

At night she sits in her room.

All to her self.

She is alone.

She cries at night thinking of the
past.

Knowing she can never go back to
the way she was.

She sits in her room.

Thinking of herself

Thinking where her life would lead
her next

She sits all alone.

6

Strength and Compassion

I HAD UNDERTAKEN THE BENSONHURST PROJECT BELIEVING MYSELF to be on high and firm moral ground. Not only was I going to help my students create good art, but I was going to help them see themselves and the world more clearly. I was going to train them to look outside themselves, to imagine the world as it seemed to other people, and to respect the authenticity and (within limits) legitimacy of other people's perspectives. I believed—and still believe—that this sort of imagination would help reduce a variety of individual and social ills, including racism and violence, that stem at least in part from a failure to understand other people's perspectives.

When my students oohed and ahed at Joey Fama's white suit and silver gun, when they took Keith Mondello's side against Gina Feliciano, I assumed that they were merely the dupes of macho culture and of Hollywood action movies. It seemed to me that all I would have to do was remind the students that Mondello and Fama were racists and point out the inarguable fact that Hawkins was a victim of the American cult of violence for them to come around to my obvious and just moral position. When this failed to happen, I concluded, to be perfectly honest, that my students were stubborn, stupid, or inattentive.

It was only as I practiced what I preached—as I read their writing, listened to what they said in class, and tried to see their points of view—that I began to understand the limitations of my own perspective. What I discovered was not so much the invalidity of my moral judgments as the privilege that made it easier for me to maintain them. It was not difficult for me to disapprove of and avoid violence. I fully expect to go to my grave without ever using a gun, a knife, or even my fists against another person. If I should be approached by someone with a gun or a knife who won't be satisfied by merely taking my wallet, well, then, I may be injured or killed—not out of any moral bravery but simply because I have not prepared myself to be violent. But that sort of violent encounter, even in New York, is statistically unlikely for someone of my class, race, and sex. The statistics, however, are not nearly so favorable for my students.

Over the six years prior to the Bensonhurst Project, the homicide rate for teenagers doubled. Adolescents were also much more likely to be the victims of other sorts of crime. Although adolescents account for less than 10 percent of the population, they make up 23 percent of the victims of assault, robbery, and rape. These are national figures. Most of my students lived in high-crime areas, where gangs—with names like Young Talented Children—engaged in constant turf battles, complete with drive-by shootings, and where a large percentage of crimes went unreported.

Not all, but many of my students really did run a much higher risk than I of winding up in situations where a lack of readiness to be violent could cost them their lives. To be ready for violence one has to have a certain level of heartlessness and a certain admiration for strength. I have no doubt that the level of violence in a society is directly proportional to the level of *readiness* for violence and that, therefore, readiness for violence is itself an evil. But nevertheless, it became increasingly clear to me after Susan's beating that there were other reasons than stubbornness, stupidity, or distraction that made it difficult for my students to commit themselves to moral choices that seemed so obviously correct to me.

As I wrote about this situation in my teaching diary the night before the final Bensonhurst meeting, I came up with an idea that was to have an enduring effect on the way I saw my work in the schools. It began with my realization that what was going on in my classroom was actually the continuation of an ancient dialogue, and that my students' respect for strength had a venerable philosophical tradition behind it. The word "virtue," after all, is derived from the Latin for "strength" or "manliness"—as is "virile"—and the traits most commonly associated with the classical understanding of virtue—courage, self-control, intelligence—are indeed all forms of strength. In my diary I called these the Virtues of Strength and saw them as opposing and balancing the Virtues of Compassion—those capacities that enable us to connect with other people, to feel sympathy, solidarity, and love. Things being the way they are, philosophers, at least from Aristotle to Nietzsche, have tended to see the manly Virtues of Strength as the essence of morality. But since one can have all these virtues and still be a drug dealer, it seemed to me that the Virtues of Compassion were the true foundation of morality; without them, courage, self-control, and intelligence had no moral meaning or focus.

The reason these ideas were so influential was, quite simply, that they made the work I was doing seem more important. Far from worrying that writing was merely a pastime of the elite classes, I could now link it to what was arguably the most crucial of human intellectual endeavors. While I would never claim that writers were more moral than any other segment of society, it did seem to me that the detailed imagination of other people's viewpoints necessary for good fiction writing was also essential for the development of the Virtues of Compassion. Although I never talked to my students about categories of virtue or the historical background of our discussion, from that night forward I became even more intent on helping students to fully imagine all the motives and responses of any character they wrote about. There was, however, one element of that night's speculations that did exert an unexpected influence on my final Bensonhurst class the following morning, and that was my observation that the Virtues of Compassion were also supported by a long, mostly religious tradition, one that found its most radical expression in Christ's injunction, "Love your enemies."

PRACTICALLY FROM THE MOMENT I READ THE *TIMES* REVIEW OF *For the Color of His Skin*, I had known that I was going to wrap up the Bensonhurst Project by having my students write letters to Yusuf Hawkins. But when I walked into the classroom on that final day of the project, I wasn't at all sure, despite weeks of consideration, that I had figured out the right way to prepare my students to produce the heartfelt, perceptive, and moving testaments that I had always imagined those letters would be.

Joan was calling out attendance. When she got to Susan Carmody's card, she just flipped past it without saying her name. Surveying the classroom, I saw that—now more than a week after the beating—Susan's seat was still empty. Had she stayed out of school because of her injuries? I wondered. Or had she simply been too humiliated to face her classmates? When Joan had finished with the attendance, I asked her about Susan, but she didn't know any more than I.

In a way I was relieved that Susan was absent. I had decided, though not without qualms, that I would not talk to the students specifically about the beating because I thought that their emotional predispositions would interfere both with their writing and with their absorption of the more generalizable principles that could be drawn from the Hawkins case. But I did hope to frame the conclusions we drew that day so that they could easily be applied to Susan—a task I felt could be accomplished much more gracefully and effectively in her absence.

I started the class by reading a few of the best dialogues from the previous week, including my favorite, one that started out as a monologue by Yusuf Hawkins and ended as a dialogue. In this piece Hawkins begins by telling about his obsession with cars and his dream of buying one with a gold-covered engine. The monologue goes on with a not particularly remarkable description of his journey to Bensonhurst and confrontation with the white gang. This writer only truly became inspired at the moment Hawkins got shot.

> . . . people kept saing stuff and suddenly something happen, bang, and I saw blood, I got fritten and felt peace at the same time dreaming of what I had and never had. what I did in my life wrong for this to happen to me and I fell on my knees with out pain just thoughts, I felt sad and happiness in my soul and heared beautiful humming and cring because I was scared I started humming and kept on going throw a path while seeing my beloved freinds standing there and the woman of my dreams that I never saw and that red ferrari with gold engine and wheels wow, but, I think I forgot about all the material for a migical feeling. I saw all my friends that I knew back then and actually I was walking fast through all my life and, it's like I couldn't stop then I stop where I died, my two buddies were crying and scared, the police and ambulance were there too. And my poor mother which was so proud of me, I never knew how much I could miss her and love her like what I feel right

STRENGTH AND COMPASSION • 115

know, camling I setled and understood that her time will come to be with me.

I met someone on my way here, he told me I could actually talk to her but only in her dreams, which I thought was kind of crazy so I was gonna try it just about now:

Yusuf: hi mom, you look so beautiful sleeping! do you miss me?

mother: of course, (and she starts to cry in here dreams and in real life) you don't know how much I love you and miss! If only I could turn back time and show you it, which I didn't really know how to do! will you forgive me?

Yusuf: of course, mama, don't think of that know and just think that you could still talk to me only in your dreams. It's really me, touch me!

mother: (she toches him) your skins feel exacly the way when you were the day you were born, oh how I love you.

The Yusuf Hawkins created by this author is so pure, childlike, and good. Even in the midst of his own death he is capable of a boyish astonishment ("wow") at a vision of that gold Ferrari engine. When he sees his mother, all the negative is gone from their relationship, and he realizes for the first time how much he loves her, just as she, when she sees him, realizes both how much she loves her son and what a loss it was that she had never been able to tell him of her love. I was so engaged by this final scene that both times I read the mother's last lines in class tears came into my eyes.

When I began this piece during my second class, Shantay, the girl who had written the dialogue about the motiveless fight between Sona and Lola ("I don't know, she's crazy.") had groaned and called out, "Bor-ing!" This was the way Shantay, who was the only girl seated among the troublemaking boys at the back of the classroom, responded to virtually every piece I read and every assignment I gave. Usually, when a piece was finished, she was the first to raise her hand, and her response was almost always the same: "Stu-pid! Bor-ing!" She was a very bright girl who, for reasons that I was never able to discover, seemed intent on sabotaging her own talent. She knew, however, that she was one of the brightest kids in the class and, I think, secretly wanted to do well. So she reserved her most vehement criticisms for the best pieces—those that were closest to what she would have produced had she ever allowed herself.

As I finished reading the above monologue, I waited to hear a second sour moan from Shantay at the back of the room. But she was completely silent.

Arnaldo called out: "That was good!"

"Why was it good?" I asked him. "What did you like about it?"

Arnaldo wilted under my attention: "It was just good, that's all."

"Anybody else?" I called. "What was good about that piece? What did you like about it? What did it make you feel?"

Angela raised her hand: "Sad."

"Okay. Why sad?"

"I don't know, I just kept thinking 'Why does he have to die?'"

"Exactly," I said. "That's just right. This piece really makes you feel what a tragedy it was that Yusuf Hawkins was killed. It really makes you feel his innocence. The kid in this monologue is such a good kid. *Why does he have to die?* . . . Do you see how much more powerful this is than just saying he was innocent?—'An innocent boy was killed; what a shame.'—Nothing! But here you feel his innocence. You like Hawkins. You are sad that he is gone. You are sad for his mother. That's how the tragedy is made real and true."

Shantay had her arm up at the back of the room. Since no one else had a hand up, I had no choice but to call on her. To my relief she only asked, "Who wrote that?"—a question that was then echoed around the room.

A skinny boy at one of the front tables shyly raised his hand and began to stand. Joan called out in astonishment, "Robert, did you really write that?"

He laughed and sat down. The author was actually the girl sitting opposite him. When I asked if the author would like to stand up, however, she remained seated and poker-faced, avoiding my eyes.

I went on to read a few more pieces, asking after each was finished, "What was good about it? Did it seem real? What did it tell you that was true? How did it help your understanding of what happened to Yusuf Hawkins? Was there anything that seemed false?" Classroom discussion was always difficult to stimulate, even at the best of times. But on this occasion it was clear to me, even from their spare, often truncated remarks, that the students had completely understood the true/false dichotomy I had established as a measure of quality. Furthermore, they understood why "good" writing was a "good" thing. Many of my students even understood how something as unrealistic as a dream conversation with a ghost could both seem real and contain real truth.

Once the dialogues had been read, it was time to introduce the lesson I had worked up for this final session. I wrote the words PERSONAL and SOCIAL on the blackboard, defined them, and then asked the class to tell me which factors led to the death of Yusuf Hawkins and what category they should be put under. As I expected, the PERSONAL side of the blackboard filled up pretty quickly, with such things as Gina and Keith's threats, Joey's insanity, and so on. The SOCIAL side remained empty for a long time until finally one boy suggested racism.

"Great!" I said, chalking the word on the board. "Anything else? What other social problems contributed to Yusuf Hawkins's death?" No answer. "Come on, what about some of you guys who were here the day of the class trip? We talked about other factors then." Still no raised hands. "Okay, think about the murder of those boys at Thomas Jefferson High School. They were all black—both the victims and the boy who killed them—so racism wasn't a cause of those murders, at least not in the way it was at Bensonhurst. What other social problem contributed to the death of those two boys and Yusuf Hawkins?"

There was a long silence. Finally a girl called out, "Violence."

"Good." I wrote VIOLENCE on the board.

It had been clear from the girl's tone that she had given me the word I was looking for only so that I would stop harping on this one point and move on. The truth is, I suspect, that she had not been alone, that many kids in the class had known exactly what I was fishing for. They didn't want to speak up because they didn't want to go where I was taking them. These abstract discussions bored them. They liked story. They liked tragedy and comedy, sex and violence. They were great on the details, but they didn't want to bother with the implications. But I wanted them to think about the implications, to understand, even be shocked by the implications. I thought: "If I can only just get them past this basic stuff into some real debate."

I pointed to the word "violence": "Okay, what does this mean?" Again, no response. Dead air. "How is violence a social problem? What about violence harms us?" Oh, no! I was getting back to the boring, obvious stuff. "I don't just mean in the obvious way. I mean . . ."

I paused for a long time, trying to find a phrase that would throw open the windows of their understanding and generate excitement, controversy.

I was stumped.

On impulse, I put down my chalk and turned away from the board. "Listen, forget all that stuff. I'm going to ask you a question that, under the law, teachers, at least in public schools, are not allowed to ask." I didn't know if this were true, but I wanted to sound dramatic. Seeing two or three pairs of eyes coming unglazed, I went on: "How many of you go to church?"

Shantay's dismissive moan sounded from the back of the room. Rosal (Diana Delacruz's friend) shouted out, "Church! Hah!"

"Come on, guys," I said. "It's a simple question. I don't mean how many of you go every Sunday—I mean how many go every once in a while?"

About two-thirds of the class raised their hands. I figured the number was probably higher, since some of the kids in the class wouldn't want to admit to anything as uncool as even occasional churchgoing.

"Okay, now you guys are all Christians, right. I don't mean funda-mentalists. I just mean Catholics, Baptists, Methodists—and fundamen-talists, too—that sort of thing. Anybody here not a Christian?" Nobody raised their hand. I heard Joan stirring at her desk beside me, not quite comfortable, I am fairly certain, about the direction my discussion was going. I have to say I wasn't 100 percent comfortable with it either. I am an atheist. As a child I had felt isolated and subtly reprimanded when teachers discussed religion. But I'd already gone too far to turn back.

"Okay," I said, "so here is my question: Who can tell me what the Ser-mon on the Mount was?"

A boy raised his hand: "It's ice."

"What?" I wasn't even sure I had heard him properly.

"It's ice. Ice on top of the mountain." As far as I could tell, this boy was not joking—in any event, nobody laughed.

"No. Come on. Who can tell me? The Sermon on the Mount. What is it?"

"Sunday school?" suggested a girl right at the front of the room.

"No."

A boy said: "It's a church. Mount Bethel Baptist Church."

I was flabbergasted. I had assumed that for a fair number of my stu-dents this question would have been as simple as "What is the Declara-tion of Independence?" (But maybe that wouldn't have been such an easy

STRENGTH AND COMPASSION • 119

question, either.) If anyone knew the answer, they weren't speaking.

Finally I said, "It's the speech that Jesus gave in which he spelled out his beliefs." (Again I heard Joan stirring.) "You've all heard, 'Thou shalt not kill,' right? Well, in the Sermon on the Mount Jesus said you should go further than that. He said, 'Love your enemies.'" Groans and a mocking cluck of tongues rose from various parts of the room. I continued: "He also said that if your enemy slaps you on one cheek you should turn the other one to him and let him slap you again."

This assertion was met with exclamations of derisive astonishment: "Come on!" "What!" "Je-sus!"

Surprised yet again at their lack of familiarity with this doctrine, but pleased that I now clearly had the attention of the whole room, I continued: "He also said that if your enemy asks you to walk one mile, you should walk two."

More derisiveness. Arnaldo called out, "That's not fair!"

"Why?"

"Because your enemy should walk as far as you."

The boy sitting next to Arnaldo laughed and slapped him on the head, "Boy, you are such a dummy!" Arnaldo looked back at him with uncomprehending irritation.

"No," I said to Arnaldo's neighbor. "What he's said is very interesting. It's unfair. Does anybody else think it's unfair?"

There were nods and "yeah's" from all around the room.

"Why?" I said.

"Because you shouldn't let your enemy run your life."

"All right. That's a good point, but—"

Shantay cut me off: "That's all crazy!"

"What is?" I asked.

"Love your enemy and all that."

"Why is it crazy?"

"Because it is."

"What do you think you should do to your enemy, then?"

"Get him back."

"You mean get revenge?"

"Yeah."

"Let's talk about that," I said. "Before we were starting to talk about social problems. Let's think about what you're saying in terms of the whole society. Do you think that a sane society is one where everybody is always going around getting revenge and an insane society is one in which everybody is turning their cheeks and trying to love their enemies?"

"Yeah."

"Why?"

"I don't know."

I turned to the rest of the class. "Let's try to think only about Bensonhurst then. Suppose everybody in Bensonhurst had turned the other cheek. What would have happened?"

Michael said, "They get beat up."

At that moment the classroom door opened and in walked Susan, leaning on a cane, but otherwise looking fully recovered from her injuries. (As I would later hear, the beating had exacerbated a preexisting back problem and caused a weakness in one leg. She had, indeed, had a concussion, but no broken ribs or punctured lung.)

Susan was clearly embarrassed by all the eyes turning in her direction. I did my best to help her—as she gave her late pass to Joan and went to her seat—by trying to draw everyone's attention back to our discussion. But the momentum we had built up was now thoroughly dissipated, not in the least because I didn't feel that I could explore the topic much further with Susan in the room. Still, I had to draw it to a conclusion.

"But what I mean is suppose *everybody* at Bensonhurst was following that doctrine—*everybody*. What would have happened?" No answer. "Do you think Yusuf Hawkins would have gotten killed?"

A general "no."

"Do you think it would be possible for people to live like that?"

"No."

"Do you think that you could live like that?"

"No."

"Okay. That's interesting. I want you to think about that when you write. We know that there's a way that people could behave that would end violence, but we also know that we can't behave that way, even if we might want to, even if we think we should. How does that make you feel about the violence at Bensonhurst and the violence you see all around you? How does that make you feel about your own role in the violence?"

The discussion was over. I was relieved but pleased by the way it had gone, in part because of all the uncertainty I had felt getting into it. I have always had a deep ambivalence about Christ's radical injunction. Whenever I have imagined putting it into practice in the real world, the word "love" has always seemed to become degraded to something like a Jesus freak's kiss-me-I'm-saved grin. Also, I strongly believe that there are people—Hitler and Stalin spring first to mind—who should remain the enemies of all decent human beings and never be treated with any sort of understanding that even verges on forgiveness, let alone love. But at the same time, I have always felt a magnetic attraction to the concept of meeting hatred with its opposite. I'm not sure why. Maybe because it would be such a relief if evil could be disposed of so decently. In any event, it was largely on account of this deep ambivalence that I had been so anxious about where the discussion might lead. But in the end, I felt that I had used Christ's radical injunction in the best way I could, not as a rule for life but as a proposition that would make my students think, that might help them see their own opinions and actions in a different light. I was still uneasy about Susan's having heard even the little she had, and I was sure that Joan now thought I was a closet fundamentalist. But these were not major worries.

I told the students that I wanted them to write a letter to Yusuf Hawkins telling him what they felt and thought about what happened to him and about what his death meant for society. Once before—at P.S. 313, in fact—when I had asked students to write letters to their future children, many had balked, saying "Uh-uh—that's voodoo! You go to hell for writing a letter like that!" So I told my Walt Whitman students that they didn't have to write as themselves. They could pretend that one of the people at Bensonhurst was writing the letter, or Martin Luther King, or Malcolm X, or God, or anyone else they chose.

As they wrote I went around the room telling certain kids who had gotten started on promising dialogues that they could finish them if they wanted rather than write the letter. Susan was sitting glumly at her desk with her folder closed. I asked her how she was feeling. Her expression became pained: "Fine." Then she asked what she should write. She hadn't done any work on the Bensonhurst Project at all. Instead she had been writing a long story about a girl who meets a boy on the street, has many phone conversations with him, and finally invites him to come to her house. I told her to keep going with that story. She opened her folder but didn't write a word.

Once I'd made a circuit of the room I went over to talk to Joan, hoping that I could somehow clear up any misapprehension she might have about me. But, since I couldn't find any graceful way of proclaiming my atheism, I just told her the kids seemed to be writing well. We talked about another teacher's kidney operation, and I went back to look over the students' shoulders, feeling that everything was okay.

As I circled the room the class discussion repeated in my mind. Once again I was astonished that the doctrine of Christian passivity espoused in the Sermon on the Mount was so foreign to these kids, many of whom, as I knew from other writing and discussions, were deeply religious. Perhaps all that had sunk in was heaven and hell, reward and punishment, those absurd and unfair contrasting fates that awaited them in the afterworld and that were hardly less unfair or absurd than the contrasts they saw all around them in the city. Perhaps Christ's injunction was too radical—or unrealistic—even for church.

I WAS DEEPLY MOVED BY AND PROUD OF THE LETTERS THE students wrote, although a few of them also disturbed me. What I learned from these letters was that despite the long silences after my questions, despite the glazed eyes, the wisecracks, the restless shifting, the students had been listening carefully to everything that was read or discussed in class, and they had taken it very much to heart. By and large, their letters were as heartfelt and sometimes as wise as I could have hoped.

Many students simply wrote to Yusuf to tell him how sorry they were over what had happened to him and how unfair it was. Many also said they wished they could have gone "back to the future" to warn him about the white gang or stop Joey Fama. Perhaps because of our final classroom discussion, many children wrote about violence, asking Yusuf, "How does it feel to be with God in a world with no violence?" or saying, "I feel like I am not safe from anything." Here are two of the most moving, the first at least starting off as if it were written by Gina Feliciano.

Dear Yusuf,

as I begin to write this letter I begin to think about what happened to you. Its to bad that I didn't get to know you and I'm sure that you were a wonderful person and I feel I'm the one to blame but lets not get into that now. as I watched the news that night I saw you mother being interviewed and she was crying and saying why, why did this have to happen to my baby and she brought tears into my eyes I could see the pain and anger she was feeling and I could see how very much she loves you and all I could tell my self is why, why do we have to live in such a rasist world why so much violence and why you. day by day the violence gets worse and ech day I begin to wonder if I'm going to make it to school and back and I think about you its as if your a part of my life now your in my mind day and night its as if you never left.

Interestingly, the year before she wrote this, this girl, who feels so unsafe and who hates the way the world is getting violent, attacked another girl with a rug cutter. The only reason she didn't cut the other girl is that her boyfriend, Austin Gonzalez ("like I said I'm crazy so I might as well shoot my self in the head. Bang") grabbed her arm and said, "Stop! You'll go to jail if you kill her."
Here is the second piece.

Hey Yussef
The world we live in is a stupid one. We walk one way it's okay The other You a damn stupid mother Fucker. You gangs and races have a place in society places. It's seems to live you must have protection and the ones who don't think this well there the victims. Color has no place in my heart but others it just the start. You talk you laugh but when your skin and background come in you aint with. You get shot at you stabed you never know what happens until you last laugh wich is your death.

The other topic that provoked the most impassioned student responses was, quite naturally, racism (and, indeed, racism was also mentioned in both of the above letters). One boy wrote:

That fucking Bastard Joey Fama pulled the fucking trigger and ended you life Just because you were black. What the fuck is the world comeing to. If this keep up Blacks are going to Vanish off the earth like Dinosaurs. Some white Dick heads don't realize we got feelings and families to. And don't realize we only live once.

Diana Delacruz's piece revealed much of the moral ambivalence and pessimism that she had shown in her play about the "Bitch and assholes with attitude" gang:

Dear yusef,

How are you doing? how are you feeling? I know the way you feel because I have friends that have gotten beat up because of raciencsm and they have gotton shot too. if you were still alive maby I could get to know you better. but since your dead and I am alive to bad. no just kidding. I really feel sorry for you I think it was wronge that you died but the problem is that I dont think that raciem is never going to stop it's just something that will never stop. and Belive me there is going to be more victims it was'nt only you.

Many, many children expressed a similar sense of helplessness before the social forces that contributed to Yusuf Hawkins's murder—which may have been another reason why they were reluctant to discuss them in class. Only one person in the whole grade, Angela Cordero, the girl whose friend had died in her arms, seemed to feel she could do anything to change the world she lived in. It should be said that, although Angela did live on one of the most violent blocks in New York City, she had a very ambitious and supportive family, who sent her to top-quality acting, dance, and singing programs after school and during the summer. Also, I had sent her piece about her friend's death to a producer at WNET, New York's public television station, who was putting together a series of thirty-second antiviolence "commercials" for television broadcast. He had loved Angela's piece and had taped her performing a vastly edited version of it just days before the final Bensonhurst class. Her letter to Yusuf concludes:

I'm going to try to change this tirrible but wonderful wold were liveing in. After I have finished my dancing and acting I am going to go into politics and so far I want to become the first women president of the united states because let me tell you something before I die there will be a difference in this world.

It was Angela's piece that, by contrast, drove home to me the hopelessness of so many of my students. I was especially saddened when I thought back to my own suburban childhood when my friends and I—at least by the late sixties—were all convinced that the power to change the world was entirely within our grasp, that we were going to end the Vietnam War, end racism, and build a culture of tolerance and compassion, perhaps before we were old enough to vote. Such optimism looks rather pathetic in hindsight, but with all of the disappointments and rude awakenings I was to experience, it was the momentum that I built up during those early, ignorant years that I am still drawing on as I work in the public schools and write books. And I can't help but worry about the future of these children whose momentum seems to be carrying them in such a different direction—toward a life of misery and hopelessness that, to an extent, will be the creation of their own expectations.

Some students did try to imagine mending the rupture in the moral fabric caused by events at Bensonhurst, but generally they chose some sort of eye-for-an-eye, tooth-for-a-tooth restoration of balance. Several students wrote as Gina Feliciano, who, blaming herself for Hawkins's murder, said that she either wished she could die in his place or that she wanted to commit suicide. Other students tried to restore equilibrium by having various members of the gang repent. Here is an example.

Dear Mr and Ms Hawkins

I'm writing to you to tell you how I feel about your sons deaf. I'm sorry what happened to him and I know it won't bring him back. But if I can give up my life for his life back I would! When I shot him I didn't know he was not involve. I just seen my friends surrounding three black kids. I thought it was the kids we were waiting for.

But I know if you do the crime and you pay the time. I wish I can go back in the future and know what I now and I would of prevented all what happened.

Other students presented their villains as unrepentant, and perhaps found their consolation by writing from the point of view of power. The following was written by an African American girl.

Dear Yusuf,

I'm just writing to tell you that I dont regret having you killed I just want you to know that if I had a chance to do it all over I would. It's making my life a little easier with one less nigger on this earth that I'll have to deal with. Now all I have to start getting rid of is those spicks.

from youe enemy,

Keith mondello

(P.S I hope your having fun with your nigger friends).

At least a couple of boys wrote letters that, along with some sympathy, expressed anger at Hawkins for having allowed himself to become a victim.

Dear yussef,

you should of just killed a man. That fukin white boy actually shot you. you got bucked by a White Boy. I hope your feeling all-right. don't worry those white boys will get what they deserve. But if you dont think they do you could always come down to earth.

Dear Yussuf Hawkins,

Hope you having fun in Heavin or Hell hope God or the Devil are treating you right hope you haven't got hurt even though you got bucked by Joey Fama. I really miss you. I think you died because your black and these whiteys are fuckin racist. I miss you. I'm going to try to get that trader Joey Fama bucked.

This last letter is in some ways the strangest of all. It was written by Ali Ahmed, the birdlike, brown-eyed Syrian boy who had written a monologue (quoted in Chapter 4) in which Hawkins was fierce, undaunted, and vengeful. "[H]e better fuckin kill," Ali's Hawkins says to himself, "or else Im fuckin comeing back witt a Tek 9 and bustin 12 clips in that fuckin whiteys ass." For the most part, Ali's letter is sympathetic to Hawkins, although there may be a note of reproach in, "hope you haven't got hurt even though you got bucked by Joey Fama." What is strange about the piece is that, despite his sympathy, Ali doesn't automatically place Hawkins in heaven, as did almost every other student who wrote about Hawkins's afterlife. The type of Yusuf Hawkins that seems to have captured Ali's imagination had a deeply ambiguous moral nature. Ali also portrays heaven and hell as having an equal potential for being fun, and God and the devil as being equally capable of treating Hawkins well. Such lack of distinction might only be the result of sloppy writing, but it could also arise from a real indifference or confusion regarding the separation of right and wrong, good and evil.

The day after Ali wrote the above, I was sitting in the writing room a little after 3 P.M. when I heard some voices in the alley outside the window. A boy was shouting, "Come on, let him kiss you! That was the deal! You got to let him kiss you." Opening the window and leaning out, I saw a girl backed up against the wall directly below me and a boy, standing right in front of her, apparently about to kiss her. I had never seen either of them before. With them, but standing somewhat apart, was Ali Ahmed, who apparently had been the one shouting. The girl looked up at me without the slightest hint of distress in her expression, so I decided to go back to my work and keep my ears open in case things did start to get out of hand. Before I could even say, "Excuse me," however, Ali had picked up a rock and thrown it at me, shouting, "Get back inside! Leave us alone!" I was so astonished that I didn't take him seriously at first. I couldn't believe he would actually want to hit me.

"Hey, what's going on!" I shouted, trying to remember his name (at any given time I have about two hundred students at P.S. 227/WWA, and unfortunately I have never had a good memory for names).

"Go on, get out of here!" he shouted, seemingly incensed and hurling another rock at me.

"Hey . . . hey . . . ," I stuttered, still trying to remember his name.

A guttural roar rose from deep in his throat and he flung another rock, shouting, "I'm Yusuf Hawkins!" The rock flicked my ear, shot through the window, and crashed into the ceiling just behind me. If it had hit me in the face I would have been badly injured. I leapt back to the far side of the room. By the time I dared to poke my head out the window again, Ali and his friends were gone.

I didn't report him to the principal, as perhaps I should have. That wasn't a part of the role I saw myself playing at the school. I was an outsider. I got through to the kids because I was different from their other teachers—a not inconsequential part of that difference being that I was disconnected from the hierarchy of authority. Deciding that it would be better for me to deal with Ali directly, I waited until I met with his class the following week and then took him out into the hall for a talk. He was very apologetic. He told me he hadn't known what he was doing, and I half believed him. I told him that if I ever caught him doing anything remotely like that again, he was going straight to the principal's office. He nodded comprehension, blinking his big brown eyes. I sent him back to his desk and never had trouble from him again.

DESPITE ITS APPARENTLY ADEQUATE RESOLUTION, I REMAINED disturbed by that incident. Although I had no doubt that on the balance the Bensonhurst Project was an enormous success, I did begin to wonder if it hadn't backfired with some students, if it hadn't glamorized the violence instead of made it seem appalling. I will never know what collection of impulses caused Ali to shout out that he was Yusuf Hawkins—the victim!—as he flung his rock at my head. Clearly, for whatever reasons, he was fascinated by violence, and fascinations find sustenance where they can (we all know how the adolescent mind can transform an encyclopedia into a work of pornography). I think I was so disturbed by the incident with Ali— and also by Susan Carmody's beating—because, still in a state of surprise over the success of the Bensonhurst Project, I hadn't yet learned the limits of its success. Or perhaps, more to the point, I hadn't yet realized what sort of success would satisfy my ambition to make writing "matter."

On This Day a Poor Day a Poor Boy Died:

THE

MURDER OF

YUSUF HAWKINS

BY THE SEVENTH AND EIGHTH GRADES
AT THE WALT WHITMAN ACADEMY

OVER THE WEEK FOLLOWING THE COMPOSITION OF THE LETTERS to Yusuf Hawkins, I wove my students' monologues and dialogues into a play entitled *On This Day a Poor Boy Died.* With the exception of a transcription of the dialogue from *The New York Times Book Review* that inspired the whole Bensonhurst Project, the play is composed entirely of student writing.

I determined the overall structure of the play, and, of course, had to make certain adjustments in order to blend the work of twenty-six different authors into a unified composition. In some cases I attached the beginning of one dialogue to the end of another, or took lines from one monologue and stuck them into the middle of a different monologue. At the insistence of Fran Kaplan, the principal of P.S. 227/Walt Whitman Academy, who was worried about parental complaints, I also removed all the four-letter words from the script—a change which, in most cases, had no effect on the rest of the text. I was sorry to have to do this but understood Fran's reasoning and explained it to my students. Finally, I straightened out some confusing sentences, corrected spelling, adjusted tenses so that they would match, and every now and then modified a phrase or added a few words to make compositions by different students cohere. In doing all of this, I took great care to stay true to the students' language and vision.

On the Thursday following the composition of the Yusuf Hawkins letters, I distributed the play to every student in the Walt Whitman Academy and read it out loud to my eighth-grade classes. Both classes broke into applause when I finished reading, and many students seemed excited about auditioning for the play the following day after school.

On This Day a Poor Boy Died
THE MURDER OF YUSUF HAWKINS

CHARACTERS

YUSUF HAWKINS
GINA FELICIANO
KEITH MONDELLO
JOEY FAMA
CHORUS *The members of the Chorus will take turns commenting on the action of the play or playing minor characters, such as Yusuf's three friends, Yusuf's mother, Russell Gibbons, the other members of the white gang, and various shocked and shamed onlookers.*

YUSUF: *(Walking alone into the performance area)* I am just a poor black boy, minding my own business, looking for a car.
CHORUS 1: *(Following Yusuf)*

August 23rd,
1989
On this day
A poor boy
Lost his life
He could have had a home
Children
A wife

YUSUF: My name is Yusuf Hawkins. I'm the kind of guy that likes to hang out with the group.

JOEY: (*Walking into the performance area*) I am Joey Fama. No one messes with me. I have family everywhere, even in the Mafia.

YUSUF: I'm a fanatic about cars! And anything that has to do with them. I'm dreaming about having a car with an engine covered with gold.

GINA: (*Walking into the performance area*) I am Gina Feliciano. I turned seventeen that night. Everything in the newspaper and the news was all a lie. I was never a drug addict. It's not my fault what happened that night.

KEITH: (*Walking into the performance area*) I'm the flyest guy around. My name is Keith Mondello. I have all the beautiful women surrounding me wherever I go. But there is just one girl I can't stand. You know? One of those crackhead broads. She's an Italian girl who I think shouldn't even be called an Italian, but a druggie.

GINA: Everything was a lie!

KEITH: She's always bringing those niggers and spics up to my neighborhood. Now that's all over.

JOEY: (*Pointing his finger like a gun at his temple*) Bang!

YUSUF: I was mad happy when I got my license yesterday. I was even happier when my cousin showed me the newspaper ad. Money! That car looked mad dope, and it was just three thousand dollars, too. I'd been saving up for months. (*He looks around for his friend JAMES, who steps out of the CHORUS.*) Yo, James! Look at this! Look at this car in the newspaper. It's a used car, but it's on sale. And I need a car, man! My mom said I could get it. What do you think? (*He shows JAMES the ad.*)

JAMES: It's all right. Can I come with you to go pick it up?

YUSUF: Yeah, sure. Who else do you think would want to come with us to Brooklyn?

JAMES: Brooklyn! I don't want to go to Brooklyn. I thought it was here.

YUSUF: Yeah! It's right there. See. Bensonhurst, Brooklyn.

JAMES: Yo, man! There's whites that live there. And they don't like blacks much. And they will beat you down.

YUSUF: Aw, don't worry about them. They won't do anything to us. Just chill, man.

JAMES: All right. I will take your word for it. Let's go ask the guys.

I'll go with you if they want to come—All right?

YUSUF: Let's go.

JOEY: I'm nineteen-year-old Joey Fama. I don't care about anybody, not even myself. I'm that type that if anybody gives me any problems, I would just have to use my thirty-two-caliber to color him dead. Now I don't really know myself that good, because, like I said, I'm crazy. So I might as well shoot myself in the head. Bang!

GINA: *(Talking on the phone)* Hi! What's up? How are you?

FRIEND: Bien. Fine.

GINA: That's good. Guess what? I'm going to have a party and I want you to come!

FRIEND: Word! For real? You know I'm there.

GINA: I'm making out a list of who's coming and I'm 'a try to invite this guy from around here.

FRIEND: Who? Your boyfriend?

GINA: No. But I like him and I think he looks good.

FRIEND: Well, call me later and tell me more about the party, all right?

GINA: Okay. See you.

KEITH: That Gina told me she was bringing some boys to beat me up. So I rounded up my boys too. She really thought she would win. Everything just blew up in my face. I didn't really think that it would end up like this. Who knew that there was going to be a death? My intention wasn't to kill, but to hurt. Now I'm in jail and that Gina is sitting at home like if nothing happened. She's as guilty as I am! She started the whole thing anyway.

GINA: *(Coming up to KEITH)* Hi, Keith! How are you?

KEITH: I'm fine, Gina. Now leave me alone!

GINA: What's wrong? Can't a friend say 'hi'?

KEITH: I'm not stupid, Gina. I know what you're going to ask me. And the answer is no. I don't like you and please leave me alone.

GINA: Well, I'm having a party tonight and all my friends are coming.

KEITH: Don't tell me that your crackhead friends are coming!

GINA: Why can't they come? Is it against the law to bring my friends over? I don't think so.

KEITH: It's not against the country's law, but it's against my law! Gina, this is the last time I'm telling you: stop bringing your crack-head friends here or somebody's going to get hurt!

GINA: Don't talk about them like that.

KEITH: Why not? Don't you see what color you are and the color they are? You must be blind, because you are certainly not their color.

GINA: It doesn't matter to me. I don't see it like you. And anyway, it just so happens that they're coming to my party. And they know you've been talking about them. So you better watch your back!

YUSUF: As soon as I got some of my friends, we went to get the car. It was somewhere out in Bensonhurst. I've never been out that way, but my mom told me how to find my way around. I was out lookin' for the place in the ad for an hour or two. It was getting dark out, when we saw guys up ahead. They had bats . . .

(As YUSUF speaks, the CHORUS gathers around him, imitating the threatening gang of whites. JOEY stands to one side.)

JOEY: My name is Joey Fama. I'm a real clean guy! I can't stand dirt! I was hit by some dirty car when I was three and got brain damage. I always wash my hands and wear white clothes. I don't like anything that has anything to do with dirt! I hate the smell, the color, the feeling, and even the look of dirt! I killed this guy named Yusuf. I had the right to kill Yusuf. He's ugly, a baby, and worst of all, he's black! . . . I'm gonna tell you how it all started. I'd just had a fight with my girlfriend. She was mad at me because I'm almost never seeing her. Me, being a busy man, son of a Mafia family, have no time for her. I left her building furiously, got in my car, and drove to my house. There I was sitting, watching *Charles in Charge,* when I got a phone call. "Who is it?" I said.

KEITH: Yo, yo! What's up? It's me, Keith! Listen up, Joe. I've got to round up the posse because Gina's going to get her kids after me.

JOEY: *(Still speaking to the audience)* "I feel like killing somebody," I told him.

KEITH: You're in luck, Pop, because tonight's the night!

YUSUF: So we saw these guys up ahead. They had bats. When I saw that they was headin' our way I was about to be outty out, but in a second they was around us. We were surrounded. *(The CHORUS pulls tighter around YUSUF and his three friends.)* No place to run. No place to hide. My natural instinct would be to start swinging, but these guys were big. It looked like there were hundreds. So I play it cool. Try and act innocent and talk my way out, careful not to seem rude because, if I do, these cats will kill me quick and not even give it a second thought.

KEITH: *(Stepping out of the crowd)* When Gina told me those niggers and spics were going to beat me up, I got scared, even terrified. You know what those crackheads are like. That crack makes them crazy. They're not even human.

RUSSELL: *(Stepping out of the CHORUS)* I'm Russell Gibbons. You probably know that I was the only black in the white gang that killed Yusuf Hawkins. You've probably wondered why I gave those guys the bats the night of Gina's party.

YUSUF: I'm looking through all these white people. In the middle of the crowd I see a single black face. But to my dismay, he's carrying a weapon, so this means he's part of the mob. How? I don't understand how a brother could be part of this with all these whites.

KEITH: When Gina told me about her friends, I was scared, man. I called up Joey first. I knew I could count on Joey. He's cool, man. When I called up Russell, I knew I had to gas it up so he would know this is a serious situation.
RUSSELL: *(On the phone)* Hello.
KEITH: Yeah. Is this Russell?
RUSSELL: Yeah. What's up man?
KEITH: Nothing, man. I just finished talking to Gina.
RUSSELL: Why are you being so hard on her? What did she do to you?
KEITH: 'Cause she tried to threaten me, telling me that she's going to get her nigger friends to jump me.
RUSSELL: When?

KEITH: Tonight. They're coming to her party. These are major-league black dudes, man.

RUSSELL: Don't worry, Keith. I got your back. They won't mess with you no more.

KEITH: I don't think you understand. These niggers got guns and knives.

RUSSELL: I understand. Look, just meet me at the old schoolyard by Gina's building.

KEITH: Okay. I'll be there.

RUSSELL: Look, man, I gotta go. My mom has to use the phone.

KEITH: All right. Peace, then.

RUSSELL: Peace.

YUSUF: One of the white guys in the gang breaks the silence by saying, "What are you niggers doing here?" I say, "Looking for an address." Be careful, man, I say to myself. They'll kill me quick. The next few seconds felt like an eternity, until one of the members of the group replies, "This ain't them. I ain't gonna hit 'em!" Then another replied with the same word. YES! I'm thinking, safe on first! But then my safety turns to fear as I see another white face running at me, toting a weapon . . .

JOEY: *(Striding into the crowd, gun in hand)* There was a crowd in front of the black kids. I was walking like no one could stop me. I was lean and mean and matching. I had my white shoes and shirt. There was a crowd in front of me, but that didn't stop me. I got to the crowd and I was ready to punch people out of my way. But they moved out of my way. Because I am the man in POWER.

KEITH: What're you niggers doing here?

YUSUF: We're looking for an address.

CHORUS MEMBER 1: These ain't them!

CHORUS 2: They ain't going to Gina's party.

KEITH: I ain't gonna hit them. These are babies. They're kids. These ain't them.

CHORUS 3: I ain't gonna hit them either.

CHORUS 4: *(Rushing forward in the crowd with his fist back)* Is this them? Is this them?

JOEY: *(Rushing up right after CHORUS 4, shouting)* To hell with beating them up! I'm gonna shoot the nigger!
CHORUS 5: NO!

(JOEY shoots, but the gunshot should be symbolized by the sudden, absolute silence of the crowd. Perhaps they should all turn their heads away in horror and shame, except for JOEY who continues to glare at YUSUF after shooting him. YUSUF stands frozen a moment, staring at JOEY in shock, then steps toward the audience.)

YUSUF: When one of the punks in the bunch stepped up like he was gonna hit me or somethin', I was about to pop him in the head, when someone with a shiny thirty-two said somethin' about not hittin' me and then blew me in the head. I felt something moving in my head, then I tasted some chocolate in my mouth.

GINA: *(Stepping forward from the crowd)* I was in my room getting dressed for my birthday party when all of a sudden I heard some noise outside of my window. So I went over to see what the noise was and there was Keith Mondello with about thirty or forty of his friends. When I saw them, I ran to my phone and called all of my friends and told them not to come over. During that time Yusuf Hawkins came around. And then I saw Joey Fama and Keith Mondello and the other guys all around him. That's when Joey shot Yusuf. When Yusuf dropped to the ground, I closed my eyes and moved away from the window, sat on my bed, and cried.

YUSUF: Then all of a sudden this guy come to me dressed all in white and with a bright silver gun. When I saw that I froze. He started screaming, "I'm gonna kill him." They all started screaming, "No don't do it, it's not him, it's not him." He shot at me. I felt nothing. I saw blood falling to the ground. It was then that I realized it was my own. I didn't think of anger, I thought peace and my family. It was also then when I realized how much I loved them. If only I would have been able to say good-bye.

(From now on, whenever a new person speaks, he or she steps forward to form a line on either side of YUSUF.)

CHORUS 1: August 23rd, 1989.
CHORUS 2: On this day a poor boy lost his life.
CHORUS 3: Dear Yusuf, as I watched the news that night, I saw your mother being interviewed, and she was crying and saying,

"Why? Why did this have to happen to my baby?" And she brought tears into my eyes. I could see the pain and anger she was feeling. And I could see how very much she loved you. And all I could tell myself is: Why? Why do we have to live in such a racist world? Why so much violence? And why you? Day by day the violence gets worse and each day I begin to wonder if I'm going to make it to school and back.

CHORUS 4: It was messed up what happen to Yusuf. It was a sad day for everyone, just like what happened with JFK. Everyone was sad and quiet. But the world didn't end yet. Everyone is going to die sooner or later. I hope I live to the age of seventy-seven. Getting back to Keith Mondello, I like him because he was the one who organized all this.

CHORUS 5: Dear Yusuf, I feel like I am not safe from anything.

YUSUF: And then another guy said something and people kept saying stuff and suddenly something happened. Bang. And I saw blood. I fell on my knees without pain. I felt sad and happiness in my soul and heard beautiful humming and crying. I was scared. I started humming and kept on going through a path, while seeing my beloved friends standing there. And the woman of my dreams! And that red Ferrari with the gold engine and wheels. Wow!

CHORUS 6: Dear Yusuf, how are you doing? I know the way you feel because I have friends that have gotten beat up because of racism, and they have gotten shot, too. I feel really sorry for you. I think it was wrong that you died. But the problem is that I don't think that racism is ever going to stop. It's just something that will never stop. And believe me, there is going to be more victims. It wasn't only you.

YUSUF: I was walking fast through my life. It's like I couldn't stop. Then I stopped where I died. My three buddies were crying and scared. The police and ambulance were there, too. And my poor mother, who was so proud of me. I never knew how much I could miss her. And love her.

KEITH: Yo! Here I'm in jail, man. I'm upset because of many different things. One of them is I ain't got anything to do with this murder. I didn't do anything at all. I didn't even start the fight. It's horrible, man! But you'll see, I'll get out of here. And then I'm really gonna start war!

CHORUS 7: Dear Yusuf, I'm writing to say I am sorry you were killed. You were an innocent victim. These guys should go to jail for the rest of their lives. Even better, they should return the electric chair for these pathetic people. I don't even think they're human beings.

JOEY: My name is Joey Fama. I'm . . . Where's the sink? This dirt got on my hand. I better go wash it . . . I'm nineteen years old and when I was three I was with my mom, my father, my sister, and one of my uncles. We were going on a trip to see my uncle's new house up in Long Island and the . . . My hand is dirty! Look at that! Where is the sink! . . . The road was icy and slushy. My father was driving, as careful as he could, when a drunk driver just ran in front of us. We crashed into the car and another crashed into us. When I woke up, I was in the hospital. I felt kind of woozy. I started to cry for my mother. She came into the room to calm me down. She was only scratched on her forehead. When I asked her where dad was, she started crying hard . . .

CHORUS 8: Dear Yusuf, you should have just killed that white boy! That white boy actually shot you! You got bucked by a white boy!

JOEY: Ma, I'm home! Yo, Ma, you here?

MOTHER: You son of a bitch! How could you do this to your family!

JOEY: Do what? I ain't done nothing. Why you crying, Ma?

MOTHER: Because you killed someone!

JOEY: I ain't killed nobody! *(His mother slaps him across the face.)* What the heck you do that for?

MOTHER: Don't talk to me like that!

JOEY: What! I didn't do nothing!

MOTHER: Don't give me that! The whole neighborhood knows about it! How could you kill a young teenager only because he was black! You just took away his life!

JOEY: Because I don't like black people!

MOTHER: What if someone killed you because you were Italian!

JOEY: No, Ma! I look out for myself. I'm a strong Italian.

MOTHER: You think you're a strong Italian! If you were a strong Italian, you wouldn't do a thing like that! *(Crying)* Now I don't have a son, because my son would not do a thing like this.

JOEY: *(Crying)* Ma, I'm sorry! Don't do this to me!

MOTHER: If you were my son, you would turn yourself in!

JOEY: Are you stupid? I'm not going to jail. You're crazy!

MOTHER: Well, get out of my house and don't come back!

JOEY: No, Ma.

MOTHER: *(Leaves and comes back with a knife)* Fine. Then I'll kill you!

JOEY: Ma! Are you crazy? What are you doing?

MOTHER: You think I won't do it?

JOEY: I'm sorry! Please! I don't want to die!

MOTHER: Now you know how it feels. *(Lowers knife)*

CHORUS 9: Dear Yusuf, how does it feel to be with God in a world with no violence?

GINA: What happened that night wasn't my fault. I turned seventeen that night. People say that I am a drug addict, but it's not true. I can get off drugs anytime I want.

YUSUF: I met someone on my way here. He told me that I could actually talk to my mother, but only in her dreams. *(He turns to his mother, CHORUS 10, who perhaps only walks up beside him.)* Hi, Mom. You look so beautiful sleeping! Do you miss me?

CHORUS 10: Of course! *(Crying)* You don't know how much I love you and miss you! If only I could turn back time and show you. I didn't really know how to show you what I felt when you were alive. Will you forgive me?

YUSUF: Of course, Mama. Don't think of that! Just think that you can still talk to me in your dreams. It's really me. Touch me!

CHORUS 10: *(Touching him)* Your skin feels exactly the way it did when you were a baby! On the day you were born! Oh, how I love you!

GINA: Dear Yusuf, I'm so sad because of your death. I wish you didn't die. I really think that your death is all my fault. And I'm really sorry. I just feel like killing myself right now. Love, Gina Feliciano.

CHORUS 11: Dear Yusuf, I'm going to try to change this terrible but wonderful world we're living in. After I have finished my dancing and acting I am going to go into politics. And so far I want to become the first woman president of the United States, because let me tell you something: before I die there will be a difference in this world.

Chorus 12: Dear Yusuf, I am happy for my life and want to live it for the rest of my time. But no man or woman can live forever in this violent world. I can feel the sorrow of your family for you. And I feel sorry for the people who did this to you. But like my mother says, you can forgive but not forget.

Chorus 1: August 23rd, 1989.

CURTAIN

7

Hell in a Handbasket

THE MONDAY BEFORE THE AUDITIONS FOR *ON THIS DAY A POOR Boy Died,* Diana Delacruz didn't show up at school. Diana lived with her father, grandmother, big brother, and little sister, her mother having died several years earlier. When Rachel Suarez called Diana's father to check up on her, he said that she had gone out of the house as usual that morning and he professed astonishment that she wasn't at school. Rachel immediately sent for Yvette Santoro, Diana's best friend, the girl who had had an abortion over the Christmas break.

Yvette arrived in Rachel's office wearing a huffy scowl, as if she couldn't imagine why she had been called out of class. She answered all of Rachel's inquiries with a shrug or an "I don't know" or a "What are you asking me for?" But stonewalling did not come naturally to Yvette. When Rachel told her how afraid she was for Diana, Yvette relented with a sigh and said, "Don't worry. She's fine." Rachel asked her how she knew, but Yvette wouldn't say another word.

The instant assumption of anyone who heard the news of Diana's disappearance was that she had run off with her twenty-four-year-old boyfriend. During the four days that she was missing, all the teachers gossiped to one another with hushed voices and weighty gazes about this guy Darrell, who was rumored to be a drug addict by some, a drug dealer by others, and who had to be, in any event, a terrible influence on a thirteen-year-old and was possibly giving her AIDS.

When Diana turned up at school on Friday morning, the day of the auditions, and it was revealed that she had indeed been with her boyfriend, the story got a new slant. Darrell was granted characteristics of a white knight: He had a perfectly respectable job at an auto body shop in New Jersey, never touched drugs, and had let Diana stay at his apartment when she needed to get away from her father. According to some, Diana's father used to beat her and lock her in her room every night. According to others, his only abuse was to forbid her to go out with Darrell. I don't know the truth. I never spoke directly to Diana about it. I do know that she was a very somber girl and that while Yvette always gave the impression that her entrance into adulthood was, despite her pregnancy and other problems, chiefly an exciting adventure, Diana always seemed to be deriving more sorrow than pleasure from every aspect of her life.

THE WALT WHITMAN ACADEMY WAS DISMISSED AT TEN AFTER TWO on Fridays. Students interested in the auditions—each clutching a glittery bag of junk food and a soda—began to drift into the vast, shabby auditorium at about two-fifteen. I was pleased to see among the first arrivals two of my favorite seventh-grade students: Xia Sanchez, the tall, dark-skinned girl with striking hazel eyes who wrote poems in a red imitation-leather account book, and Ricky Ortiz, the big-fisted, very serious boy who had written "I am the arcade/with my blinking lights/and my bing bong tilt."

Ricky hurried down the aisle and clambered right up onto the brightly lit stage, where I was waiting with my colleague Daniel Sklar and the other members of the Teachers & Writers team: Matt Sharpe and Elizabeth Shepard, the Columbia MFA interns, and Jenifer Polatsek, a Hunter College education student who had observed a couple of my classes and had volunteered to help out with the play.

"Hey, Steve," said Ricky, "I'm going to be Joey Fama, right?"

I wasn't surprised to hear that Ricky wanted this part. Both of the monologues he had written had been for Fama, and his sister Sasha had written that first breakthrough Fama piece, the racism of which had so worried me. Ricky also looked like a Fama, with a light Mediterranean complexion and an intensity in his gaze that could seem unbalanced. The truth is that I all but made my decision to cast Ricky as Joey Fama right on the spot. But of course, I couldn't say so, not before the auditions had even begun. "I don't know, Ricky," I told him. "Anybody who wants to try out gets an equal shot at the part."

"I gotta be Fama!" he said. "That part was made for me. It's the only one I want."

I turned to Xia, who had followed him up onto the stage. "What about you, Xia? Which part do you want?"

She just shrugged shyly. "I don't know. Any part."

It was typical of Xia to be so self-effacing, but I knew her well enough to suspect that deep down inside she was considerably more ambitious. I told her to look over her script and try out for at least three parts.

As more and more students came into the auditorium, I noticed two surprising things. First, despite the fact that I had talked up the auditions to both my eighth-grade classes and many students had seemed excited about being in the play, only one eighth-grader, apparently, had been excited enough to actually show up. Her name was Tarika Murdo; she was a sweet, loud, goofy girl who had worked with Daniel Sklar the previous year and wanted to be a professional actress. I liked Tarika but was disappointed that more of her classmates hadn't come with her.

The second thing that surprised me was that, apart from Ricky Ortiz, only one other boy had come to audition: Isaac Moreno, a tall and good-looking twelve-year-old with narrow eyes, a sharp nose, and lush mahogany-colored skin. Daniel and I had already decided that—with the possible exception of Yusuf Hawkins, whom we both felt ought to be played by an African American—our casting would be color-blind. But it was looking as if it would have to be sex-blind as well—a possibility that made me decidedly uneasy. I had a strong suspicion that, for the play's adolescent actors and audience, the boundaries of gender would prove considerably harder to surmount than those of skin color.

I PUT OFF THE AUDITIONS AS LONG AS I COULD, HOPING THAT more people would arrive. But finally, at around two-thirty, as a small crowd of students—high on sugar and the impending freedom of the weekend—began chasing one another up and down the aisles and over the tops of the auditorium seats, I realized that if we didn't start the auditions right away, they might not happen at all.

Getting the prospective cast up onto the stage turned out to be no easy matter. It seemed that only half the students in the auditorium had actually come to try out for parts in the play. The rest just wanted to watch—not a very good idea, I thought, since the presence of their friends would probably make the actors too self-conscious. My announcement that everyone not auditioning had to leave was met by the predictable moans and protests, then followed by a lengthy gathering up of coats and backpacks and the exchange of last shoves, jokes, and good-byes.

I had just gotten all the prospective actors seated in a circle on the stage and was about to explain how the auditions were to be conducted, when I heard a heavy clank at the back of the auditorium. From the sudden, interested stillness that came into the students' faces, I thought I had yet another frustrating interruption to deal with. Looking over my shoulder, I saw Yvette Santoro and Diana Delacruz slipping through the heavy metal auditorium door. "Are we too late?" Yvette called out.

"Are you here for the auditions?" I asked, hardly believing they could be.

"Uh-huh," Yvette answered with a heavy nod.

"Well, hurry on up here, then. You've just made it."

This was the first time many of the students sitting on the stage and all of the members of the Teachers & Writers team, myself included, had seen Diana since her return. The students moved aside to make room in the circle for the two girls, and I went on with my introduction, but it was hard for any of us—at least for the next few minutes—to give our full attention to the business at hand. Partly we were in the grip of a natural curiosity about Diana and kept glancing at her for clues as to what had really happened during her four days away and how she had been affected by the experience. But I think that we all, in our own ways, were almost equally curious about why she and Yvette were even among us.

To the kids, most of whom knew the girls only by reputation, Diana and Yvette were celebrities—maybe a bit intimidating, even frightening, but very definitely cool. We adults were not entirely unaffected by the girls' coolness, but to us they were primarily children "with problems," children "at risk"—in other words, precisely the sort of students we most wanted to help. I know that I considered their coming to the auditions a small victory and was eager to understand what it was about the play that had made it important to them. And in a sense this was only a variation of what the students were wondering. We all, for our own reasons, believed that if we could figure out why the play mattered to these girls we would discover something about why it should matter to us.

THERE WERE THIRTEEN OF US SITTING ON THAT STAGE: EIGHT students and five teachers—Daniel, Matt, Elizabeth, Jenifer, and myself. I introduced everyone, said a few words about our production schedule and about how the auditions would be conducted, then turned the group over to Daniel.

More than just the students' roles had to be determined that afternoon. Daniel and I also had to work out the parts we would each perform in the production of the play. I had asked Daniel to be the director, but that didn't mean I had given up my strong proprietary feelings regarding the play or my very definite ideas about how it should be produced. My big worry was that I would not be able to restrain myself from butting in on Daniel's direction and that he and I would end up at odds, perhaps wrecking the play. That first afternoon, however, my complete inexperience with acting and the theater made it easy for me to restrain my natural competitiveness.

Daniel is a small man with wiry once-black hair, now mostly a steely gray. He has a rich tenor voice and speaks softly and precisely in a manner that conveys his love of his work and his respect for the people he works with. But he is also careful to make very clear what he expects (and will not tolerate) from his cast—a combination that always puts his listeners at ease.

He began the session by having us get on our feet and do stretching and breathing exercises, then led us through some standard theater games. In the most interesting of these games, one person would stand at the center of the circle and Daniel would call out: "You've just been fired!" or, "You've just won the lottery!" The person would have to respond to whatever situation Daniel suggested instantaneously with a noise and a gesture but no words. The point of this exercise was to get past self-consciousness and learn to go with the body's first and most natural impulses. After responding to the situation, the person would walk toward a member of the circle, repeating the sound and gesture with every step. The chosen member of the circle would then have to mimic the sound and gesture and take the original person's place at the center. This process would be repeated again and again until everyone in the circle had had a turn.

None of the kids, understandably enough, were eager to go first at this game. After several fruitless pleas and encouragements, Daniel finally dragged Tarika Murdo—whom he knew to be an irrepressible exhibitionist—to the center of the circle. Tarika moaned, giggled, and protested loudly, but the instant Daniel shouted, "You've just dropped your keys into the sewer," she screamed and stamped her foot, showing how eager she had actually been to play the game.

"Perfect!" Daniel said. "Now keep doing that!"

Tarika screamed and stamped with every step as she made her way toward the edge of the circle. Once Yvette realized that she was the one Tarika had chosen, a look of panic came into her face. She dodged a couple of steps out of the circle, but Daniel told her to come back. And when she made only the most feeble attempt to imitate Tarika's sound and gesture, Daniel told her to do it over again. Reluctantly she screamed and stamped a second time, then again and again and again. And gradually, as she yielded to Daniel's encouragement, an uncanny transformation occurred: Yvette lost her normal elegant reserve and took on some of Tarika's goofiness. Everybody in the group began to laugh at such uncharacteristic behavior—including Yvette herself, who then, with own her noise and gesture, passed on some of her grace to the next girl.

This game took a very long time, especially because Daniel would not let any two students exchange positions until they were exactly duplicating each other's movements. I began to worry that we would not have enough time left over for the auditions proper. But the kids were having so much fun (except for Diana Delacruz, who had to be shoved by Yvette before she would cooperate) that there was no way I could cut the game short.

When at last Daniel had finished, we gave the kids scripts and asked them each to read the opening poem ("August 23rd /1989 / On this day/A poor boy/Lost his life . . ."). It was thrilling for me to hear these words in the different accents of the children. I had, of late, become so familiar with the script that I had begun to wonder if it had any life in it at all. As soon as I heard the first child speak, however, all of my original faith and excitement was restored—and I got my first inkling of the creative art of the actor and the director. Unfortunately, reciting the poems turned out not to be an effective means of discovering each actor's particular talent since, with the exception of Tarika, who gave her performance a tad too much bounce, all the students did a good enough job to be effectively indistinguishable.

For the final phase of the auditions, we had intended to have the students each choose and read one of the letters to Yusuf, but, as I had feared, we did not have enough time. So instead I decided to use the fifteen minutes that remained before the official end of the Drama Club to find out how the girls would feel about playing boys.

This question had been gnawing at me all through the audition. If the girls proved as reluctant to cross sexual boundaries as I suspected, I would either have to find some way of luring more boys into the Drama Club or simply give up the play. To my surprise, when I introduced the possibility of transsexual casting, not one of the girls seemed the least fazed by it. And when Daniel asked them if they would like to practice walking like boys, they were all on their feet in an instant, strutting and striding back and forth across the stage, not so much imitating boys as satirizing them. The funniest was Xia Sanchez, who crossed the stage with a bowlegged, crotch-grabbing swagger that she said she had learned from Danny Amado, the seventh-grade boy who had written, "getting back to Usus Mondello I like him because he was the one who organize all this." When, for fairness's sake, I asked Ricky and Isaac if they would like to try walking like girls, they shouted, "Are you crazy!" and ran out of the auditorium as if I'd waved a gun at them.

THESE FIRST AUDITIONS MAY NOT HAVE BEEN AS WELL ATTENDED or as efficient as we had hoped they would be, but they were a great deal of fun for students and teachers alike. They were so much fun in fact, that three of the girls—Mayra, Celeste, and Xia—wouldn't leave until Elizabeth Shepard and I pushed them up the auditorium aisle and out the door.

Once the students were gone, it was time for our staff meeting. We were all very pleased by our young actors' enthusiasm but were still worried about how their classmates would respond to girls playing boys' parts. The last thing we wanted was for the girls to work hard and deliver powerful performances only to be laughed and hooted at by their classmates. I thought maybe the thing to do was stage the play in as stylized a fashion as possible, perhaps even having the kids wear masks, as in a Japanese Noh play. Elizabeth suggested that half the masks could be white and the others black. "Then when Yusuf Hawkins gets shot," added Matt, "the kids could trade their masks." We all liked this idea, even though we weren't quite sure what it would symbolize, and ended the meeting by making plans to consult the Walt Whitman art teacher about collaborating on constructing the masks.

I had been as enthusiastic about the masks as anybody but had hardly walked out the school door before I began to wonder if they were such a great idea. Would the students really be able to produce masks that didn't just look silly? And how well would inexperienced actors manage to project their voices through layers of papier-mâché and paint?

"Ah well," I thought, "we'll have time to sort out these problems." In the meantime I just wanted to enjoy my good mood. It was a golden, spring-like evening at the very beginning of April. I walked home with my coat over my shoulder, my throat sore from shouting, my head spinning with exhaustion, but feeling absolutely thrilled that after three months the Bensonhurst Project was still thriving. It seemed a miracle.

THE LAST THING I DID BEFORE LEAVING THE SCHOOL THAT evening was write a note to Joan Gold asking her to remind her classes that the second auditions would be held Monday afternoon and to encourage everyone, especially boys, to attend. Unfortunately, Joan was absent that Monday. When I arrived at the auditorium at three o'clock, I found only four students waiting for me on the stage: Xia Sanchez, Celeste Santiago, and Mayra Climente, all of whom had come on Friday, and Gina Fernandez, the eighth-grader who had written that marvelous monologue-dialogue in which Yusuf Hawkins's mother tells him that his skin is as soft as it was when he was a baby.

I was glad to see Gina, who was one of the eighth-graders to whom I had issued a special invitation, but was nevertheless disappointed at the low turn-out and especially at the complete absence of boys. I was still worried that, although the girls had not had any trouble satirizing boys, they might yet prove too self-conscious—especially in front of their peers—to authentically portray boys. I was also worried that if the play were seen as too much of a "girl thing," the boys might simply dismiss it, which would mean that for 50 percent of the student audience, the Bensonhurst Project would have an anti-climatic conclusion.

When I expressed some of these worries to Daniel, he sighed and said, "Look, Xia, Celeste, and Mayra are clearly going to be the core of our troupe, and this will give us time to give them more special attention. You'll see. It will work out for the best."

We started the rehearsal by having the girls read their chosen letter to Yusuf. After each reading Daniel would ask the girls what they had felt and thought about as they read, and suggest that they try doing the letter in different moods, or at different speeds, or even in different positions.

I had hoped that Gina Fernandez would be perfect as her namesake, Gina Feliciano. But no matter what Daniel did with her, she couldn't put any feeling into her performance. She was too self-conscious, too cerebral—qualities that had helped her create vivid characters on the page but that made it impossible for her to think with her body and her voice (her "instrument," as Daniel would say) when she had to act.

Mayra Climente was a small, stout girl with a rich baritone voice that occasionally cracked into a soprano and a cloud of black hair that wafted around her head like smoke from an oil fire. Her problem was exactly the opposite of Gina's. She was a good actor who could not write or even read very well. The first time she performed her letter to Yusuf, she was so halting and made so many mistakes that she asked if she could go off by herself and study it. "Sure," I said, though not with any great hope of her improvement. Thus I was amazed when she came back and gave a fluid, heartfelt reading. Mayra was to become one of our best actors, a hardworking, absolutely reliable girl.

Celeste Santiago was a sparrow: light as air, never still, always chattering, bouncing, giggling, laughing, teasing. She had a long face with a prominent mouth and high, African cheekbones. Her skin, however, was an ashy white—not at all healthy looking. Her eyes were like two chestnut brown marbles. All through Gina's and Mayra's performances she had been poking Xia, whispering, making jokes, and generally making a pest of herself. Partly just to shut her up, Daniel told her, "Okay, Celeste, you've been so busy commenting on everybody else's work, let's see what you can do."

Celeste got up with her script and said she was going to read Chorus 3's speech:

Dear Yusuf, As I watched the news that night, I saw your mother being interviewed, and she was crying and saying, 'Why? Why did this have to happen to my baby?' And she brought tears into my eyes. I could see the pain and anger she was feeling. And I could see how very much she loved you. And all I could tell myself is: Why? Why do we have to live in such a racist world? Why so much violence? And why you? Day by day the violence gets worse and each day I begin to wonder if I'm going to make it to school and back.

It is often remarked that it is a class's worst-behaved and brightest students—not, by any means, mutually exclusive groups—who get all the teacher's attention, while the cooperative, middling students get ignored. Wild as Celeste may have been at Drama Club, in the classroom, among children with whom she perhaps felt less comfortable, she was subdued to the point of being somber. Her writing was not particularly imaginative or expressive, but it wasn't truly horrible, either. It was merely unremarkable. The result was that, although I had taught her class for three months, I hardly knew her. I hadn't even remembered her name when she showed up at Friday's auditions. Thus I was quite unprepared for her waifish, thoroughly honest, and compelling performance of Chorus 3's letter.

When she was done, Daniel and I turned to each other and nodded. This was certainly a potential Gina Feliciano.

"That was really good, Celeste," said Daniel.

"Yes," I said. "Fabulous."

Celeste gave a little leap of pleasure.

Daniel went on: "I would like you to do it again, but let's see what happens if you do it in a different mood. What mood were you feeling then?"

Still smiling, Celeste shrugged. "I don't know—sad?"

"All right," said Daniel. "What other mood could you do it in?"

She looked baffled.

"Think about it," said Daniel. "What other kind of feeling could you have about what happened to Yusuf?"

"Depressed?"

"That's the same as sad, isn't it?"

"No, it isn't."

"Well, it's close. What's a really different feeling that you could have?"

Celeste just shrugged. Clearly this grilling was undoing the pleasure she had gotten from our compliments.

"What about angry?" said Daniel.

"Oh. Okay."

Celeste did her monologue again, more or less exactly as she had done it the first time. Sad—or depressed—and vulnerable, but not angry.

"Let's do an experiment," Daniel said when she had finished. "Put down your script." She gave him a puzzled look. "Just drop it on the floor. Good. Okay, now you're not an actor reading a script anymore. You're Celeste Santiago. You've just heard that an innocent boy was gunned down by racist thugs in your neighborhood. You've just seen his mother crying on television. I want you to tell me about all of that and how you feel about it in your own words."

Celeste was utterly unable to accomplish this task. She kept wanting to go back to her script, and Daniel kept saying, "Just tell me how *you* feel. Just tell me what happened."

Watching all of this, I realized that Celeste was having the same sort of problem she had when she wrote. What we were asking for was verbal expression—not at all Celeste's forte. We might have had better luck had we asked her to dance what she felt. I decided that here was a case where my expertise was useful. "Celeste," I said, "we talked a lot about the murder of Yusuf Hawkins in class. You really know what happened. How does it make you feel that such a thing could happen in this city?"

"Bad."

"When this sort of thing happens, what does it tell you about the world?"

"That everything's just getting worse and worse—"

"That's for sure," Xia called out.

"—and there's nothing you can do about it," Celeste continued.

I was intrigued that Celeste's remark had been significant enough for Xia to want to second it. "Is that what you really believe?" I asked not only Celeste but the other girls as well.

"Yes," said Celeste.

"The world's just going to hell in a handbasket," said Xia.

"And you really think there's nothing you can do about it?"

"Of course!" exclaimed Celeste, as if shocked that I could ask such a question. The other girls agreed with her.

"Well, I think there's plenty that can and should be done." A speech rose up inside me as I made this remark. But this was not the place to get preachy, nor did we have enough time.

Clearly Celeste had gone as far as she could with her performance, so we let her off the hook and gave Xia a turn. Xia read the same Chorus speech as Celeste, also playing it as sad, but not quite so vulnerable. She was more straightforward, more matter-of-fact, which transferred some of the tragedy from the grieving speaker to the crime itself. I liked that effect.

Although I had always imagined that the actor who played Gina Feliciano would also do the Chorus 3 speech, I now wondered if we could split the speech from the role and give it to Xia.

Much as I liked Xia's performance, I couldn't see her as Gina Feliciano. My reasons, I now realize, were borderline racist and very definitely sexist. Despite Daniel's and my resolution about color-blind casting, all the girls I was thinking of for the part were very light skinned, and Xia's skin was a rich coffee black. But more important, although I had never seen a picture of the real Gina Feliciano, I had always had it in my mind that she was very beautiful, that she looked, in fact, quite like Yvette Santoro. I suppose that I possessed some of the notions I had once attributed to my students; that is, I too assumed that Feliciano's sexual attractiveness must somehow have helped inspire the chain of events that led to Hawkins's death. Complete nonsense, of course, but just because a man knows the truth doesn't mean it governs his thoughts.

For better or for worse I wanted a beautiful Gina Feliciano. Xia had gorgeous, nearly golden eyes, but her face was small and tight, and she was very tall, broad shouldered, and somewhat ungainly. If glamorous Yvette Santoro didn't work out, I wanted to go with waiflike Celeste. Daniel concurred.

DANIEL AND I HAD ORIGINALLY PLANNED TO ANNOUNCE OUR casting decisions at the regular Drama Club meeting the following Friday—which happened to be the day before the weeklong spring break.

But so far only nine students had tried out for parts. Since we were likely to lose at least three of these students, that hardly gave us enough actors to do the play. Daniel and I talked this situation over after the Monday audition and decided to put off making our decisions until after we had held a final audition at the Friday meeting.

I left another note for Joan, who, this time, was not sick and graciously passed on my message to her classes. For good measure, Matt, Elizabeth, and I also talked about the play and auditions in our Walt Whitman classes and were especially encouraging to boys.

When I walked into the auditorium on Friday, I was pleased to see that Xia, Mayra, Celeste, Ricky, Yvette, Isaac, and all the rest of our original candidates had returned, as well as four new students, one of whom was a boy—a fifteen-year-old seventh-grader named Cullen Williams. Cullen was tall, good looking, and very dark skinned—a definite possibility for Yusuf Hawkins.

"Cullen!" I said, patting him on the back, "I'm glad you came!"

Wincing under my attention, he stepped away, muttering shyly, "I'm just here with Natalie."

Natalie Nanterre, Cullen's girlfriend, was a sweet, pretty, thoroughly Americanized Haitian—to my monomaniacal eyes an intriguing possibility for Gina Feliciano. But when she heard what Cullen told me she said, "I'm just here with Shanequa and Yolanda."

None of this sounded good. "But you guys are going to try out for parts, aren't you?"

Cullen shrugged. Natalie said, "Yeah. I guess." I gave them both scripts and hoped for the best.

I didn't have high expectations for the two other new candidates, Shanequa Franklin and Yolanda Castro. Shanequa was a big, square, spacy girl with a surprisingly high voice. Throughout the whole writing phase of the Bensonhurst Project, she had produced only one good line—the play's opening, "I am just a poor black boy, minding my own business, looking for a car"—which she had simply copied over and over again in her every composition for a solid month. As for Yolanda, I had known her ever since she was in fourth grade. She was a small, pudgy girl who was bright and could write very well but was prone to sulky fits, during which she wouldn't write at all. Most of the present year she had written only the most insipid compositions (lists of her favorite songs and friends, silly rhymes, and so forth), as if she had been trying to bore everyone, including herself. I had talked to her a couple of times, but to no avail, and so had written her off. Thus I was surprised by her apparent interest in the play and gave her and Shanequa warm welcomes and a couple of scripts.

As I turned away from the girls, Daniel walked up to me and, raising his eyebrows and pointing at Yolanda, said: "She's really good!"

"Oh, yeah?" I said dubiously.

"She wrote the most amazing play for me last year. And she's a *real* actor."

I decided to wait and see.

It was a testimony to the students' dedication that they had chosen to postpone the start of their spring vacation an extra hour and a half so that they could audition for the play. But it was, I suppose, unreasonable of me and Daniel to have expected that they would repress all of their excitement about their week off merely because they were still in school. The auditions were, in a word, wild. None of the students could keep still or quiet—especially Celeste, Ricky, and Shanequa.

At one point, Daniel and I were doing our best to hear and see twelve-year-old Mayra Climente as sixteen-year-old Keith Mondello when Ricky came charging across the stage in his giant white sneakers, with Celeste running after him, shrieking and batting at his head with a rolled-up script. They disappeared behind the curtain, where they bellowed and squeaked and thumped one another, until I went back there and told them they would have to leave unless they calmed down. I gave Ricky a new script and sent them each into opposite corners of the huge auditorium to study their monologues.

Patient Mayra had just transformed herself back into Keith Mondello when, with fabulous flourish and a sound like a cannon shot, Tarika Murdo fell off her chair, causing Shanequa to laugh so hard she poked Xia in the eye with her script. While Xia jumped theatrically around the stage, Shanequa and Tarika rolled on the floor in equally theatrical hysterics. It was getting hard for me to contain my exasperation. "What are you doing on the floor, Shanequa?" I said. "You're up next. I want you to try out for Keith Mondello. You sit here and practice this speech until I call you."

Shanequa gave me a snappy two-fingered Girl Scout salute. "Yes sir!"

I went back to Mayra, who started her monologue over for the third time and, against all odds, managed to get all the way through, doing a very impressive Keith Mondello.

Now it was time for Shanequa to go on, but she was not where I had left her and was nowhere in sight. When I called her name, Celeste shouted out, "She went to the bathroom!" And Natalie said, "She's gone home." I was just about to call Ricky Ortiz when there was a tremendous thumping from the stairwell up to the writing room (where there was indeed a small bathroom) and Shanequa shot across the stage, the pages of her script fluttering one at a time onto the floor in her wake, and came to a stop directly in front of Daniel and me. "Here I am!"

A couple of sentences into her reading I realized that she was not doing Keith Mondello, as I had instructed her to, but a Yusuf Hawkins monologue.

"Wait a second," I said, "Didn't I ask you to do Keith Mondello?"

"No."

"Yes, I did. Five minutes ago I told you I want you to do Keith Mondello."

"But I don't like Keith Mondello. I'd rather be Yusuf Hawkins."

"But you've already tried out for Yusuf Hawkins."

"Can't I try out again?"

Before I could answer this question, Ricky Ortiz, experimenting with the light switches, plunged the stage into total darkness.

The mayhem was relentless. By the end of the auditions Daniel and I and all the other members of our team were so tired we could hardly lift ourselves out of our chairs to go home.

Cullen was the biggest disappointment. Merely standing in front of an audience, even an audience of his fellow actors, all but struck him speechless. The best he could manage was to mumble haltingly through a monologue with the script right in front of his face.

Sadly, Yvette was also a big disappointment. It was clear that she wanted to play Gina Feliciano almost as much as Ricky Ortiz wanted to be Joey Fama. But whereas Ricky could slip right into character with an almost chilling ease, Yvette seemed unable to let go. In everything else she did Yvette was striking for her poise and grace, but when she acted she wore lead boots: Every gesture was forced, every modulation of her voice somehow awkward and wrong.

Shanequa, on the other hand, despite her unceasing antics, was a wonderful surprise. Without seeming the least unnatural or affected, she made a slinky, soulful dance out of her recitation of the "August 23rd, 1989" poem. And when she performed one of Yusuf Hawkins's monologues, she gave him a funky grace without detracting in the least from the gentle earnestness we were looking for.

I find it hard to resist the idea that Shanequa came by her talent—for this play in particular—in the womb. During a lull in the auditions, Shanequa had come up to Matt and, pointing at the photograph printed on his tie-dyed T-shirt, said: "I know who that is! That's Jimi Hendrix."

Matt asked, "You like Hendrix, Shanequa?"

"He's my great-uncle," she said. "See, I even look like him." And she crouched, turned her head to one side and put on a sullen expression that exactly matched the face on Matt's shirt.

A little later, after Yolanda Castro had finished reading the same Hawkins monologue as she herself had read, Shanequa said, "You know, Yolanda, you too small to be Yusuf Hawkins. He wasn't no little guy. He was a *hunk*. I got a picture of him. He was my cousin."

"Wait a second, Shanequa," I said. "You mean that you are related to Jimi Hendrix *and* Yusuf Hawkins?"

Shanequa nodded. "Uh-huh."

Matt laughed and said, "That means that Jimi Hendrix and Yusuf Hawkins are related."

Shanequa shrugged and turned her long fingered hands palm-up. "I guess so."

I didn't know what to think about these claims. Daniel, however, seemed to have no trouble with them.

"Shanequa," he asked, "do you think you could bring in that photograph? Maybe we could use it in the play."

"Okay. I got to ask my mom for it. He's her cousin."

Daniel asked for the photograph on many other occasions, but it never showed up. Does this mean that Shanequa was lying about these celebrated relatives? I don't suppose I'll ever know, but I have to say that when she crouched beside Matt's T-shirt, she really did look like Jimi Hendrix.

Even if Yolanda Castro wasn't anything close to a *hunk,* she gave a compelling performance as Yusuf Hawkins. When Daniel announced it was her turn, she stepped to the center of the stage with perfect seri-

HELL IN A HANDBASKET

ousness and self-assurance. Celeste and Shanequa shouted out mock encouragements to her as she searched her script for the beginning of her monologue ("Go girl! Show'm what you can do!"), but when she found her place she gave herself entirely to the words, becoming a quiet, vulnerable Yusuf Hawkins who seemed still in shock, not only over what had happened to him but at the magnitude of the racist hatred in the white gang.

Daniel was clearly very happy with Yolanda's reading. I, too, thought it was good, though not better than Shanequa's—or even Xia Sanchez's. Just as she had with the Chorus 3 monologue, Xia had given us a straight-from-the-shoulder Yusuf Hawkins, whose sensibleness highlighted the madness of what had been done to him. I would have been happy if any of these three girls played Yusuf, and I was pleased at the depth of acting talent we seemed to have in this little troupe.

We did get two pieces of bad news during these auditions, however. The first came from Isaac Moreno, whom Daniel and I had all but settled on for Keith Mondello. At ten minutes to three, he came up to me and said he had to go. "What do you mean you have to go?" I said. "Drama Club's not over until three-thirty."

"Yeah, but I have to go to swimming practice."

"Swimming practice!"

"I'm on a team. I have to be at the Y at three-thirty."

"Does this mean you're going to have to leave every Friday at ten to three?"

"I guess so. Yeah."

"Isaac! What did you try out for Drama Club for if you can't come to the meetings?"

"I want to be in the play."

"But you can only stay for half of a meeting. Sometimes we don't even get going until nearly three. How are you going to rehearse?"

A baffled, helpless look came onto his face, as if he had never thought of this before. Finally he said, "Look. I gotta go. I'm gonna be late."

I told him to go ahead but warned him that if he didn't find some way to stay for the whole meeting next time he would have no chance of getting a major part.

"I can't," he said, already hurrying off the stage. "The practices always start at three-thirty. Besides, my mom doesn't want me to be an actor."

With that he zipped down the steps and up the aisle, and I shook my head, thinking that I had lost not only a good Keith Mondello but one of my boys. I did not have high hopes for Cullen sticking around. But if he left, too, how would I ever hold on to Ricky Ortiz—who, as it turned out, was everything I could ask for in a Joey Fama.

I CONCLUDED THE AUDITIONS BY REMINDING THE CAST THAT AFter the spring break we would have only two weeks to rehearse before the twentieth-anniversary celebration on May 8—not nearly enough time to do a top-quality job, especially when no one knew what parts they were playing yet. In order to make sure that we did get enough time, Daniel and I had scheduled two-hour rehearsals for Monday, Tuesday, and Wednesday mornings during the vacation. It was as I was giving the students letters about the rehearsal and permission slips for their parents that I got the second piece of bad news.

Accepting her letter, Xia Sanchez told me that she needed to have a private talk.

"Of course, Xia," I said. I asked Elizabeth to hand out the rest of the letters and walked with Xia to a deserted corner of the dark auditorium.

She spoke without meeting my eye. "I just wanted to let you know that I might be a little late for the rehearsals, because my mother has to go to the hospital."

"That's fine, Xia. No problem. I'm glad that you've told me." After a moment's hesitation, I added: "I hope that your mother's not too sick."

"Nah. She's not sick or anything. It's nothing like that."

I was too conscious of the limits of my role to ask the questions that were on my mind, but Xia saw my curiosity.

"She's gonna go to a drying-out clinic," she said. "Because she started drinking too much."

I understood right away—either because she felt embarrassed or because that simple phrase "she started drinking too much" conjured up too many unpleasant memories—that Xia regretted having spoken.

"That's hard," I told her. "I know what it's like because my father is also an alcoholic. I brought him to a drying-out clinic a few years ago, and it completely changed his life. He doesn't drink at all any more."

I had hoped that by exposing this detail from my own personal life I would make Xia feel better about what she had told me, but perhaps it only embarrassed her further. I don't know. She didn't respond to it, just shuffled from foot to foot without looking me in the eye.

"Well, see you on Monday," I finally said, patting her on the shoulder.

She gave me a quick glance, said, "Bye," then hurried over to join Celeste.

I watched the two girls walking up the aisle, one stately and tall, the other a mere wisp of flesh and bone. I thought about how amazing it was that Xia could seem so levelheaded and sweet when her mother had been enough of a drunk to have to go to a drying-out clinic. If my own experience was any indication, life at Xia's home must have been hell, especially since her father wasn't around anymore. I hoped that she didn't feel too bad about having given me such personal information.

8

Whites

A NEW MEMBER JOINED THE WALT WHITMAN TEACHERS & WRITERS team at the final audition on Friday. Jessica Sager was a Barnard College drama major who had been working as an intern with Teachers & Writers' publishing division, but had been given permission to spend part of her internship helping out on the Bensonhurst Play.

Jessica and Daniel had already worked together on another of his drama projects, but I had never met her before. In fact, it wasn't until she walked into the auditorium on Friday afternoon that I had any idea she would be joining us. Despite her youth—she was only twenty-one—Jessica was extremely confident and made excellent suggestions to our actors about how they could improve their performances. She was also very enthusiastic and compassionate—instantly winning the trust of the cast members, girls and boys alike, and becoming a key player on our team.

AN HOUR BEFORE THE START OF OUR FIRST VACATION REHEARSAL, Daniel, Matt, Jessica, and I met in a Latin pastry shop near the school to finalize our casting decisions. Most of them were pretty easy. Everyone agreed that Ricky Ortiz should get his wish and play Joey Fama. We all also thought that Mayra Climente, the stocky, stalwart girl with the hair like black smoke, would be a perfect Keith Mondello and that waifish, birdlike Celeste Santiago would make a sad and compelling Gina Feliciano.

We had our first disagreement over Shanequa Franklin, the Hendrix look-alike. Matt wanted her to play Yusuf Hawkins. "She made him really *black*," he said. "That was one cool Yusuf."

"She was very good," I said. "But the problem with Shanequa is that she's not reliable. I mean, she's come to only one audition and already she was a prima donna. She couldn't stand it when our attention was on anybody else. I don't think we can give the main role to somebody like that. Yusuf Hawkins must have fifty percent of the lines in the script. If she decides to throw some kind of petulant fit on us she could ruin the whole play."

"What about if we make her the Chorus Leader?" suggested Daniel. "She could lead the Chorus around the stage. She's got all those slinky moves. I bet all the kids would end up imitating her, and they'd look like they were doing a dance up there."

We all liked this idea and gave Shanequa some of the key chorus speeches as well, including the poem ("August 23rd / 1989 / On this day / A poor boy / Lost his life . . .") and also the tiny role of Russell Gibbons, the black member of the white gang.

This decision out of the way, I said: "So now we're down to Xia or Yolanda for Yusuf."

Since neither Matt nor Jessica had particularly strong feelings about either girl, this was essentially a conflict between Daniel and me—the first issue on which we had any clear disagreement. I am sure that Daniel would have gone along with me if I had really insisted on Xia, but I decided not to. He was the director. He should make the decision. All I said was, "It just doesn't seem fair to me that Xia should get left out of the major roles. She's really good and she's so excited about the play."

"We can give her a whole bunch of the best Chorus speeches," said Daniel.

"Maybe she could be James, Yusuf's friend," said Matt.

So that was the decision: Yolanda got Yusuf Hawkins and Xia got James and some of the better Chorus speeches, including Chorus 3's letter to Yusuf, the one that contains the lines that she and Celeste had both read so beautifully, "Why do we have to live in such a racist world? Why so much violence? And why you?" I wasn't happy with this decision, but put my trust in Daniel's greater experience.

After that, it was a simple matter to give Tarika the role of Joey Fama's mother, and Yvette Yusuf Hawkins's mother. I worried that we might lose Yvette by giving her so small a part, but everyone agreed that by comparison to Celeste she had seemed to sleepwalk through her Gina Feliciano monologue. We also gave Tarika and Yvette a couple of Chorus speeches and divided the remaining ones among Isaac, Natalie, Cullen, and Diana.

When the casting was taken care of, Matt said, "Jessica and I were talking earlier about how we need to come up with some sort of overarching vision for the play."

"Something to unite all the performance and production decisions," Jessica explained, "so that all the parts of the play are working together and making the same points."

I was interested in this concept. It was not something that had ever occurred to me.

"So, we were kicking around some ideas," said Matt, "and we thought it would be interesting if we didn't do the play on the stage but did it someplace where the kids could mix with the audience."

"Like the cafeteria," I said. "That's where the twentieth-anniversary party is going to be. We could just have it right there."

"And the kids could clear the performance space themselves," said Matt. "They could just come out of the audience."

"Oh, you mean like the old guerrilla theatre?" said Daniel.

"You mean," I said, "they'd just elbow everybody aside, saying, 'Outta my way, whitey!'"

"I like that idea," said Daniel. "Why don't you guys talk to the kids about it, see what they say."

CELESTE AND MAYRA WERE ALREADY IN THE AUDITORIUM, SITTING on the edge of the stage when we arrived. As soon as she saw me, Mayra called out, "Xia's not coming."

"Yes, she is," I said, walking up beside her. "She's just going to be late."

"No she's not. Her baby brother had to go to the hospital because he had a heart condition."

"I thought it was her mother who was going to a clinic."

"She is," said Mayra. "That's why Xia had to go out to her grandmother in Queens. Her mother has to stay at the hospital with her little brother."

I was now thoroughly confused. I wondered if Xia had made up this story about her brother because she was embarrassed to admit the truth to her friends. Not wanting to breach her privacy, I decided to go no further with the discussion. "Well, let's see. All I know is that she told me she was coming but that she would be late. Maybe it was because she was going to have to come all the way from Queens."

While we were talking, Yvette arrived and told me about another dropout: Diana Delacruz had decided she no longer wanted to be in the play. This news was a relief, because it meant that I had more Chorus parts to divide up. I especially wanted to give Tarika additional lines, since she was nothing if not enthusiastic about the play, even if her enthusiasm tended to get in the way of her acting.

The rehearsal was supposed to start at ten o'clock. By ten-fifteen the entire cast had arrived except for Xia, Cullen, and Natalie. I considered this attendance almost miraculous given the normal reluctance of children to come to school during their spring vacation, and decided that it was just as well that we hadn't been able to announce the parts on Friday as we had planned.

I was also surprised at how well the cast took their assigned parts. Yvette and Tarika's faces visibly fell when I said that Celeste was going to be Gina Feliciano, but neither of them murmured a word of protest. Celeste, on the other hand, leapt up from her seat on the stage floor, bounced up and down squealing, and gave us all hugs. Only Shanequa complained about her parts: "I don't want to be no Russell Gibbons— that Uncle Tom, that Oreo, that traitor!" But she accepted the role when we pointed out that we could easily give it to someone else.

When I'd finished announcing the parts I turned the floor over to Matt and Jessica. Matt summarized the points he and Jessica had made in the pastry shop and then asked the cast what they thought the purpose of the play was. Yolanda spoke up first, shyly as always. "I think what we're trying to do is change people's minds on racism."

Shanequa shouted out, as she too always did: "We want to stop the violence!"

Yvette said: "We want to end prejudice."

I was happy to hear the kids saying these things, even if, to a certain extent, they were only regurgitating what they had heard from me, Daniel, and the rest of the team. What was different about this discussion was how willingly the kids were participating in it. In all but my very best junior high classes, I had often suspected that the students were answering my questions because their embarrassment at their silence was worse than their embarrassment at speaking. But this time there was no sense of compulsion. The kids were speaking because they wanted to and because they felt free to, which reflected well on both the mission of the play and the atmosphere we had created in the Drama Club.

"So, how to you want to present this play?" Jessica asked. "We've talked a little about what we're saying, but who are the people saying it? How do you want to present yourselves to the audience? Are you kids? Are you grown-ups? Are you rappers, like on MTV? Homies hanging out on the street? Are you angry? Sad? What?"

Again Yolanda was the first to speak: "We just want to make a tribute to Yusuf."

Mayra raised her hand. "We're just kids that care."

At first I was bored by Mayra's suggestion. It seemed an insipid evasion of the soul of the play. But then I realized that she was actually making two important points—as, to a lesser extent, was Yolanda. First, she was saying that she thought that they should present the play as what it was, a statement that the cast members themselves were making. And second, as a part of this conviction, she was rejecting the images of city kids as tough, angry, possibly violent but always stylish homies and rappers—images that are pervasive on TV, in movies, and even in the minds of liberal white do-gooders. This was a lesson to us all. The kids just wanted to do the play as themselves. A very wise decision, as it turned out, and one that led me finally to reject the idea of masks.

DURING THE VACATION REHEARSALS, WE DIVIDED THE CAST UP into small groups. Daniel, Matt, and Jessica each worked with two or three students, while I worked exclusively with Yolanda, who, as Yusuf Hawkins, had by far the biggest, most complicated, and most important part in the play. (Elizabeth, the other Columbia intern, and Jenifer, the volunteer from Hunter College, couldn't make these morning rehearsals.)

Despite Daniel's confidence in Yolanda, I still had many reservations about her. She seemed to be taking the play seriously, but I knew that she could be moody and flippant. And I was especially worried about her tendency to sabotage her own work in the face of a challenge. We had hardly begun our first rehearsal, however, before she had completely won me over. Not only was she talented, she seemed determined to do everything possible to improve her performance. She listened carefully to my suggestions, never complained when I asked her to do a scene over again, and was willing to rehearse for more than an hour without a break.

Yolanda played Yusuf Hawkins as a ghost who had come back to earth partly to relive the last moments of his life, partly to show other people what his experiences meant about violence and race relations in our society, and partly to convince himself that these events really had happened. She had great limitations as an actress—as most twelve-year-olds would—and especially had trouble with more emphatic emotions: anger or joy. But she was excellent at expressing Hawkins's subdued, otherworldly astonishment at the grim and the beautiful details of life. There were times, listening to her, when I felt chills at the poignant dignity of her performance. By the end of our three days working together, I had only the greatest respect for Yolanda and felt we had established a rapport that was rare between teacher and student.

Much of my direction consisted of trying to help Yolanda expand the range of emotions she brought to her role. We spent a lot of time working on the scene in which Yusuf encounters the white gang:

YUSUF: So we saw these guys up ahead. They had bats. When I saw that they was headin' our way I was about to be outty out, but in a second they was around us. We were surrounded. *(The CHORUS pulls tighter around YUSUF and his three friends.)* No place to run. No place to hide. My natural instinct would be to start swinging, but these guys were big. It looked like there were hundreds. So I play it cool. Try and act innocent and talk my way out, careful not to seem rude because if I do these cats will kill me quick and not even give it a second thought.

KEITH: *(Stepping out of the crowd)* When Gina told me those niggers and spics were going to beat me up, I got scared, even terrified. You know what those crackheads are like. That crack makes them crazy. They're not even human.

RUSSELL: *(Stepping out of the CHORUS)* I'm Russell Gibbons. You probably know that I was the only black in the white gang that killed Yusuf Hawkins. You've probably wondered why I gave those guys the bats the night of Gina's party.

YUSUF: I'm looking though all these white people. In the middle of the crowd I see a single black face. But to my dismay, he's carrying a weapon, so this means he's part of the mob. How? I don't understand how a brother could be part of this with all these whites.

It seemed to me that Yusuf's last speech, in particular, required—or at least offered the opportunity for—a variation in emotional tone. It is hard to imagine even a ghost not having some sort of response to the sight of a black face in that white crowd. But in all of our rehearsals Yolanda kept reading these final lines in the same wounded, ethereal monotone she had used in most of the rest of the play. "Let's stop right here," I said to her one morning. "What do you think Yusuf is feeling in this last speech?"

"I don't know."

"Think about it. Read that last speech over again."

She did, then shrugged.

"Okay," I said. "Let's work on this together. If you were Yusuf, what would be your first thought when you saw that black face in the white crowd?"

"I don't know. I guess I'd say, 'What's he doing there?'"

"All right. That's good. But before that. You're surrounded by whites who are talking about killing you, then suddenly you see a black face—what would you feel?"

She looked at me, baffled. She was waiting for me to give her a clue as to what I was expecting.

"Just think about it," I said. "Just try to put yourself in the scene."

She thought a moment, then said, "I'd wonder what he was doing there?"

"Let's look at the script. 'To my dismay . . .' What's 'dismay' mean?"

"He's disappointed."

"Right. What's he disappointed about?"

Yolanda's answer was almost a question. "That the black guy isn't going to help him."

"Right! Exactly!"

A big grin came on to her face.

"So that must mean that just before, when he first saw that black face in the crowd, for a split second he must have thought, 'Oh good. He'll help me.' Right? So how did he feel during that split second?"

"Happy?"

"Right. Happy. A little excited—then disappointed. Do you think you could let those feelings come into your voice?"

"Yeah."

"So, where would you sound disappointed?"

"When he says, 'to my dismay . . .'?"

"Maybe. But what about here?" I pointed at the script: "How? I don't understand how a brother could be part of this with all these whites.' Don't you think that's the moment when he would be the most disappointed? The moment when he really understands the truth."

"Yeah."

"Okay. So read it for me again. And try to think about that little moment of hope and then the disappointment. Let that disappointment and anger come into your voice."

She performed that section for me again with maybe slight improvement.

"That was good," I said. "Better. There was more feeling in it. But let's think about some of the individual words a bit. He says, 'I don't understand how a *brother* could be part of this . . .' How does he say 'brother'? He's amazed, right? Astonished. A black man—not just a black man, a *brother*, someone he should be able to trust—is helping the white gang to, maybe, kill him. That's astonishing. You've got to let some of that astonishment come into your voice."

"Okay."

I couldn't tell from this response whether she really understood what I was saying. I continued: "Now, how would he say the word 'whites'? He'd have to say it in a way that made it clear why he is so astonished that a *brother* would be with these people. How does Yusuf feel about that gang? He hates them. He thinks they're animals, worse than animals. They disgust him. Maybe not all whites disgust him. But that group sure does. And that's why he's so astonished to see Russell in with them. You've got to show that astonishment and you've got to let that hatred, that disgust come into your voice when you say the word 'whites.'"

• • •

IT MAY COME AS A SURPRISE TO READERS TO HEAR THAT I thought of this conversation as one of the high points of my teaching career. While Yolanda and I went over Yusuf Hawkins's speech in a dim corner at the back of the musty auditorium, a nearly euphoric excitement rose within me. And it was largely on the basis of this excitement that I came to conclude that Yolanda and I had established so rare a rapport.

Some of what I was feeling was simply satisfaction at the way the Bensonhurst Project was continuing to thrive and was becoming an ever richer experience for everyone involved. Despite all of Yolanda's limitations as an actress, I knew that her performance was adding a haunting sadness to the play that I had never seen in it before and that could not fail to move the audience at the twentieth-anniversary celebration. I was also very excited by what I was learning about the arts of acting and directing. I had never understood so clearly how performance could transform a written text and felt that I could have a whole new appreciation of the movies and plays I went to. But more than anything else, my near euphoria grew out of my feelings about race and race relations.

In many ways, our conversation was precisely the cathartic one I had hoped to initiate that chaotic day Brenda Brodsky told her story about her niece. It had seemed to me, as Yolanda and I both tried to look into Yusuf's heart and mind, that the difference in the color of our skin didn't matter at all (Yolanda is a very dark-skinned Latina), that we couldn't have been more united in our abhorrence of racism and of what racism had done to Hawkins. And, of course, the grim events we were discussing only made our transcendence of racial barriers seem even more auspicious and right. But what especially pleased me about our apparent rapport was how naturally it had grown out of our shared task, without premeditation or self-consciousness—except for the self-consciousness represented by the mere fact that I found it so pleasing.

Did Yolanda share in my pleasure? At the time, in the midst of the self-centeredness that is a part of any intense emotion, I simply took it for granted that she did. I am sure that Yolanda must have derived some satisfaction from our work together—my judgment could not have been so far off. But when I consider those vacation rehearsals in the light of subsequent events, I am afraid that I may largely have been alone in my estimation of our rapport and that, in particular, what I had thought of as a transcendence of racial barriers might very well have been more like its opposite, that talking so frankly about racial hatred with an older, male, white teacher had only made Yolanda uncomfortable. I'll never know. It's so hard to guess what goes on inside the minds of children like Yolanda, who are so shy, silent, and watchful.

9

We're Gonna Save This Girl

THE SPRING BREAK REHEARSALS HAD BEEN AN IDYLL. THERE HAD been disappointments—Xia hadn't come to any of them, and Yvette hadn't come after the first day, when her face fell so visibly on hearing that she would not be Gina Feliciano—but there had been such a good spirit among the cast members who had come. Daniel, Jessica, Matt, and I all felt we had made steady progress and established solid relationships with the students we had each been coaching. The idyll came to an abrupt end with the resumption of school on Monday.

Now that our rehearsals were restricted by the students' schedules and the demands of teaching, I became particularly aware of how little time—a mere two weeks—there was before the twentieth-anniversary celebration and how much work yet remained to be done. Daniel, Jessica, Matt, and I may have been very pleased by our progress with our individual students, but we had never had the whole cast do the play from start to finish, which meant that we had no idea how well our independent performance decisions would work together. Nor did we know whether a play that relied so heavily on monologues could build up the dramatic energy to interest and move an audience. Worst of all, we hadn't even begun to work out the blocking (the positions and movements of the actors within each scene), a very important and time consuming task for a play like this one, in which all of the actors would be onstage all of the time.

The rapid approach of the twentieth-anniversary celebration was also geometrically escalating the amount of work I had to do independent of the play. I spent that first Monday morning after the vacation writing letters and making phone calls to track down former P.S. 227 teachers, students, and T&W members, and also calling media contacts, to whom I had already sent publicity releases, and finally making sure that everybody down in Teachers & Writers' main office knew what exhibits, food, drink, and film clips to bring to the celebration. After lunch I went to the school and, list in hand, shot up and down the stairwell, making sure that janitors would clear out the cafeteria for us on the afternoon of the celebration, scheduling a security guard so that the school could legally stay open after 3 P.M., and generally taking care of as many as I could of the thousand trivial yet all-important other details that had to be attended to. Somehow, with every task I accomplished, I only felt more rather than less anxious. So I was in no state of mind for the news with which I was greeted on my arrival at the three o'clock rehearsal.

I found Daniel and Isaac Moreno sitting alone on the brightly lit stage. The rest of the vast, dim auditorium was empty and utterly silent.

"Where is everybody?" I asked.

Daniel shrugged. "Ricky and Shanequa are out on the street looking for them. Cullen and Natalie were here a minute ago. I don't know where they are now."

"What about Yolanda, Xia, Mayra, and Celeste?"

"Apparently Xia wasn't in school today."

"Neither was Yvette," said Isaac, flipping his baseball hat up into the air and punching it as it fell.

"And nobody knows where Yolanda, Mayra, or Celeste are," said Daniel. "Ricky says that Tarika just went home. He doesn't know why."

I flung my scripts and notebook down on the floor and dropped into one of the wooden audience seats, suddenly exhausted. "What are we going to do?"

"We'll see."

Just at that moment, Yolanda walked into the auditorium, sucking on a carton of orange juice. A few minutes later Ricky, Shanequa, Cullen, and Natalie returned, all carrying sodas and bags of potato chips. I was glad to see them. I had been afraid they might simply have given up on the rehearsal. But even with the appearance of these cast members, we were missing nearly half our actors, including two of our four leads.

There was no way we could do all the work on the play I had been planning.

On reflection I wasn't surprised that Xia was absent yet again. Something crazy was going on in her personal life, although I still wasn't quite sure what, and I had begun to reconcile myself to the fact that she probably wouldn't be in the play. Several times over the vacation I had tried to call her at her grandmother's house (she didn't have a phone at her own), but the ring had a funny, muffled sound and no one ever picked up. On Wednesday Daniel had drawn Cullen and Natalie aside to talk about taking over Xia's parts.

I also wasn't surprised about Yvette. The truth was that I had never had much faith that her commitment to the play—even if she had gotten the role of Gina Feliciano—was strong enough to overcome the lure of that uptown life complete with twenty-something boyfriends that had already reclaimed Diana Delacruz.

I was fairly sure that Celeste's absence was only temporary. There was no question of her dedication to the play. She was completely focused when we asked her to perform, pouring herself into the heart and mind of Gina Feliciano, listening and responding to direction. But whenever Daniel or I were not giving her undivided attention, she was wildly out of control, constantly teasing other cast members, playing tag behind the stage curtains, giggling, shouting, and generally making such a nuisance of herself that we would have to stop the rehearsal time and again to yell at her. I think that she had so little flesh on her bones because she couldn't stop moving; she may even have been borderline hyperactive. I was sure that she had only gotten caught up in one of the dozens of social transactions that occurred every afternoon on the sidewalk in front of the school and that she might even turn up later in the rehearsal.

It was Mayra and Tarika's absence that most puzzled me. They had always been so enthusiastic, so dependable, and had never missed an audition or rehearsal.

"It's nerves," said Daniel. "The kids always start getting jittery around this time."

This made perfect sense to me, given the state of my own nervous system. "So, now what? We want to do a run-through of the play on Friday and half our stars aren't here."

"We'll do blocking. We don't need the whole cast for that. You'll see. It'll be fine."

It was a disaster.

We spent the whole rehearsal just blocking out the cast's entrance into the performing area and their formation of a phalanx behind Shanequa, the Chorus Leader. The biggest problem was trying to figure out what position they should all stand in while Shanequa delivered her "August 23rd, 1989" speech. We tried various rigid, militaristic postures: at attention, then legs spread and arms folded across the chest, then legs spread with hands behind the back. When none of these seemed right, we tried a variety of more freeform postures, but with no more success, partly because we could never get all the kids to stand in the same position at the same time and so could never evaluate the visual effect of any particular posture.

For the first time Daniel lost his patience with the cast: "I don't see what's so difficult about doing this!" he said. "All I want you to do is put your hands on your hips! . . . Look, just do it! Like me. Everybody stand like me: hands on your hips! . . . Come on! We're not going to do anything until everyone has their hands on their hips! . . . Believe me, this is just as boring for me as it is for you!" And so on.

After a while, we decided to give up on dictating body postures and just get the kids to express a mood, figuring that the mood would automatically inspire the appropriate posture. "Look angry," Daniel said. "Look determined." Angry they may have been. Determined they definitely were not. And they expressed their anger or whatever else they may have been feeling only in sighs, moans, slack shoulders, and wisecracks.

Isaac refused to cooperate at all. He spent the whole rehearsal just sitting on a sawhorse at the back of the stage, his baseball cap first on backwards, then sideways, and a skeptical, bored expression on his face. "This is stupid," he called out at one point. "We're not getting anything done."

"We would if you would only cooperate," said Daniel. But this line of reasoning didn't carry much weight with Isaac or with any of the other kids either.

"Why don't we just do the play?" complained Shanequa. "We don't need everybody to be here. I know the whole play by heart."

"Yes," I said, "but you *don't* know where you're supposed to move on the stage, do you? How do you think you're going to look when you're performing in front of your friends and you're all bumping into each other or talking to empty spaces?"

"Stu-pid!" called Isaac from his sawhorse.

"That's exactly right. So let's get going."

But we didn't.

In the midst of this agony, I looked away from the cast and saw Rachel Suarez hurrying down the auditorium aisle. I could tell from her face that she was upset, and jumped off the stage to meet her.

"Have you seen Yvette?" she called before she was even halfway to the stage. When I told her I hadn't seen Yvette for almost a week, Rachel said, "I'm frantic. She hasn't been at her placement since Friday."

"Placement! What placement?"

"She lives in a battered women's shelter! It's a horrible place for her. There are no rules there. It's not meant for young girls like Yvette. It's for adult women who can take care of themselves."

"Why isn't she at home?"

"She got beat up by her mother. Brutally. Last November. It was horrible."

This was a complete shock to me. I had never suspected that such a history could lurk behind Yvette's placid sweetness. "Was it because she got pregnant?"

"No. It was before that. Her mother just doesn't have any control. It's not that she's a monster or anything. But life is hard for her. She says to me, 'I'm Hispanic! I've got a right to beat my daughter when I get angry! It's part of my culture.' They have a terrible relationship. Yvette will do anything to get at her. I look at the two of them and it gives me nightmares. I think about my own little girl and how she's going to get on with me."

"Isn't there any way to get Yvette out of this placement?"

"No. She loves it!"

"She loves it?"

"There are no rules! She can do anything she wants! I thought maybe she might have come here, since she's so excited about being in this play."

"Have you talked to Diana?"

"Diana won't speak to me. She hates me since I broke things up with her twenty-four-year-old boyfriend. I called him up and said, 'How'd you like to do ten years in prison for statutory rape?' That took care of him. I tried the same thing with Yvette's boyfriend, but he wouldn't even listen to me. He's a real low-life, let me tell you."

Rachel hurried off. When I turned back to the stage I saw that the rehearsal had come to a complete standstill. Daniel and the cast were all looking at me, waiting to hear what Rachel had said. That was it for the day. All anyone wanted to do was talk about Yvette, though none of the students admitted to knowing where she was.

TWO DAYS LATER, ON A WEDNESDAY, I CAME TO SCHOOL TO WORK with Yolanda but stopped off at Rachel's office first to see if she had any news about Yvette. Peering through the window, I saw that Rachel was talking to a heavy, dark-haired woman. I knocked and stuck my head in the door.

"Oh, Steve," said Rachel. "Come on in. This is Yvette's mother."

I was surprised by how little of Yvette's beauty and delicacy her mother had. She leaned in her chair like an overstuffed duffel bag. Her brows were puffy, her expression haggard, her hair a black tangle. Life had indeed been hard on this woman. Rachel told me that Yvette had returned to the battered women's shelter the preceding night and had told them she was coming to school today, but so far neither she nor Diana had shown up.

By this point Yvette had missed so many rehearsals that I was beginning to wonder, with only a week and two days before opening night, whether I could keep her in the play. When I mentioned this to Rachel, Yvette's mother squeezed her lips together and sighed. She looked on the point of tears. "Let's see if she comes to rehearsal this afternoon," Rachel suggested. I said that maybe I could hold the part until Friday. As I left the office I met Yvette's mother's eye. I both hated her for what she had done to her daughter and felt terribly sorry for her. "I hope everything works out," I said, instantly feeling the remark's absurd insufficiency.

YOLANDA HAD TOLD ME THAT SHE WOULD BE IN HER FAMILY LIVING class at eleven, but when I went to the classroom, I found the door locked and the desks vacant. I wandered the halls, asking students if they knew where Yolanda's class was, and finally learned that they were in the gym.

When I walked into the bright, airy, tan-tiled gym I found Yolanda's class engaged in six separate basketball games, one at each of the gym's backboards. I spotted Yolanda immediately at the big room's farthest corner, and she saw me. But instead of responding to my smile, she turned her back and pretended to be absorbed in her game. When I reached her, she acted surprised to see me, and I acted as if I hadn't noticed anything odd about her behavior. "So, you ready for a little practice?" I asked.

"I can't," she said.

"Why not?"

"Because I'm in gym."

I sighed impatiently. "Come on, Yolanda, you know this is much more important than gym."

There was no way she could argue this point, so she came with me.

Elizabeth was working in the writing room with Tarika and Ricky, so Yolanda and I had to practice in the dim stairwell that connected the writing room to the auditorium.

It was not the best of rehearsals. We went back to that troublesome section where Yusuf first encounters the white gang. Yolanda still couldn't get any feeling into the line about the "brother" and the "whites," but I decided that we had worked that one to death. Instead, I concentrated on a passage a little farther on, where, on hearing a couple of members of the gang say, "These ain't them. I ain't gonna kill 'em," Yusuf reacts as follows: "YES! I'm thinking, safe on first!" Yolanda simply could not get any of Yusuf's relieved and hopeful joy into her voice. She was especially embarrassed by the word "YES," which, in accordance with the rules of the then fashionable slang, had to have an extended hiss at the end of it and be accompanied by a tight swing of the fist. She wouldn't do either of these things. Her "YES" was grudging at best, as if she were admitting after a long interrogation to having committed some minor indiscretion.

Still, she had made good progress at memorizing her lengthy part. And, I thought, even if she never got down the fine points of expression, her subdued, earnest intensity would go a long way toward carrying off the performance, as would her physical presence: she was small, pretty—a trifle overweight—and very dark. It was painful even to think of such a child as the victim of racist brutality. All this being true, that day I entered my first negative remark about Yolanda into my diary: "She's such a self-conscious young girl, very much a one-note actress."

THAT AFTERNOON'S REHEARSAL THREATENED TO BE AS PAINFUL AS the previous one. By five after three, the only cast members who had come to the auditorium were Tarika Murdo and Mayra Climente. I made a run out onto the sidewalk in front of the school to see if I could catch any straggling cast members and spotted Celeste and Natalie in the thick of a crowd of girls on the far side of the street. When I called out to them to come, Celeste shouted back, "We can't. Natalie's had her first PMS." I took this to mean that she had had her first period, and while it didn't seem to debilitate Natalie enough to prevent her from being the excited center to a crowd of her friends, I figured it was not my place to interfere with one of life's great moments of passage. So I shouted back to Celeste, "Okay, but there's nothing stopping you from coming."

Ricky, Cullen, Yolanda, and Shanequa were also out on the sidewalk. When I had gathered them together, they begged me to let their friends come and watch the rehearsal. My first thought was that the cast would be distracted by the presence of their friends. But then, touched that these kids were all so eager to see the play, I wondered if the cast mightn't actually try harder in front of an audience. So, with some reluctance, I agreed to the request and walked back into the building in the midst of a crowd of about twenty kids. One of them was Ricky's sister, Sasha, who asked me: "When are you going to get this play over with, already?"

"A week from Friday," I told her.

"Thank God. Ricky's been running around the house acting like Joey Fama for a month now. It's disgusting. I'm afraid he's gonna kill me." Later I was to hear that Ricky was indulging in the same behavior at school. During the two weeks before the performance of the play, he picked fights with five different boys. What is more, he was bragging about these fights to Elizabeth and Jessica in a way that made it clear to both of them he thought they would find these macho encounters sexy.

As I escorted the crowd of kids back to the auditorium, Celeste fell into step beside me, and I asked her where she had been for the last two rehearsals. With perfect simplicity she said, "My mom had to go to a mental hospital."

Once again I was shocked. It was a moment before I could ask, "Is she all right?"

"Yeah."

"What was the matter with her?"

"She just got depressed." (I remembered how Celeste had corrected Daniel when he had said "sad" and "depressed" were the same thing.) "Sometimes she'd just sit in one chair all day long and not do anything."

"Is she still in the hospital?"

"No. They brought her home. I think they just gave her a whole lot of drugs."

"Who took care of you?"

"Nobody. I had to take care of my sister and brother. That's why I couldn't come to rehearsals."

"Couldn't your grandmother take care of you? Or your father?"

All Celeste said to this was, "My father died when I was a baby."

Figuring I had pried enough, I just patted her on the shoulder and said, "Well, I'm glad to have you back with us."

WHEN WE FINALLY REACHED THE AUDITORIUM, I SAW XIA UP BY the stage talking to Daniel. Celeste caught sight of her and ran ahead, calling out her name. The story as I got it from Xia now was that her little brother had indeed had heart trouble but that it had turned out not to be serious—"just a heart murmur"—and that she had spent the last three weeks with her grandmother out in Queens, not going to school so that she could help take care of her little brother and sister while her mother was in the drying-out clinic. But now everybody was home, life was back to normal again, and not only would Xia be able to attend rehearsals, but she had already found out what her parts were from Mayra and had memorized them all.

"What a girl!" I said, giving her a big pat on the back and instantly forgiving all her absences.

While Daniel called everybody onto the stage and explained what we were going to do that day, I surrendered to a moment of distraction during which my brain tried to catch up with all the astonishing information it had taken in over the last couple of days: Xia's mother had gone to a drying-out clinic, Celeste's was in a mental hospital, Yvette was in a battered women's shelter because her mother beat her, and Diana had run away from home for who knew what reason—so much tragedy in so small a cast! Was there more? Were Ricky, Cullen, Natalie,

Mayra, and the rest nursing wounds that simply hadn't yet come to light? And then there were my other students: Susan, who had been beaten up; Denise, who had helped beat her and whose mother had tried to make her a ward of the state; Taletha, the bright, obstreperous girl in Yvette's class ("I want to shoot them muthafuckin' white boys!"), who, I had just found out, was pregnant; Ingrid, the girl who had been writing me suicide notes and who, I had discovered on reporting them to Rachel, had seen her own mother blow her brains out with a pistol; and Enrico, the boy who used his writing folder for a series of confessions about how his father had beaten him and his brother senseless. But again, these were only the tragedies that I had heard of. How many other students were harboring similar horror stories? As I stood there beside the stage, I realized yet again how enormously I had misunderstood my students and their world. And there was still so much I didn't know. Was such density of suffering a statistical anomaly or merely normal for such a cross section of kids at an inner-city junior high?

IT TURNED OUT THAT MY FIRST INSTINCT HAD BEEN CORRECT: letting outsiders watch the rehearsal was a big mistake. Rather than spurring the cast to greater effort, the presence of their friends made them self-conscious and embarrassed. Cullen, in particular, felt he had to show off by blatantly defying Daniel's every request. Finally, I had no choice but to provoke the wrath of everyone in the cast and their classmates by telling the observers to go. This turned into an absurd ordeal, with the kids in the cast whining, "Oh, come on! Why can't they stay? We want them here. We won't make any noise." And me repeating over and over: "No. Absolutely not! Everybody out, now! I mean it! Let's go. Out! Out! Out!"

I ended by—mostly in jest—having to physically shove a couple of kids out the auditorium door. I was walking down the aisle thinking that here was yet another rehearsal ending a total shambles when I heard Celeste call out from the stage, "Look!" and I turned around to see Yvette and Diana walking down the aisle behind me.

The whole cast bounded off the stage to gather around the two girls, hugging Yvette and patting her on the back. I was pleased to see the solidarity that had developed among them all, especially since most of the seventh-graders had hardly known Yvette (an eighth-grader) before the start of rehearsals. I was also pleased to see that Yvette really had cared enough about being in the play to come to rehearsal even in the midst of whatever turmoil had absorbed the rest of her life.

Yvette herself seemed surprised and very pleased by her reception—although she also looked tired. There were dark circles under her eyes.

Her entrance couldn't have come at a better time. All the bad feeling of minutes before was completely gone. To have Yvette and Xia return on the same day buoyed everybody's spirits. We ended by having a fabulous rehearsal that lasted until five o'clock. At one point, while Yvette, as Yusuf's mother, was blocking out her final scene with her dead son, I looked around to see Rachel standing by the stage, grinning with her arms folded across her chest. She gestured for me to come over. Jerking her head in Yvette's direction, she whispered in my ear, "We're gonna save this girl!"

Because of their absences, neither Yvette nor Xia had had a chance to have individual rehearsals with any of the T&W team, so Jessica made appointments with both of them for the following day. I remember thinking it strange that Yvette couldn't remember what room she would be in at the time of her appointment, but chalked it up to distraction resulting from the chaos that seemed to have absorbed her life. As she was leaving the auditorium I pulled her aside and said, "Are you sure you're all right?"

She smiled, seeming touched and flattered by my concern. "Yeah."

"I just want to make sure, because we're all worried about you."

"Don't worry. Everything's fine!" There was a strange excitement in her expression as she said that. Then she hurried away, seeming, as I wrote in my diary that night, "thrilled by her sudden plunge into life's adventure and perhaps a little in love."

As Xia prepared to leave, she hefted a big black plastic garbage bag onto her shoulders.

"What's that?" asked Jessica.

"Sandwiches left over from the class trip we took today." (From its bulk, the bag looked as if it contained twenty or more heros.)

"What are you doing with them?"

"I'm bringing them home for my family and the other people in my building. Otherwise they'd just get thrown away." Swinging the bag onto her shoulders, Xia followed her friends out of the auditorium.

• • •

THE FOLLOWING MORNING, I WENT INTO MY EIGHTH-GRADE CLASS and Joan Gold told me that Yvette was missing again. As soon as that class was finished, I went across the hall to talk to Rachel, who told me that she had been calling Yvette's "placement"—the battered women's shelter—all morning and that they wouldn't tell her anything except that she had last been seen leaving the shelter at ten o'clock the previous night. "They don't want to cooperate," said Rachel, "because they're worried that they might be liable for her."

"Is she staying with her boyfriend?" I asked.

"She can't. He's married. But he's got her an apartment somewhere up in the Bronx. Let me tell you, this guy is real scum. There's nothing good about him. He's a drug dealer. He's got a lot of money, so putting her up in an apartment is nothing to him."

I just shook my head. It was so sad and strange to think of one of my students living in such a world.

"She's just doing it to get back at her mother," Rachel continued. "There's nothing I can do about it. She's digging her own grave. She's trying to kill herself. I swear, I expect to hear nothing about her for five years and then I'll get an invitation to her funeral."

I had to hurry back across the hall to teach my second eighth-grade class, the one in which Diana was a student. After presenting the writing idea for the day, I took Diana out into the hall to see if she knew anything about Yvette. She kept her head down, never once meeting my eye, and claimed she hadn't spoken to Yvette since leaving the rehearsal yesterday and had no idea where she was. Then she went back to her desk and wrote the following:*

Diary

I am so stupid. Darrell called me yesterday, and I hanged up on him. and I left school yesterday because I was so just, so angry that I left so I started crying. I don't know I wasn't thinking right. So I called him collect and he accepted the call then I told him to come around [. . .] street but I forgot to tell him [which avenue] I was on. you know so I hang up so I waited there for half an hour so then I left to my sister school Then we went to Jose's house. We were with all those guys we had fun. So we left then he called me and I

---

*Place names have been removed for the sake of privacy.

hang up I dint even give him a chance to talk I just went CLICK
and hang up so he called back Then I told my brother to tell him
that I don't live here no more but I love him and I want to be with
him no matter what but I dont care I will promise you that I am
leaving far with him very far that no one will ever no where I am I
don't care about no one except him I dont know why but I think
it's love and some little voice inside of me tell's me to go with him
stay with him, run away, kill yourself, die, you dont need to be
alive, Why tell me a good reason why it's it good to live when they
are seperating him from you. But I will fight that voice and will
obey it in only one thing which is run away but only with him
that's it I am really saying the truth but first I want to graduate then
I will plan it and my plan will reveal and then I will strike and leave
4 ever no one will ever, ever, ever, ever, ever, ever, ever, ever, ever,
ever, ever, ever, ever, ever, ever, ever, ever, ever, ever, ever,
ever, no where

I AM

So much for Rachel's claim that she had broken Diana and Darrell up
with that threat about statutory rape! You do your best for these kids,
but ultimately, they run their own lives. Oddly, this thought was a comfort to me as I contemplated Yvette's situation for the remainder of the
day. Yvette may have been troubled, but that didn't mean she was incapable of taking care of herself. She had, after all, never struck me as
self-destructive, and I didn't think that she would ever do something
she *knew* to be dangerous. The big question, of course, was how much
she did know about the world in which she was traveling. Pretty terrible
things could happen to a beautiful, naive fifteen-year-old girl on her
own in this city. As Daniel said when we talked about it later that day,
"It makes you want to cry."

IT WAS FRIDAY—EXACTLY ONE WEEK UNTIL THE TWENTIETH-
anniversary celebration. As soon as I arrived at school I stopped off to
see Rachel, but she still didn't have a clue as to where Yvette might be
and hadn't had time to call the battered women's shelter. I taught my
classes in a state of distraction, worried about Yvette, but also wondering if Xia could take over Yvette's part. I knew that Xia could handle it,
but I was worried that the audience might become confused if the same

actor who played Yusuf's friend was also his mother.

After my morning classes, I went to pick up Yolanda for our practice—only to hear her tell me that she didn't want to go. When I asked her why she said, "I just don't want to be in the play anymore." That was all. No other explanation.

Such was the state of my nerves at this moment that my first response was to become hugely furious at her. I managed to contain my anger, however, and instead of yelling, gave her an inspirational lecture about how bright and talented she was, about what a great opportunity this performance would be for her, about how she would kick herself if she didn't take advantage of it, and, most important, about how it was too late for her to quit, because no one else could learn her part in the time we had left. "If you quit now," I concluded, "you'll let down all of your friends and ruin the whole play."

"Shanequa knows the part," she said.

"That's beside the point," I said. "No one can play Yusuf Hawkins as well as you. And anyway, you've got to learn to keep your promises. When you agreed to take this part, you were promising me, Daniel, and the whole cast that you would do it. You can't let us down now."

I was proud of this speech and in the end Yolanda seemed convinced by it. I decided not to rehearse with her that day, however, both because I felt that she was under enough pressure and because I had so many other things to do.

I ended up having no time for lunch, so I ran out to the grocery across the street to get a bag of nuts and a cup of tea just minutes before rehearsal time. On my way back I met Daniel, who was just arriving at the school. As we walked up the block, I filled him in on Yolanda and Yvette. We agreed that if Yvette didn't show, we would give her part to Xia and let Cullen play Yusuf's friend, James—a part he had already begun to learn during Xia's absence. Neither of us could figure out what to do should Yolanda quit on us. Shanequa had been having a terrible time with the Russell Gibbons part, so it was hard to believe that she could know all of Yusuf's lines. But even if she did, who could possibly match her performance as the Chorus Leader? Her slinky catlike strut had become increasingly central to the whole look of the play.

We walked into the auditorium to find Yvette sitting on the edge of the stage, drumming her heels against the wood paneling beneath it.

While Daniel went to put his stuff away in the writing room, I talked to her. "Where have you been all day?"

"At the doctor's."

I wasn't at all sure if I should believe this, but once again I did notice that she had very dark rings under her eyes. "Are you okay?"

She shrugged. "I got these headaches. And this pain in my stomach." She pressed her hand over her liver. "And I keep vomiting up this green stuff with lots of, like, white pus in it."

"What's the doctor say?"

"He says they got to do some tests. He says it's probably on account of my mother beating me up."

"Still!" I said. "That was such a long time ago." It was seven months, to be exact.

"Yeah. Well, I been having all this stuff ever since then."

I couldn't talk to her anymore because the rest of the cast had begun to arrive. Looking down at the far end of the stage, I saw Daniel and Elizabeth in deep discussion with Yolanda. I hurried down there and found that, just as I had feared, Yolanda was indeed telling Daniel that she didn't want to be in the play. Once again I gave her my inspirational speech and once again she relented.

"Good job," Daniel said as Yolanda walked away, but I had little confidence that she would remain convinced by my arguments.

As I walked toward center stage to get the rehearsal going, Celeste came up to me and said, "Steve, you better get home as fast as you can."

"Why?"

"Don't you know? They're beating up white people on the streets."

Hearing this, Tarika broke in: "Don't say that to him! It's not polite."

"That's all right, Tarika. She can say anything she wants."

This was Friday, May 1, 1992, the day after the four policemen who had beaten Rodney King were found innocent of criminal wrongdoing, and south central Los Angeles had erupted in the worst outbreak of looting, vandalism, and violence since the Watts riots of nearly thirty years before. This morning the whole of the nation, and perhaps New York in particular, had woken up wondering if the violence in L.A. would spread to other inner cities—but I had been too obsessed by the play to give it more than a passing thought. Throughout the day, however, I had heard rumors of rioting on Herald Square and Times Square, although these, too, I had dismissed as inconsequential.

"Anyhow, it's all happening in midtown," I said to Celeste, "we don't have anything to worry about here."

"Oh, yes we do," said Celeste. She spoke with great assurance about rioting only a few blocks away. When several of the other cast members, who had gathered around us, confirmed what she had said, I began to get worried, not so much about us white folks as the kids, many of whom lived right in the area of the supposed looting.

"You hear anything about this?" I asked Daniel.

"I heard that somebody got killed on Times Square," he said. "But I just came through there on the subway and everything seemed perfectly normal."

"I hear the worst of it is at Union Square," said Elizabeth.

Matt, who had just come into the auditorium, said, "I was just in the office and the secretary says they've been getting calls all afternoon from parents who have heard there is rioting and want to bring their kids home early."

I asked if he had been told anything about the neighborhood where Celeste had said there were riots.

"Yes," he said. "Apparently some people have called in and said there's looting there."

With this independent confirmation, insubstantial as it may have been, I realized the time had come to take this situation seriously. One thing was clear, the kids were all so worked up about it that we wouldn't have been able to get them to rehearse anyway.

"All right," I said, not without a twinge of excitement. "No rehearsal today. I want you guys to be very careful going home. Is there anyone who doesn't have someone they can walk home with?" Nobody raised a hand.

Looking around the room I saw that everyone except Shanequa had come to rehearsal, even without my having to get them off the sidewalk. This struck me as a sign that the play really mattered to the kids, that in some way they all believed being together and working on this play was a way of responding to the racial turmoil that apparently surrounded us. No sooner had this thought occurred to me than, quite spontaneously, Natalie said, "I can see the connection between this play and what happened to Rodney King."

"What is it?" asked Matt.

"Some white cops beat Rodney King and some whites killed Yusuf Hawkins."

"The difference," said Matt, "is that the killers of Yusuf Hawkins got sent to jail, but the cops in L.A. went free."

"We're all angry about what happened in L.A." I said. "But looting and killing are not the right response to it. Isn't that what this play tells us? Doesn't this play show us how evil it is when one group of people takes out its rage and fear on another? It was wrong to beat Rodney King. And it was wrong to kill Yusuf Hawkins. But the beating and the killing that might be going on right now are also wrong, and for exactly the same reasons. There are other ways to deal with evil and injustice. One way is to make sure that everybody knows about it so that it will never happen again. I want you all to remember that when you practice your lines this weekend. This play is part of the struggle to make sure that there are no more Yusuf Hawkinses or Rodney Kings."

I had felt that, as the leader of this group, I was obliged to make some sort of statement about our work and the events we were ostensibly in the middle of. The statement quoted above was simply the first thing that came into my head. It doesn't seem all that bad to me now, given the circumstances. At the time, however, no sooner had I shut my mouth than I felt fatuous and narcissistic for attempting to inflate our little school project by linking it to the social turmoil that, by all reports, was engulfing the city. Such second-guessing and self-consciousness were very much the mode of that unreal afternoon.

AFTER THE STUDENTS HAD GONE, THE T & W STAFF—ALL OF US lily white—held a brief meeting. Jenifer, the volunteer from Hunter College, said that she had heard that *two* people had been killed on Times Square. Daniel and Matt, who lived on the same block in Greenwich Village, decided to share a cab home. Jessica had been planning to go to work at the T&W offices on Union Square, but decided she wouldn't after hearing Elizabeth's report of the rioting there.

A subtle hysteria was slowly taking us over as we sat there on the stage. I talked about the looting I had witnessed during the black-out of '77, in particular about a man I had seen staggering in the street, covered with blood, trying without success to get a passing car to take him to the hospital. Jessica said that in L.A. the rioters had burned down three schools and that she figured that the auditorium was the safest place to be if this school caught on fire. Daniel and Matt talked about the white truck driver in L.A. who had been dragged onto the street and hit on the head with a brick.

Twenty minutes earlier, no one had been taking the possibility of racial violence in New York City terribly seriously, but now, as the time for our departure rapidly approached, we all felt a clammy uneasiness in our guts. I jumped off the stage and declared, "Okay, everybody, practice your commando tactics!" and got a much bigger laugh than the joke deserved. We picked up our things and headed out of the auditorium. Daniel said, "Maybe we should all hang little signs around our necks that say, 'Don't kill me, I'm a liberal.'" More anxious laughter.

On our way out of the school, we stopped by the main office and found the principal, Fran Kaplan, and the school secretary standing behind the desk. "Have you heard anything about what's going on outside?" I asked. Fran simply pointed out the window to where two police cars, dome lights flashing, were stopped in the middle of the street, causing a traffic jam. "Apparently they're arresting a single looter."

The computer teacher, who had just been outside, came into the office. "They say that this guy came running down the block after trying to loot a store. But there was nobody else. I mean, there wasn't a mob or anything."

After that we left. The weather outside was beautiful, but a little dimmed by high, rusty haze, which in this context gave the whole scene an apocalyptic air. I looked at the traffic jam and said, "The rats fleeing!" Then: "Really, I've never seen the traffic this heavy." No sooner did I say this than I wondered if it were true. I had never really paid attention to the volume of traffic on this street at 3 P.M. Now everything seemed significant: The normally tired or bored faces on my fellow pedestrians looked like the brave, beleaguered, and wary faces of combatants, and the scant children, on bicycles or in strollers, seemed the most vulnerable of innocents.

The longer I walked, however, the more normal things began to seem. I glanced down the street where the looting was supposed to have occurred and saw absolutely nothing out of the ordinary. People were browsing at the fruit stands, pouring out of the subways. None of the shop owners had pulled down their shutters. On the corner of my own street, I saw three police cars with flashing domelights, each with one or more young black men in their back seats. Was this normal too? I wondered.

Later that night, when the big news on television was that there was no news, that there had been no rioting on Times Square or Herald Square or Union Square and that nobody had been killed, I thought about how the euphoria that I had experienced so often during the Bensonhurst Project was the mirror image of this non-news, about how there would have been no reason to feel euphoric if I hadn't, on some level, always possessed a terror about what might happen between blacks and whites in this country, the same terror that had made so many New Yorkers rush to save themselves and their loved ones from the riots that never happened.

1 0

You Can Do Anything You Want with Your Life

THREE-TEN P.M. ON MONDAY, MAY 4. FOUR DAYS REMAINED BEFORE the twentieth-anniversary celebration. Daniel, Jessica, Matt, and I and the entire cast were sitting on the stage waiting for Yolanda. None of the kids knew—or would admit to knowing—where she was or why she hadn't come to rehearsal. I made my usual run out to the sidewalk in front of the school, but she wasn't there; no one had seen her. I sent Tarika into the girls' bathrooms, but Yolanda wasn't there either.

Daniel and I exchanged grim glances on my return to the auditorium. We decided that the kids were getting too restless and that we had too much work to do to postpone the rehearsal any longer. Daniel called everyone together to start the warm-up exercises, and I asked Xia if she could read Yusuf's part until Yolanda showed up. Xia's face lit up at my request. "Sure. I already know a lot of it from when we were trying out." By this I understood that, despite her self-effacing claim that she would have been happy with any part, she had wanted the lead all along—and I was now very sorry that we hadn't given it to her.

We did a quick reading of the whole play, with the kids sitting in a circle on the floor, just so we could get a feel for its dramatic momentum. Then we went into a more complete rehearsal of the last third of the play, which we had often not had time to get around to in other rehearsals. Daniel and I were working on the blocking for the shooting scene when the auditorium door clanked and Yolanda slipped into the large, dim room. "Let's go, Yolanda," I called out. "You're late!" This was an understatement. It was now nearly four o'clock.

Yolanda walked slowly down the aisle without saying a word.

"I'll go see what's the matter," Jessica whispered and, leaping from the stage, hurried toward Yolanda. I suppose that Jessica intended us to go on with the rehearsal, but none of us could pay attention to anything except our wavering star. Daniel and I gave the cast a break and climbed down from the stage ourselves.

Jessica was wearing a resigned expression when we joined her and Yolanda. "Well," she said, shrugging her shoulders, "she doesn't want to do it."

"Is this true, Yolanda?" I asked.

Yolanda didn't look me in the eyes. She just said, "Shanequa can do it."

Shanequa had come running up behind me. "Yeah, I can do it! I already know the whole part."

Shanequa had been complaining about playing Russell Gibbons from the moment the part had been assigned to her. It was, of course, perfectly understandable why she might feel uncomfortable playing a turncoat "brother." Jessica, Daniel, and I had taken pains to make it clear to her that the part in no way reflected on her own character and that everyone would understand she was just an actor playing a role. We had even let her rewrite Gibbons's lines so that he appeared more aware that he had done wrong. This had seemed to appease Shanequa, and she had played the part without complaint for the last few rehearsals. But at the same time she had been letting us know repeatedly, one way or another, that she had memorized the whole play, and Yusuf Hawkins's part in particular.

I had dismissed these claims as irrelevant braggadocio, but now, as she and Yolanda stood side by side and as Yolanda said, "Yeah, you should let Shanequa do it," I suddenly realized that the two girls must have been plotting Shanequa's taking over the role at least since Friday.

It was clear to me that, even if Yolanda could be persuaded yet one more time to resume her role, she simply could not be counted on. Were she to quit again tomorrow or the day after, the play would be hopelessly sabotaged—if it hadn't been already. And it was also clear that our easiest and perhaps best option would be to go along with the girls' suggestion. But giving in to their manipulations would have been too much like rewarding Yolanda for her irresponsible, cowardly, and self-defeating behavior. And I especially did not want to reward Shanequa for whatever encouragement she had given to Yolanda to quit so close to opening night, even if it was only by expressing her readiness to take over the part.

"Look, Shanequa," I said, "just butt out of this, okay. This is between me and Daniel and Yolanda."

Jessica put her arm around Shanequa's waist and led her and the rest of the cast back up onto the stage.

"What do you think we should do?" I said, turning to Daniel, whose face mirrored my own baffled frustration.

"I don't know," he said after a bit. "We'll have to discuss it . . . But we don't have time to discuss it now."

"Okay," I said, turning to Yolanda. "You take a seat in the audience until the end of the rehearsal, and then we will discuss your request. Until that time, *you're still Yusuf,* so go over his lines. Also think one last time about whether you want to quit. This is a great opportunity for you, Yolanda. You could really shine. I would hate to see you lose it."

I meant what I said. I was pained by the thought of Yolanda giving up the part that, despite my recent qualms, she had done so well. But I also strongly suspected that, as I had seen with so many other kids in this school, Yolanda was terrified by her own gifts and the elevated expectations they evoked in everyone around her. She didn't want to fail—not by a long shot. What she wanted was to be invisible, to just get by.

Nobody saw her go, but sometime during the rehearsal, Yolanda simply disappeared.

As the kids were gathering up their things to go home, Daniel pulled Shanequa and Xia aside to tell them that we were considering offering one of them the role of Yusuf. I was surprised that he didn't just give the role to Shanequa, since she did seem to have the best grasp of it, but his circumspection turned out to be wise.

After the cast had all gone, we held a staff meeting and came to the unanimous conclusion that we should give the part to Xia. She was smart and hardworking and, even if she had missed several rehearsals, she had had good excuses. As for Shanequa, we simply didn't want to reward her for what was at least a tacit conspiracy with Yolanda. Daniel made the point that if we gave in to their pressure, it would diminish the whole cast's confidence in our ability to lead them and might stir up all sorts of anxiety. And besides, there was no one who could even come close to duplicating Shanequa's performance as the Chorus Leader.

Our big worry was whether Xia could learn in four days a part that Yolanda hadn't been able to master in four weeks. Jessica, whose classes at Barnard had already ended for the year, said she would come to the school every day to work with Xia. And Daniel said, "If she has to carry a script with her during the performance, that's not the end of the world. We'll just have to explain that there were unforeseen circumstances."

ON WEDNESDAY MORNING I CAME INTO THE SCHOOL TO SET UP A series of displays for the twentieth-anniversary celebration, the most important being the Poetry Wall—a twelve-foot-long, four-foot-high display of writing by present P.S. 227 and Walt Whitman Academy students. I didn't have a key to the school's storage room, however, so Rachel Suarez came along to unlock and lock the doors for me, which gave us an opportunity to talk.

She told me that Yvette's medical problems were very real, that she had been in pain and bleeding for the whole seven months since her mother beat her. She also said that just the previous day doctors had found some sort of a shadow on Yvette's liver. Neither of us had any idea what that meant, but it sounded scary. And finally Rachel gave me a bit of bad news about Joan Gold, who was upset because when she talked to her students about the L.A. riots, they had said the rioters were right to burn and loot and to beat up innocent white truck drivers. Joan felt that the Bensonhurst Project had incited the kids to this heartless and irresponsible attitude. Although I remembered my own concern that the project might have encouraged Ali Ahmed's violence, I told Rachel that if the Bensonhurst Project had had any effect on the kids, it had only helped them feel free to say what they really believed. Still, I was sorry to hear that Joan had not been happy with the project, and surprised as well, since she had never breathed a word of criticism to me. I hoped this wouldn't damage Teachers & Writers' reputation at the school.

My wife had been helping me meet the demands of the celebration and the play by doing the lion's share of afternoon child care during the preceding weeks, but her semester was also coming to a close and she couldn't take any time away from her own teaching the Wednesday and Thursday before the performance, so I had to bring our five-month-old daughter, Emma, to both rehearsals. This meant that I wasn't able to participate quite as fully as I would have liked to, but the kids loved getting to meet Emma. Yvette and Celeste in particular couldn't keep their hands off her, each of them stealing her away to coo over in a remote corner of the room—which made me very happy. Once again I felt barriers were breaking down between my students and me, that the nature of our relationship was becoming—perhaps not familial, but certainly more neighborly.

Wednesday's rehearsal was our first in the cafeteria, where we would actually be performing the play. It went fairly well, although there were still many glitches. Xia was carrying her script but able to do long stretches of the play without even glancing at it. I was impressed and very relieved, as I think were the rest of the cast. A good spirit had developed among the kids. They had become partners and friends. That evening, I wrote in my diary, "I have a real affection for these kids—the first word that came to mind was 'love', but that's too strong."

XIA AND I HAD ARRANGED TO DO A REHEARSAL ON THURSDAY, but when I went looking for her after my eighth-grade classes, Celeste told me that—shades of Yolanda!—she hadn't come to school. I couldn't believe that Xia would buckle under the pressure. But I did worry that some new calamity with her mother or baby brother would prevent her from coming to the rehearsal or even the play. Celeste hadn't heard anything from her, nor had Mayra.

I went home and tried calling her grandmother's number, but once again there was no answer. I was getting desperate. The celebration was tomorrow. I decided to seek Xia out at her home. If she wasn't sick, if her mother was just keeping her home to baby-sit, perhaps I could help them make some other arrangements. It also occurred to me that her mother might simply not know how important this performance was to Xia. During the time when I was arranging the "famous writers" reading series, I had had to deal with more than one set of parents for whom their child's education was simply a second or third priority. Had school not been mandated by law, had it not been free day care, they might well not have bothered with it. If Xia's mother was at all of this persuasion, I hoped that my coming to her house would, if nothing else, shame her into letting Xia attend the play.

I called the school and got Xia's address from her files. She lived only about ten blocks away from me, an easy walk on this bright spring day. Unfortunately, it was now my turn to take care of Emma, and as I drew closer to Xia's building, I became increasingly anxious about taking my baby girl inside, especially if, as it appeared from the address, she lived in one of the projects.

I was ashamed of my anxiety, which seemed irredeemably middle class, racist even. Half my students lived in the projects. Most of them walked in and out of these big bland brick buildings every day of their lives without ever having a problem—most of them, that is, but not all. Ten percent, or 5 percent, or 20 percent—I have no idea of the actual proportion—had indeed been mugged in the elevator, raped in the stairwells, or had friends or parents or cousins gunned down on the surrounding sidewalk. As ashamed as I may have been, I couldn't stop myself—as I pushed Emma's stroller down the street—from remembering the many horror stories I had picked up from my students, the newspapers, and local gossip.

At last I was standing outside the address I had scribbled on a piece of note paper: a project building indeed. Xia lived on the nineteenth floor. The cornerstone of the building had the date 1963 on it. The front entrance had been renovated some time in the eighties, but already it looked like the hull of a long submerged ship: sooty, streaked with rust-oozings from its small roof. Several glass tiles had been bashed in. Where the lock on the front door ought to have been, there was only a dented hole.

As I stood on the sidewalk, alternately gazing at the front door and my sleeping baby's face, a black woman and her young child strolled into this building as casually as I would have gone into my own home. That was it! Enough middle-class squeamishness! I pushed Emma's stroller toward the entrance, deciding that, if nothing else, I could call up on an intercom.

Just inside the entryway, a phone receiver hung over the raw hole where the intercom's guts had been. There was a place for name labels, but it was empty. The lock on the inside door had also been bashed out. I pushed open the door to look into the dim but not unclean lobby.

A stainless steel elevator stood open, perhaps waiting for me, perhaps permanently broken. I hesitated and pulled Emma's stroller back out onto the sidewalk, telling myself that I couldn't be too cautious when it came to the safety of my child, but feeling doubly ashamed because I wasn't at all sure I would have gone into that building even if I had been alone. (As I was to find out a few days later, going into that building would have been an exercise in futility. Xia and her family had moved to a far scarier welfare hotel a few blocks away because they could no longer afford the rent in the projects.)

I walked directly from Xia's building to the school, where I found Daniel waiting for me in the auditorium. I filled him in on Xia's absence and was just about to confess my shameful cowardice when Xia herself walked in the door.

"Hey, Xia!" I shouted. "I am *so* glad to see you!" She came down the aisle, a shy but proud smile on her face, clearly happy at the greeting she had gotten, not only from me but the whole cast. I continued: "I was afraid when I heard that you weren't in school."

"I had a headache all day. I still have it, but . . ."

Good old Xia.

I didn't have to go out to grab anybody off the sidewalk that day. The only cast member who didn't show up was Natalie. Cullen (who had an ongoing flirtation with her) told us that she had gone to New Jersey and would miss the performance. She had only a couple of lines. Daniel said we could just drop them. This meant losing "Dear Yusuf, I feel like I'm not safe from anything," a line near the end of the play that had always struck me as especially poignant. But what else could we do? When we did the rehearsal, however, and got to the part where Joey shot Yusuf, nobody shouted "No!" That had been Natalie's line. Instead of assigning the line to someone else, we decided that the whole cast should shout "No!" at once. That worked far better, giving Yusuf's slow cringe at the silent gunshot a heartrending eeriness. I couldn't stay for the whole rehearsal because I had to pick up my son from his after-school program.

FRIDAY, MAY 8. THE DAY OF THE PERFORMANCE. I GOT TO THE school at about ten-thirty and spent the morning stapling, taping, hammering, and otherwise putting the final touches on the twentieth-anniversary displays. My third-grade class canceled, which was fine by me. I took a long lunch at a nearby diner, where, over a meatball hero, I rewrote my notes for the speech I was going to give that evening, making sure to put in the names of all the people I had to thank.

I was very happy about how much interest the celebration was generating at the school. Kids had been coming up to me all day, telling me that they were planning to attend—something that had never happened with the reading series. I overheard a couple of teachers discussing the party in the teachers' lounge, and one of them shouted out, "Oh, you have to come. All the old teachers are coming back. Everyone's so excited about it!" I was sure that, as a party and a reunion, the twentieth-anniversary celebration would be a big success. But as for how the play would go over—well, that was a different matter.

Daniel told me that the rehearsal hadn't gone well after I'd left to pick up my son. The kids had been skittish. Ricky had been talking in almost a falsetto, forgetting many of the lines he had known before. From Ricky himself I heard that Celeste had been bossing everybody around and forgetting her own lines. "She's so temperamental!" he said. After working with her that morning, Elizabeth said to me: "That girl is a bitch!" None of this sounded good.

Roger, the chief custodian, had promised to meet me at one o'clock in the cafeteria to have his men clear away the tables. At one-fifteen he still wasn't there, just his second in command, Oscar, and another man, who were mopping up. Roger had told me that his men folded up all the tables every Friday, but nothing in the behavior of these two men indicated that any such labor was in the offing. Finally I said, "Roger told me that you guys were going to fold up the tables. Are you going to do it? Or is that going to be my responsibility?" Oscar seemed to think that this was very funny. After a long, raspy "oh, ho, ho" laugh, he looked at his friend and exclaimed, "We gone put up those tables!" More laughter from both of them. That was as much of an answer as I got. I spent the next half hour flipping the folding tables into eight-foot-high Formica gravestones and wheeling them into the most remote corner of the cafeteria.

I HAD JUST GOTTEN THE LAST TABLE OUT OF THE WAY WHEN Daniel and the rest of the T&W team came in with the cast. I had too much work to do putting up decorations even to pay much attention to this, our last rehearsal. The little I did see, however, gave me considerable cause for worry. The kids were simply too excited to do what Daniel told them. I had never seen him yell so loud or get so red in the face. Several times I had to stop what I was doing, come over, and back him up. By the time the rehearsal was over, all of us adults had sore throats and headaches.

The celebration was to begin at six. Our plan had been to keep the cast at the school until that time, doing last minute touch-up rehearsals and decorating the cafeteria. We had also ordered them pizza and soda and brought along my son's boom box so that they could dance. No sooner did the clock strike three, however, than the cast all began to disappear: Shanequa and Celeste had to walk their little sisters home—I couldn't object to that—but the rest just fled. At first I tried to keep them at the school, afraid they would not get back in time. Then I gave up. I just didn't have the strength to ride herd over them for three hours. I was glad to get them out of my hair.

I was alone in the cafeteria hanging a mural that was to be the backdrop for the play, the only scenery or prop we were going to employ. The mural had been painted by a few students in the eighth grade under the direction of the artist Christine Slessinger, who was working at the school as a part of LEAP (Learning Through an Expanded Arts Program), an artist-in-residence organization like Teachers & Writers. The mural was beautiful—grim and very moving. At the bottom, Yusuf Hawkins lay on the street, blood trickling from his head into the sewer, the half-eaten Snickers bar in his hand. At the top of the mural, in a puffy cloud, was the inscription, taken from the play script, AUGUST 23RD, 1989, ON THIS DAY A POOR BOY LOST HIS LIFE. Between the dead body and this cloud there were brown and pink faces in a crowd, red buildings, a starry blue night sky fading to lavender, a silver escalator to symbolize the ascent of Yusuf Hawkins's soul, and, sticking out of the bottom of the puffy cloud, a blue sleeve and a brown reaching hand. Just over the heads of the crowd there was a blank space in the picture, where the artists wrote, "Why do we have to live in such a racist world? Why so much violence? And why you?" then signed their names.

I was just applying the last pieces of duct tape to the jerry-built structure supporting the mural when Yvette came up to the bottom of my ladder and asked if she could go home and get a black dress. "I'm supposed to be in mourning," she said, "but I forgot my dress at home." She told me where she lived and said, "I can just take the train and be back in a few minutes." The address she had given me was nearly fifty blocks away—a good deal farther than a few minutes' journey—but my nerves were so overstrained that I couldn't bear a confrontation. "Okay," I said.

Fifteen minutes later I came across Yvette and Diana Delacruz sitting in the hallway. "Back already?" I asked.

"I didn't go. I called my mother and she's bringing it right down."

An hour later Yvette came up to me again, "Have you seen my mother? She still hasn't come with my dress."

I hadn't seen her, but another forty-five minutes or so later (at five-thirty) I came across the poor, bewildered-looking woman standing in exactly the same place where I had seen Yvette and Diana. She was wearing a tight black dress of her own, and thick silver blue eye shadow. Her hair, which had been in such a tangle the day I saw her in Rachel's office, was combed neatly back into a ponytail. In her hand she held a crumpled plastic bag, out of which protruded a slim wedge of black.

"Boy," I said, "Yvette sure will be happy to see that!"

"She don't want it," her mother told me, giving the bag a fitful shake. "She said to bring it down and now she don't want it."

Later, when I went up to the writing room, where the reassembled cast was enjoying a pizza dinner, I asked Yvette, "Don't you want to put on your dress?"

"Nah! She brought it too late. She told me she was going to bring it, but she didn't come. So I called her and there was no answer. I let the phone ring and ring. Then I called her again later and she tells me she didn't answer 'cause she fell asleep. She fell asleep! She's supposed to bring me my dress and she fell asleep! I'm not going to take that dress now. No way! It's too late!"

It was not too late, of course. Yvette had plenty of time to get into her dress before the performance. But she was intent on making a statement to her mother, and there was nothing I could do to change her mind. An hour and a half later Yvette was a mother herself, standing in the spotlight, in jeans and a T-shirt, stroking her dead son's cheek, and I was wondering what was going through her mind as she spoke the lines "I love you so much. I didn't know how to show you that I loved you when you were alive."

• • •

THE REUNION WAS TO START AT SIX O'CLOCK, BUT PEOPLE BEGAN arriving by five-forty-five. Although I was nominally the host of the event, I didn't have to play much of a role, at least in this early part of the evening. The whole Teachers & Writers' administrative staff had come to manage the bar, the hors d'oeuvres, and the book displays. They knew most of the P.S. 227 Teachers & Writers veterans better than . I did.

I got down from the writing room to find that my predecessors as directors of the program, Phillip Lopate and Alan Ziegler, had arrived. They were each going to reminisce briefly about their years at the school before I introduced the play. I gave them programs so that they would know when they were going on.

The room was filling rapidly. I saw twenty- and thirty-year-old former students, many of them looking up at the ceiling, as if amazed at how small and dark their old school had become. Legendary T&W members whom I recognized from photographs taken when they were themselves in their twenties and early thirties—often bearded, braided, and beaded—came into the room looking like parents. Some of the guests stood against the walls, clearly wondering why they had come. Others screamed and hugged, shouting out, "I can't believe it! I can't believe it!"

At one point I looked over and caught a glimpse of Celeste slinking through the crowd. Our plan had been to keep the cast in the writing room until just before the performance. I wondered how she had slipped out. A little later Yvette strolled by carrying what looked like a glass of wine, but so casually that no one, myself included, questioned her. After the performance I heard that Celeste, Yvette, and several of the other performers had managed to slip glasses of wine upstairs to have with their pizza.

Finally, at five to seven, I called out for everybody's attention, helped by the school's supplies clerk—maybe I should call her our quartermaster sergeant—who shouted at the top of her healthy lungs: "Hey, everybody, shut up! The show's about to start." I introduced Fran Kaplan, the principal of P.S. 227 and the Walt Whitman Academy, then Phillip Lopate, and finally Alan Ziegler. All of them seemed to speak well and got plenty of laughs, though, to be honest, I hardly heard a word. My thoughts were too preoccupied with the play. I did, however, hear Phillip say that his twelve years at P.S. 227 were the richest, most integrated period of his life, the time when everything made the most sense, when "I felt I was the hero of my own life"—a remark that, for better or for worse, I understood perfectly at that moment.

ALTHOUGH YOLANDA NO LONGER HAD A SPEAKING PART IN THE play, she had agreed to be the prompter. Her job was to follow along in the script and tip the actors off with a whispered word or two if they seemed to have forgotten their lines. When I realized that Alan Ziegler was drawing his speech to a conclusion, I sent Yolanda to signal the cast to come to the cafeteria doorway.

As the cast assembled I told the audience a bit about the origin of the play, talking about the astonishing wisdom and passion the students had displayed in their writing, their classroom discussion, and in rehearsal. Then I stepped into the crowd, and Yolanda turned on my son's tape deck, which played at top volume the hypnotically tense instrumental version of the rap "Self-Destruction" by the Stop the Violence Movement.

AS SOON AS THE KIDS CAME INTO THE PERFORMANCE AREA, ALL of them strutting to the rhythm of the music, I saw that they were completely absorbed by their roles. They were serious, slinking, urban. When they started to speak, I saw an engagement that I had only glimpsed in scattered moments during rehearsals. "They're doing it!" I thought. "They're really doing it!" And they kept on doing it. The play was better than I had ever dared hope it would be.

There were moments when I held my breath as the actors seemed to search for their lines, but they almost always found them. The only person who seriously blanked out on a line was, uncharacteristically, Mayra. It happened in the scene where Gina and Keith were just about to have their fateful squabble. Mayra, playing Keith, was introducing the scene by saying: "That Gina told me she was bringing some boys to beat me up. So I rounded up my boys too. She really thought she would win. Everything just blew up in my face . . ." Mayra had been speaking her part perfectly, without the slightest hesitation. In fact several people told me she gave the best performance of the night. But when she said, "blew up in my face," her mouth opened for the next word and nothing came out, just silence and then a stuttered "uh . . .

uh . . . uh." I looked over at Yolanda to find that she was yacking away to a couple of friends and not paying the slightest attention to the play. I had to rush around behind the audience to where she was sitting, look over her shoulder at the script, find the place where Mayra had gotten stuck, and speak her line to her—a process that took a good twenty seconds.

I worried that Mayra's fumble—and Yolanda's dereliction of duty—would set off a collective collapse of confidence that I had seen destroy other student productions. But nothing of the sort came to pass. The play worked. The kids worked. I think they all discovered their talent in front of one another, in the midst of their performance, and it inspired them. In the end nothing mattered, nothing even existed for those eight young actors except that work of art they were bringing to life on the stage.

Ricky, as Joey Fama, was especially good during his hand-washing scene, switching eerily from his tragic narration to his neurotic, twitchy obsession with his hands. I have to say that as I watched, the thought flashed through my mind: Is this real? Has Ricky crossed completely over into his role? I remembered his sister Sasha's story about how he had been Joey Fama at home for the last month and all those fights he had been getting into.

Shanequa was hypnotic in her dark-mirrored sunglasses and backwards baseball cap as the Chorus Leader and also, despite all her reservations, as the sadly vulnerable Russell Gibbons. It was through her performance especially that I saw the real advantages of having girls play this largely despicable group of boys. It gave them all slightly vulnerable, likable sides that heightened the pathos of what they were saying and doing. *Children* really did commit these atrocities. A *child* really was killed. That aspect of the events at Bensonhurst would not have been nearly so apparent, had boys been playing all the roles, and the play would have lost much of its power.

The most remarkable performance of all was Xia's. She hesitated a few times but never forgot a line and never dropped out of character. She seemed so honest, so humble. Her voice and body said: "This is it, folks. This is what happened to me. This is how I died. Yes, I'm angry. Yes, I'm sad. But that's not what matters. All I want is for you to know what happened to me, what people in our own city can do."

What was most astonishing, of course, was that she learned this huge role in a mere four days. How could she do it with so much to struggle against—an alcoholic mother, no father? Where did she get her strength?

I thought, Xia is a miracle—and it was an impression that would only be confirmed time and again during the remaining year that I would work with her.

"AUGUST 23RD, 1989." SHANEQUA SPOKE HER LAST LINE ALMOST IN a whisper and joined her fellow cast members in front of the murals. The play was over. A first solitary clap was instantly drowned by whoops and a storm of applause that got louder and louder until it seemed it would never end. And in the midst of it all, the eight young actors stood blinking in astonishment and pride at what they had done.

THE FOLLOWING MONDAY RACHEL HAD A LONG TALK WITH YVETTE about what she would have to do, given her many absences, in order to graduate from Walt Whitman and about her desire to attend the High School of Fashion Industries, one of New York's specialized high schools. Then Yvette simply disappeared from both the school and the battered women's shelter.

She was still gone on Wednesday, when the cast performed for the fifth, sixth, seventh, and eighth grades. Jessica, script in hand, filled in for her.

On Friday we had our cast party. I brought along inscribed copies of my book of stories to give to each of the cast members. I had brought one for Yvette, as well, just in case she conformed to her old pattern and showed up without having bothered to attend school. And that was just what happened. She told me that she had been absent because the doctors had given her medication that made her throw up all the time, but now she was better and she wouldn't miss any more school until the end of the term. She didn't tell me why she hadn't been at the shelter, and I didn't ask.

I had written in her copy of my book: "Thanks for all the hard work and thought you put into the play. You can do anything you want with your life. Good luck."

I have always hated inscribing books. I can never come close to representing my real feelings about whomever I am writing to, be they intimates or acquaintances. What I wanted to tell Yvette was that I was afraid for her, that hard as life had been on her already, it could be a lot harder. I wanted to tell her that, angry as she may have been at her mother or the world, she should not let that anger destroy her. I knew that sometimes she felt her life was a trap. I wanted to remind her that the way to escape that trap was simple, if not easy. She should begin by taking care of herself. She should stay away from everybody and everything that might hurt her. She should have a good hard think about exactly what she wanted in life, and then she should go for it, single-mindedly. One thing she had to do was graduate from the eighth grade, then go to high school, then college, if she could—because in this society freedom comes with education. I wanted to tell her that she was a good kid, that she had all the brains and talent she needed to make a perfectly fine life for herself, that I had faith in her, that she should call me if she ever needed help . . .

A speech very like this came into my mind as I watched Yvette chatting to her friends at the party. I decided that I would wait until she was between conversations, then take her out into the hall for a private talk. The longer I thought about it, however, the less confident I became that my earnest speech would have any other effect than to make Yvette uncomfortable and cause her to write me off as another naive, meddling teacher. There were several moments during the party when both she and I were idle and I could easily have taken her aside for our talk, but I let them pass. Then, finally, I looked around and she was gone.

In a way, my failure to connect with Yvette typified my last moments with everyone in the cast. There was so much that I wanted to say to each and every one of them, so much feeling that I had built up for them over the last months, that it was impossible, maybe even slightly inappropriate, to express it. In the end I settled for standing by the wall, a dazed smile on my face, looking on while these kids yammered, shouted, laughed, flirted, and stuffed their mouths with pizza, potato chips, and cookies.

Then it was over. The room was cleaned up. Daniel, Matt, Jessica, and I were out on the sidewalk in front of the school, not knowing quite what to do. All at once Daniel said, "Look at us, we're just standing here, not going. We just don't want to let go of it." I said, "That's exactly how I feel about it." And Jessica: "I know! I know!" But then the awkwardness came back. We stood there a moment more, blinking, smiling, sighing.

Then we hugged and said good-bye.

I MADE ONE LAST VISIT TO THE SCHOOL IN MID-JUNE AND HEARD from Joan Gold that not only was Yvette missing from school again but she had gotten pregnant and was determined to keep the baby. Yvette was graduated in absentia. "It's our gift to her," Rachel said.

When I went to see Rachel at the start of the following school year, she told me that Yvette was living with the mother of one of the two men who might have fathered her child. This sanctuary was provisional, however. If the child was the "wrong color," she would have to leave. Where could she go? "No place!" said Rachel. "She can't go back to her mother! I don't know what she's going to do!" Rachel didn't have time to talk to me, however. "This is the craziest week of my life!" she told me. "Diego just broke down in my office because he saw his mother for the first time in nine years and she's a bag lady! A hopeless wino! No one ever told him before. His grandmother's been taking care of him, but she never said a word!"

Just at that moment a parent knocked on the door and Rachel told me she'd have to talk to me later. I walked out into the hall and bumped into Celeste. "Steve!" she cried and threw her arms around me. "Welcome back! Are we going to be doing another play this year?"

"You bet!" I said.

PART THREE

Will My Name Be Shouted Out?

I Can Be Hurt by You

THE 1992–93 SCHOOL YEAR COULD HARDLY HAVE GOTTEN OFF TO a better start. I was eager to work with the Bensonhurst cast again, and they seemed eager to work with me. We greeted one another in the hallways like long-lost friends. We eyed one another across classrooms, waiting for my assignment presentation to be over, so that I could stroll around to their seats for more intimate conversation. What is more, our excitement seemed to be shared by the whole school. Students were always coming up to me and asking if I were going to do another play or if they could join the Drama Club. They didn't seem half as embarrassed about raising their hands in class. I heard many fewer moans, sighs, and wisecracks and saw far fewer students who seemed only to be doing imitations of staying awake. In previous years I had felt that I had to fight to gain the respect of my students. This year I knew I had it from the very first moment I walked into the classroom.

Perhaps the best thing about the beginning of the year was the news I heard from Rachel Suarez when, finally, we had a chance to speak. Every one of the Bensonhurst cast members, she told me, had raised his or her grades after beginning to work on the play, with Celeste and Xia showing the most marked improvement. Celeste had even been given the job of delivering newspapers to all the classrooms in P.S. 227 and Walt Whitman, a position that was normally reserved for the best and most responsible students, and one that also earned her pocket money. What was more, the cast members' rising grades had been accompanied by rising ambitions. Xia, Celeste, Ricky, Mayra, and Isaac all wanted to go to LaGuardia, the top public high school specializing in visual and performing arts—a school that they all, except perhaps Isaac, would have considered way out of their range before joining the Drama Club.

The elevated confidence upon which these new ambitions were founded was also having an effect on the cast members' social status. Again Celeste was the greatest beneficiary. When she had first enrolled at Walt Whitman the previous year, kids had made fun of her because she had only two dresses and these were rarely laundered (Joan Gold had felt so sorry for her that she had given her clothing passed on from friends with teenaged daughters). Celeste and Xia, especially, but also Mayra and Ricky were still among the poorest children in the school. Now they were no better able to afford the clothes, jewelry, sneakers, or CD players that are important status props in adolescent society, but they were no longer nonentities—or in Celeste's case, something close to an outcast. Their merits were widely recognized; they too no longer had to fight for the respect of their classmates. They had only to be themselves.

I couldn't have been happier at this news. It had been all too easy during those moments of grim reckoning at 4 A.M. to wonder if my pride in the success of the Bensonhurst Project wasn't based largely on my own sentimental and self-serving exaggeration. But here was proof of that success—just the sort of proof that educational experts and bureaucrats value most—higher grades, higher ambitions, and higher social status. I'd felt good about my work in the schools before. I'd had former students come up to me on the street or in the subway to tell me that they had loved my course and to thank me. But I had never had such concrete evidence of the benefits of my teaching, especially for students whom I cared so much about. As I sat beside Rachel's desk, I was all but levitating with pride and had to fight to restrain my smile, lest I appear conceited. And then Rachel hit me with the bad news.

In a sense the bad news was really old news. During my first two years at P.S. 227 and the Walt Whitman Academy, the school had enough money to fund the Teachers & Writers program at record levels, allowing us to teach for a total of 112 days, or 3 days a week for the whole school year. During my third year running the program, New York City's growing financial troubles meant that the school had enough money only to fund Teachers & Writers for 87 days. And by my fourth year, the year of the Bensonhurst Project, we were at the school only for 73 days—2 days a week from October through May. The bad news Rachel gave me during our conversation was that, despite all the successes of our program, the city had cut the arts budget yet again, and the school had enough money to fund us for only 61 days—slightly more than half the number of days the program had run just three years earlier. This news might not have been so depressing had I not heard even worse earlier that morning.

The salaries of the Columbia creative writing MFA student interns working with T&W had been paid by the Urban Corps, a sixties-era program that gave students financial aid in exchange for career-related community service work. During my first years running the P.S. 227/Walt Whitman program, the Urban Corps funded six internships, which allowed the T&W staff to work with every teacher in the school who wanted our services and to do a lot of team-teaching and special projects, like novel-writing clubs and video dramas and documentaries.

The year of the Bensonhurst Project, the city slashed the Urban Corps budget so severely that it could fund only two interns—Matt Sharpe and Elizabeth Shepard (Jessica Sager, the Barnard drama student, and Jenifer Polatsek, the Hunter graduate education student, were essentially volunteers—Jessica was paid for a fraction of her time—and they both helped only with the Drama Club). This two-thirds cut in my teaching staff meant we could no longer work with every teacher in the school who wanted us; video projects were out, so was team teaching, and our students got a lot less individual attention. Still, that year, we had managed. We had done the Bensonhurst Project, after all. But it had been a big strain. And some students and teachers, especially in P.S. 227, had felt shortchanged.

Thus it was with some trepidation that I called up my contact at the Urban Corps the morning of my meeting with Rachel. What I was dreading was that further city budget cuts would reduce my staff to one intern. What I heard instead was a recording telling me my contact's phone had been disconnected. A couple of phone calls later I discovered that the entire Urban Corps had been eliminated, which meant that now, suddenly, I had no staff at all. With a single stroke of a bureaucrat's pen, Teachers & Writers' "flagship program," which had just been feted for twenty years of educational innovation, had been reduced to an ordinary one-writer residency. "That's the way they always do it in the public school system," said Rachel when I had finished telling her my news. "They reward hard work and success by taking things away!"

It was on the basis of the residency's twenty-year success story that, a couple of days after my conversation with Rachel, I was able to convince Teachers & Writers itself to provide enough money for one internship, which I decided to split into halves, so that I would have two interns, each working half-time (ten hours a week rather than the usual twenty). Matt and Elizabeth, having received their degrees, were no longer eligible to work with the program, so I hired two new Columbia MFA students: Erin Donovan, a fiction writer, and Siobhan Reagan, a poet. Jessica was able to come back, though still mostly on a volunteer basis. Daniel too would be able to work with the Drama Club, but only until Christmas, after which, alas, he would be moving to France. The program was going to survive another year, but we would be seeing a third fewer students and have a lot less time and energy to devote to them.

MY FIRST PRIORITY FOR THAT YEAR WAS TO HELP XIA, CELESTE, Ricky, Mayra, and Isaac get into LaGuardia High School—not so much because I wanted any of them to become actors as because I thought LaGuardia offered them the best chance of escaping the poverty they had been born into. Most of the other high schools they were considering were little more than brick holding pens for confused and bored adolescents. LaGuardia, by contrast, was solid academically—its advanced placement program in particular was about as good as could be found at a New York public high school. More important, however, it was filled with talented and ambitious kids. It was a place where my students' newfound ambitions would be given an opportunity to flourish rather than be dismissed as dumb fantasies.

Ambition is another word for hope. As I was growing up, my ambition to be a writer gave meaning and purpose to every minute of my life and made so many of my biggest choices clear. I wanted my students to have a similar hope around which to build their own lives. Even if that hope ultimately had to yield to less glamorous career plans, it would still offer the students a strong defense against the many temptations and traps that lay ahead of them during the next few years. These were all good kids, but the world they lived in was terribly dangerous and confusing. I was afraid for them and wanted them to have all the help they could get.

The first meeting of the Drama Club was only for the LaGuardia applicants. Jessica, who was herself a graduate of LaGuardia and who had even helped judge the drama admissions auditions, did most of the talking, while I sat in the corner, taking the opportunity to observe these very familiar but surprisingly transformed girls and boys.

They all seemed to have inflated slightly in the four months since we had last been together. They were taller. Their faces were bigger but also more distinct, as if by having lost some childish softness, they had come more sharply into focus. Their behavior also was subtly different. They were all a bit more fashion conscious—the girls constantly adjusting their elaborate hairdos and the boys casting admiring glances down at their big, brand-new, blinding white sneakers—and all a bit more studied in the way they sprawled across their chairs.

I could see that they were happy to be together again in the writing room with Jessica and me, that they considered this talk a kind of a privilege. But at the same time it was clear that for all of them this was also just another form of schoolwork, something to be endured but impossible to wholly pay attention to. Even Xia seemed lost in a glazed passivity.

What Jessica was telling them was important, though at the time, none of us had any idea how important it would turn out to be. She was explaining that, on the first weekend after the Christmas vacation, they would have to go down to LaGuardia High School and perform two short monologues in front of a committee of faculty and students. Those applicants who most impressed the committee would be invited to go on to a second part of the audition. "If they don't invite you to the second part," Jessica said, "it means you haven't made the cut and you won't be going to the school." In the second part of the audition the candidates would have to read a script with a current LaGuardia drama student. "The judges don't expect you to have your part down perfectly when you do this reading," said Jessica. "What they are mostly interested in is how at ease you are on the stage and how naturally you work with other actors."

I was encouraged by this news, because the thing that had most impressed me when I first saw each of these students perform was how easily they seemed to step into their roles and how well they could react to one another's performances. The only person I thought might have trouble with this phase of the audition was Mayra, who, because of her dyslexia, always stumbled through her initial reading of a script. My hope was that the first part of her audition would be so strong that she would be forgiven any awkwardness during the second.

The biggest obstacle that all of these students faced was their grades. Even with the improvement of the previous spring, their academic records were shoddy at best. And what was more, Walt Whitman, while not a bad school, did not rank even in the top half on citywide public school reading and math tests and fell even farther behind the many private schools whose students would also apply to LaGuardia. While, in theory, a fabulous audition could compensate for a mediocre report card from a mediocre school, it would mean that for any of these students to get into LaGuardia, they would have to be among the very best young actors in the whole of New York City.

Were any of them that good?

My hopes were highest for Xia, who, in my opinion, was the brightest of the applicants and the most talented and who, with Celeste, had the greatest need. Maybe Ricky, too, had the talent to be among the one-tenth of applicants admitted to LaGuardia. His grades had never been terrible. Over the summer, with Daniel's help, he had gotten a part in an NYU student film, and the director apparently thought him very talented. (Ricky himself was certainly proud of his performance in the film. It was the only thing he would talk about at the start of the school year.) Then there was Celeste. Maybe she too had the talent—

But I couldn't go on with this line of speculation. The truth was that I couldn't bear to think of any of these kids not getting into LaGuardia. I couldn't bear to think of all their new hope and pride being stifled so soon.

After Jessica had finished talking, she and I passed out books of monologues and made arrangements to meet with each of the kids for weekly practices. I would work with Xia and Isaac. Jessica would work with Celeste, Ricky, and Mayra.

• • •

DANIEL WAS GOING TO SPEND THE SPRING AND SUMMER IN France, which meant that I would have to direct the new seventh and eighth grade play on my own. Shortly after the LaGuardia meeting, I visited Daniel's apartment in the West Village to talk about what we were going to do with the Drama Club that autumn. What we needed was a project that would engage the club members as much as the Bensonhurst play had but that would reach a satisfying closure before Christmas so that we could start rehearsing the new play afterward. No small order! After discussing the possibility of helping club members write and perform their own brief monologues or do a short one-act play by an adult author, Daniel had the idea of having the club perform three plays about families that had been written by three of his former students—one of them being Yolanda Castro, whose play Daniel had referred to when he first told me what a good actor she was.

Apart from the fact that I still bore a mild grudge against Yolanda for dropping out of the Bensonhurst play so close to opening night, I thought this was a wonderful idea. Two of the plays were about divorce, and one—Yolanda's—was about a basically happy family that squabbled all the time. There was plenty of material to engage the adolescent imagination in either of these situations. So it was decided: the Drama Club would spend the autumn semester rehearsing the three family plays and perform them at a one-act play festival just before Christmas.

Daniel had another interesting question to discuss with me. A friend of his was looking for a wiry, tough-talking thirteen-year-old Hispanic girl to star in an off-Broadway play she was directing. "Celeste would be perfect," I said before he even mentioned her name.

Daniel nodded but didn't quite seem to share my enthusiasm. "What about if she doesn't get it?" he asked. "How would that affect her?"

Although I knew that there was a possibility that she wouldn't get the part, in my heart I was sure that no one would be able to resist Celeste. "How can we not give her the chance?" I said. "Think how wonderful it will be if she does get the part. And if she doesn't . . . Well, at least she'll know that *we* thought she was good enough."

Daniel agreed and said that he would talk to Celeste about the auditions privately at the next Drama Club meeting—which would be the first meeting open to students other than those applying to LaGuardia High School.

•   •   •

SINCE THE AUDITORIUM STAGE WAS BEING USED EVERY DAY AFTER school by one of the school's extended-day child care programs, Joan Gold kindly offered to let us hold Drama Club meetings in her classroom.

About eight kids came to our first meeting, including both of the seventh grade's only white girls, Arlene Salter and Anna Harris, and one of its two Asians, Lily Choi. I was pleased by the turnout and by the enthusiasm of the students but disappointed that once again we had only one boy, Isaac Moreno.

After a round of exercises and theater games, Daniel and I told the students about our plans for the semester, passed out copies of the three family plays, and then had the students choose parts and give the plays a quick read-through. At the end of the meeting Daniel took Celeste out into the hall to tell her about the audition with his friend's play. When Celeste came back into the room to get her coat, she was walking with an uncharacteristic—almost dazed—tranquility, her face lit by an enormous smile.

THE FOLLOWING WEEK IN MY SEVENTH- AND EIGHTH-GRADE classes (I was teaching all four of them myself this year), I talked with only slight exaggeration about how wonderfully the first Drama Club meeting had gone and about how moving and witty the family plays were. "If anyone wants to try out for the club," I said, "our second and final auditions will be held this Friday." Of course, no one who wanted to join the Drama Club would ever have been turned away, whether they came that Friday or any other time. But I felt that it couldn't hurt to make membership seem something of a privilege. During writing time I also made individual invitations to a number of the boys, including Ricky Ortiz.

Despite his improved grades, Ricky was once again sitting at the back of the room with the troublemakers. Taking the vacant seat beside him, I asked, "You coming to the Drama Club this afternoon?"

"Uh . . . yeah," he said, then looked quickly away. He drew his breath as if he had something else to say, but then just let it out in a long sigh.

"What?" I asked.

"Nothing."

His skin had a slightly yellowish cast and there was a strange fixity to his expression. Recently I had learned from Rachel that Ricky was an epileptic. Just before the start of school, he had begun taking a new medication that was either causing or simply not preventing frequent momentary petit mal seizures. As Rachel explained it, Ricky ought to have gotten frequent blood tests over a period of at least a couple of weeks, so that a doctor could determine exactly what dosage was right for his body. But Medicaid wouldn't pay for so many tests, so Ricky was having to take a dosage that had been little more than his doctor's educated guess. The medicine was apparently also causing his beard to grow prematurely, although this was not a side effect that Ricky minded. He was growing a neatly trimmed goatee and was constantly complaining to his baby-cheeked peers about the nuisance of having to shave every morning.

"You all right?" I asked Ricky.

"Yeah, sure," he said impatiently.

I got up from my chair. "So, I'll see you at two-fifteen?"

"Right."

My sense that Ricky was not being straight with me was only heightened at the end of class when, as he was leaving the room, he stopped and told me that he might be a little late to Drama Club. When I asked why, he said something about having to get his working papers filled out but concluded, "Don't worry. I'll be there."

He wasn't.

Nor was Isaac, who was back on the swimming team and didn't see the point of coming to Drama Club if he had to leave early every week.

Although all of the kids at Drama Club knew exactly where Ricky was that afternoon, none of them would say a word about it. As I would find out the following week, he had gone to the playground to have a fight with a boy—a bit of irony here!—named Yusuf.

Yusuf was extremely bright and a good writer, even if he almost never put a word on the page. "He's so full of himself that he thinks he doesn't have to bother," was Joan Gold's analysis when I complained about him one day.

To a certain extent, Yusuf and Ricky were simply victims of the ancient and ironclad rules of urban confrontation. The fight became a possibility one lunchtime when Yusuf said something insulting about Ricky behind his back, and it became inevitable when a couple of boys, perhaps for no other reason than to watch the familiar mechanisms come into play, instantly reported Yusuf's remark to Ricky. "You gonna let him get away with that?" Ricky's friends asked him, knowing that, given his reputation, there was only one possible answer that he could give, something to the effect of "If he doesn't take that back I'm gonna beat the shit out of him!" Yusuf too could say only one thing if he didn't want to lose face: "I ain't afraid of him. If he wants a fight, I'm ready." After several more of these exchanges, some of them face-to-face, it was arranged that the boys would meet on the playground on Friday after school, during Drama Club. This confrontation, however, amounted to little more than a trade of additional threats and insults. The fight didn't happen until Monday at lunch, and then it was almost by accident.

I don't think that either of the two boys wanted to fight. They had been good friends before and would be again, and they were both bright enough to know that they really had nothing to fight about. But at the same time, they lived in a world where often the only way to feel safe was to prove to everyone, including themselves, that they had no fear. Ricky apparently felt that he had accomplished this end when he and Yusuf met in the playground that Monday after school. Yusuf, however, seemed to have quite different feelings. He was so frightened that when Ricky drew his finger across his own throat and said, "Let's cut it"—meaning, "Let's stop the fight"—Yusuf thought he was about to draw a knife and so flew at him with all his might. The boys punched and wrestled until they were pulled apart by teachers. Neither was badly hurt. They were both given detention for a week. But this was Ricky's second fight of the year—at least the second I'd heard of. I worried about what might happen if one of his opponents in these fights— perhaps having the same fear as Yusuf—brought along a knife or gun. I resolved to talk to him as soon as I could.

THE DRAMA CLUB MEETING THAT RICKY MISSED WENT VERY WELL, even without any boys. Daniel had us break up into three groups to rehearse the three plays. Thanks to our shortage of males, I was given the role of the father in a play about a father and daughter who don't get along. Xia played the daughter. Siobhan Reagan, one of the new Columbia interns, was the director.

A couple of years before the opening scene of the play, the father had left the girl's mother and married another woman, with whom he had recently had a new child. The daughter, Bibi, was deeply ambivalent about her father. She wanted to love him but was furious at him for leaving and for not seeming to care enough about her. The father was incapable of handling the situation. Whenever Bibi tried to talk about her feelings, he either threatened to slap her or protested, "I love you! How can you do this to me?"

Siobhan began by having Xia and me read the play aloud—which took no more than five minutes. Then we each talked about our characters. I had taken a great dislike to the father. He seemed selfish and sentimental and not really to love his daughter so much as want her to love him. When we did the play again—this time really acting rather than simply reading our parts—I was surprised to find myself much more sympathetic to the father, feeling pangs of sadness whenever Bibi told him what she thought of him. That surprise, I realized afterward, somewhat to my chagrin, was at least in part the result of my almost total ignorance of the art of acting.

Having never acted before, except in pretend games of childhood, I had never fully understood the degree to which the performance of a role was a form of thought—one that employed not only the analytical faculties but the body, voice, emotions, and whole history of the actor. By engaging in that kind of thought, I had come up with a far more nuanced and complex portrait of the father than I had when simply using those skills honed during a lifetime of reading and a couple of years in graduate school. Until that performance with Xia, I had always taken a rather condescending view of actors as the drones of the playwright. Now I was a bit humbled, as well as excited, to discover how similar the art of acting was to the process by which the playwright—or the novelist—created a fictional character.

The art of acting was to give me another—somewhat disconcerting—surprise only a few minutes later, when Siobhan asked Xia and me to put down our scripts and try an experiment.

Although, under the letter of our contract, I was the one meant to be training the Columbia interns, Siobhan actually had far more experience in the theater than I. She had performed in several plays in college and had taken a couple of acting classes since moving to New York. What she wanted Xia and me to do, once we had put our scripts aside, was perform an exercise she had learned in one of her classes. "It's really very simple," Siobhan began. "Just sit directly opposite one another, look into each other's eyes and repeat over and over, 'I can be hurt by you.' Just that one phrase, over and over, for as long as you can do it."

I went at the exercise in the spirit of good fun and so was startled by how quickly the more serious reverberations of looking into Xia's hazel eyes and saying, "I can be hurt by you," began to build up in me. I think Xia felt the same way. Neither of us could get through more than six repetitions without bursting into embarrassed laughter. Finally we gave up, pretending the whole venture had just been a ridiculous joke—but I, at least, felt strangely disconcerted by the degree to which the exercise had caused us to transgress the normal boundaries between teacher and student.

We didn't get a chance to read the play again, but we did talk about it. Xia said: "This play is sorta like my father and me, because my father doesn't live with us."

"Oh, really?" I asked, although I already knew this fact. "Do you and your father get on?"

"Oh, yeah. We get on fine. It's just that I don't see him that often. You know, I have to go all the way up there to see him."

I wanted to ask Xia more about her father and, specifically, find out where "up there" was, but at that moment Daniel called the three groups together so that we could perform our plays for one another before finishing up for the day.

Xia and I went last.

Once again in the middle of the performance I felt my understanding of the character deepen and become more sympathetic, partly as a result of Xia's deepening understanding of her own character. This time, however, I was more aware of how different acting, fundamentally a collaborative art, was from writing. Xia and I were developing our characters together, each responding to the emotional situation the other created. Though I don't make any claims to being much of an actor, I do think it is a real testimony to Xia's talent that, despite the differences in our levels of maturity, she could go right along with me throughout the play without my ever feeling that she was inhibiting my performance. When the play was over, the other club members clapped and clapped, and Xia, after first looking astonished, the way she had the night of the Bensonhurst performance, slowly began to smile.

• • •

All the performances were over. All the kids were gone. Daniel, Jessica, Siobhan, Erin (the other new Columbia intern) and I were gathering our belongings, straightening desks, and conducting an extemporaneous postmortem of the Drama Club session. I was recounting what Xia had told Siobhan and me about her father when Jessica interrupted. "Oh, so that's what started it!" She explained that while the first group had been getting ready to perform its play, Xia had come up to her and, apropos of nothing, spilled out the following, at least as Jessica reenacted it: "I'm a lot like the girl in my play because I don't get to see my father very much because he's in jail. But I like him. He's not like this father at all. I love him. I was so disappointed because I went up to see him on his birthday and they wouldn't let me. I don't get to see him that often and he won't get out of jail until I'm twenty-five. But we have a real good relationship. It's my stepfather I can't stand. He's a real jerk. He's just like the father in this play."

Her father wouldn't get out of jail until she was twenty-five—not for another twelve years. I never found out how long he had been in jail or of what crime he had been convicted (I didn't want to pry), but it must have been very serious. As I listened to Jessica recite this speech, I thought of Xia's hazel—almost golden—eyes as she had been repeating to me and I to her: "I can be hurt by you. I can be hurt by you." So much tragedy in this poor girl's life! How did she stay so even tempered, so smart, so responsible?

On Wednesday of the following week, Celeste auditioned for Daniel's friend, who was directing the off-Broadway play. On Thursday, hearing that Celeste did not get the part, Daniel immediately called me. Apparently his friend had found Celeste too sweet to be the tough-talking street kid she had in mind. Daniel thought the problem was that, because Celeste had come to the audition with her mother, she had been too embarrassed by the script's many swearwords and frank sexuality. Daniel tried to convince his friend to give Celeste another try, but without success.

This was very bad news. Just that morning Rachel had told me Celeste had been flying high all week, telling her friends that she was going to star on Broadway. Remembering how I had privately dismissed Daniel's suggestion that she might not get the part, I now saw clearly that, given her exaggerated responses to virtually everything, Celeste would not take her failure at all well. Far from being a consolation, the fact that Daniel and I had believed in her might only make her feel worse, since it would mean that she had let *us* down as well as herself.

Unfortunately, Celeste didn't have a phone, so Daniel couldn't give her the news in the privacy of her home but would have to seek her out the next day for a hurried conversation between classes. Daniel knew that I would be seeing Celeste first thing in the morning when I taught her eighth-grade class and made me promise not to tell her anything. He felt that he should be the one to break the news.

As soon as I walked into Joan's room the next morning, Celeste ran up to me: "Steve, did I get the part?"

I decided to play it stupid: "What part?"

"In the play Dorothy is directing!"

Dorothy, I took it, was Daniel's friend. "Oh. I don't know. I haven't spoken to Daniel all week. I didn't even know you'd tried out." Celeste was so hyped up that even this news brought a crushed look onto her face. I hated having to lie to her and felt that I should at least prepare her for what was coming, if only by reminding her of the reality of the audition: "How do you think you did?"

"Good! Everybody was so impressed by me! But that girl I was playing had such a bad mouth!"

"Well, Daniel will be in at about one. If he knows anything, I'm sure he'll tell you then."

Celeste went to her seat and took out her folder on which she had written, "I love Teachers & Writers and the Drama Club." Her crushed expression had been replaced by her former avidity. I dreaded seeing her after Daniel had given her the news.

THIS WAS THE MORNING I INTRODUCED THE EIGHTH GRADES TO the playwriting unit I had developed for that year. I had contemplated a variety of subjects for the play including the Los Angeles riots, a murder at Brooklyn's South Shore High School, and the tragic shooting of a crack-addicted daughter by her mother. All of these topics were terribly grim, however, and only presented African Americans as two of their worst stereotypes—victims and perpetrators. For a while I thought of basing the plays on the life of either Martin Luther King or Malcolm X but suspected that my students would be turned off by the very elements that made the lives of these men attractive to me. Writing about heroism would seem too goody-goody, too much like schoolwork to twelve- and thirteen-year-olds who—via Bart Simpson and the Terminator—had perhaps absorbed modernism's antiheroic aesthetic a bit too well. Besides, Martin and Malcolm had ultimately become victims themselves.

In the end I settled on the shooting at Thomas Jefferson High School that we had discussed the previous year. One reason why I was attracted to this event was that the newspapers contained a wealth of information about the families of the victims. I liked the idea of having the seventh- and eighth-grades write a play that carried on some of the themes of the family plays that the Drama Club was working on. But I also nourished a slim hope that the students might become so inspired by the plight of the family members—some of whom seemed quite admirable and strong—that the shooting might fade into the background and the play end up being about the families' attempts to surmount their grief and the brutality of urban life.

Paradoxically, I was also attracted to the Thomas Jefferson incident by the rather puzzling scarcity of information about the two murdered boys and their killer (I could only assume that the two boys were less than innocent victims and that the newspapers had withheld damning information about them out of respect for their obviously decent families). One of the great regrets I had about the Bensonhurst Project was that, between the limitations of the facts and my role as editor of the play, the students had not had much freedom to forge their own plot. In the case of the Thomas Jefferson shooting, however, the fact that the news clippings I had seen said nothing whatsoever about the killer's motives or the relationship between the three boys meant that my students would have no choice but to make up a considerable portion of the plot themselves.

In the final analysis, the single factor that most influenced me to settle on the Thomas Jefferson murders was the poem, written by one of the victims, that has given this book its title. When I came across it in a *Newsday* article, I not only was moved by its awkward earnestness—so like writing I read every day at Walt Whitman—but felt that it would clearly illustrate for my students the value of writing as a means of exploring and expressing one's deepest feelings and understandings.

What follows is the text of the handout I gave to my seventh- and eighth-grade classes at the start of the Thomas Jefferson High project.

FEAR

What I fear began when my grand-
    mother died
Obviously, it was the fear of death
Death is something I just can't handle
When she died, it was so unbelievable
I fear death because I don't know
What will happen when I go.
It is something I can't face.
When I die, will I be thought about?
Will my name be shouted out?
Death will come at any time
No matter how far you're up the ladder.

This poem was written by Ian Moore, one of the two boys killed at Thomas Jefferson High on February 26, 1992. Ian wrote the poem to read at his grandmother's funeral when he was sixteen, and it was read again a year later at his own memorial service.

Ian and his best friend, Tyrone Sinkler, sixteen, grew up together in East New York's Linden House projects. They were shot in a crowded school corridor early on the morning that Mayor David Dinkins was to speak at the school. In anticipation of the Mayor's visit, police had been stationed all over the school, but apparently they were not on the scene at the time of the shooting.

Ian and Tyrone were shot by fifteen-year-old Khalil Sumpter, who claimed that he had been told that the two boys were planning to kill him. He said that he was so afraid of them that he took a different route to school that morning. As soon as he saw them in the corridor, he pulled out his gun and fired. He then fled the school and was caught a few blocks away, with the gun.

Obviously Khalil wanted to make himself seem innocent, but so far no one in Ian or Tyrone's families has contradicted—or con-firmed—his story. Instead, at the boys' joint memorial service (where the poem was read) the minister and their parents talked about all the terrible problems that young African American men face in our society. At a demonstration held shortly after the killing and attended by 2,000 people, the two murdered boys once more were not portrayed as innocent. Rather, the speakers urged the crowd to "stop the violence!" and "stop lynching our brothers and sisters!" and sang "We Shall Overcome."

Thomas Jefferson High School, called "TJ" or "Jeff" by students, certainly is a very rough place. In the three months before the killing, 32 knives and guns were confiscated by teachers and police, and 89 weapons were found on school grounds. During the previous five years, 227 Thomas Jefferson students had been killed. Earlier that same year a teacher had been shot in the hallway and, on the very same day that Ian and Tyrone were killed, another boy accidentally shot himself to death. It was because the school was so rough that Mayor Dinkins had decided to come there and make a speech. His speech was canceled after the killing.

The boys' families each responded very differently to their losses. Tyrone's parents, Ethel and James Sinkler, are suing the school for not protecting students. They have also spoken to the press, at Senate hearings, and to the parents of other children killed in NYC high schools. Tyrone's older brother, James, has also spoken to the press. He said that he and Tyrone used to dream about making enough money to move the family out of the Linden House projects. After the memorial service the family sent Tyrone's body back to his father's hometown, Pinewood, South Carolina, to be buried.

Ian's parents, Linda and Victor Rowe, have dealt with their grief more privately. Linda has been going to a therapist ever since her son's death, and she says she spends most of every session crying. She also visits his grave in Evergreen Cemetery in Queens every weekend with Ian's little brother, Patrick, who was only one at the time of the shooting. Patrick has apparently only just understood that his brother won't be coming back. For a year he kept asking his mother, "Where's Ian?" but last month on a visit to the cemetery he finally said, "Bye-bye Ian," and kissed his mother twice. Linda says that she was not told of the killing by the school or the police but by a student who called her house.

Khalil's parents haven't spoken to the press, so we don't know their names. He is being held without bail until his trial.

Before reading this handout aloud to each of my classes, I had written my trusty equation, FICTION = LIES = TRUTH on the blackboard, discussed how it could possibly make sense, and then explained that we would be using our imaginations to try to reach as complete an understanding as we could of what might have happened at Thomas Jefferson High School. As I had during the Bensonhurst Project, I decided to begin with a controversial question: "How many people believe that Khalil Sumpter was telling the truth when he said that he was afraid that Ian and Tyrone were going to kill him?"

To my astonishment, this question could hardly have been less controversial. Not a single person in all four classes raised his or her hand in response to it, whereas in every class, when I asked, "How many think he was lying?" hands went up all over the room. I was astonished, if for no other reason than that I thought I had implied Ian and Tyrone's guilt pretty forcefully in my handout. I was also surprised, however, because my students' assumption of Ian and Tyrone's innocence seemed so innocent in itself—certainly much more innocent than many of these same students' admiration of Keith Mondello.

When I asked why they doubted Khalil all of my classes said pretty much the same thing: "Because that's what killers always say"—a good enough point and one that, in my last eighth-grade class, I managed to employ for pedagogical purposes.

"So what you are saying is that Khalil's defense is a cliché?" I asked. No response. "Who can tell me what a cliché is?"

Although most of these students had heard me talk about clichés scores of times, probably no more than a handful had remembered what the word meant, and these were too embarrassed to reveal their knowledge in front of their classmates.

After another silence, I defined the term and made it clear how Khalil's defense could be called a cliché. Then I said: "But if what you are saying about Khalil is right, then doesn't that present us with another cliché? Can anybody see it?" Apparently nobody did. "Isn't it also a cliché that victims are always innocent? And when you say that Khalil had nothing to fear from Ian and Tyrone, aren't you also saying that they were innocent?"

The word "no" rose from two or three parts of the room. A boy at the front called out: "Khalil was lying!"

Good. Now I was getting some controversy.

"All right," I said. "If Khalil wasn't afraid of Ian and Tyrone, why did he kill them?"

"To get respect," said Ricky Ortiz.

I was surprised and troubled by this remark, which made pretty clear at least one of the reasons why Ricky had been getting into so many fights.

I said: "Do you really think a boy would kill his friends for no other reason than to get respect?" Ricky just shrugged. I continued: "It's perfectly possible that getting respect was one of the reasons why he shot them. But how much respect is a kid going to get if he just shoots two of his friends for no reason? He had to have another reason."

A boy named Hernan called out: "Maybe they were picking on him."

"Do you think he would shoot them just because they were picking on him?"

Hernan shrugged: "Some kids might."

"But is that really likely? I mean, isn't it more likely that Ian and Tyrone were doing something a lot more serious than just picking on him and that he was really afraid?"

One way or another I got around to making this point in all four classes. And, likewise, I went on to say something about which I would later have second thoughts (the decision was made in my first seventh grade, but I repeated it in my three other classes because I wanted them all to write the same play): "I don't know for sure, and it will be up to you if we write the play this way, because you're the writers, but I think that Ian and Tyrone were *not* entirely innocent. I think they did something that gave Khalil a real reason to want to shoot them."

On the whole the kids seemed surprised to hear me say this. I think that most of them had a strong need to see Ian and Tyrone as innocent, if for no other reason than that the story would be impossibly bleak without someone to sympathize with. I felt bad for depriving them of this consolation and, despite my claim to the contrary, for making it all but impossible for them to decide to portray the boys as innocent. I made this statement because I was convinced that it was true but also because I thought that the play would be more complicated and compelling if the villain were not wholly evil and the victims not wholly innocent. Given the students' reaction, however, I realized that I would have a hard time getting them to see—and write about—the killings as I thought best and that, furthermore, if I pushed my point of view on them, I would be violating my resolution to allow them maximum imaginative freedom. Thus, I was very happy and excited when the question of Ian and Tyrone's innocence ceased to be a matter of opinion.

In my last eighth grade, as I revealed my suspicions about Ian and Tyrone, a shy boy named Dashawn, who heretofore had not participated in the discussion, raised his hand and said, "They used to beat up on Khalil."

"Well, that's a possibility."

"No. They did. My mom knows Ian Moore's mom. And she told me Tyrone was always beating up on Khalil, and Khalil used to beat up on Ian to get him back. And I think they were all in a robbery together, but I don't remember."

Dashawn promised that he would talk to his mother and tell me everything she knew the following week. The assignment for that day was to write a monologue in which a relative of one of the three boys told about the moment in which he or she heard that his or her son, brother, cousin, or nephew had either been shot to death or arrested for murder.

WHEN THE CLASS WAS OVER I PULLED RICKY ASIDE AS THE OTHER students were filing out into the hallway. "Look, Ricky," I said, "I care about you a lot. I think you are a very talented writer and actor and a smart guy. But I'm worried about you too. I'm worried because of all these fights you get into."

"But I wanted to stop this one."

"I know, I heard about that. But you get into a lot of fights. And I want you to think about what you're doing. Fighting may seem cool to you now, but when you look at what happens to fighters in life, you'll see that fighters are losers. Just look around you. People who fight all the time don't succeed at anything. I don't want you to get into that kind of trouble. You're in the middle of a dangerous time of life right now. You know that?" He nodded. "I just don't want you to make the wrong decision."

I don't know how seriously Ricky took my advice, but he was clearly touched that I had troubled to speak to him. When I asked him if he was coming to Drama Club that day he said, "Yeah. I'll be there."

And this time, he was.

When Ricky walked into Joan Gold's classroom all the other members of the Drama Club cheered—bringing an embarrassed but happy grin onto his face. In order to insure that he would keep coming to meetings, Daniel and I made some quick casting revisions and offered him the plum male role: the father in the play I had read with Xia. We had already decided to give the role of the daughter to Celeste, partly in compensation for her not getting the part in the off-Broadway play.

According to Daniel, when he had broken the news about his friend's decision to Celeste earlier that afternoon, all she'd done was shrug and say, "Oh, well, I never really wanted to be in the play anyway." And indeed, at the Drama Club meeting that day, she was her normal self, constantly bouncing around the room, laughing with Xia and Mayra, teasing Ricky. I was greatly relieved but still couldn't quite believe that she could be so indifferent to getting the part. I decided not to say anything to her about it unless she mentioned it to me first.

Celeste and Ricky gave fabulous performances that afternoon. Each of them seemed to be living their part. I was almost at a loss as to how I should direct them and found myself just sitting back and imagining the amazed expressions of the audience as they watched these two perform on opening night. It was thrilling to see how they had matured over the summer. Ricky in particular had become almost professional in his approach to acting, perhaps as a result of his role in the NYU film.

FROM THAT AFTERNOON ON, RICKY SEEMED TO REFORM. HE hardly missed a Drama Club meeting and, as far as I know, stopped getting into fights. I would like to believe that this transformation was due to my influence, but I am afraid that it was primarily the result of his having fallen in love.

At every Drama Club meeting, Ricky would work with great concentration for the first forty-five minutes or so. Then, starting at around three o'clock, he would become noticeably distracted, compulsively asking me for the time every two or three minutes and constantly darting to the window to look out onto the street. Finally, always at about three-twenty-five, he would see what he was looking for: a slim girl, dressed all in black, with a doughy complexion and long black hair, standing beside the mottled plane tree just across from the school's front door. This was Ricky's girlfriend, Isabel. As soon as he would spot her, he would fling open the window, call out her name, and wave. Once, to my amazement, he even shouted, "I love you!" Sometimes we would invite Isabel to come up and sit in on the club, but nobody—and Ricky in particular—could perform with any concentration when she was around.

Ricky had nothing to do with the Thomas Jefferson project or any other assignments I gave that year. All he wrote were love poems. Here is one.

> I was on the dark street
> only lit by a few street lights.
> Also the light of cars
> as they passed.
> I ran throw all of the light
> across the street.
> I saw her
> just as my foot hit the sidewalk
> I saw her turn that head
> with that sweet smile.
> Her long dark hair waved in the wind.
> Uncovering those eyes
> those baby brown eyes.
> As she turned.
> God I knew then
> we would spend the rest of our life
> together.

ONE OF THE THINGS THAT USED TO AMUSE AND AMAZE ME ABOUT Ricky's performance of the father was that, just as when he portrayed Joey Fama, there seemed to be no distance between him and his character. For at least the duration of Drama Club meetings, and possibly longer, Ricky *was* the father. When I would ask him questions about his character, he would get defensive, just as the father did when Bibi, the daughter, tried to talk to him about their relationship.

Once, for example, I asked Ricky why the father would get so angry at the Bibi. "Because she's always talking back to him," he answered.

"Is that all?"

"Yeah." Ricky looked uncomfortable.

"He doesn't have any other reasons?"

"I don't know," he answered impatiently.

"What about Bibi? Why is she so angry at him?"

"Because she wants him to buy her things and he won't do it." This is just what the father said in the play, and it is the only explanation Ricky ever seemed to accept for Bibi's behavior.

"Don't you think," I said, "she might also be angry at him for leaving her and her mother, and for never coming to visit, and even for getting remarried and having a new baby?"

"Well, yeah," Ricky muttered uneasily, then suddenly became irritated. "But she still shouldn't talk to him like that!"

Ricky's blindness to the failings of the father by no means excluded a sophisticated understanding of his feelings. At one point, after slapping his daughter, who has insulted him, the father says, "But I love you!" I asked Ricky what the father was feeling. Ricky said, "Guilt. And anger. The anger hangs around a bit even after he calms down."

"Does he feel any love?"

"No. Not then."

In all of my readings of this part I had always made the father rather pathetically express and desire real love at that moment. Ricky's reading was exactly right. That was why he could be so convincing when he threatened to slap Bibi and I couldn't. Ricky's voice as he said, "I love you," had an undercurrent of calculation and fury, even if it was also true that on some level the father he portrayed actually did love his daughter.

RICKY AND CELESTE CONTINUED TO GIVE FABULOUS PERFORMANCES as father and daughter. On the day of the conversation quoted above— Ricky's third Drama Club meeting—Celeste had been more than usually manic, giggling at every mistake either of them made and constantly poking and swatting at Ricky with her script in a manner that was decidedly less playful than she pretended. For most of the rehearsal she had been sitting on a chair that was pressed right up against Ricky's, her foot inserted between his legs and resting on his chair rung.

After my conversation with Ricky, I decided we should do the play over again from the top. The play opens with the father kissing his daughter hello. In the past, Ricky had handled this moment by placing an awkward air kiss about a foot and a half to the right of Celeste's cheek, and this had seemed to suit her fine (it was the one weak spot in their performance). But on this occasion, when Ricky aimed his lips at the air beside her face, Celeste swatted him with her script. "What's the matter?" she asked with a tight-lipped grin. "You afraid to kiss me?" She swatted him again and turned to me. "Steve! Tell Ricky he's got to give me a real kiss, right on the lips!"

I laughed and said, "That's up to Ricky!"

"Oh, no!" Ricky howled and covered his face with one big hand. "Don't make me! Please!"

Deciding the time had come to settle this problem, I said, "Look, Ricky, you don't have to kiss her. You can just give her a hug." (I hugged Celeste.) "The father is awkward and shy with his daughter anyway. You can be shy if you want."

We went on with the rehearsal, but Celeste couldn't concentrate. She kept giggling for no reason and jerking her bony body around in her chair. At one point her foot slipped off Ricky's chair rung and left a gray smear across the toe of his creamy white sneakers.

"Are you crazy!" he shouted, instantly pulling up his foot and trying to undo the damage with the tail of his shirt. "What's the matter with you today!"

I didn't have a lot of sympathy for Ricky's sneakers, but I did think that Celeste was beginning to get out of hand. "Look, Celeste," I said, "you're a really good actress—both you guys are really good. But you can't keep goofing around like this. You've got to be serious." She was grinning. She lifted her script up and covered her face. I pulled the script back down and said, "Celeste, I mean it. If you don't take the play seriously and you screw it up, you're only hurting yourself." As I spoke I saw her face go from silly grin to sullen. Then she jumped up from her chair, threw down her script, and saying, "I don't want to talk about it," ran out of the room. I ran after her, making it out the door just in time to see her zip into the stairwell.

"Wait!" I cried. "What's the matter!" By the time I got down the first flight, she had vanished. I looked for her on the street, but she wasn't there. None of the kids hanging out on the school steps had seen her. Daniel went out looking for her, too, but with no more luck than I. Finally Jessica found her in the girls' room, sitting on the window ledge with her face in her hands. She wouldn't look at Jessica or answer any of her questions, except by nods. When Jessica asked her whether it was the play itself that upset her, she didn't respond in any way. But when Jessica asked if she was upset because of Ricky, she nodded. And when Jessica asked whether Ricky had done anything to her, she shook her head.

After getting this report, I went in to speak to Celeste myself, but she just sat there staring with trancelike fixity at her feet, not responding to any of my numerous queries or attempts at sympathy. When I said to her, "Come on, Celeste, you're not being fair," she slid off the ledge and ran out of the room.

Jessica finally convinced Celeste to go out for a hot chocolate but didn't get much information. Returning to the school just as Daniel, Siobhan, Erin, and I were packing up to go, Jessica told us that Celeste's main complaint had been that Ricky was a bully. Daniel pointed out that the previous year Ricky had threatened to beat up her little brother. Jessica also said that Celeste had been freaked out by my having come into the girls' room.

I wasn't sure that Celeste had been honest on either count. She and Ricky had seemed to be getting on fine in the hallway before the Drama Club meeting. And Ricky was the elder brother of her best friend, Sasha. It seemed quite possible to me that what was really going on was that she had a crush on Ricky and didn't want to admit it. Daniel, however, thought that she might have a crush on me. I didn't know what to do. I didn't want to reward her for sulking, but if something deeper was going on, I didn't want to abandon her. Given what Daniel had suggested, however, I didn't think I was the best person to deal with her, so I asked Jessica to give her some extra attention. Meanwhile we decided to have Celeste and Xia switch roles. Xia would return to playing Bibi, and Celeste would play the dreamy artist father in a comedy about a divorced couple who, at their daughter's twelfth birthday party, decide to remarry.

1 2

You've Got to Show Them the Way Out

DASHAWN, THE BOY WHOSE MOTHER KNEW IAN MOORE'S MOTHER, kept his promise. At my next meeting with his eighth-grade class, in his easy, soft, always slightly bemused voice, Dashawn recounted everything he could remember of what his mother had learned from Linda Rowe.

As Dashawn told the story, Ian, Tyrone, and Khalil had all committed a robbery together. Dashawn didn't know what sort of robbery it was or why only Tyrone got arrested for it. Tyrone was, apparently, in jail for only a very short time. When he got out he told Ian that he thought it was Khalil's fault that he had been arrested. Dashawn's mother didn't know for sure whether Ian and Tyrone had really planned to kill Khalil in revenge, but apparently Khalil heard rumors that they had and decided to make a preemptive strike.

Sketchy as this account may have been, it was an irresistible foundation for the play. It had thrills (the robbery), mystery (Did Khalil really rat on Tyrone? Did Ian and Tyrone really plan to kill him?), and most of all, it provided the class with a simple and comprehensible chain of events with which to explain the tragedy of friend turning against friend. Another attractive feature, from my point of view, was that it enabled us to bypass what I had come to realize would have been an extremely time consuming, complicated, and potentially divisive process of extracting a single plot from the work of 132 students. With

238 • *Will My Name Be Shouted Out?*

Dashawn's account, all the major plot decisions had been decreed by fate. The students hadn't made them; I hadn't made them. Nobody had to feel bad because I had rejected his or her plot idea. Nobody could even protest that the plot was stupid, because, as far as we knew, it was the simple truth. In a mere five minutes Dashawn had knocked two or three weeks off the writing phase of the project. Our narrative explorations were over; now we could start working on the play itself.

All that remained was to fill the major holes in the story, which, for efficiency's sake, I did by vote in Dashawn's own class. First the crime: "What should they have robbed?" I asked. One kid called out, "A bank." Another, "A liquor store." A third, "A jewelry store." Other students suggested a restaurant and an apartment. I wrote all the suggestions on the board. When it came time for voting, I gave the students the following advice: "Remember, with this play we are trying to tell the truth about life in this city. When you choose the location of the crime, it should seem realistic. If your audience doesn't believe that the kids could rob this place, then they are not going to believe the truths you have to tell them. And also, if you have the boys robbing the vaults of the king of Mars"—I chose a fantastic example because I didn't want to impugn any of the ones on the board—"then you probably aren't going to have a whole lot of truth to tell about life in New York City. At the same time, however, the robbery should be interesting. Think about how you would write about a robbery at each of these locations. If one of them starts giving you good ideas, that's probably the one you should choose—as long as those ideas are believable. Again, you may get a lot of good ideas about robbing the emperor of Mars, but they aren't going to work in this story, because we're not trying to write science fiction. *Interesting* and *believable,* those are the two variables you need to consider."

We held the vote and the liquor store won.

Then we had to figure out why Tyrone was the only one arrested. Again I asked for suggestions, but this time I was more dictatorial. A couple of kids made more or less the same suggestion, that Khalil would have called the police to get back at Tyrone for something he had done, but I rejected these out of hand, explaining that if Khalil had called the police, then he would have risked getting arrested himself, since he had also participated in the robbery.

Then a girl named Raquel suggested: "Maybe they were doing the robbery and the police arrived and they all ran away, but Tyrone got caught."

"That's good," I said. "That sounds perfectly possible. But why would Tyrone blame Khalil?"

Raquel took this question as a rejection of her idea and turned a sullen gaze down at her desk.

"I like this idea," I emphasized. "But we have to come up with a good reason why Tyrone would blame Khalil."

"Khalil tripped him," said one boy.

"Maybe."

Another boy said: "Maybe Khalil was an undercover cop, and he was setting them up."

"No. That's too complicated. Besides it's not believable. Why would an undercover cop want to trap some ordinary teenagers? They're usually after drug dealers."

Then someone suggested that they be drug dealers. I was tempted by that idea but once more decided that it would be too complicated and that we should just stick with our first decision, that the crime should be robbing a liquor store. "It's simple and it's believable," I said. "The cops come. The kids run, but Tyrone gets caught. Why does he blame Khalil?"

A long silence. The class was stumped and, frankly, so was I. I was about to suggest that they work out their own ideas as they wrote when Raquel raised her hand a second time: "Maybe Khalil was the lookout and he wasn't paying attention."

It took a moment for this to sink in, but then I said, "All right. That's it. That's perfect. We'll go with it."

The only remaining hole to fill was whether Ian and Tyrone had actually planned to kill Khalil. But at this point I suffered what was to prove a particularly consequential moment of confusion and insecurity about my pedagogical responsibilities.

As I have said, I believed that the two boys probably *were* after their friend. I couldn't see any reason apart from sheer terror why Khalil would have committed so desperate and dumb an act as to shoot Ian and Tyrone on the day of the mayor's visit, when the school was crawling with cops. But obvious as Ian and Tyrone's villainy may have been, something about it made me uncomfortable.

In a way, I suppose, I was no different from my students. I too preferred my victims innocent. At a primitive and irrational level, I felt that if Ian and Tyrone were authentic villains, then there was something sick about the balance of good and evil in the universe. Our play might have had more truth in it—and might even have been more interesting—if I had asked the students to explore how Ian and Tyrone could have come to the point of wanting to kill Khalil, but I was reluctant to further depress children who already had so grim a view of life. Believing I was granting my students an important imaginative freedom, I decided to let them determine Ian and Tyrone's motives and morals for themselves and hoped I wouldn't get too many incompatible monologues and dialogues. Little did I realize that it would be precisely my reluctance to play the literary and moral dictator that, at a much later date, would force me to be far more dictatorial than I had ever been with the Bensonhurst play.

I set the students to work, and they wrote eagerly for the remainder of the period.

It was clear to me right from that first class that the focus of the play had shifted away from the families' grief to the boys and their two crimes (the robbery and the killings). I was sorry that this play wouldn't become quite so coherent a follow-up to the three family plays the Drama Club was working on, but I couldn't stand in the way of inspiration.

The truth was that the students had begun to grow tired of writing monologues for mourning mothers, fathers, and brothers. But now that they were free to investigate the murder and the robbery, and also the history of Ian and Tyrone's long friendship and their more ambiguous relationship with Khalil, they began to write with the same enthusiasm and talent that had so thrilled me during the Bensonhurst Project. Not everyone wanted to work on the play, of course. Some students—like Ricky Ortiz—found their inspiration elsewhere. Others never found any inspiration at all. But as the weeks went by, I watched the student folders swell with reams of work that was always as good as and often superior to the Bensonhurst writing. Once again I felt as if I were presiding over a small-scale miracle.

ONE DAY I WAS IN THE P.S. 227 LIBRARY MAKING ARRANGEMENTS with Doris Catello, the school librarian, for some of my fourth-grade students to read their work on WNYE, the Board of Education's radio station. While Doris riffled through her calendar, I noticed a tall woman with long, dark hair at the far end of the library counter, sorting books into stacks. I had never seen this woman in the school before. Observing that she worked with a degree of energy and efficiency that clearly distinguished her from the ordinary public school employee, I decided that she must be a parent volunteer.

After we had finished our arrangements, Doris introduced me to the woman, whose name was Beth Rogovin, and explained that she was a coordinator of New York public school library programs. Beth apologized for having eavesdropped on our conversation but said she was interested in hearing more about my work. Normally this was just the sort of request that I was eager to accommodate, having found that my stories about the Bensonhurst and Thomas Jefferson projects were surefire hits at cocktail and dinner parties, but something in Beth's manner made me wary.

I had only gotten halfway through my usual spiel about the projects when she interrupted me. "But what are you going to do about the despair? These children are already so overwhelmed by it. You can't just take them deeper into it; you've got to show them the way out."

"As a matter of fact," I said, with somewhat forced confidence, "tomorrow I'm going to wrap up the Thomas Jefferson Project by having the students write speeches or poems that could be read at the funerals of the two victims. And in these speeches I want the students to talk about why tragedies like these murders happen and what could be done to make them less likely."

"But the problem with that," Beth said, "is that the kids will just tell you, 'People should be nicer.' That's not enough." (I had to admit, at least to myself, that there was truth to this.) "What you should do," she continued, "is get some of the crisis mediation people at the school to come into your classroom and hammer at the kids to make them think."

The crisis mediation counselors visited the school weekly to train a group of students—Xia among them—to intervene in disputes before they became violent and to help their fellow students solve conflicts by discussion and compromise. The idea behind this program—perfectly valid in my opinion—was that fights often started simply because students didn't know any other way of dealing with conflict.

I had no doubt that the training these students received really did help with playground and hallway conflicts, but I felt strongly that inviting crisis mediation counselors into the classroom would be a violation of the tacit pact I had made with my students that they could write anything they wanted, no matter how unpleasant or socially unacceptable it might be, as long as they were trying to tell the truth. Bringing in the counselors would be like bringing in socialist realist censors. It would be saying: "Oh, no, you can't tell just any truths; you have to tell only these truths, and your stories should only have these particular morals." Whenever, as a student, I had felt teachers imposing similar limits on my honesty or imagination, I had always reacted by intentionally defying them. I suspected that many of my students would respond in exactly the same way to the crisis mediation counselors and that others would simply turn off, labeling my class just "more school bullshit."

The problem with such arguments was that I myself wanted the students to recognize certain truths and consider certain morals. My belief was that I could do this in a way that did not contradict the principles of imaginative and individual freedom that were at the heart of my teaching method. But as I listened to Beth Rogovin, I began to worry that I was only deceiving myself.

"My students *have* been thinking about these problems," I said. "It's not like I'm going to spring them on them all of a sudden. And we'll discuss them again tomorrow before they write. But anyhow, it's too late to bring in the crisis mediation people. The project will be finished on Friday."

"You could bring them in next week. That's soon enough."

Now I was getting annoyed. It was clear from her tone of voice that Beth thought I was just one of those spaced-out, everything-is-wonderful school poets. "My main hesitation," I said, "is that I don't think that the crisis mediation people have any real solutions to the problems the kids face either. What do you think should be done about all the violence and drugs?"

"Well, yes . . . ," she said, clearly at a loss. "I hate it when curriculums are oversimplified, too. But these crisis mediation people are really getting into these problems in a serious way."

The conversation finally ended when I said that I might ask them to talk to the students after the presentation of the play, as a way of getting the discussion going.

I brought up Beth Rogovin's suggestion at the regular T&W staff meeting on Friday, and Daniel, Jessica, Erin, and Siobhan all derided it

vehemently, echoing my own beliefs that the crisis mediation counselors would kill the students' creativity with a bunch of heavy-handed
clichés. Rather than reaffirming my beliefs, however, the very unanimity
of this response only made me wonder if we might all be laboring in
the service of heavy-handed—if highbrow—clichés of our own that
were causing us to deny our true moral and social agendas and to neglect an important obligation to our students. The reason for my sudden
suspicion of principles I had long taken for granted was that in the two
days since my conversation in the library I had given my seventh and
eighth graders their final Thomas Jefferson lesson and had discovered
things about their lives that had once again thrown me into a crisis
about my roles as teacher and writer.

Despite my show of confidence, I had come away from my
conversation in the library convinced of the futility of my ambitions for
that final lesson. I was facing the same problem that I had had last year.
One session simply was not enough time to get my students to think
deeply about the social dimensions of the individual tragedies they had
been exploring for so many weeks, especially not deeply enough to affect the way they saw themselves and their responsibilities to the society in which they lived.

Why, then, was I even bothering to go ahead with a lesson I knew
was doomed to failure? Partly it was the resurfacing of my old ambition
to make writing "matter." I didn't believe that our purely individualistic
exploration of the Thomas Jefferson tragedy had had enough of the
"political and social importance" I felt ought to belong to my craft. But I
also had another, far more irrational, far stronger, and, from a pedagogical point of view, not entirely proper reason for being unable to turn
my back on my probably futile lesson.

Deep in my heart I wanted to rabble-rouse. I wanted, in a single class
meeting, to inspire in my students the passion for social reform that had
been missing from this country throughout the whole of the Reagan and
Bush years—since the end of the Vietnam War, really. That the accomplishment of such an ambition was wildly beyond my abilities or anyone
else's didn't diminish it in the least, just as the fact that I don't have wings
has never diminished my desire to fling myself into the air and fly.

In the grip of such an irrational impulse, I arrived at Joan Gold's classroom with a couple of questions that I hoped were controversial enough to provoke, if not a passion for social reform, then at least a passionate discussion:

1. If you committed a crime and someone told the police about you, how would you respond?
2. If you heard two dangerous young men wanted to kill you, what would you do?

To my surprise and disappointment, these questions provoked hardly any controversy at all. Most of the seventh-graders seemed to take it for granted that they should try to kill anyone who planned to kill them and that likewise they would have been justified in doing practically anything to a stool pigeon. If any students disagreed with these ancient, cardinal laws of street life, they didn't feel that they could express their disagreement and retain their dignity.

My hope had been that when my students got fired up debating the merits of revenge and the legitimacy of self-preservation, they might be intrigued when I asked them, for example: Why did Ian, Tyrone, and Khalil live in such fear? What things about their environment would have had to be different for them not to be so afraid or self-destructive? What if guns had not been so easily available? How attractive would drugs and drug dealing be if there were decent, well-paying jobs available for everyone who needed them?

Without the hoped-for passionate discussion, such questions were greeted by shrugs and glazed eyes. In the end, largely just to fill the dead air, I gave the students a hasty, oversimplified, liberal-left lecture about how programs like socialized medicine, cheap and widely available daycare, and better funded public schooling could help reduce urban violence and make it easier for people to escape poverty.

Then, when this speech was no more successful in stimulating discussion than my questions had been, I hurried to the relative safety of the day's assignment: I asked the students to write speeches and poems that could have been read at Ian and Tyrone's funeral. I told them that if it would help, they could write in the voice of a minister, or even Malcolm X or Martin Luther King.

As I made the circuit of the room I came to the desk of a very bright but harried-looking boy named Fernando. Normally he had no trouble filling a page, but today he sat in front of a completely blank piece of paper, looking more harried than ever.

"What's the problem, Fernando?"

"Nothing." He didn't look at me.

"Then how come you're not writing?"

"I don't know. I guess I don't feel anything about violence in the city."

"Have you ever seen any violence?" I said.

"Well, one time me and my father were driving in his car and we got caught in the cross fire between two gangs. They just started shooting at each other right across the street."

"Did anything happen to you?"

"No. My father told me to duck down, and then he just drove out of there real fast."

"All right," I said. "That's a good story. Write about that. Forget Ian and Tyrone. Write about what you felt when you were caught in the cross fire."

As I spoke Fernando underwent a whole-body wince and said, "Uh-uh. No way. I don't want to write about that."

So much for not feeling anything about violence.

I told him he could write about anything he wanted, even if it had nothing to do with violence or Jefferson High—hoping that giving him this freedom would make it easier for him to go back to the topic.

Leaving Fernando's desk, I headed for the back of the room, where one table was talking much too loudly. Generally I tolerate conversation during writing time, as long as it's not so loud it disturbs the other students. Often the kids discover their inspiration by talking to one another, and if I want to establish an atmosphere in which my young writers feel free to follow their fancy, I can't be too much of a totalitarian. But this conversation, between Rahel, Diego, and Cassandra, had gone many decibels beyond the acceptable limit.

As Diego saw me approaching, he called out: "Steve, it's because Eve ate the apple, right?"

"What is?" I asked.

"Adam ate it too!" Rahel shouted.

"Quiet," I said softly. "You guys have to keep it down."

"Didn't Eve eat the apple?" asked Diego.

"Well," I began, not knowing quite what I was getting into, "Eve and Adam both ate the apple."

"Yeah," said Diego, "but she made him. If she hadn't done that, he wouldn't have eaten it, and then we wouldn't have any violence."

"That's what I'm saying," said Cassandra. "It's because Adam ate the apple that we have so much violence."

"No it isn't," said Diego.

"Yes it is. You said it yourself."

"Yeah," seconded Rahel.

"It's 'cause Eve ate the apple, right, Steve?" said Diego.

"First of all," I said, "it's just a story. Not everybody believes it. But second of all it's because Adam and Eve *both* ate the apple that the human race was kicked out of Paradise."

"There, you see, it's *both*," said Rahel, and that seemed to end the discussion.

"What makes you think violence started with Adam and Eve?" I asked.

"'Cause it did," Rahel answered. "My mom told me that the reason there's so much violence is because we're being punished for what Adam and Eve did."

"Don't you think there are any other reasons?"

"Nope," said Rahel. Neither of the other two contradicted her. That showed how effective my hasty liberal lecture had been.

"Well, how do you explain the fact that the cities weren't always as violent as they are now?" No one volunteered an answer. They were waiting to be enlightened. "Violence in the cities got much worse during the nineteen sixties. My father grew up in the city. When he was a kid there were gangs and kids got into fights all the time, but it was nothing like today. Do you know why? It was because the Mafia hadn't brought heroin into the city yet and because hardly anybody had guns. Guns and drugs. Those are the main causes of the violence we have now." This was an argument I hadn't made to the class as a whole. Perhaps it would have had a deeper effect than my more abstract pronouncements about poverty and despair.

But then again, perhaps not.

"Yeah, but it wouldn't have happened if Eve hadn't ate the apple," said Diego.

"Adam ate it too!" Rahel and Cassandra said simultaneously.

Clearly this disagreement had too much energy to be altered by anything I said. I moved away from the table, saying, "You guys can keep talking about this, just keep your voices down."

I drifted across the back of the room until my eyes lit on Lily Choi, who was sitting at her desk, her face crushed between her fists, looking as if the world were about to end. This was a common expression for Lily. She was a new member of the Drama Club, and I couldn't understand why she had joined, except perhaps to be with her friends Arlene Salter and Anna Harris—the two white girls.

Acting seemed to be profoundly unpleasant for Lily. Whenever she had to perform, she either doubled over in a fit of nervous giggling or threw a sulk, causing her directors and her fellow actors no end of frustration. But on the other hand, she seemed to take great pride in belonging to the Drama Club and never missed a meeting. Apart from when she was acting, she was a kind and generous kid, so I felt a special loyalty to her.

"How's it going?" I said, crouching beside her desk.

"Hunh?"

I saw that she was holding a crumpled piece of paper in her hand. This too was typical of Lily. She sabotaged her writing in much the same way she sabotaged her acting. "Having difficulty getting started?"

"What are we supposed to do?"

Patiently I told her once again about writing the speech for Ian and Tyrone's funeral. When I finished she uncrumpled the paper and handed it to me. "Is this okay?"

In very light pencil across the top line of the paper was this sentence fragment: "When my brother die six months ago . . ."

"Is this true?" I asked.

She nodded.

"How did he die?"

"He was in a gang in Chinatown and . . . they just shot him."

I was stunned. We had been working together for three months, and she had never given me the slightest indication, either in her conversation or her writing, of anything like this in her background.

"I'm very sorry to hear that." She shrugged, seeming near tears. I looked again at her half sentence, neatly written in pale pencil. "This is fine, Lily. Go ahead. Tell the story if you want to. Sometimes it helps to put it down on paper."

She pulled the crumpled page out of my hand and immediately got to work, hardly lifting her head for the remainder of the period. When I came around to collect her folder, she told me that she hadn't finished and asked if she could take her composition home. I said okay, although when kids took their work home I usually never saw it again. She promised she would bring it to Drama Club the following afternoon.

After class I asked Joan if she had known about Lily's brother. She hadn't and was astonished by the news, as was Rachel when I spoke to her later.

"A lot of these kids have had things like that happen," said Rachel. "Have you heard about Cesaré Lopez?"

"No."

"Her sister was shot by her husband in August. We only found out when, at gym, Cesaré threw a tantrum because she had left her watch in her classroom and the teacher wouldn't let her go back for it. She became like a wild animal. She was cursing, blubbering, kicking. Nobody could get near her. Finally, when she calmed down, she told us that her sister had been killed and that this watch was the only thing she had of hers."

THE FOLLOWING MORNING I FOUND LILY WAITING FOR ME OUTSIDE Joan's room with not one but two compositions about her brother's death. She explained that when she had finished the first one she thought it was terrible, so she had rewritten it as a play, but she thought that was terrible too. I told her I would read them both before Drama Club and give her my opinion.

Entering Joan's classroom, I found it in complete chaos. Joan was absent, just as she had been absent the previous year on the last day of the Bensonhurst Project. While Rachel went to find the substitute and then while the two of them calmed the class, I had time to read both of Lily's pieces. Here they are.

When my brother die six months ago, I was thinking of what is going to happen to our family without my brother?
who is the next person to die in the family?
Am I going to die the same way as he did?
There was whole bunch of questions I needed to be answer. but who can answer it for me?
When I hear about my brother death on June 5, 1992, I was shocked. I was crying in my room telling myself that "the person who die yesterday is not my brother." Since that day I was angry to my friends.

Than on June 8, 1992, I had to go to the funeral. and I miss one day of school which I never do.

After I came home from the funeral that night, everybody in my family was talking about how he die, and how it all started.

I was in my room listening. And then I realize that he die because he was being helpful.

He was helping one of his friend getting out of trouble And for no reason that guy just shut my brother and shut his friend too.

The next day I went to school, my teacher ask me "you all right"? I just said "yeah" which is not true.

I kept thinking that why it happened to him and not to me? And I still thinking about it now. but not as much as I use too.

Life is not fair. why the peoples that is being helpful and nice have to end up dead.

And the peoples that kill other people just for money and do other bad things have to end up in jail, in stay being dead? I mean, when they come out of jail, they will still be the same person. they not going to change just because they got lock up in jail once.

no matter how many times they go behind bars, they will not change there life for something else because they got use to what they do already.

What I think we should do is that the people that kills another people should lock up in jail and not be free. they will be in there for the rest of there life. once they get in, they can not come out. so the people that being helpful can end up happy and don't worry about getting robbed.

place: Chinatown (in an gangble place) on the second floor.
time: 10:15 p.m.
Date: June 4, 1992
raining day

A bunch of people walk in and start pushing Martin around.

Joey: pay up my man.
Martin: what you talking about
Joey: the money you own me last week.

Louis: what's going on here?

Joey: none of you business so butt out.

Martin: Joey, don't talk to him like that, he's my friend man.

    (Joey and the guy walk out.)

    (15 minutes later)

    (Joey walk in with a gun in his coat pocket)

Joey: Look, pay up or you are a dead men.

Martin: Come on, don't be like this. we're buddy, remember.

Joey: If you really want to be my buddy why don't you pay up first.

Louis: Look man, he try to be nice to you, why don't you give him a few more day, and I premiss he'll pay you back.

    (Joey start yelling at Louis)

Joey: why don't you just shut up. (in high tone)

Michael: Look man, I'm just try to help here, you don't have to yell at me like you are my father.

    (in an high tone)

    (Joey pull out his gun and start shooting at Louis)

    (Three gun shut.

    first at the heart

    second shut went

    through the cheek and

    comes out from the side

    of the life eye.

    third shut went right

    through the brain.)

Than Joey turn around and saw Martin try to run away. and Joey went after him. when Martin was at the middle stair and Joey was still at the top stair,

    Joey shoot down right at Martin.

Martin fall down the stair. And laying facing the floor on the bottom stair.

    Joey start running.

    so did the rest of

    the peoples in there.

    By the time the

      cops came nobody is

        in there,

        the room is empty

> And there was two
> body on the floor.
> And it was Louis
> and Martin.
> It was 10:30 p.m. when
> Louis die.
> And he was 17 yearsold.

This was by far the most detailed and heartfelt writing Lily had ever given me. I was saddened to learn not only of her grief but of her fear and her sense—which ran fairly deep, I believe—that life was not fair. But I was also pleased that she had felt comfortable enough to write about this private trauma in my class, and especially that the form of writing we had been working with—the play—had been useful to her in dealing with her brother's death.

I was struck by the fact that in neither of her compositions had Lily mentioned, as she had told me in class, that her brother had been a member of a gang—though her play was set in "a gangble place." I was also struck by the precision of the killing—the bullets through the heart and brain—which made Louis's death seem more like an execution than the act of spontaneous violence Lily represented it as being. I know nothing of the murder apart from the details mentioned above, but it did occur to me that Louis might not have been quite as innocent as Lily wanted to believe. And I wondered if she hadn't chosen to rewrite her first composition primarily to correct her own lack of confidence in the explanation for Louis's death she had developed the day of his funeral: "he die because he was being helpful." If this was the case, it meant that, rather than using the dramatic form as a means of uncovering the truth, which was the way I had always talked about it during the Thomas Jefferson Project, Lily had imagined her brother's death in the detail necessary for a play chiefly so that she could substantiate a more comfortable fiction.

It was not my place to question the integrity of Lily's vision of her brother, nor did it even make sense to offer technical criticism of these compositions, since, one way or another, they really mattered only as a means for helping her heal her emotional wounds. When I saw Lily that afternoon at Drama Club, I told her that I had been very moved by both pieces and that, rather than one being better than the other, I thought that they had both worked together to make a whole that was far more powerful than either would have been on its own. While this was an exaggeration of my best feelings about the pieces, it made Lily blush and smile with pride. I also told her that she should feel free to write more about Louis's death if it would help her. But in my class, she never committed another word to paper about any aspect of her personal life.

LILY'S COMPOSITIONS ONLY CONFIRMED THE DECISION I HAD made the previous night about how to alter my final lesson. And perhaps they gave me the greater strength of conviction that enabled me to perform the miracle of getting the class's attention, despite their substitute.

I began by asking my students how many of them had ever had a gun pointed at them. Six kids raised their hands. Two of them had had the guns pointed at them by friends playing with their fathers' guns. One boy's own father aimed a gun at him, but he was just "playing around" (responsible guy!). But the father of a girl had wanted to train her not to panic when someone threatened to shoot her. Ricky Ortiz told about playing Russian roulette with a friend. And another boy described being held up at gunpoint in the subway.

Next I asked my students how many had friends or relatives who had been shot. To my amazement, virtually everyone in the class raised his or her hand. I asked for details. The first few students who spoke told me about friends, cousins, brothers who got shot because they were drug dealers. Surprised by the apparent level of involvement of my students' families in the drug trade, I asked how many had drug dealer friends or relatives, and a small, spunky black girl named Keisha Damar laughed at that question.

"What's so funny?" I asked.

Becoming embarrassed, she said, "I don't know."

"No, really," I told her. "I want to know."

She shrugged and said, as if it were the most obvious thing in the world, "Because we all do."

I asked for a show of hands, and she was absolutely right.

A chilly feeling came over me as I looked out at the forest of black and brown hands. I had been so worried about depriving my students of their innocence and, especially since talking to Beth Rogovin, the library coordinator, about rubbing their faces in the grim facts of city life—but here I was discovering that I was perhaps the most innocent person in the classroom, that nothing I had asked my students to write about was any grimmer than what most of them had experienced in their own families, and some of them in their homes.

Retrospectively, it is hard for me to understand how I could have been so innocent about the lives of my students. I already knew most of the statistics I have mentioned in the introduction to this book. I had read all the stories in the papers about crime and drugs and the life of the very poor. I had even lived on the very block where Angela Cordero's friend had been gunned down. I myself had seen two bodies on the sidewalk in front of the local drug kingpin's restaurant headquarters. I myself had walked into the middle of a gunfight and had been shoved aside by a fleeing gunman, who was then chased by two other young men with drawn pistols. It had, indeed, been partly my experience in that neighborhood, as well as all the horror stories I had read in the newspapers, that had made me want to work in the schools. But still somehow, while standing in front of a classroom or crouching beside the desk of one of my young writers, I had managed to keep all that knowledge at a distance. Some part of me simply did not want to believe that people whom I knew and liked, even liked a great deal, could lead such blighted lives. And in that way I was no different from so many other Americans who read the papers and watch the news every day but have never let themselves truly imagine what it means to grow up poor in this country.

Feeling like a child in front of the upraised hands and wise faces of my students, I didn't see that I had anything more to tell them. Rather, I wanted to hear what they could tell me, and to that end the assignment I had come up with the previous night seemed more apropos than ever. Passing out the class's writing folders, I told my students that we were done writing about Ian and Tyrone. What I wanted everyone to do now was tell me about *their own* experiences of violence.

That night, as I read the accounts produced by both eighth grades (the discussion in the second class had virtually duplicated the first), I began to realize why, naive as I may have been, it had been so important for me to bring the grim facts of Bensonhurst and Thomas Jefferson High into the classroom. Partly out of a desire to foster empowerment and to "ac-*cen*-tuate the positive," the students at Walt Whitman Academy had been given virtually no opportunity to grapple honestly and without oversimplification with the insanity of their life outside of school. The reason they had written so powerfully and willingly about Thomas Jefferson High and about Bensonhurst was that, like Lily Choi, they had all had many experiences and fears that they needed to explore, understand, and express their feelings about.Here are a few of the pieces the eighth-graders wrote for me that day.

What I'm about to write is true. It happened June 4, 1990. It was about 11:00 P.M. and me and my father was coming from parking the car. My father was singing to me and as we went in the building I asked him for fifty dollar's. He asked me for what and then I told for some sneakers so He gave it to me, I was real happy but as we went up the stairs I saw some one come in the building, I was still happy so I just looked at him right away because I was counting the money and then it happend, a gun shot ran off and I just ducked, my mother came out, she was screaming to come in I ran in the house, my mother asked me where's my father, I was saying I don't know, I don't know, then thats when I realized that my father has gotten shot, I went crazy, I was going wild, my brother got my father's gun from the house looking for someone that killed my father, I couldn't believe it until like a month later, I don't know where the world is going to but if it keeps on like this, the world is going to end.
　　—Cornell Vargas

My sister was shot and killed by her husband. I was away at camp and I came home two days later. My mother didn't want to tell me or my sister 'cause my sister would not have been able to drive to pick me up. But when I came in the house everyone was crying. I didn't know what they were crying for, so I asked them. They told me. I didn't cry at first. But I cried later on, when I was alone.*
　　—Cesaré Lopez

Violence

It was over the summer in mid-july, It was me a some of my friends We were walking up on [. . .] street And as we were walking We

---

*This is an edited version extracted from the Thomas Jefferson play. I no longer have the original.

saw these two guys fighting then some guy out of Nowhere shot them both. They fell to the ground and some of my friends screamed I just stood there for a moment then we ran All you saw when they got shot was blood ever were and as we where runing we heard 2 more gun shots. And after that I never went over there again Because that could happen to me Just as easyly.

—Shanequa Franklin

On the night of some years ago. I went to a friends house to pick some things up he put his hand in his cabinet and pulled out a revolver and put it to my head. He said are you scared to die? I said no in a low voice Then I heard a click and then the gun was right to my temple. then pulled the triger and . . . It was empty.

One night I had a fight with a kid and he pulled a knife and then my friend gave me my skull shape handle knife and we went on. by the way I lost the knife. I went in and got stabed in the face. I got him back and won but till this day I still regrate that day. In these days that how it is you have to fight or die. That's all these animals leave you to do.

—Ricky Ortiz

I was in my cousin's house and it was holloween. The door Bell rings, my cousin open's the door and two teenager's in mask's. They come in and lock the door. me and my two cousin's are eating. The man pull's out a gun and points it at my cousin's head, they open the closets were my aunt keeps the drugs and the money and take everything, Me and my two cousin's are lift scared. The reason why those two robber's broke in was becuse they knew that there was drugs. Drugs are the reason ther is violence in the world. If don't have money they steal to buy drugs. But the most worst thing is that you can't do nothing about it because if you try the people will do it more because you're trying to stop it.

—José Figueroa

It was a friday Night and I was spending the night at my uncles house. I was in the hallway talking to my boyfriend and my uncle came out of his house with the gun and said "Didn't I tell you either come in the house or stay your ass out this building"!! by the time he said that my boy friend had went in his house. I ran behind my uncle cause I knew he was drunk so, he shot three times in the air and Said "now get you fuckin' ass in the house". I didn't know how to feel because to me it was normal, I have a gun but I leave it with my uncle. I only carry it with me to Partys.

—Keisha Damar

1 3

Hoping to Be Free

ALL THROUGH THE FALL SEMESTER, WHILE I WAS WORKING ON THE Thomas Jefferson play with the seventh and eighth grades and while the Drama Club continued to have its regular Friday afternoon meetings, Jessica and I met weekly with the students applying to LaGuardia High School to help them practice their monologues. Toward the end of November, Jessica told me that Celeste and Mayra were coming along beautifully but that Ricky hadn't yet even settled on the first of the two monologues he would need for the audition.

Even though Isaac had dropped out of the Drama Club, there had never been any embarrassment or bad feelings between us. He showed up in the writing room promptly every Friday and had memorized both of his monologues within the first two weeks. In the Bensonhurst play, his swimming practice had meant that his only speaking parts had been a few of the Chorus speeches. I had been impressed by the earnest passion he had given to them but, when I began working with him on the LaGuardia monologues, I discovered that earnest passion was all he could do. He had no understanding of the ironies or emotional subtleties in his monologue. His performance was forceful but flat-footed.

Xia, the other student I was coaching, was an entirely different story. She had an instinctive understanding of the character and situation of each of her monologues, and her presentation, at least on her good days, was rich with nuance and moving implications. The main problem

with Xia was that she was absent at least every other Friday and sometimes two Fridays in a row, which meant that she frequently missed
both her LaGuardia practice and Drama Club.

For her first monologue she edited together beautifully, and entirely
on her own, three Yusuf Hawkins speeches from the Bensonhurst play.
Her performance had lost none of its power. All I needed to help her
with was blocking and the masculinization of her accent and gestures.

It took Xia a while to settle on a second monologue, but finally she
chose Angela Cordero's piece about seeing her best friend shot as they
went out to the grocery store. I was pleased that Xia seemed to be
more moved by her fellow students' writing than by any of the monologues written by professional playwrights that Jessica and I had given
her. But even so, while I had no doubt that the LaGuardia judges would
be impressed by her ability to play a male as well as female role, I did
worry that her monologues were too similar and, perhaps, too mawk-
ish. But once Xia had made her decision, she was adamant, so I went
along with her.

When we first started working on Angela's monologue, Xia was a little stiff. I wanted to help her gain access to some of the powerful emotions latent in the story and began by asking her why she had chosen it.
"I don't know," she said. "It just seems real to me, I guess."

"Have you had any experiences like this?"

She took a deep breath, then spoke in that thoroughly matter-of-fact
manner of hers, though with the faintest smile: "Oh, I've seen lots of
people get killed."

"Anyone you know?"

"Yeah. My cousin. He was playing around with some friends and he
went into his father's bedroom. And . . . See, that's where his father
keeps his gun . . ." She paused. "And one of his friends picked it up and
accidentally shot him."

"Oh, God! That's horrible. I'm sorry."

Xia shrugged.

I tapped her copy of Angela's piece. "Have you ever seen anyone get
shot like this?"

"Well, one day I was walking down the street with my friend and her
father. And this man came out of a store and started to argue with him.
Then the man went back into the store and came out with a knife and
just stabbed him to death."

"You were there?"

"Yeah. He stabbed him right in front of his daughter."

"What did you do?"

"I ran screaming around the corner and called my mother."

"How did you feel."

"Pretty scared. You know, she was my best friend, and I knew her father real well too."

Curious as I may have been about other killings Xia might have seen, I worried that recalling such memories would upset her. I stopped questioning her and, instead, asked her to read the monologue once again, letting her feelings about the deaths she had witnessed flow into Angela's words. This time her performance was so powerful that it brought tears to my eyes—perhaps precisely because it brought none to hers. There was little sadness in her voice when she said, "She died and that day a part of my heart died too"—only deep weariness and a fatalism that was chilling in a child so young.

THE FOLLOWING FRIDAY, DURING MY REGULAR TEACHERS & Writers session with her class, I noticed that Xia was absent yet again. As the students crowded out of the room at the end of the class, I asked Joan, "Do you have any idea what's going on with Xia Sanchez? She's hardly ever here anymore."

A light went on in Joan's eyes: "Oh, Steve, don't get me started! Look at this." She flipped open her roll book and pointed to the entries beside Xia's name. "She's never here! Look, this month and last month she was absent more than she was at school." Looking at the roll book I saw that Xia had missed close to two-thirds of each month. Joan continued: "And when she does come, she's always late. Every single day she comes waltzing in five minutes after the bell, ten minutes after the bell. And she acts as if it doesn't matter that the whole class has to stop and watch her take her coat off and get into her seat. Every day, five minutes! Ten minutes! Why can't she just come on time!" Joan snapped her book shut and looked me in the eye: "Are you doing something special with her this year? I know you're doing something special. Well if you are, you should drop her from it right away. She doesn't deserve the privilege."

Nothing could have been farther from my intentions or from my way of dealing with difficult students, as Joan must have known. She didn't wait for an answer: "And you know, she's a liar. She collected thirty-nine dollars for the candy she sold to help pay for the Christmas dance, and then she said somebody stole it from her. And then the other day I asked her for her homework and she started looking through her notebook, acting like it was there. Then she said she must have left it home. But when I asked her a couple of questions about it, it became clear that she hadn't done it."

Although I was sure that Xia's absences and her missing $39 were not the product of the arrogant disregard to which Joan attributed them, I did become much more afraid for Xia after this conversation. Here was a girl who had so much of what it took to do well in life—to do far better than either of her parents—but she was still so vulnerable. I was sure that her absences had something to do with her chronically sick mother or grandmother. But even so, they were serious business. How was she ever to win the grades she needed to be admitted to LaGuardia if she continued to miss two out of every three days of school, or if she continued to alienate Joan Gold? As for the missing $39, could Xia and her mother and stepfather possibly have eaten up thirty-nine giant-sized chocolate bars? Maybe so, but what was so unbelievable, in a neighborhood like Xia's, about a thirteen-year-old getting mugged?

The worst result of my conversation with Joan was that, despite all the possible explanations for Xia's transgressions that I could come up with, I couldn't help beginning to wonder if the impression I had built up of her as a very talented and heroically dedicated girl had been nothing but wishful thinking and sentimentality.

The next time I saw Xia, the following Friday, during her regular Teachers & Writers class, I found myself watching her with what amounted to suspicion. Even her physical appearance seemed different to me: she was a tall girl with broad shoulders; I had always seen her as statuesque, but now she looked thick, thuggish. And I found myself getting irritated when I noticed that she was not listening to my presentation with rapt attention.

During the writing time, I stopped by her desk and said, "So I'll see you later for LaGuardia practice?" She answered me only by shifting her eyes away and giving me a noncommittal nod.

Had my change in attitude shown in my expression or voice? Had she taken my question as an accusation? I don't know. But I do know that Xia had never behaved with me like that before and that I was disturbed. I resolved to go talk to Rachel about her and find out what was going on in Xia's life outside school.

When I saw Xia for the LaGuardia practice, she was very distracted, agreeing with me somnambulistically when I made suggestions, as if she just wanted to shut me up.

We were working on Angela's piece and Xia was having trouble getting any feeling into the last paragraph, a hopeful assertion that violence can be stopped by people working together. All at once, as Xia was reading, I remembered that the last paragraph had been added on for the *Crimebusters* commercial and didn't really belong with the rest of the piece. I told Xia that if she wanted to leave it off, she could. She shrugged her shoulders and said, "Okay."

"Do you *want* to leave it off?" I asked. "You don't have to."

Another shrug. "I do."

But then she did a second reading and left the last paragraph in. She didn't even seem to notice. When I pointed it out she said, vaguely, "Oh, yeah."

I put my own copy of the piece down and looked her in the eye. "Listen, Xia, is anything wrong?"

A shrug. She lowered her gaze to the floor. "No."

"I know that Ms. Gold is mad at you. But I was wondering if anything else was bothering you."

"Mrs. Gold! She wants me to stay after school because I was five minutes late! She wants me to get my mother to sign this paper, but my mother won't sign it. She says that I should only have to stay as long after school as I was late."

I pointed out that being late disrupted the class.

"But I never miss anything. She hasn't even called the roll when I get in. I'm just two minutes late."

"Well, that's between you and Ms. Gold. I just want to make sure that nothing else is bothering you."

"No."

I didn't believe her but couldn't force her to talk to me. So I just said, "Listen, Xia, I want you to know that you are one of the best students I've ever had. I care a lot about you. If you are ever in any trouble, you can always come to me. I'll do anything I can to help you." She grunted. Maybe the faintest smile flickered on her face—not, I suspect, because of any pleasure at what I had said, but only because she knew a smile was expected.

After our session together, I went to talk to Rachel, who said that all the teachers were complaining about Xia. Rachel thought that Xia's problems had to do with her family moving out of the Pantheon.

The Pantheon was the welfare hotel a short distance from the school where Xia had actually been living at the time I made my cowardly attempt to visit her the previous year. It was a horrible place, filled with burnt-up, angry people. On two separate occasions, as I was walking past it, bottles had hurtled from upper story windows and crashed to the sidewalk beside me with such force that they left only star-shapes of white crystals on the pavement.

I had visited the Pantheon once at the end of the last school year, to drop off a video of the Bensonhurst performance for Xia. The clerk at the reception desk must have weighed three hundred pounds. He had a Fu Manchu mustache. A huge mirror-bright hunting knife lay open beside his hand on the counter. In a room behind him, two men in their mid-twenties, who had been moving a set of heavy shelves, stopped to stare at me. As I explained to the clerk what I wanted, my gaze occasionally strayed over his shoulder and, every time, I saw these two men staring hard right into my eyes. I was getting the same treatment from another youngish man, who leaned against the wall a few feet away from me. I felt like a fresh convict making his first entrance into the cell-block, and was glad to get out of there.

I would have thought Xia too would have been glad to escape that building, but Rachel said her stepfather had told her that the apartment Xia's family had moved to was in such a bad neighborhood that he never let Xia out to see her friends. The move also meant that she had to take two buses to get to and from school every day, which partly explained her lateness. As I spoke to Rachel I realized that this stepfather was a new thing in Xia's life. She hadn't mentioned him the previous year. I told Rachel what Xia had said about her stepfather being like the father in the play, and we agreed that it would probably be a good idea if the social worker who visited the school twice a week spoke to her.

That night I wrote in my diary: "There has always been a depth of unresponsiveness in Xia. She has, at times, the low affect of a trauma victim, or at least of someone who is used to hardship. You say something to her and it seems to slip into a void behind those ever watchful eyes. Her response always comes half a beat too late and always seems considered, calm, matter-of-fact—at least in some moods. I think that she is a very smart girl bearing an enormous burden, who has known sadness and horror that I can only have nightmares about. Her heart is good, but she is being put to a tremendous test right now, and I don't know what it is all about."

The following week Xia was not in her class again. Rachel told me that her stepfather had come to pick her up at school that morning because her mother had had to be rushed to the hospital with liver pains. This was terrible news because it meant that Xia's mother was probably still drinking heavily and might even be in danger of dying.

I WAS NOT XIA'S SOCIAL WORKER OR THERAPIST. I WAS HER teacher. If something seemed to be interfering with her schoolwork, I could venture a personal question, but I could not pry, no matter how concerned I may have been about her. There was one means, however, by which I might discover clues to her true state of mind: I could look through her writing folder, which I did many times that year. And because Xia was not only a good actor but an extraordinarily prolific writer, reading her work carefully gave me many insights into her character—especially into her fears and ideals—that I had not gained through my encounters with her.

Apart from her Thomas Jefferson work, most of the writing in Xia's folder was love poetry, all of it pretty generic. Some of the poems were even copied—with attribution—from the folder of a friend, and for the life of me, without that attribution, I wouldn't have been able to tell which poems were Xia's and which her friend's. I do not know to what extent Xia was involved in romance, but the poems do show that love—and more than just romantic love—was very important to her. Here is how she put it.

What is Love

Love is within our hearts,
not within sex.
Love is when two people care
for each other.

When two people know that without,
each other they'll never make it.
Love isn't a toy, nor a game,
Love is a gift, a gift from the heart

This poem could hardly be more trite, especially for an adolescent, and its triteness makes it hard to pay attention to what it says, or to know how seriously Xia meant it. The lines that most strike me are "Love is when two people *care / for each other. /* When two people know that without, / each other *they'll never make it.*" I could have written this myself when I was thirteen, and the lines would have been empty treacle, borrowed from half a dozen pop songs and Hallmark cards. But Xia's life had been very different from mine, and I suspect that the words "they'll never make it" meant something much more serious and frightening to her than they ever could to me.

The importance of caring for other people comes up again and again in her writing, most notably in a rambling piece that she wrote at the conclusion of the Jefferson High project.

Violence affects us in many ways. People just don't care anymore. First of all, I think that children are taking drug, shooting people and robbing, raping etc. . . . because of the parents. They feel that if their parents can do these thing, that they have the right to do it too.

I remember the day my cousin died. I was outside playing around when my cousin and some of his friends were playing around the house. One of his friends found a gun that was left in the house and thought it was a toy and shot my cousin in the chest, My cousin died in my Aunts bed.

I don't think Id ever forget that day, even if I wanted to.

I think people are killing because they want revenge. I say that because if a white man kills a black man a black man will go kill a white man or a domincan man kills a puerto rican man then it'll go on and on. An probably if someone does it once and doesn't get caught then he'll do it again and again.

People just don't care any more. All they care about is themselves.

I think that every one should intergrate and try their best to fight violence with love and may be we will win our country back and there wouldn't be so much violence.

"Fight violence with love": that sounds like something Xia might have heard in church or from her grandmother. But obviously it made sense to her. She did not reject it. It is reflected in the point she makes twice in the piece—"People don't care anymore"—to which, on its second appearance, she appends: "All they care about is themselves." The obvious implication of these statements is that if people cared about (or loved) other people, there wouldn't be so much violence and, consequently, such a need for revenge. What is interesting, however, is that Xia never actually says this. The only cause for violence that she mentions explicitly is the bad example of the parents. People "feel that if their parents can do these thing [take drugs, shoot, rob, and rape], that they have the right to do it too."

With a mother who, at the very least, abused alcohol and a father serving a twelve-year—or longer—jail sentence, it is easy to imagine why Xia might blame parents for not being the right sort of role models. It is also easy to speculate that Xia's parents were deficient in the love they gave her and that this is why she saw a lack of love as a cause of violence and drug addiction. But I don't think that was the case. For one thing, if Xia had not been given love, it is unlikely that she would have known what love is or have been capable of loving. For another, in my two telephone conversations with Xia's mother I felt that, while she may have been disorganized, weak willed, and overwhelmed by the strains of her life and her health, she was not unloving. She was clearly proud of Xia and kept talking about what a "good kid" she was.

I think that Xia's confidence that she was loved and worth loving are reflected in the following poem, but so is her anxiety about how little her virtues might count for in the world in which she lived.

Lonely in the dark

I walk around the street feeling
kind of good about myself,
But its all a lie.
No one cares about the way I
feel.
No one gives me a second chance
in life.
No one excepts me the way I am,
they want me to be the way

they are, they want me to look
like them, dress like them, act
like them and even ditch school
with them.
But no, there is no way I'm going
to be like them, cause I'm me,
smart and reliable.
Well, I guess I like to feel that
I am.

Whenever she was absent from school, Xia told Rachel and Joan either that she was sick or that she had to take care of her mother, her baby brother, or grandmother. The reference to ditching school makes me wonder if all of her absences weren't quite so defensible. If Xia was less resistant to the pressures of her crowd than this poem would indicate, she clearly was struggling against those pressures and used her writing both to examine the dangers she felt she was facing and justify her resistance of them.

As a result of the Thomas Jefferson Project and her involvement in the Drama Club, Xia became increasingly interested in writing plays as the year went on. The piece of writing she was most proud of that year was the following play that seems to spring from the central preoccupations of "Lonely in the dark."

The Drug Journey

DEMETRIUS—STAR		NATALIE	FRIENDS
MIKE			OF
TONY	} DRUG USERS	NANCY	DEMETRIUS
SHAMEL			

CELESS*—Co-Star—4
months pregnant

Setting:

       At the Pit (Hang Out)

---

*I have changed the name of this character to Celess because I do not think it insignificant that that character's original name differed by only one letter from the real name of Celeste.

Time:

8:30 AM

Scene ONE   (At the Pit)

Demetrius: Yo whats up? (Shaking hands with the guys and hugging girls).

Mike: Yo Demetrius Listen up. Come with us we're going to Central Park man. I got blunts* and the whole nine Yo.

Demetrius: I don't know man I got to go to shcool.

Mike: Come on man. We gonna have fun. Your mother never know less somebody tells her. So what you getting all scared about?

Demetrius: All right man. But make sure no body catch us O.K.

Shamel: Come on man just chill out and losen up. We got girls blunts and the whole nine. What more can you ask for?

Natalie: Come on are we going or not? It's getting kinda cold standing here

Other girls: Yeah man hurry up!

Mike: All right lets go.

Central Park
Scene two:

Natalie: Yo let me get a beer.

Tony: Here. You wanna blunt too? It'll cool you down

Natalie: Sure. Hay Nancy do you want some? This stuff is good.

Nancy: Yeah. Oh Demetrius why don't you come over and join us.

Demetrius: It's O.K. I don't smoke but I will like to have some beer

Mike: Here take the beer. Whats the matter? You scared a little blunts going to kill you.

Demetrius: No I'm not scared.

Mike: Then take the blunt!

Demetrius: Alright. (He smokes it) This stuff isn't so bad.

Shamel: See I told you. You just have to losen up a little and join the fun man.

*Blunts are a type of Phillies cigar that drug users often fill with marijuana.

Demetrius: Yeah I guess you were right. (Pauses). Yo Celess hows the baby.

Celess: The baby's doing fine.

Demetrius: Have you gone for a check up.

Celess: No! I don't need no check up.

Demetrius: What the hell you talking about, the baby could die if you don't take care of it

Celess: What is it to you it's not your baby?

Demetrius: You want to know what it is to me! Well you know what it is, it is that I care for you and I don't want any thing to happen to you.

Celess: Yeah thats nice thanks for the sympathy. (Walks away).

Demetrius: Celess! (Yells) (Celess keeps walking)

Nancy: I know you care for her and everything but foget about her for now and lets have some fun.

Demetrius: Your'e right. You know I think I could used another blunt.

Natalie: I have something better than blunt. It'll really cool you down.

Demetrius: What is it.

Natalie: Yo man you blind or something. It's coke.

Demetrius: Yo man that's too much for me!

Tony: Let a man show a little boy how it's done. Give me some Natalie. (He sniffs it).

Demetrius: Listen man I'm just getting sick of you and Mike alright. I see you later because I have more important things to do.

Tony: Well you have it your way (Demetrius leaves and looks for Celess)

[In "Scene 3" Demetrius hears from Natalie that Celess was killed in a "drunk driving car accident" and that her funeral is on Friday.]

Scene 4   After Funeral

Mike: Yo man the funeral's over so lets get something that will cool us down.

Tony: How 'bout some blunts and a *"40"**

---

*A "40" is a forty-ounce bottle of beer.

Mike: Yup I think that'll do me fine.

Demetrius: What the hell is your problem.

Mike: What the hell you talking 'bout.

Demetrius: Celess's dead and y'all acting like nothing happened.

Tony: Come on man just chill. She's dead and its over and done with. Don't worry 'bout her any more.

Mike: Yeah man just losen up.

Demetrius: You know what Im tired of both of you's. You don't know a dam thing about losening up. All you know about is smoking and drinking. (Pauses) Hate to see the day you two die. (Demetrius walks away, Tony, Mike walk away in opposite directly—curtains go down the End)

The main thing that strikes me about this play is how consistent it is with Xia's poems. Demetrius's strength is that he "cares" about Celess, his self-destructive friends, and himself. What his caring amounts to is a willingness, in all but one instance, to recognize and fully feel reality. His friends are always desperately trying to escape the reality of their situations by "cooling down" with drugs and drink. Celess is so "cooled down" that she doesn't "care" even when her friends offer sympathy. She dies in an accident that is associated—albeit unclearly—with drinking.

One of the reasons why Xia seemed to be so remarkably strong—or, as she put it herself, "smart and reliable"—was precisely that her ideas were so consistent. This girl knew what she thought about life, which was much more than many of her classmates, who were perfectly capable of wanting and believing utterly contradictory things simultaneously. But her faith in her own worthiness of love, her honesty, and the integrity of her beliefs by no means made her invulnerable to the dangers of city adolescence—as she was well aware. Her alter ego, Demetrius, does indeed succumb to the temptation to take drugs, and this play illustrates that Xia was at least familiar with marijuana. She could hardly not be. One of her classmates once told me that 80 percent of his friends smoked blunt.

While I am not comfortable drawing biographical conclusions based on any author's writing, I do believe that Xia's work tells us a lot about her ideals and her ideal vision of herself. In a thirteen-year-old, ideals and an idealized vision of self are not nearly such insubstantial attributes as they are in adults, because they are still capable of shaping the person the child will one day become. I worried, after talking to Joan, that I had sentimentalized Xia. Once I took a close look at the work in her folder, however, I realized that even if my vision of Xia was sentimental, it was also something more than that. One of the reasons I was so afraid for her was that I was afraid of what the strains she had to suffer in life would do to her ideals.

Here was a girl who, despite all the terrible things she had seen and experienced, was strong enough that she did not feel that she could only be strong—she was strong enough not to have wholly surrendered the Virtues of Compassion to the Virtues of Strength. Unlike many of her other classmates, who were unwilling to say that people really ought not be so violent or heartless to one another, she was not embarrassed by these beliefs. She did not consider them hopeless, a sign of weakness, a source only of despair. Rather, ideally at least, she was resolved to live according to them and to fight for them. That sort of clear-headed, optimistic resolve is all too rare among my students, especially among those whose lives are as hard as Xia's. In a very real sense my fears for Xia were fears for the human spirit.

Here is how Xia saw her main struggle.

Life in the Darkness

Sadness . . . Hoping to be free
from . . . this violence.
Wanting peace to take over and
stand up for its rights.
Realizing that just sitting down
and doing nothing isn't going to
change a thing.
Its time to wake up from
the darkness and fight for what
I believe in!
And during that fight If
I don't make it,
at least I know I tried
to achieve my goal for peace.

1 4

Miracle Workers

THE FAMILY PLAYS WERE TO BE PERFORMED IN THE SCHOOL library on Monday, December 21, three days before the start of the Christmas vacation. Most of the members of the Drama Club worked hard on their parts and approached the plays' "opening" with a surprising calm. Dependable Mayra Climente came to every meeting and had her part down perfectly weeks before the performance, as did Arlene Salter and Anna Harris, the two white seventh-graders. Lily Choi continued to alternate between giggles and sulks whenever she was asked to perform, but since she had a very small part, her behavior didn't detract much from the rehearsal of the play. The big problems were Ricky, Xia, and Celeste—the very children who had given the strongest performances in *On This Day a Poor Boy Died*.

As the fall semester wore on, Ricky started coming to rehearsals less and less often. In part this was because Xia's attendance was so irregular. Many an afternoon, Ricky and I would wait for Xia to show up, then finally give up and do the play ourselves. Ricky learned his part well this way, but it was hard for him to work up the right emotional responses with a six-foot-one male teacher playing the part of his little girl. Also, he—and I too, I must confess—began to wonder if there was any point in continuing to rehearse the play if it wasn't at all clear that Xia could be relied upon to show up for the performance.

When Xia did come to rehearsals, however, she was, as always, ex-

271

cellent. She and Ricky clearly enjoyed working with each other, and each brought out the best of the other's talent. They were also able to throw themselves completely into the father-daughter dance of bickering, begging, and betrayal without any of their negative feelings spilling over into their interaction outside the play—as had happened when Celeste played the daughter part.

But even so, Xia was a changed person during these last weeks of the semester. There was no playfulness in her, no excitement. She was still "smart and reliable"—at least on those days she did come to Drama Club meetings—but she was not happy. When she and Ricky were taking a break, or if I would have an extended conversation with Ricky about his performance, Xia would drift to another part of the room, sit on a desk or look out the window, her arms folded across her chest, her expression a mix of anger and exhaustion. There were times when I would talk to her about her performance and I would have the sense that she was getting so annoyed by all the demands that such conversations inevitably made of her that she was about to scream. She never did, however. She would always listen quietly, nod at appropriate moments, and answer my questions in a patient, even voice. Then she would resume her performance, always with a level of skill that I couldn't complain about, but without any evidence that she had heard a word I had said. I would watch her, wishing that I knew more about what was going on in her life and why she was absent so often, my attitude toward her wavering uncertainly between irritation and concern.

Celeste, also, was impossible to figure out. Although she never acted up as wildly as she had that afternoon she fled the Drama Club, she, like Lily, alternated between manic goofing and bleak sulks. During her rare moments of control, however, her performance was wonderful.

She had a real comic gift that hadn't been apparent during the Bensonhurst play. She had the role of the alcoholic artist father in the play about the divorced parents who reconcile at their daughter's birthday party. Throughout the play the father would have telephone conversations with his daughter, during which he would profess love and give her advice about life—all of which Celeste would transform into marvelous hypocrisy by having the father sip beer, dab at his canvasses, and perform other activities that clearly engaged him more than anything his daughter said. Good as these touches may have been, Celeste simply couldn't memorize her part. Right up until our final dress rehearsal, the day before the performance, she refused to go onto the stage without the script in her hands.

The difference between Celeste and Xia was that, although Xia did not come to Drama Club nearly as often as she should, when she was there, her performance was as good or better than it had been in *On This Day* . . . Celeste, on the other hand, knew that, despite her good moments, between her moods and her inability to memorize her lines, she was in danger of delivering a vastly worse performance than she had in the Bensonhurst play. Even when she was at her jokey wildest (slyly slipping other kids' props away just at the moment they needed them; emitting croaking belches in the middle of heartfelt speeches), I could see her own disappointment with herself in her eyes—a disappointment that only intensified the extremes of her moods, which in turn caused her to feel even more disappointed and, perhaps worst of all, to panic at how little control she had over herself.

Daniel, Jessica, and I were bewildered by the change in these kids with whom we had shared such an ecstatic triumph the year before. This was not at all the way any of us had imagined our relationship continuing with Celeste, Xia, and Ricky, and it was hard for us not to feel that we had done something wrong or had not done enough. Our staff meeting the Friday before the performance was gloomy. Between Xia's and Ricky's absences and Celeste's inability to memorize her lines, it was looking possible that the two best of our three plays might not be able to go on. Daniel said that Jessica or I could fill in for absent or panic-stricken actors—but that was hardly a satisfactory solution.

As soon as I arrived at school on the morning the plays were to be performed, I ran into Xia and Celeste in the hall. Both of them were holding on to plastic bags that contained their costumes and were giggling and bouncing around just like their old selves. I was about to ask them if Ricky had come to school when I saw him strolling down the hall wearing the green fedora that he had told me he was going to borrow from his grandfather to make himself look more mature. Seeing that he too was smiling and was clearly—in his own low-keyed way—excited about the performances, my own spirits began to pick up.

The plays were to be performed in the library at one-fifteen for the seventh grade, at two o'clock for the eighth grade, and at six in the evening for the cast's parents. As we had had only one previous opportunity to rehearse in the space where the plays were actually going to be presented, I had booked the library for the whole day, beginning at 10 A.M., so that Daniel and Jessica would be able to do at least two or three intensive rehearsals of each play. Unfortunately, I had to teach my regular P.S. 227 classes that morning, so I was able to visit the rehearsals only intermittently.

Just as on the day of the Bensonhurst performance, Daniel made substantial last-minute changes in the blocking of all the plays, but especially Xia's and Ricky's, which, because of their absences, had never been thoroughly blocked. Once again I worried that all these changes would confuse the kids but was comforted by the obvious good spirits of everyone in the room—even frantic, overworked Daniel.

DANIEL, JESSICA, SIOBHAN, ERIN, AND I WERE STILL HELPING THE cast members get down their cues and most difficult lines when the seventh grades began to file into the library. Within minutes the room was filled with a noisy but expectant audience, and there was no more time to rehearse. Ready or not, the plays had to go on.

The kids were fabulous. Just as with the Bensonhurst play, everyone's performance was far better than it had ever been in rehearsal, and with every performance the actors got deeper and deeper into their roles.

The only exception was Ricky. Before the first performance (for the seventh grade) he had beads of sweat on his nose and was annoying all the other cast members by bossing them around. As the lights came up at the start of his play, he hesitated a long moment on the edge of the performance area and let out an extended, openmouthed "ah" before making his entrance. All through his performance he would stop midsentence, seeming to have forgotten his line, only to complete the sentence perfectly a moment later and blink anxiously at the audience.

After the first performance, I took him out into the hall and asked him what was the matter. He pushed back his fedora, scratched his aspiring goatee, and looked down at the floor. "Well, see, I got, like, this thing . . . epilepsy."

Ricky and I had never talked about his illness before. I said, "I know. Ms. Suarez told me."

"And my medication's all messed up and I keep having these little tiny seizures. You wouldn't even notice them. I just kind of stare for a little bit, and then they go away. But they get worse when I'm nervous."

To my knowledge, I had never seen anyone have a petit mal seizure before. His behavior on the stage had looked like simple nerves to me, so I wondered if he wasn't using his epilepsy as an excuse. This didn't really matter, however, since one way or the other his confidence was clearly a determining factor in his performance. While the two other plays were being performed for the eighth grade, I stayed out in the hall and read the daughter's part in Ricky's play so that he would be sure of his cues. We read through the play twice and he didn't make a single mistake. When at last it was time for him to go on, he entered the stage without hesitation and, like all the other club members, gave a performance that surpassed all of his rehearsals. His classmates filled the room with claps and shouts, while he and Xia took their bows, clearly the hits of the afternoon.

As with the Bensonhurst performance, we kept the cast at the school until the evening show, feeding them pizza and soda and letting them dance to my son's boom box and tapes. At one point, while we were all sitting around in the writing room, Celeste announced in a tone of mischievous conspiracy: "I'm going to let you all in on a secret. My mother promised me she was going to come to this play tonight, but she said she didn't have anything to wear. So I went down to the store and bought her this really nice two-piece outfit, with this little black skirt and this really cute little black jacket that goes with it. And I didn't tell her nothing about it, just put the package on her bed for her to find. So this is it: I want everybody to watch and see if she wears it when she comes! You'll recognize it right away. It's this really nice, cute outfit!"

I interpreted this whole speech as Celeste's way of expressing her anxiety about whether her emotionally disturbed mother would come at all, and so I spent the rest of the evening wondering what would happen to Celeste's performance if her mother didn't show up.

At quarter to six, the actors' parents and other family members began to filter into the library. Ricky's mother, father, sister, and grandparents came, as they had to the Bensonhurst play. Mayra's mother hadn't come to the Bensonhurst play, but she came this evening, escorted by Mayra's older brother, who was wearing a trim, colorful Marine Corps dress uniform. Xia's mother didn't come to either performance, with the same excuse on both occasions: "She's too sick."

Xia and Celeste stuck together as the other cast members' families arrived. Celeste's pale face was fretful and drawn. Xia was all assurance and smiles. "Don't worry," I heard her tell Celeste. "She's coming. She probably just got lost."

"I wonder where she is?" Celeste said anxiously, having not heard or not taken seriously her friend's consolation.

Xia didn't say anything, just patted Celeste on the back.

By six o'clock, most of the seats in the library had been taken and the room burbled with conversation. Celeste was constantly darting out into the hall to see if her mother had arrived and returning with increasingly unhappy expressions on her face. For her sake, Daniel and I decided to delay the start of the program as long as we could. At five after six I stepped out of the library, for no other purpose than to see if Celeste's mother was coming.

There is nothing more still than a public school hallway at night. During the day there is always a child hurtling out of the stairwell, or a teacher rushing to her classroom, arms stuffed with worksheets, or a couple of little children holding hands as they return from the lavatories. Every few minutes a whole class will appear, straggling double-file behind a teacher on their way to or from the cafeteria, the gym, a class trip. Even when the hallway is empty, there is always motion, noise and light spilling out of the open or shut classroom doors. But at night, all the classroom doors are closed and dark. There is not a sound. If a breeze is blowing it makes no visible sign. By contrast to the day, the hall at night is so still that it seems to have become a photograph of itself.

This was just the scene I saw when I stepped out of the library at five after six. I was already heading back inside when I heard the squeak of the stairwell door. Taking a second look down the hall, I saw a lost-looking woman in a slightly-too-small black skirt and jacket hesitating outside the stairwell. Sending Arlene inside to get Celeste, I hurried toward this woman, who looked forty, but may have been a lot younger. "Hello! Are you Celeste's mother?" I asked. She smiled gratefully and stepped toward me extending her hand. But before we could introduce ourselves, Celeste had run down the hall and thrown her arms around her mother's neck.

"Mamí, you came!" Stepping back, she nodded at her mother's clothes. "How do you like it! Isn't it beautiful! Weren't you surprised!"

I don't know how I expected this woman to behave, after all the stories I had heard about her anger and her desolation, but as she and Celeste walked arm in arm into the library, she looked for all the world like any other proud and happy mother.

Xia was still sitting on the table where she and Celeste had spent much of the evening and hardly seemed to notice as the other cast members crowded excitedly around the excited Celeste. But then, with a slight pursing of her lips, she slid off of the table and, taking hold of Celeste's mother's hand, kissed her on the cheek.

AFTER THE PERFORMANCE, DANIEL, JESSICA, AND I WENT OUT for a celebratory drink. We were happy—not as deliriously happy and proud as we had been after the Bensonhurst performance, but pleased with how well the kids had done and how excited they had been. But at the same time we felt that we had had a near escape, that any number of things could have—and nearly had—gone disastrously wrong. These were the wages of experience. We now understood that we were not miracle workers, just teachers doing our best in difficult circumstances. I felt this more than anyone, perhaps, because I knew that the biggest challenge of the year—the production of the Thomas Jefferson play—was ahead of us and that Daniel wouldn't be there to help me. We toasted the kids, then toasted Daniel—wishing him a happy and productive stay in the south of France—then hurried off to our separate dinners, families, friends.

I SPENT MUCH OF THE CHRISTMAS VACATION EDITING AND TYPING the Thomas Jefferson play, which I distributed to the seventh and eighth grades on my return to school. Before I could turn my attention to the production of the play, however, I had to attend to some unfinished business.

The first Friday after the vacation I met with Isaac and Xia for a final coaching session before their auditions for LaGuardia High School that weekend. Isaac's performance was fine. With the help of his mother, he'd done a lot of work on the monologues over the vacation and made some effective changes in the blocking, though none that helped make his two ostensibly comic pieces any less humorless.

Xia, on the other hand, reeled off her monologues as if they were grocery lists that she had been forced to memorize as a punishment. Nothing I said could induce her to perform them with any more feeling. I was very worried when she left the writing room. I didn't know what was going on with her, but it was clear to me that if she didn't pull herself together, she wouldn't have a hope of getting into LaGuardia.

Just before the Drama Club meeting that afternoon, I ran into Jessica in the writing room stairwell. She too was in a state of panic over her LaGuardia candidates. Ricky not only hadn't memorized his monologues; he still hadn't even chosen one of them. But worst of all, Celeste, who had been doing wonderfully during her practices, had now decided that she did not want to apply to LaGuardia at all. Jessica was absolutely baffled by this reversal. Celeste's only explanation: "I just don't want to."

That afternoon's Drama Club meeting was supposed to be the cast party for the family plays, but the pizza, cookies, and soda were gobbled up so fast that it soon became obvious that we would have to come up with some other activity if we wanted to last the hour or so that remained of the club's normal running time. Partly with the idea of convincing Celeste to recant, I suggested that the LaGuardia applicants might benefit by practicing their monologues in front of a larger audience. Mayra and Xia seemed excited by the idea. Ricky said, "I can't do it. I don't know my monologue" (I told him he could read from the script), but Celeste didn't respond to my suggestion at all.

While I got the other kids to clean up some of the garbage and push back the desks to clear a performance area, I heard Jessica trying to talk Celeste into auditioning. "This is important," she said. "We're not talking about some little performance here. We're talking about the next four years of your life."

I came over and interjected. "It's not just the next four years; it's the whole of your life. I've lived long enough to see how decisions that may seem insignificant when you are very young can change the course of your life. And this is one of them. If you don't get into a good school, a whole series of doors are just going to slam in your face. You have real talent, Celeste. Don't waste it."

"But I don't want to go to LaGuardia," Celeste said. "I applied to eleven other schools besides LaGuardia, including Fashion and Seward

Park." (These were the two others that Xia had applied to.) "I don't want to go there."

"Look," I said, "nobody says you *have* to go to LaGuardia, but why cut down your options? LaGuardia really is a very good school. Go to the audition. If you get in, then decide if you want to go. If you don't, well, you haven't lost anything except a Saturday morning."

Celeste looked away from me and, in a very weak voice, said, "I don't want to."

I thought perhaps the weakness of her denial meant that Jessica and I had made some progress, but when I said, "Come on. Why don't you just do the monologues for the club?" she answered, "I hate my monologues!" It was clear that there was no use protesting. Jessica and I let her sit by herself and went to watch the other students.

Xia went first, performing both her monologues with real feeling—not as well as she was capable of, but well enough to revive my hopes.

Ricky did a fabulous reading of a speech from the play *Search and Destroy,* in which the character (a woman in the play, but the sex wasn't important) tries to sell a Hollywood executive on his idea for a lurid and grossly sexual science-fiction horror movie. Ricky summoned up just the right degree of enthusiasm for the movie's most awful details to make the monologue sickly funny—but alas, he was only doing a reading and had nothing to follow it up with.

Mayra was the great surprise of the afternoon. I often underestimated her, in part because her dependability meant that I simply didn't have to give her much thought, but also because her small smile, nestled like a button between her pudgy little-girl cheeks, and her voice, which would alternate between baritone squawks and soprano squeaks when she got excited, made it difficult to take her seriously, at least until you saw her act. Mayra was dependable and a hard worker, but she also had soul. She was able to give herself entirely to her part and play it with all of her heart.

She began her performance with a monologue from *Angie's Song,* in which a teenage girl describes how a blow from her father caused her to have a miscarriage but how she still sometimes talks to her baby and knows that it would have become a smart and good girl. Then, in only the time that it took to deepen her voice and throw back her shoulders, Mayra transformed herself from this frail, tragic girl to Keith Mondello, "the flyest guy around." I couldn't believe that the judges could witness so thorough a transformation and not be impressed. For the first time I thought that Mayra had a real chance of getting into LaGuardia.

Celeste sat out all the performances behind Joan Gold's desk. But after hearing Mayra and Xia do speeches from the Bensonhurst play, she came up to me and asked me if I could give her a script so that she could practice her old Gina Feliciano monologues. I borrowed Mayra's copy of the script and xeroxed the relevant pages for Celeste, telling her that I thought she should stick to at least one of her original monologues, since doing two Gina Feliciano monologues wouldn't show off her real talent. Her only response was to wrinkle up her face and tell me, for the second time: "I hate my monologues."

As I walked home after Drama Club in the flat, frigid winter dusk, I thought a lot about the limits of my relationship to my students. I had spent a semester trying to help Celeste, Xia, Mayra, Ricky, and Isaac get into a better school—and now they were on their own. I could do nothing more. Perhaps Jessica and I had done enough for Isaac and Mayra. They seemed as ready as they would ever be. But something had gone wrong with Xia, Ricky, and Celeste. Maybe there was something else we could have done to help them. Maybe not. But in any event, it no longer mattered. It was too late.

That night I wrote in my diary, "In the end I can't save these kids from drowning. I can hold out my hand to them, but I can't make them take it." In retrospect this remark seems arrogant and naive to me because it implies that I actually had the power to save my students, whereas, in fact, my extended hand only signified my desire to help, not my ability to actually make a difference.

IT DIDN'T TAKE JESSICA OR ME LONG TO DISCOVER THE TRUE limits of our abilities. Although the LaGuardia admissions wouldn't be announced for months, we learned everything we needed to know the following week.

Total disaster.

Mayra had been cut off before she'd even finished her monologue from *Angie's Song.* The judges never got to witness her stunning change of sex and mood. Neither Jessica nor I had known that there was a one-minute time limit for each monologue. Mayra had been cut off after exactly two minutes.

Celeste, as we had expected, didn't even go to the auditions. Ricky had gone but hadn't brought his proper papers, so wasn't allowed in. Isaac had gone, brought his papers, done both his monologues, but predictably, the judges were not impressed. He wasn't invited to do a reading with a current LaGuardia student.

The most frustrating story was Xia's. She *had* impressed the judges and *had* been invited to the second reading. "They begged me to come," she said. "They loved my monologues, but I couldn't stay. I had something to do that afternoon, so I left."

"You left?" Jessica said incredulously.

"Yeah. Well, I'd already finished the audition. And I had somewhere I had to go."

Xia seemed truly not to understand that this invitation to do a reading was a part of the audition—the most important part. I remembered that first Drama Club meeting of the year, during which she and all the other applicants had seemed only to endure rather than actually listen to Jessica's explanation of the two phases of the audition. Perhaps Xia had not taken in the importance of the second phase of the audition then, but I too had mentioned it several times during our weekly coaching sessions. It was possible that I hadn't gone into it in detail, because there wasn't much I could do to help Xia prepare for it, but could she really have failed to understand that the reading with the LaGuardia student was essential?

In the end, neither Jessica nor I bothered to disabuse Xia of her misconception. Jessica called her contacts at LaGuardia but was told it was too late; the records of all the candidates who did not go on to the second phase of the audition were discarded immediately. Xia was no longer a part of the process, and there was no way she could be brought back in.

I don't know how the kids felt about not getting into LaGuardia, but Jessica and I were devastated. We blamed ourselves completely for what had happened to Mayra and, to a lesser extent, to Xia. We felt terrible about all those doors that had just slammed in our students' faces, especially since every one of the students (with the possible exception of Isaac, whose mother had a good job with the city government) needed all the help they could get to escape the fear, frustration, and simple deprivation they had been born into.

But most of all, we were astounded. Ricky, Celeste, and Xia—our best actors! Our greatest successes! The kids to whom we were most attached! They had all panicked, wilted, failed! It was a grave lesson in humility.

Xia's case was the most mysterious. Remembering her depressed performance the day before the auditions, I couldn't help feeling that her failure to go on to the second phase was somehow a product of fear, that she had known she should accept the judges' invitation but had used the vagueness of her memory about what Jessica and I had said as an excuse to give in to fear—to feign ignorance, even to herself, and leave. I might have been wrong. Perhaps Xia's was just a case of normal adolescent absentmindedness. But that was my gut feeling.

Ricky and Celeste clearly panicked at the last minute, just as Yolanda Castro had the year before on the eve of the Bensonhurst play. This is a dynamic I have witnessed again and again in my teaching: exceptionally talented or intelligent children collapsing in the face of challenges they might well have met if only they had had more faith in themselves. This is perhaps the most insidious heritage of poverty: this dry rot of confidence, this deep-seated belief of even some of the brightest poor and minority children not only that they can't succeed but that they don't deserve to.

When I went to talk to Rachel Suarez about the results of the auditions, she leaned back in her chair and said, "Look, Steve, it's for the best. These kids would have died at LaGuardia. They don't get the kind of training at a small school like this to handle a big, demanding school like that. They need to be coddled—*you* know that. At LaGuardia they would just fall through the cracks."

I left Rachel's office greatly comforted by the knowledge that she didn't blame me for what had happened, but I couldn't entirely accept her rationale.

Maybe she was right about LaGuardia. But did she really think that the kids would get any more coddling at whatever high schools they went to instead? Also, I couldn't help wondering if the mere fact that a prestigious institution like LaGuardia had recognized their talent and offered them time to pursue it, wouldn't have been all the coddling our students—and Xia in particular—might have needed.

But most of all I objected to the class agenda implicit in Rachel's resignation. It seemed to me that part of what she was saying (although I know that she never would have meant to say this) was that, at La-

Guardia, Ricky, Celeste, Mayra, and Xia would have been like so many Leonard Basts, the working-class character in E. M. Forster's *Howards End,* whose taste in art led him to mix with a higher social class, bringing disastrous consequences on all involved.

I have always hated Forster's veneration for upper-class refinement and tradition. And I have always believed that, significant as class distinctions may be—even here in the United States at the end of the twentieth century—we must never grant them legitimacy and must resist them at every turn. To a certain extent, all of my work in the classroom had been an attempt to help my students transcend the limits of their social position. And I had truly believed that of all my students, Xia, at least, possessed the talent and the strength to overcome whatever obstacles class might have put in her way at LaGuardia. Perhaps that was innocent and romantic of me, perhaps not. In any event, when I left the school after my talk with Rachel, I had to face the fact that I had failed in one of my dearest ambitions for my students, even if they had not necessarily failed themselves.

Will My Name Be Shouted Out?

BY THE SEVENTH AND EIGHTH GRADES
AT THE WALT WHITMAN ACADEMY

I EDITED *WILL MY NAME BE SHOUTED OUT?* FROM STUDENT WORK over the Christmas vacation. This play proved far easier to assemble than *On This Day a Poor Boy Died,* in part because the seventh and eighth grades had both worked on the play for the whole duration of the project, so I had much more material to choose from. But the Thomas Jefferson writing was also considerably more powerful and coherent than the Bensonhurst work had been. The eighth-graders, in particular, seemed to have learned a great deal from their work on the earlier play.

I did, however, have one grim moment during the vacation. I spent a whole day rereading the students' compositions, extracting the best of them, and putting them into piles on my living room floor according to where they fell in the narrative. Only after I had gone through every single folder in all four classes did I notice that, where the scene explaining Khalil's fear of Ian and Tyrone ought to have been, there was nothing but a patch of empty rug. This was the moment when I first recognized the consequences of my reluctance to play the literary and moral dictator.

It seemed that my students had indeed been just as uncomfortable as I with the idea of Ian's and Tyrone's villainy. While many students had written monologues in which the two boys professed innocence, and several had had Khalil express his fear that his friends wanted to kill him, no one had written a monologue or a scene that gave Khalil the remotest reason to be afraid.

I don't know how I had failed to notice this gaping hole in the plot when the students were still working on the play, but my discovery left me with only two alternatives.

I could delay assembling the play until after the vacation, when I could ask one or more of my classes to write the missing scene. That, however, would have meant postponing the play tryouts at least a week and thereby cutting down the time left to rehearse the play.

Or I could shamelessly usurp my students' imaginative authority by writing the missing scene myself.

It is with some hesitation that I confess I chose the latter alternative. I simply didn't want to lose precious rehearsal time, and I was fairly certain that, as successful as the Thomas Jefferson Project may have been, my classes would balk at going back to work they thought they had already completed.

I did my best to minimize my own contribution to the play by searching the students' work for passages that I would only have to alter slightly. I finally settled on the following lines from a monologue spoken by Tyrone: "It was Khalil's fault I got arrested. If only he warned me on time! But he was a punk. He so scared, man, he just run without saying nothing." Out of these lines, I constructed the following dialogue, spoken while, unbeknownst to Ian and Tyrone, one of their classmates was listening:

IAN: It was Khalil's fault. If he only warned us on time!
TYRONE: I told you he was a punk. Man, he's the one I oughta be smoking!
IAN: That's the truth! He so scared, man, he just run without saying nothing.
TYRONE: Yeah, he let us both down. You and me, we both oughta smoke him.
IAN: Yeah . . .

Since, apparently, nobody in any of my classes had wanted Ian and Tyrone to be guilty of actually plotting Khalil's murder, I went on to completely fabricate the following bit of dialogue, which reestablished their innocence. It was to be spoken after the classmate had run off to spread the fruits of his eavesdropping all over the school.

[IAN continuing from above:] How'd you get out of jail?

TYRONE: Bail. My moms got up the money.

IAN: *(Pause. Thinking.)* You don't really want to buck Khalil, do you?

TYRONE: I don't know.

IAN: 'Cause the truth is, he wasn't any more punk than the rest of us. We was all scared. That's the truth, man.

TYRONE: I guess you right, man.

The rest of the play was constructed out of the students' monologues and dialogues in exactly the same fashion as *On This Day a Poor Boy Died,* except that, because the work was so much stronger, I didn't have to meld separate monologues and dialogues together quite so often. Again, as in the Bensonhurst play, I did remove all four-letter words from the characters' speeches and I made a few small edits and other adjustments so that the play would seem to be one continuous composition. Because Khalil's mother's name had not been printed in the clips I read, my first seventh-grade class gave her the name Alexandra.

Will My Name Be Shouted Out?

CHARACTERS

IAN MOORE

TYRONE SINKLER

KHALIL SUMPTER

LINDA ROWE (IAN'S MOTHER)

ETHEL SINKLER (TYRONE'S MOTHER)

ALEXANDRA SUMPTER (KHALIL'S MOTHER)

MIKE—IAN AND TYRONE'S FRIEND

LIQUOR STORE CLERK

STUDENT 1

STUDENT 2

MINISTER

ASSORTED FUNERAL GUESTS AND STUDENTS

The stage is dark. At lights-up there are three chairs on the stage, two of them side by side, about five feet apart, and the third placed some distance away, perhaps at an angle.

IAN enters from offstage, walks slowly to center stage, faces the audience, and pauses a moment before unfolding an ordinary piece of school composition paper.

IAN: This is a poem I wrote to read at my grandmother's funeral about a year before I got shot myself. It's called "Fear."

> What I fear began when my grandmother
>   died
> Obviously, it was the fear of death
> Death is something I just can't handle
> When she died, it was so unbelievable
> I fear death because I don't know
> What will happen when I go
> It is something I can't face
> When I die, will I be thought about?
> Will my name be shouted out?
> Death will come at any time
> No matter how far you're up the ladder.

(At the conclusion of the poem there is a short moment of silence, then CAST MEMBER 1 enters and begins to tell his story as he makes his way across the stage to take his place beside IAN. The same is done by all succeeding Cast Members, who, forming a line on either side of IAN, eventually fill the whole stage.)

CM 1: It was about 11 P.M. and me and my father was coming from parking the car. My father was singing to me, and as we went into the building I asked him for fifty dollars. He asked me for what and I told him for some sneakers. So he gave it to me. I was real happy. But as we went up the stairs, I saw someone come in the building. And then it happened. A gun went off and I just ducked. My mother came out. She was screaming to come in. I ran in the house. My mother asked me, where's my father? I was saying, "I don't know. I don't know." That's when I realized that my father had gotten shot. I went crazy. I was going wild. My brother got my father's gun from the house and went looking for the man that killed my father.

C M 2 : My sister was shot and killed by her husband. I was away at camp and I came home two days later. My mother didn't want to tell me or my sister 'cause my sister would not have been able to drive to pick me up. But when I came in the house everyone was crying. I didn't know what they were crying for, so I asked them. They told me. I didn't cry at first. But I cried later on, when I was alone.

C M 3 : About two months ago I was going back to my house. It was about 4:15 P.M. I entered the 7 train at Times Square. I was not alone in the car. There was at least seven others. Two guys came into the car. One sat next to me and said, "Hey, kid, give me your money." "I don't have any money," I said. At that moment I saw the gun. He put the gun in my head and said again, "Give me your money kid." "I don't have any money," I said. He searched me and found nothing. He and his friend left the train. Nobody asked me if I was okay and no one took any action.

C M 4 : Two years ago my grandmother and I went to buy something. When we came back, my grandfather was standing outside with his hand over his mouth. We asked him what happened and he said, "We got held up. They tied me up." When we went upstairs the girl that was renting a room was crying. She was nearly raped.

C M 5 : I know this boy who got shot in the face. They tied him up and put him in the back of his own car.

C M 6 : I was walking on the street with my friend and all of a sudden two guys pulled out guns and started firing. My friend and I ran. I never said nothing about it to my grandmother, because I knew she wouldn't let me go down again. To this day no one in my family knows.

C M 7 : I live in the projects and I hope I don't get caught in the cross fire. My building was almost burned down because crack addicts were in the stairway smoking from a pipe, which they left there. Every day I walk home with my head down and my hood over my head so that they can't get a new customer.

C M 8 : My cousin and some of his friends were playing around the house. One of his friends found a gun that was left in the house and thought it was a toy and shot my cousin in the chest. My cousin died in my aunt's bed.

CM 9: I went to a friend's house to pick something up. He put his hand in his cabinet and pulled out a revolver and put it to my head. He said, "Are you scared to die?" I said, "No," in a low voice. The gun was right to my temple. Then he pulled the trigger . . . it was empty.

CM 10: I was at my cousin's house and it was Halloween. The doorbell rings. My cousin opens the door and two teenagers come in and lock the door. Me and my two cousins are eating. The man pulls out a gun and points it at my cousin's head. They open the closets where my aunt keeps the drugs and the money and take everything. Me and my two cousins are left scared.

CM 11: I was spending the night at my uncle's house. I was in the hallway talking to my boyfriend and my uncle came out of his house with the gun and said, "Didn't I tell you either come in the house or stay out of this building!" By the time he said that my boyfriend had went in his house. I ran behind my uncle 'cause I knew he was drunk. So he shot three times in the air and said, "Now get in the house." I didn't know how to feel because to me it was normal. I have a gun, but I leave it with my uncle. I only carry it with me to parties.

CM 12: When my brother was shot six months ago I was thinking of what was going to happen to our family. Who is going to be the next person to die? Am I going to die the same way he did?

ENTIRE CAST: *(Loudly, with a seriousness bordering on anger)* WHEN I DIE WILL I BE THOUGHT ABOUT? WILL MY NAME BE SHOUTED OUT?

(Lights down)

(At lights-up, the cast has all taken places. IAN and TYRONE are seated in the two adjoining chairs, each with his mother standing beside him. KHALIL, with his mother at his side, is sitting in the separate chair. The other members of the cast are scattered around the stage, murmuring as if making small talk at a funeral. As IAN'S mother, LINDA, steps forward to speak, all fall silent.)

LINDA: I come home exhausted from work. I go in my house and go to the kitchen to get a glass of water. Suddenly I hear the phone ringing. I didn't feel like talking to anybody, but for some reason I felt like if this might be important. I pick it up. The person on the phone sounds nervous and asks me, "Are you Ian's mother?" I say, "Yes." He says, "Well I just want to tell you that your son got shot." Then he hanged up! I start thinking for a minute and sit down. Then I hear the phone again. I pick it up and say, "What do you want from me?" Then they ask me, "Is this Mrs. Rowe?" I say, "Yes." "This is the police and we want to inform you that your son Ian is dead." *(Steps back)*

ETHEL: *(Stepping forward)* I knew it would come to this. All the time I have been going to Tyrone's school because he got in trouble with other kids. I tried to help him by keeping him out of the streets, but he always seemed to get in trouble. And it came to a point where I just didn't know what to do. *(Pause)* When the phone rang I thought it was my boss. Maybe he didn't want me to work today. I could hardly hear what the person was saying. It was like he had an apple in his throat. Then I heard it. My son was dead. I hanged up the phone. I thought it was a joke. I started to sweat, tremble, and cry.

ALEXANDRA: *(Stepping forward)* All these thoughts spinning in my head. With Khalil in jail and can't be bailed out. I just want to drop right here on this floor. But I can't because Khalil is my son and I have to take care for what's goin' on right now. I remember when I first saw him after his arrest and him asking me, "Mom, you don't blame me for shooting them, right? I mean, don't you think they had it coming?" And all I remember is me saying, "It's too late for you to ask me that now. What's been done is already done and I don't know if I can do any more but pray . . ."

LINDA: Oh, Ian! I remember when you were a little baby, you looked so adorable. You always liked to smile. You were always happy. I remember when we were at the park and we were playing tag, and you would say, "Boo!" when you saw me. I loved you so much.

ETHEL: I still remember a lot of crazy things Tyrone did as a child. He was born here in Brooklyn—Linden House projects—which wasn't too bad when we first came here but is now very bad. When Tyrone was about eight years old he met Ian . . .

(At the beginning of ETHEL's last sentence, IAN and TYRONE rise from their chairs and move toward center stage. All the rest of the

cast, including KHALIL, step back to form a ring of observers around center stage. MIKE steps out of the crowd dribbling a basketball. IAN walks around the inner edge of the crowd as if he hasn't noticed the other two.)

TYRONE: Mike, you can't shoot a basket for your life!

MIKE: I'm better than you, you fat slob.

TYRONE: I bet you that kid coming down the block is better than you.

MIKE: Then call him.

TYRONE: Hey, boy, come over here!

(IAN walks toward them.)

MIKE: Can you shoot hoops?

IAN: Hell yeah!

TYRONE: What's your name?

IAN: My name is Ian.

TYRONE: Do you want to have a shootout with my friend, Mike?

IAN: Okay.

MIKE: You go first, Ian.

IAN: No, you go first.

MIKE: Okay. *(Shoots five times. Shows frustration on missing twice.)* Three out of five! Beat that!

IAN: *(After shooting five baskets)* Hah! I beat you! I got five out of five.

TYRONE: *(Pats IAN on the back)* Good shooting!

(Lights down)

(At lights-up IAN is alone in center stage as he was when he read his poem. All the rest of the cast is offstage.)

IAN: My name is Ian Moore. I live in a rough neighborhood in Brooklyn. Where I live there is a lot of killing, robbery, and drugs. When I go to bed at night the only thing I hear is gunshots. At this moment my family is in bad shape. My mom is on welfare and my father works for the city. He is a garbage man. My best friend, Tyrone, has big problems at his home too. His father is alcoholic. One day I was walking home with Tyrone. When we went to his house, Tyrone saw his father beating up his mother. Tyrone started crying. Then his father said, "Shut up! Your mother is a ho!" Then Tyrone started fighting with his father.

TYRONE: *(Entering)* My friend Ian wrote a poem about dying and I admire it. But in a way it gets me scared. But I'm not going to worry about it.

(The WHOLE CAST enters the stage and starts walking back and forth as if they were in a crowded school corridor. There is some shoving, some anger displayed, and some flirting. TYRONE joins in with the crowd, leaving IAN alone at center stage.)

IAN: Today is me and Tyrone's first day in Thomas Jefferson High School. I hope I like it here. Tyrone told me that he was going to try to be a big shot and show that no one can mess with him. But I don't think he should do that because there are other people with guns and knives. Tyrone can be such a jerk at times.

(IAN joins the crowd. The stage clears and LINDA enters.)

LINDA: I wish we didn't live in this neighborhood. That way this wouldn't have happened. But we don't have enough money to live in a better place. I remember when Ian was just a baby, my husband left us. I got a job, but still couldn't make enough money to take care of us. That is why I got married again. For the past months I've been thinking about this. I grew Ian up the best way I could . . . but I guess that wasn't enough.

(LINDA exits. The crowd returns. IAN emerges from the crowd to resume his position at center stage. Something in his clothes and manner makes it clear to the audience that he is older than when he last spoke.)

IAN: My name is Ian Moore. Me and Tyrone have been brothers for a long time. We were raised up together in the projects in East New York. Not such a great neighborhood. But I got my props and I'm not gonna have no problems. Me, my gun, and Tyrone have gone a long way. *(The crowd thins. TYRONE is working the combination to his locker. As IAN approaches, continuing his monologue, TYRONE opens the locker.)* One day a new kid came into school. He was dressed kind of flavor, but I'm not gonna sweat it. I met Tyrone at the lockers to put my gun inside . . . You know, just in case we have beef. Then I left my homeboy and went to my class, but I couldn't stop thinking about that new kid. Somehow he interests me. There's something about him that I like.

(IAN and TYRONE exit in opposite directions. The stage clears completely, then KHALIL enters.)

KHALIL: My name is Khalil Sumpter. I'm the kind of person who trusts no one. Of course I have friends, but not the kind I would trust. *(The crowd filters back, including eventually IAN and TYRONE.)* When I first walked into T.J. High I saw a whole lot of kids. It was jam-packed inside that school, man! I saw homies selling guns, also selling drugs. I saw girls fighting over boys, ripping each other's brains out . . . Damn, there were a lot of cuties in that joint! *(IAN and TYRONE block KHALIL's path, cutting off his speech abruptly.)*

IAN: What's your name?

KHALIL: Khalil. Why?

IAN: We're just asking.

TYRONE: What're you looking for?

KHALIL: I'm looking for this room number.

TYRONE: It's over there. I'm going right there now.

(KHALIL and TYRONE exit together, leaving IAN onstage.)

IAN: After that we started hanging out with Khalil. We went to parties and we stayed at each other's home once in a while. Then, a month later, we were playing basketball.

(Enter KHALIL and TYRONE with the basketball.)

TYRONE: My ball!

KHALIL: Let's shoot for it.

IAN: Okay.

(They play a bit, then, exhausted, sit down.)

IAN: You want to get buddha?

TYRONE: Why not? Wait, who's gonna buy the weed and the Phillie?

IAN: I'm not. I'm broke.

KHALIL: Me either. I'm broke too.

TYRONE: *(To IAN)* If you're broke, then why'd you come up with the idea.

IAN: I don't know. And what you talking to me like that for?

TYRONE: Just forget it.

KHALIL: I'm tired of this.

TYRONE: Tired of what?

KHALIL: Can't you see we don't have any money? Let's do something crazy.

TYRONE: Like what?

KHALIL: I don't know. Don't you see how messed up it is with no money?

TYRONE: That's true. Look at my clothes and my house.

IAN: Yeah, man look at the neighborhood we live in. And then look at Washington, D.C.!

TYRONE: Ay-yo, you know what I want to do, man?

IAN and **KHALIL:** *(At the same time)* What?

TYRONE: Let's rob a liquor store, the one on the corner.

KHALIL: What! Is you stupid?

TYRONE: No, man. Come on—just to get a little cash, man. Then we could buy bags and smoke them, B.

IAN: Nah. I'm not with that money, 'cause if we get caught or something, I don't want to go to jail.

TYRONE: But, yo, think about it B. You know know how much money liquor stores be having?

IAN: Ay-yo! *(Thinks)* What the hell, man. Let's do it.

KHALIL: Yo, B. I don't know, man . . . *(He looks at Tyrone and Ian.)* Okay, man, I'm down.

TYRONE: All right. Yo. This is how we're going to do it. Tomorrow at twelve midnight we meet here. And bring your piece, Ian. And Khalil, I'll lend you one of mine.

(They all slap hands. TYRONE exits.)

KHALIL: Ay-yo, Ian man, I don't really want to do this.

IAN: Ah, don't be a punk, man. Don't worry. Nothing is going to happen.

KHALIL: But still, I don't think I'm doing—

IAN: *(Shoves him)* You punk!

KHALIL: Don't push me! You punk man! I'm being out. *(Exits.)*

IAN: *(Calling after him)* At least think about it, B!

(Lights down)

(Empty stage. Enter ALEXANDRA.)

ALEXANDRA: Khalil is a pain in the butt. I know that. But I never thought he'd kill a man, much less two men. When he was younger I knew he was in a lot of trouble at school . . . I mean, of course he would get into trouble. What little kid wouldn't? But to think that now my little boy had a gun in his hand and not a rubber ball—it's depressing and sickening. Once a little boy and now a grown criminal! I guess I ignored the warning signs. I mean he would go out and stay out for . . . Oh, I don't know . . . Some mother I am, don't even know how long he was out for. He wouldn't talk to me. Wouldn't smile at me. He just left and walked out into the world.

(Lights down)

(As the lights come up IAN and TYRONE are waiting for KHALIL, both wearing sweatshirts with hoods and with guns bulging in their pockets.)

TYRONE: Yo, Ian, I don't think this punk is going to show up, money.

IAN: He has to. He's not that much of a punk.

TYRONE: What makes you think he's going to show up? It's already 12:10 A.M.

IAN: True. Yo, forget that dude. Lets be out. Lets do this by our own selves.

(They start to walk away. Enter KHALIL.)

KHALIL: Yo, Tyrone! Ian! Wait up for me.

IAN: I knew you was comin'! Let's go!

(Lights down.)

(Lights up. LIQUOR STORE CLERK is behind a counter. Enter TYRONE, IAN, and KHALIL. They stop just outside the store.)

TYRONE: Okay . . . Now put up your hoods. And Khalil, you'll be in the door for the lookout while me and Ian get the money.

(KHALIL stays at the door. TYRONE and IAN rush into the store, guns drawn.)

TYRONE: Yo! Pops! Guess what?

CLERK: What?

TYRONE: You robbed! Put the money in a bag.

CLERK: Paper or plastic?

IAN: Don't give us any trouble or I'll blow your freakin' head off!

TYRONE: Hey, pops, would you hurry up! We ain't got all night, man. I'm going to be eighty-three when we get out of here.

CLERK: I'm going just as fast as I can.

IAN: Man a snail can go faster than you!

KHALIL: (*Looking offstage*) Yo! . . . The cops! Yo! The cops are coming! Run for it.

IAN: Yo! Tyrone! Yo! Take the money and run for it! Come on!

(*IAN and KHALIL run offstage. CLERK also exits, leaving TYRONE alone in centerstage.*)

TYRONE: Something happened. I don't know what. But then I started hearing sirens and I just felt like killing myself. Ian was not very scared at all. He left with Khalil. I just stood there thinking and feeling nothing but fear. Then the cops came in. I got caught because Khalil and Ian left me. Man, I thought Ian and I was best friends. I was wrong, real wrong. They took me away and all I saw was Ian and Khalil's eyes in a dark alley looking at me. I had tears to my eyes, but didn't show it.

(*Lights down*)

(*The next day. IAN and KHALIL in their hangout.*)

IAN: Why did you do that, leaving us there alone? I swear, man.

KHALIL: (*Very anxious*) I don't know. I left when I saw the cops coming. (*Pause*) I'm nervous about Tyrone getting caught.

IAN: Why?

KHALIL: Because he might tell the cops that we was with him when we robbed the liquor store.

IAN: Now that you say that, I'm nervous.

KHALIL: I'm nervous too. That why I'm telling you this. But we still have to stay on top of things and be aware of what's going on.

IAN: You right. No problem. He might and he might not. But if he do and the cops come for us, if they get you before they get me, don't tell them where I live and I won't tell them where you live.

(*Lights down*)

(*Lights up. ETHEL and LINDA are onstage.*)

LINDA: Oh, Ian! I loved you so much. I remember when you liked that girl Shanice, but you didn't know how to have a relationship, so you came to me and I told you. Then the next day you asked her and she said, "Yes." You were in the sixth grade and she was the only thing you ever thought about. I also remember when you had a loose tooth and you were running all over the house because you thought that if I pulled it out it would hurt. Why did it

have to be you who got shot! For God's sake, man, what is wrong
with this world!

ETHEL: I knew I shouldn't have let him hang out with his
friends. I knew something was going to happen to him. I just knew
it but I didn't know it was going to be so soon.

LINDA: This can't be happening! No! Not to me! Not to Ian! I'm
sure that any minute now he's going to walk into this room and tell
me, "Oh, Mama, I'm all right. I'll never leave you . . ."

ETHEL: I knew something was going on when I found a twenty-
two gun under his mattress.

LINDA: Then he'll give me a big hug and a kiss and tell me how
much he loves me and he'll never leave my side, never!

(Lights down)

(Lights up. IAN is walking along the street. TYRONE enters.)

TYRONE: Yo, Ian!

IAN: *(Startled)* Yo! Yo, Tyrone, man! What's up?

TYRONE: What you mean, what's up! I been in jail, that's what's
up!

IAN: I know, man. I'm sorry.

TYRONE: Sorry! Man, I don't care if you sorry! Where were you
when I needed you? Man, you lucky I didn't just smoke you when I
seen you!

IAN: I swear, man, I didn't want you to get busted. Didn't you
hear me call out to you when the cops was coming?

TYRONE: I heard you. It was too late by then, man. The cops already had me surrounded.

*(MIKE enters and stands behind IAN and TYRONE, close enough to
hear, but is not seen by either of them.)*

IAN: It was Khalil's fault. If he only warned us on time!

TYRONE: I told you he was a punk. Man, he's the one I oughta
be smoking!

IAN: That's the truth! He so scared, man, he just run without saying nothing.

TYRONE: Yeah, he let us both down. You and me, we both
oughta smoke him.

IAN: Yeah . . . *(Pause, during which MIKE exits)* How'd you get
out of jail?

TYRONE: Bail. My moms got up the money.

IAN: *(Pause. Thinking.)* You don't really want to buck Khalil, do you?

TYRONE: I don't know.

IAN: 'Cause the truth is, he wasn't any more punk than the rest of us. We was all scared. That's the truth, man.

TYRONE: I guess you right, man.

(Both exit. MIKE and STUDENT 1 enter from opposite sides of the stage and meet at center stage.)

MIKE: Did you hear? Ian and Tyrone are going to shoot Khalil 'cause Tyrone got arrested.

STUDENT 1: Really?

(Exit MIKE. Enter STUDENT 2.)

STUDENT 1: Did you hear that Ian and Tyrone are going to get Khalil?

STUDENT 2: Yeah. That's the rumor.

(Exit STUDENT 1. Enter KHALIL and TYRONE from opposite sides of the stage. KHALIL, who hasn't seen TYRONE since the robbery, rushes over to him.)

KHALIL: Yo, Tyrone! What's up?

TYRONE: You will be if you don't get out of my sight! *(Exits.)*

KHALIL: *(To STUDENT 2)* What's up with Tyrone?

STUDENT 2: He's planning to kill you. Ian is too.

KHALIL: Seriously? Oh, no!

STUDENT 2: Wait! Where you going?

KHALIL: To get some protection. *(Exits.)*

(STUDENT 2 shrugs and exits in the opposite direction. Lights down.)

(Lights up. KHALIL in center stage.)

KHALIL: I had to do it. I was too scared. I mean, those guys had to die or they were going to kill me. I was friends with them. I wouldn't just kill them for nothing. Okay. We did rob a liquor store together, but I know it wasn't my fault for Tyrone to get caught. And if it was, I swear, I was really sorry. I only wanted to do something for my friends. But they wanted to kill me. I had to protect myself. I swear, it wasn't really me who killed them. It was my nervousness, my fear, man. *(Enter ALEXANDRA, who mimes making* *breakfast, getting milk out of the refrigerator, etc.)* I thought about it all that night. I didn't get a wink of sleep. When I came down to breakfast, I hardly knew where I was. *(Sits, as if at table.)*

ALEXANDRA: Hi, sweetheart. How are you this morning? *(KHALIL doesn't answer. He starts to lift the spoon for his cereal, then pushes the bowl away. Alexandra speaks after a puzzled pause.)* Aren't you gonna eat your breakfast?

KHALIL: I'll be late for school.

ALEXANDRA: Khalil, it's only 7 A.M.! You live three blocks away from school.

KHALIL: Yeah, what does that have to do with anything? *(He stands.)* Look, I have to go to school now.

ALEXANDRA: Khalil, what is wrong with you? Why are you mad?

KHALIL: You're too protective of me, Mom.

ALEXANDRA: I care for you. I'm your mother.

(A long silence. KHALIL sits back down.)

KHALIL: Mom.

ALEXANDRA: What?

KHALIL: Can I ask you something?

ALEXANDRA: Go ahead.

KHALIL: Why is this world so cruel?

ALEXANDRA: I don't think I can answer that question. That is one of the questions that can't be answered.

KHALIL: I hate this world! I hate this life! *(He exits. Lights down.)*

(Lights up. KHALIL is downstage, facing the audience. IAN and TYRONE enter upstage, walking diagonally toward KHALIL. TYRONE speaks just at lights-up.)

TYRONE: Yo, Khalil, man, I wanna talk to you.

(A pause. KHALIL is quivering. The audience can see how frightened and distraught he is. All of a sudden he draws his gun, wheels around, and levels it at IAN and TYRONE. Everyone freezes for a long moment. Lights down.)

(Lights up. The three boys are sitting in their chairs as they were at the beginning of the play.)

TYRONE: Me and Ian were walking to homeroom when I saw

Khalil coming toward us. I thought he was smiling. I wasn't sure. I thought that was the phoniest smile I had ever seen. I yelled out, "Yo, Khalil, man, I wanna talk to you!" He put his hand in his pocket. When he was about ten feet away from us he pulled out something black. The sun reflected off it and my whole body started tingling. I pushed Ian and tensed up. I didn't even hear the shot. All of a sudden everything went quiet. I looked at Ian. He looked as shocked as I felt. There was blood coming down the side of his shirt. I tried to reach out to him. I felt that if I could just touch him one more time everything would be okay.

IAN: I felt the bullet enter my body. I felt the bullet just stop my whole body. I mean everything in my body just stopped. Then I realized I was on the ground dead. I knew I was dead because I could feel myself coming out of my body. There was a whole big crowd over me.

TYRONE: Down Ian went. And I went down. Blood was everywhere. I felt my body in an ambulance riding away to death. Ian was my friend after all. I felt his body next to mines. He was with me all the way.

(A long silence.)

KHALIL: It was my nervousness, my fear, man. I took the gun, but it wasn't to kill them. It was just to scare them. But I was so scared of them killing me that when I saw them, I couldn't move. I was paralyzed. But I managed to pull out the gun, to scare them only, but my hands were shaking like a power drill and my finger just went off by itself. I didn't know what to do. Now I was really scared. I was going crazy. My whole body was shaking. I was so nervous that I felt like killing myself, man. I swear, I loved those guys.

(Another silence. Enter LINDA, who takes her place beside IAN.)

LINDA: I didn't want to talk to anybody. But for some reason I felt like this call might be important. The person on the phone sounded nervous. He said, "I just want to tell you that your son got shot." I started to think. I sat down. I said, "How did this happen? Are you sure? It's not true! My baby Ian will come home any minute. Why do you kids play around like this?" He said, "I'm not playing around, miss. Your son was shot today. I don't play with death." I said, "Yes, yes, yes, you do play with death! You kids are always joking around! You just don't know when to stop. Well let me tell you something: don't do this to a mother! Don't play around like this, okay." *(Enter ETHEL.)*

ETHEL: *(Taking her original place beside TYRONE)* I want to know what parents have to do to keep their kids alive. *(Enter ALEXANDRA, taking her place beside her son.)*

ALEXANDRA: *(Mimes slamming down a telephone)* Oh no! I can't . . . I can't believe . . . I can't believe this! My baby a criminal! Not . . . no, not my baby! They must be mistaken. But what if they're not mistaken? Why? . . . Why? . . . Why did he do it? It's a hard world out there. He had to do something. I can't believe this! Oh, my God! Lord, please stay by my side and my son's. We need you. I really need you. Please, Lord, bless us! Stay by our side. You're the only one that can make it better. I know he had a reason. I hope he had a damn good reason! He better had. I will kill him! I thought he was different. I knew I should have just sat down and talked to him about this. Especially this. It's my fault. I should be the one going to jail Not my baby . . . Not my baby. In reality, I'm the one really guilty. *(She falls to her knees.)* Lord, I know I was young when I had him and he wasn't brought up too good, but do me a favor—take him! He can't live like this. Either he will die in jail or die after he come out. Lord, take him. He can't survive like this. He can't survive. He needs you to take him. I love him to death, but, Lord, take him please, so it can be peaceful for me . . . and him.

(Lights down.)

(The whole cast is on the stage, murmuring as if at a funeral. As the MINISTER walks toward center stage, everyone falls silent.)

MINISTER: This world is like an endless stream of violence. These two boys were caught up in this stream, and like many other people, they drowned. Ian and Tyrone were best friends. They did everything together. They went to school together and they died together. May God guide them to hope and happiness in a world of peace. I also hope that Khalil learns. And may God forgive his soul, because he's only a child and he did not know what he was doing. *(Exit MINISTER.)*

(From now every speaker will exit after completing his or her speech. At the end, only IAN will be left onstage.)

CAST MEMBER 1: I can't believe Ian and Tyrone are gone. I feel so out of control, like I can't do anything to end this violence we live in today.

CAST MEMBER 2: I don't know where the world is going, but if it keeps on going like this, the world is going to end.

CAST MEMBER 3: I am really scared about this violence that is going around. I get very scared every morning when I have to go down the stairs and there's no light. And I thank God every day that I get home safe from school.

CAST MEMBER 4: Violence is the main thing that exists in our world today. There are people blowing each other's heads off for drugs, money, or sometimes just for laughs. I'm not really afraid of violence because I feel that if I keep my mouth shut and mind my business, I won't have a problem. But if someone's gonna kill me, I will fight for my life and if I die, at least I died fighting.

CAST MEMBER 5: I feel violence would not have been in the world if it was not for Adam and Eve.

CAST MEMBER 6: I think that all this violence comes from us. We created this. It comes from inside us. The only thing we can do to resolve this and protect ourselves is to carry a gun. That's the only solution.

CAST MEMBER 7: The messed-up thing about it is that blacks are killing blacks. It's sad because myself and my children will have to grow up worrying about whether they will get shot, beat up, or killed. They should be worrying about their schoolwork. I wish things will change. If things don't change, me and other people will have to make it so that it can change.

CAST MEMBER 8: I think that everyone should integrate and try their best to fight violence with love.

CAST MEMBER 9: I think they should put all the drug dealers in jail. I think they should have policemen all over the place. I feel sorry saying this because most of my friends are drug dealers.

CAST MEMBER 9 (KHALIL): People think that violence is the answer to their problems. Violence just leads to more violence.

CAST MEMBER 10 (TYRONE): I wish that everyone would stop hating each other and get along.

(IAN is now alone on the stage. He gets up from his chair, walks to center stage, and unfolds an ordinary piece of school composition paper.)

IAN: What I fear is not death.
What I fear is life.
The pain of violence,
The terror of each day.
Death comes when you least expect it.
Life only comes when you want it to.
Some provoke Death.
Some try to erase it.
Death comes from violence,
Sometimes racism.
I want to have racism gone,
Banned from the world forever,
I want us to live in harmony.
But peace only comes
When we really want it.
Peace is a foreign thing
To human beings.
When I think of harmony
I think of all the voices of the world
Singing together as one.
One person, one being.
People don't want that.
People want power.
People want.
People WANT.
That is all people do:
Want, want, want.
Material things have taken over.
People kill over material things.
I want love.
I want happiness.
I want that convertible.
I am no different.
I enter the race
To have material things,

To be rich,
To be loved by millions.
I am only human.
I do not fear death.
I fear life.

CURTAIN

There's Never a Good Day, No Matter What

THE FIRST THURSDAY AND FRIDAY AFTER THE CHRISTMAS VACATION, I read the whole of *Will My Name Be Shouted Out?* aloud to my seventh- and eighth-grade classes and gave every student a copy. Each class listened to the play in attentive silence, amazed—as had been the Bensonhurst authors before them—by what a moving and coherent story their work had amounted to. My second eighth grade, which had provided the largest portion of the writing included in the play, cheered and applauded when I finished. And in every class, after the reading, several students asked me if they could try out for parts.

There was so much enthusiasm about the play those first two days that I was almost sorry I had promised that Friday to the family play cast for their cast party (this also turned out to be the day that Mayra, Ricky, and Xia performed their LaGuardia monologues). But I figured that students who were genuinely interested in being in the play would be just as enthusiastic the following Friday, the date I'd scheduled for the first Thomas Jefferson auditions.

In my second eighth grade, after I had finished reading the play, Joan Gold pulled me aside and asked me to talk to a student named José Figueroa about applying to LaGuardia High School.

"The auditions are tomorrow," I said. "Has he gotten all the paperwork he needs from LaGuardia? Has he prepared his monologues?"

"No," said Joan. "He hasn't done any of that."

"Well, then it's impossible."

"I know," she said, turning up her hands to indicate helplessness. "He just won't listen to me. Could you please talk to him?"

I told her I would, and ten minutes after the end of the class this persistent thirteen-year-old and I were in two identical chairs, facing each other across the narrow width of the writing room.

JOSÉ FIGUEROA WAS A TOUGH LITTLE KID: JUST BARELY FIVE FEET tall and skinny enough to slip through a basketball net with hardly a riffle. His laugh was a loud, flat "hah!" His eyes were sly and deep brown, often all but squeezed shut under the pressure of his huge but always worldly-ironic grin. He was a cross between the comic mania of a Groucho Marx and the New York swagger of a Sylvester Stallone.

I have never had a student who revised his work as assiduously as José. Not only would he follow the suggestions I wrote in the margins of his first draft, but he would then revise his second draft on the basis of my new suggestions. I was amused and amazed by him: at first I didn't know whether he was utterly devoid of ego or simply determined to improve himself. He was certainly not the former, but it is a testimony to the quirkiness of his character that I cannot imagine what it was in addition to the latter that made him so willing to follow my every bit of criticism—at least regarding his writing.

The dialogue in *Will My Name Be Shouted Out?* about buying "buddha" (marijuana) that ended with the line "Yeah, man, look at the neighborhood we live in. And then look at Washington, D.C.!" was José's and, in a way, typical of him, since few other members of the eighth grade had enough political savvy to see injustice in the disparity between the lifestyle of the elite and that of the people in their own neighborhoods. José was also the one who wrote Cast Member 10's first speech, about being at his cousin's apartment on Halloween when two masked teenagers came in with guns. But once the Thomas Jefferson unit was over, José wrote almost nothing but love poems. He was obsessed, in a deeply passionate but always good-natured way, with a bright, charismatic, though not especially good-looking girl in his class who wouldn't even glance in his direction. All of his poems were about the day this girl told him she didn't want to go out with him. He had little talent as a poet—but I was always impressed by the gentlemanliness with which he accepted the finality of this girl's "no."

As we sat facing one another in the writing room, I told José what I knew about LaGuardia, but made it clear that it was all moot in his case, at least as far as the following year was concerned, because there was no time for him to get the necessary paperwork done, even if he could manage to perfect two monologues by the following morning.

This was all I had to say on the matter and assumed that José would understand our meeting was over. But he just kept sitting in his chair after I had finished talking, as if waiting for me to really get down to business. I had a lot of work to do, but I liked him, so I said, "Why do you want to go to LaGuardia?"

"'Cause I want to."

"Why do you want to?"

"I don't know."

"What do you want to be when you grow up?"

"Well . . ." An expression of discomfort came onto his face. "My folks want me to be an architect or a lawyer."

"What do you want to be?"

Now he leaned forward, glancing warily right and left, before looking me in the eye and speaking in a low, emphatic voice: "I want to be an actor."

"Have you ever done any acting before?"

"No."

"Why do you want to be an actor?"

"I just do. I know I'd be good at it."

I couldn't help smiling at this. "You going to try out for the Thomas Jefferson play?"

"Yeah," he smiled broadly, almost proudly. "I want to be Ian."

"Great. But you better try out for a couple of other parts because there's no guarantee that you'll get the one you want. Ian is the star of the play, you know."

"Nah." José shook his head dismissively. "It's Ian or nothing!"

THE AUDITIONS WERE HELD A WEEK LATER IN JOAN GOLD'S ROOM. By comparison to the Bensonhurst tryouts they were a huge success. At least three times as many kids came, and at least a third of them were boys. Also, the overall level of talent was much higher than in the Bensonhurst rehearsals—so high that Xia, Celeste, and Mayra didn't seem quite as exceptional as they once had. Mayra in particular didn't look good, but then she always had trouble with the first reading of a script. I knew she would pull through in the end.

Perhaps the most exciting moment of the auditions was when three African American girls—Keisha Damar (the spunky girl who had laughed when I asked her class if they knew drug dealers and who had said she kept a gun at her uncle's house), Tunisia James, and Chantell Williams—performed the scene in which the boys plot the robbery. These three girls gave the boys a wry, funky style of talking and moving that was tough, humorous, and absolutely authentic. When I saw them working together, I thought half my casting decisions were over. I didn't see how anyone else could do a better job.

But that was before I saw José's rendition of Ian Moore.

José had stage presence. There was nothing shy or muted about his manner as he stepped in front of an audience. If anything, he seemed to become more intensely himself, sly, funny, brash, and thoroughly engaged in what he was doing. When José spoke Ian Moore's poem, it lost all its whininess and incoherence and became the blunt statement of a young man who was too tough and honest to lie about death. When José did the first basketball scene with Tyrone and Mike (played by Xia and Keisha), he seemed so engaged by the game and so bemused at his own victory that it was easy to see why Tyrone would fall for him. Watching José act was like experiencing one of those moments in my own fiction writing when my characters would suddenly take on a life of their own, becoming more complicated, intriguing, and meaningful than I had ever planned them to be. I knew right away that José was going to be Ian, although this was a decision I had to keep secret for at least a week.

Xia was also fabulous as all three of the boys. But she worked best as Alexandra, Khalil's mother, who had a pronounced hysterical edge to her that a lesser actor might easily have overdone. Celeste gave a moving performance as Linda, Ian's mother, bringing out Linda's edgy vulnerability. Arlene Salter, who had delivered an extremely polished performance in the family plays, also did a great job on Linda, giving her a more neurasthenic air. Arlene's friend Anna Harris, the only other white student at the audition, was dead set on playing Khalil. She was big and did a convincing male street accent, even if it wasn't nearly as authentically black as Keisha's, Tunisia's, or Chantell's.

By the end of the audition, I was very happy. Even if a good many of the kids who had tried out ultimately drifted away from the Drama Club, I had such a deep pool of talent that there was no way I wouldn't be able to put on an extremely powerful production. There were only two disappointments.

The first concerned Celeste, who informed me, as we were all gathering our coats and bags to go, that she was starting a new baby-sitting job and from now on would have to leave the Drama Club at three. This meant that she would miss half our rehearsal time, because, although the club officially began at two-fifteen, we never got down to work until two-thirty, and we quit at three-thirty. I understood that Celeste needed money, but I had to tell her—as I had told Isaac the year before—that if she couldn't find a way to stay later, at least on Fridays, I simply couldn't offer her a major part. Celeste said she would talk to the child's mother and see if she could change the schedule, but she wasn't optimistic.

The other disappointment was the failure of Ricky Ortiz and Cornell Vargas to come to the auditions as they had both promised. When I asked the other kids where Ricky and Cornell were, I was answered at first only by patently false professions of ignorance and a collective exchange of glances. Finally Celeste blurted out, "They're at the rumble."

THE PLAY'S OPENING MONOLOGUE, ABOUT THE BOY WHOSE FATHER got shot after giving him $50 for sneakers, was written by Cornell Vargas. Cornell was an excellent writer, one of the best I have ever worked with. Close to a quarter of the Thomas Jefferson script consists of his work. I could have included more, but I wanted to get as many students' writing into the play as possible. The remaining three-quarters of the play was drawn from the work of twenty-one other students—which gives an idea how out of proportion his contribution was.

Here is a piece Cornell wrote the day I read *Will My Name Be Shouted Out?* to his class.

Being a Kid

Being a kid is pretty hard these days, especially for me. I travel alot going up and down on trains and I'm always worring about some guys coming and trying to start trouble with me but I'm always ready for something like that, cause I know how to fight back or get away. So. its' even to travel.

I live in a block of violence and drugs. so in a neighborhood like this you have to know everyone to have props. Me I have a big brother so everyone knows me as little Ike. And no one ever messes with me. But still its' messed up because anything can happen like just the other day I was chillin on the corner with my boys and my brother and cops raided all of us and they checked everyone and They let me go and my brother. this just a example of a few hard things to be a kid. So as I was saying, its' like theres never a good day, no matter what, something has to happen. Sometime's people I don't know come around my block and act hard so so you have to look at them hard so they can know its' your block. A few weeks ago, I was coming out of the candy store with my friends and this kid starts looking so I say what hell are looking at and he was about to argue with me or fight until my friends turned around and he probably got scared so he turned around, thats' how you show someone you got props. Some kids that are like punks don't even look at people like me cause they probably think that If they look at me I'm going to hit them and they know I'll hit them that's why I don't mess with them cause it must be hard for them.

This piece surprised me at first because Cornell was not, by any stretch of the imagination, a thug. He was nice looking, short, slender (almost waiflike), bright, and well mannered—certainly not someone other kids would be afraid to look at. On a closer reading, however, it is obvious that, with all of its braggadocio, "Being a Kid" is not the work of an authentic thug. Cornell shows too much discontent with the world he has no choice but to inhabit and too much sympathy for punks who can't even summon up the toughness to *act* tough. But the fact that Cornell neither thought nor looked like the tough character he claims to be did not, of course, detract in the slightest from his desire to seem tough—a desire that, inspired as it may have been by the need to protect himself, might easily one day get him into big trouble.

The rumble that kept Cornell and Ricky away from the auditions began with a sadly typical inner city adolescent confrontation.

On the Monday before the auditions, three of the previous year's eighth-graders had come back to visit the school. They were Bianca Chavez, the girl who had beaten up Susan Carmody; Shantay Fredricks, the loudmouthed girl who had told me it was crazy to "love your enemies"; and Chris Wood, who because he was very big and very dark skinned—and because we live in a racist world—was widely thought to be tough but was in fact, in the words of Rachel Suarez, "nothing but a teddy bear." Both girls were carrying knives. Chris was unarmed.

While these three were hanging out in front of the school after dismissal, talking to some of the current eighth-graders, a group of kids from nearby Susan B. Anthony Junior High came down the block and the inevitable confrontation ensued. At first it seemed to focus on the two visiting girls—probably because they both had wicked tempers and tongues. One of the kids from Susan B. Anthony pulled out Bianca's earrings, splitting her earlobes, and another ripped out a hank of Shantay's hair. When Chris tried to intervene to protect the girls, he got stabbed in the chest—not deeply, but he had to be taken to the hospital.

The stabbing ended the confrontation, but both sides seemed to feel a state of war now existed between their two schools.

On Friday, the day of the auditions, a rumor circulated in the school that a gang from Susan B. Anthony was coming to have a rumble with the kids from Walt Whitman. Getting wind of this rumor, Fran Kaplan, the principal of P.S. 227 and Walt Whitman Academy, asked the police to park one of their cars in front of the school as a warning to both groups. Apparently Fran's strategy worked. There was no rumble that afternoon and no trace of the kids from Anthony. Nevertheless, several boys from Whitman, including Ricky Ortiz and Cornell Vargas, felt honor bound to patrol the streets just in case any of their counterparts from Anthony were lurking in the neighborhood. This venture resulted in no confrontations, but it did keep both boys away from the audition.

I spoke to Ricky and Cornell during the following week, and they each promised that they would come to the second audition. During my conversation with Ricky, I warned him that, despite all the good work he had done in the Drama Club, I couldn't hold a part for him if he didn't come this time; it wouldn't be fair to the other kids. He swore that he would be there, that he really wanted a part in the play. But then, as we were about to part, he added, apropos of nothing: "I just been having a lot of trouble with my medication. I still keep getting all these seizures." Whether it was the seizures or not, I don't know, but Ricky didn't show up at the next audition—and that was the end of his membership in the Drama Club.

Cornell did come to the audition, however, and was nearly as good an actor as he was a writer. On the idea that it would lend the play extra emotional power, I had hoped that he would want to perform his own monologue about the death of his father, but Cornell wouldn't even consider it—for perfectly understandable reasons—though he had no objection to its being in the play. There was only one part he wanted to play: Ian.

I wasn't going to announce my final casting decisions until the following Friday's meeting. All through the intervening week, kids would ask me which part I was giving them, and I always gave the same answer: "You'll find out on Friday." I was being hardnosed about it because I knew that many kids who were disappointed by the parts I had given them wouldn't bother to come to the meeting and thus would never have a chance to discover whether they could enjoy playing the parts they had been given.

No student badgered me more often than José Figueroa. Every time I saw him it was: "Hey, Steve, am I Ian?" or, "Come on, can't you even tell me if I'm close?" One time he rushed up, rammed his index finger against my temple, and quoting Ian's lines from the robbery scene, said, "Hey, Steve, 'I'm gonna blow your freakin head off!'"

When I announced that he had gotten the part, he jumped into the air and did a little dance. Siobhan, Erin, Jessica, and I had been unanimous in our decision. We all saw that he would give the play a strong, charismatic focus.

I offered Cornell the role of the Liquor Store Clerk and a few choice Cast Member speeches, but he wasn't interested and left. I was disappointed, but not—as I would have been the previous year—worried that the flight of one talented actor threatened the whole play. If anything, we had too many talented actors that year. There was no way that all the girls and boys looking at me so expectantly would be satisfied by the roles I had to give out.

Of the three African American girls who had so impressed me at first, I cast only one of them as one of the boys: Keisha Demar got the role of Tyrone. She gave the part a hard, smart, and angry edge—and struck me as someone I could trust to come to all the rehearsals and not crack on opening night.

Chantell Williams got the role of Ethel Sinkler, Tyrone's mother. Ethel was the toughest of the mothers, and I thought that Chantell, a big girl with a gentle tenor voice, could give her just the right blend of maternal grief and frank, sometimes brutal, realism.

I was strongly tempted to give the third girl, Tunisia James, the role of Khalil. She would have made him edgy, volatile, and intense—a perfect combination for a boy who would one day gun down his friends. But those same qualities, which were very much a part of her everyday character, made me wonder if we could depend on her as an actress. Already she had proven to be a moody and troublesome member of the Drama Club, talking during other kids' performances, mouthing off or making faces at me when I asked her to be quiet, and generally refusing to respond to any of my requests until she had driven me to the point of anger.

Such behavior was typical of Tunisia during the three years that she had been my student. Although she was relatively bright and not at all a bad writer, she was one of those kids who would routinely tear up her writing, say it was no good, and not even look at me when I tried to talk to her about it. I didn't think I could risk giving one of the three main roles in the play to someone so temperamental and self-defeating. When I told her I had given her some of the choicest Cast Member speeches, she said, "I don't want those stupid parts!"

"Fine," I said. "I'll give them to someone else if you don't want them."

She crossed her big arms across her ample chest and jerked her chin around so that I could see only the side of her face. I took her silence as a tacit acceptance of her parts but had already begun calculating who I could pass them on to if and when she quit.

Anna Harris got the role of Khalil. As I have said, she played a very convincing boy but retained a feminine softness that made Khalil more sympathetic and therefore tragic. I have to admit that I had reservations about casting a red-haired, freckle-faced white girl in one of the lead roles when there were black girls—Tunisia in particular—with just as much talent. But I felt it was important to maintain the tradition of color-blind casting and that having a white girl playing this black boy could symbolize the fact that, despite the huge barriers that American society has erected between the two so-called races, blacks and whites are vastly more alike than different.

I saw Xia's face fall as I assigned each of the roles of the three boys. When I gave her the part of Khalil's melodramatic mother, Alexandra, she managed a trouper's smile. I made a mental note to tell her that I had given her the part because I thought she should have a chance to play a female role for a change and also because none of the other students would have been able to handle Alexandra's lines without overblowing the emotion.

Mayra was also disappointed to get only the role of Mike and a few of the better Cast Member speeches. I felt bad, too, but given the mix of talent we had, I just didn't have a choice. I had wavered a long time about giving her the role of Khalil but ultimately decided that Anna would be a more forceful presence. The truth was that I had given Mayra a smaller part because of her dependability. I knew that she would never quit the Drama Club. And I was just as certain that, as we drew closer to our performance date, one of the lead actors would pull a Yolanda Castro. Mayra was my insurance. As soon as a starring role opened up, I knew she would be right there, ready to act with all of her heart and intelligence.

When I told Celeste that she was going to be the Minister (a small role with great possibilities) and the Liquor Store Clerk, her eyes went dull and her whole body wilted. I took her aside and explained again about not being able to give her a big role, because then the whole cast wouldn't be able to rehearse important scenes when she wasn't around. She nodded but didn't speak and didn't look at me. Later, when I asked the cast to gather in a circle and do a reading of the play in their newly assigned roles, she wouldn't join the group and left at three without saying a word. I was worried about her and wished that I could call her at home to make it clear that I had given her the Minister because the part required a powerful actor, but she still did not have a telephone. The following Wednesday, Jessica saw Celeste and said that she was in a great mood, full of laughs and excited about her part. I chose to take this as encouraging, though so radical a shift in mood did seem peculiar.

ONCE AGAIN OUR PRODUCTION SCHEDULE WAS VERY TIGHT. THE positioning of the winter break in mid-February coupled with the shorter number of days that T&W was contracted to be at the school meant that we would have only five regularly scheduled Drama Club meetings before the first performance—and that included the meeting at which the parts were announced. I intended to buy us more time by having a pair of two-hour rehearsals over the break and by rehearsing on three afternoons during the two weeks before the performance.

As I worked this schedule out, I realized that I was going to have severe staffing problems. Thanks to the demise of the Urban Corps, my budget for the Columbia interns had been cut in half. This meant that I had just barely enough money to pay Siobhan and Erin for their regular teaching hours and the weekly Drama Club meetings. Any additional time they put into the play, including attending its two performances, one at the school and the other in the evening at the Teachers & Writers main office, would have to be entirely on a volunteer basis. Jessica too had been volunteering all of her time at the school outside of the regular Drama Club meetings. Just before Christmas, however, she had been graduated from Barnard, and now, with four years of student loans about to come due, had to begin looking for paying work. She planned to make as many of the rehearsals as possible but warned me that she was bound to miss some of them, including the Drama Club meetings, because of job interviews and auditions.

I had been anxious enough about directing the play without the support of Daniel's expertise and philosophic calm, but now I felt a positive dread at the prospect of those rehearsals when I might have to manage the cast entirely on my own. How on earth was I ever going to give due concentration to the performances of the two or three performers in any given scene while a dozen other energetic, egocentric, impatient, and sometimes terrified adolescent actors chased one another up and down the aisles, moaned in boredom, and otherwise clamored for my attention?

I am grateful to report that my cast and I were spared such extremes of chaos by the unexpected addition of a fifth member to our team. The very day that I first recognized the full extent of my staffing woes, Fred Glover, a scriptwriter and playwright, having been referred by Teachers & Writers' main office, called me up and said that he would be interested in working with the Drama Club an afternoon or two a week in fulfillment of the public service requirement of the New York Foundation for the Arts grant he had received that year. As luck had it, whenever Jessica, Siobhan, and Erin were all unable to attend a rehearsal,

Fred was always free. While not quite a substitute for Daniel, Fred was much more than just a baby-sitter. It was a great comfort for me to have a professional with whom to discuss my directoral ideas. He was a nice guy, with a set of biceps and pectorals that made quite an impression on several cast members and a couple of their mothers.

DURING THE TWO REHEARSALS BEFORE THE MIDWINTER BREAK, I had the usual behavior problems. José and Keisha, talented as they were, soon proved themselves to be a couple of prima donnas who couldn't stand it whenever I wasn't devoting myself to them. They gave me the most trouble during the blocking—or choreography, really—of the high school corridor scenes, which was especially tedious, both because the actors' movements were so intricate and because the entire cast had to participate.

Normally I try to keep idle cast members from getting bored by having them practice lines with one or another member of the T&W team, but this was impossible during the high school scenes. So there were many occasions when the whole cast had to stand around getting increasingly irritated while I instructed—or yelled at—one or two actors at a time.

I had decided to symbolize the corridor by having some of the actors stand in two parallel lines, between which the remaining actors would walk back and forth briskly to suggest the chaos of class-changing time. Getting the actors to walk back and forth at the right speed so that they always kept the corridor full was no mean feat, especially when José was constantly pulling pranks: sticking his foot out to trip other students or intentionally bumping into a student when it was his turn to walk through the corridor.

The first time he bumped into one of the students, he put his hand to his mouth and said, "Oops! Sorry!" It looked to me as if the collision had been intentional, but I couldn't resist that merry smile of his. "Okay, José," I said. "Let's just do it over." But when he bumped the same student the second time, even his smile wasn't enough to save him. "Come on, José! Cut out that garbage! Let's just do it and do it right so that we can move on to something else."

"Yeah, José," Keisha called out, "you always wasting our time with all this foolishness! I'm sick of it! I don't see why we got to wait around while you do all this dumb stuff all the time!"

"Enough, Keisha!" I said. "José knows what he has to do. Now let's just get on with it."

"Yeah, Keisha!" José said, stepping toward her. "Just because you got the loudest mouth around don't make you the director."

"All I'm saying is you just do what you supposed to do, instead of acting like some kind of clown all the time. I don't see what's wrong with that."

"Keisha," I said, raising my voice: "Be quiet! Now *you're* the one wasting time."

"Yeah, Keisha!" said José, "why don't you keep that big mouth shut and stop—"

"JOSE!" Now I was getting angry. "You too!"

"Come on!" moaned Tunisia. "Let's get going! Can't you keep them under control?"

Turning to Tunisia, I said, "Now, don't you start!" Tunisia never lost an opportunity to complain.

"Well, what am I supposed to do if you can't keep them under control?"

"They *are* under control! The only one talking now is you."

"Look," declared Keisha, "I don't have time for this! Would everybody just be quiet!"

"You too motormouth!" said José.

"Well, why don't you stop stop goofing around, acting like some kind of—"

"EVERYBODY QUIET!" I shouted. "I don't want to hear another word!"

"He's talking to you, Keisha," said José.

"I'm talking to EVERYBODY!" I said.

"This is so stupid!" moaned Tunisia.

Turning huffily on her heels, Keisha said, "I'm leaving! I got better things to do than stand around here while everybody's yelling at everybody else!"

I watched her stamp down the stage steps and head toward the chair where her coat and backpack were heaped. I half thought I should just let her go and be rid of one of my headaches. But of course I couldn't let the kids determine when they had to be at rehearsal, so in my most authoritative voice, I told her: "KEISHA, IF YOU TOUCH THAT COAT YOU ARE OUT OF THE PLAY! Now, get back up on the stage and let's finish this scene, and I don't want to hear another word out of you."

To my astonishment, she turned to me with a perfectly pleasant smile and said, "Okay. If you say so."

She came back up on the stage and we finished the scene without a hitch—except that José made an exaggerated loop around the student he had bumped twice before, giving me another irresistibly good-natured, if mischievous, smile.

Such scenes were frustratingly common throughout the whole production of *Will My Name Be Shouted Out?* José acted up, I believe, simply because he wanted the attention. So did Keisha, but she also had a second agenda that she shared with Tunisia. I think that both of these girls were somehow made uneasy by my preference for maintaining control by appealing to the goodwill and rationality of the cast rather than by the simple assertion of my authority. Particularly when they got anxious about the play or their own performances, Keisha and Tunisia seemed to want me to be a much harsher—and therefore, in their eyes, stronger—leader. They would goad me until I became furious and only then comply with my wishes—Keisha, usually happily, as in the above case, but Tunisia, only sullenly. Tunisia was never happy; she hardly ever smiled.

But even on the worst of days, someone would always deliver a performance that took my breath away, and I would see that despite everything, the kids really wanted the play to work—at least most of them did, most of the time. There were days when I left the rehearsal so exhausted I would stagger home like a drunk, but I always knew that *if* I could only get this fractious group working together, they would deliver a performance that would make the Bensonhurst play look like amateur night—although it was clear right from the very beginning that this was a rather significant "if."

My only real disappointment in the cast was Chantell Williams, who had the part of Tyrone's mother. Chantell was a model student. She always did her work, which was competent if not outstanding. She would speak in class and usually had good points to make. She was considerate, well spoken, polite. As far as I could tell, she was happy with her part, but although she didn't miss a single day of school, she didn't come to either of the rehearsals before the winter break. The Friday after she had missed her first rehearsal, I talked to her about it in class. She apologized, said she had been busy—though she didn't say with what—and promised that she would come to that afternoon's rehearsal.

But once again she didn't show up. When I asked her friends Keisha and Tunisia why she hadn't come, they professed to have no idea.

TO INSURE THAT ALL THE CAST MEMBERS WOULD COME TO OUR two winter break rehearsals, I sent them home with letters explaining the importance of the rehearsals and including permission slips for their parents or guardians to sign. When all but three of my students returned their signed slips to me, I thought it was a done deal that enough of the cast would attend the rehearsals for us to make some real progress. Thus it was not only with disappointment but with surprise that, on Tuesday, I attended the first of the rehearsals to find that only Mayra, Anna, and Arlene had shown up. Xia had called me the night before to say that she wouldn't be able to come, because, as seemed always to be the case during school breaks, she had to stay with her grandmother in Queens. But otherwise I hadn't heard from a single one of the eight other cast members.

My main ambition for that rehearsal had been to finish once and for all the blocking of the school corridor scenes—but that was impossible with only a quarter of my cast. I was very disappointed. I had been eager to get these important but troublesome scenes behind us.

I decided to make the most of the situation by doing intensive work with the three girls who had come, all of whom were excellent actors. At the end of the rehearsal, I told them to make sure they got all their friends on the cast to come to Thursday's rehearsal, otherwise we would fall way behind in our schedule. I also told Mayra to start practicing Chantell's part, because, unless Chantell had a very good excuse for her absences, she was out of the Drama Club.

That night I tried calling the absent cast members, only to discover that half of them didn't have phones and that the rest had the wrong phone number listed in the school's directory (usually because, hounded by rent or bills, their families moved a lot, or because they had listed a false address to be eligible for the school). I was able to get through only to a kittenish but depressive seventh-grader named Julie Madera, who told me that no one in her family had been able to bring her to school that day, but that maybe her uncle could bring her to the next rehearsal. I hung up the phone, never expecting to see her.

But Julie did come to the rehearsal. And so did Mayra and Arlene, but not Anna or any of the other cast members. This time I was not only disappointed but worried. Our first performance was to be in exactly three weeks, and I had been able to reserve the auditorium for only five more rehearsals—not nearly enough time to do all the work that needed to be done, especially the all-important but ever-frustrating blocking. The only way to make up for the time we had lost by the cast's failure to attend these vacation rehearsals was to set up rehearsals during school hours. I didn't want to do this, because it would require taking the cast out of their classes and because the only spaces that would be available to us during school hours would be the corridors, where we would be guaranteed to have only the most chaotic and distracted of rehearsals.

I also had personal reasons for not wanting to schedule additional rehearsals. Thanks to the budget cuts, I was already not going to get paid for all the time I put into the play, and with a second child and rising bills, it was getting ever more difficult to justify working for free. The truth about leaner and meaner public service budgets is that they make leaner and meaner public servants.

As I sat on the edge of the stage that morning, growing increasingly worried, angry, and depressed, I became possessed by the harsh spirit of this budget-slashing age. I thought: "I ought to just can the show and teach these kids a little responsibility! They aren't going to learn anything if I keep giving in to their laziness and rude behavior. I've got to show them that their actions have consequences. That's the best thing I can do for them! That's the only way to help them grow into responsible adults!"

Canning the show was impossible for the obvious reasons: it wouldn't have been fair to those members of the cast who had come to the rehearsals, who had called me, or who would turn out to have had legitimate excuses; and it would have made me and the whole T&W program look bad. But the most important reason for not canning the show was that it wouldn't have taught the students anything about living up to their responsibilities. It would only have confirmed their sense of the inevitability of their failure.

These were frightened children, angry children, lonely children—children who through no fault and no choice of their own had been born into a world where the people they needed most were often taken away from them by guns, drugs, drink, or despair; where people like themselves were portrayed as subhuman and even evil in the songs they had been taught to love, on television, in the halls of government, and by so many people in their own country; where nothing they came into contact with worked right, looked right, or was the way it was supposed to be, not their buildings, or their schools, or the police, or the criminal justice system; where the only people who succeeded were the ones who broke the laws; and where the only way to feel safe was to be stronger and more deadly than the Mac 10–toting, 4x4-driving thugs who terrorized their neighborhoods. These were children who had never had a fair shot at the reward the "invisible hand" was supposed to bestow on all as they deserved. My job was not to slam yet another door in their faces and tell them yet again how stupid, lazy, and undeserving they were. My job was to help these children succeed, to get them, despite all of their handicaps, including sometimes the handicaps of their own characters, to work hard enough and have enough faith in themselves and one another that they might actually accomplish something they could legitimately feel proud of.

But even knowing all this, it was hard for me to work up any sympathy for my students and their troubles as I sat on the stage that morning . . . at least until Jessica mentioned she had gotten a message on her phone machine from Celeste after Tuesday's rehearsal. "All she said was that she couldn't come to Drama Club anymore and that she would call back to explain why—but so far, she hasn't."

On hearing this, Mayra exclaimed, "Oh! I forgot to tell you: Celeste's mother put her in a home."

"A home?" I asked. "What kind of home?"

"I don't know. A foster home I think."

"Why?"

"I don't know. All I know is that that's why she can't come to rehearsals. She told me to tell you."

"Is she still going to be going to Walt Whitman?"

Mayra shrugged. She'd told us all she knew.

On Monday I went into school to track down my delinquent cast members, get their excuses, and arrange to work with them individually in the writing room. Chantell had no excuse for her absences but said she had memorized her part. On working with her, I found it was true. Taking this as a sign of dedication, I decided to let her keep the part but told her that from now on if she missed one single rehearsal, she was out.

José, Keisha, and Tunisia explained to me independently that they had tried to come on Tuesday but had been told by the school security guard that there was no rehearsal. I had reason to believe this story. On leaving the school after Tuesday's rehearsal I had discovered that the guard whom I had informed about the rehearsals had gone off duty just after my arrival and hadn't bothered to convey any of what I had told him to his replacement. In any event, I didn't see what could be gained by calling José, Keisha, and Tunisia liars. What I needed to do now was get them rehearsing. I was pleased to find that they all seemed eager to get to work, and began to feel optimistic again . . . until I ran into Rachel in the hall.

"Steve!" she called out. "I was just going to call you at home. Have you heard from Celeste?"

"No. What's happened to her?"

Rachel only gestured for me to follow her into her office. She closed the door.

"You hear about her mother threatening to kill her?" Rachel said, taking her seat behind her desk.

"No! All I heard was that her mother put her in a home."

"It was much worse than that. Apparently her mother flipped out over the vacation. She started smashing up the apartment and told the police that she was going to kill Celeste."

"Why? What happened?"

"Well, she's been under a big strain lately because her husband, Celeste's stepfather, has been gone."

"I didn't even know Celeste had a stepfather."

"Oh, yeah. For the last year or so he's been a real stabilizing force in that household. Everything's been much better for Celeste, her little sister, and brother than it has been for years. But then he had to go down to Honduras on family business and somehow messed up on his papers, so they wouldn't let him back into the country. This has been—I don't know—maybe three months now." Hearing this, I began to understand at last why Celeste had become so bizarrely moody during the previous semester. "Anyhow," Rachel continued, "Celeste's mother just can't handle it with him not around and possibly never coming back. So apparently, over the vacation, with all her kids at home, she just lost it. She got drunk. She started screaming and yelling and smashing everything. Celeste is the linchpin in that family. You know, typical child of an alcoholic, carrying all the responsibility on her shoulders. So when her mother started acting like this, Celeste got afraid, went next door to the neighbors, and called nine-one-one. When the police arrived, Celeste's mother thought her own daughter had turned her in. She freaked out even more and started screaming at Celeste that she was going to kill her."

"Do you think she really meant it?" I asked.

"The police took it seriously. That's why Celeste is in a foster home. And she's taking it seriously, too. When she called me, she wouldn't even tell me where the foster home was because she was afraid her mother might come after her. She wouldn't even give me her telephone number."

I remembered how excited Celeste had been the day the family plays were performed about the little black suit she had gotten for her mother. I remembered them walking arm in arm into the library, both seeming so happy. How could so much have changed in so short a time? Or, perhaps more accurately, how could one relationship contain such extremes?

Rachel shook her head. "This kind of stuff kills me."

"What's going to happen to her? Is she going to come back to school?"

"She doesn't want to come anywhere near the school. She's afraid her mother might be hanging around. She says she's going to go to a school near the home."

"Poor Celeste! How's she going to handle all this in a family of strangers, starting a new school, cut off from her friends? Has anyone even talked to her mother?"

"I don't know. I haven't had a chance to talk to her social worker. You're right, though. We've got to get her back to this school." Rachel leaned forward and pounded her desk blotter with her index finger for emphasis as she said: "I mean, this school is the one thing going right in her life!"

I knew that Rachel was talking, at least partly, about the benefits Celeste had derived through her membership in the Drama Club, and I flushed momentarily with pride. But I also knew that Rachel suffered from the same do-gooder's disease as I and that a large part of the reason why we both wanted Celeste back at the school was that we wanted to be her saviors. I had hardly left Rachel's office before the egotism of our shared desire began to trouble me. And for the remainder of the day I was in a very strange, gloomy state, partly on account of Celeste's terrible situation but also because her plight made me hypersensitive to the ambiguities of my generosity and the limits of my compassion. In particular I remembered the afternoon I had informed her that her job made it impossible to give her a major part.

I had felt strong as I spoke. I had felt virtuous. My voice was full of understanding as I told Celeste about the limitations of our rehearsal schedule and of my obligations to her fellow cast members. I have no doubt that everything I said and did, in and of itself, was right. What was not right, however, was the private thrill the exercise of my own virtue gave me, a thrill that was enhanced—though only slightly; I don't want to exaggerate—by my knowledge that my words caused Celeste pain.

It was impossible to work with a girl like Celeste, a girl on kinetic and emotional overdrive, without sometimes getting angry at her. As much as I respected and liked her, I had been angry at her many times. I had also felt betrayed by her the day she ran out of the Drama Club without explanation and steadfastly refused to let me comfort her—to let me be her savior. I understood full well that there were countless reasons why an adolescent girl might not, and even should not, want to confide in a male teacher. But there it was: I had expended much time, much energy, and much thought to help this girl, and I wanted her gratitude. I wanted her to let me continue to help her.

I do not expect myself to be perfect. I do my best to restrain my less generous emotions—and, in particular, the secret selfishness of my generosity—but I do not expect those emotions to go away. Had Celeste's mother not threatened to kill her, had Celeste not been put in a foster home, I might never have given a thought to that private thrill I got from the exercise of my virtue or to any of the other times my lingering anger or sense of betrayal might have caused me to be more irritable with her or less encouraging than I would have been otherwise. But as I walked home that afternoon after my talk with Rachel, I worried that I had brought unnecessary pain into a life already so full of suffering and, worse, that the division between Celeste and me since the day of my private thrill might limit my ability to give her the help she now needed so desperately. I even worried that I didn't have the right to help her.

But these were not the ambiguities and limits that were to trouble me most. Those didn't become apparent until that night, over dinner, when I told my wife what had happened to Celeste and we began to talk about offering to let her stay in our own apartment, perhaps even adopting her.

The truth is that I brought up these possibilities only because I felt obliged to and not because I was ever, even for an instant, serious about them. My home was my sanctuary from all the turmoil I lived with at P.S. 227 and the Walt Whitman Academy. I could not bear the thought of bringing Celeste's misery into the middle of my family's happiness—although this was not a factor my wife and I discussed. We talked instead about the difficulty of putting Celeste up in our living room. We talked about the complications of her future relationship with her mother and her brother and sister. And we talked about our children. This was where we found absolution. Whatever we might have felt about Celeste, we couldn't risk our children's happiness or safety. That was obvious. That was legitimate. No one could blame us for thinking about our children. Even though we both knew that having Celeste in our home probably wouldn't have much effect on our children's happiness or safety, that it might even be good for them to witness and participate in such an act of compassion and social responsibility, and that whatever suffering my family might endure would probably be outweighed by the benefit Celeste would derive by being rescued from the instability and indifference of New York's foster care system and being brought into a happy and loving family.

So there it was: I was talking about my children, but in my heart I had recognized the degree to which my own comfort mattered more to me than alleviating the desperate suffering of a sweet girl I liked to think I cared about very much.

When my conversation with my wife had reached its inevitable conclusion, I felt that I had to do something more. So I called a friend who had an extra room and who had once said she would be willing to take in one of my troubled female students. I had only gotten out the words "Remember that time—" when she said, "Oh, no! I know why you're calling." She listened patiently while I explained the situation. She asked intelligent questions. There was a long silence during which she seemed to be seriously considering the possibility. But finally she said, "I can't. I've got to think about my own children." I was immensely relieved. Perhaps it had even been, secretly, to experience this relief that I had called her. She was no more virtuous than I on this count. Now it was my friend's turn to feel guilt. Over and over again she repeated: "Oh, I feel so awful!" And I was able to be a paragon of moral generosity and levelheadedness. "Oh no, you have to draw lines," I said. "If I didn't draw lines every time I went into the school, I wouldn't be able to do anything at all." I think that my friend was comforted by my words, but on at least two other occasions, she asked me about Celeste and told me how guilty she felt.

My friend also suffers from the do-gooder's disease. And this is its downside, this is why it is a disease: as soon as you decide to help other people, as soon as you allow yourself merely to understand that there are desperately suffering people whom you could help, you are doomed to self-hatred. Because no matter what you do, you can never do enough. Even if you fully alleviate one instance of suffering, and even if you feel a just satisfaction at what you have done, there are always millions of other cases as bad or worse that you not only could or should, but that you *must* also do something about. But you don't. You draw a line. And you start to hate yourself a little. This is one of the reasons so many teachers burn out after a few years. They end up trying to escape their self-hatred either by hating their needy students for their very neediness, or simply by quitting, moving to the country and taking up gardening. Rationalizations like "You're only human" or "You're only one person" are never adequate protection, because they do nothing to change the fact that, no matter how legitimate the indulgence of one's own comfort may be, it is finally always a matter of fiddling while someone else's Rome burns.

BY WEDNESDAY CELESTE STILL HAD NOT RETURNED TO THE school. Sasha Ortiz, Ricky's sister and Celeste's best friend, had a more complete version of the conflict between Celeste and her mother than Rachel's. Sasha told me that Celeste had slept over at her apartment without telling her mother and that it was on Celeste's return home the following day that her mother had flown into a rage.

Rachel told me that as far as she could tell, Celeste was going to stay with her foster family and go to a new school. But on Thursday I came out of the stairwell onto the third floor, and there was Celeste standing in the middle of the hall, talking to Mayra. When she saw me she called out my name, ran over, and taking a little leap, came to a halt right in front of me. "I'm back!" she declared with effervescent pride.

"I see you are," I said, somewhat taken aback by her manner. "I'm glad to see you. I was worried. How are you doing?"

"Fine," she said with a grin. She was acting as if she had suffered nothing more traumatic than a week in Florida.

She had been showing Mayra something when I came upon her, and now she showed it to me: a small gold-colored tin broach with a five-pointed star dangling by a tiny chain off one end. "My foster sister gave it to me," she said. "Isn't it beautiful!"

1   6

I Don't Want to Relive My Past

CELESTE RETURNED TO SCHOOL EXACTLY TWO WEEKS BEFORE
Will My Name Be Shouted Out? was to open, on March 11, in an afternoon performance before the sixth, seventh, and eighth grades. The
play would be performed one more time on Friday, March 12, in the
evening, at Teachers & Writers Collaborative's offices on Union Square.

Friday, February 26
During my regular T&W session with Celeste's eighth grade, I asked if
she wanted to come to the writing room after class and work with me
on her parts—the Minister and the Liquor Store Clerk.

"I can't," she said. "I'm too busy."

Figuring that on account of her family turmoil she probably had appointments with Rachel or with the guidance counselor, I asked: "Well,
can you make it to rehearsal this afternoon?"

"I got my baby-sitting job, remember?"

"Sure, but you can still come at two-fifteen, right?" She nodded. "Get
there on time and I'll make sure we do your scenes first."

"All right."

As I stood up to move on to the next student, I asked, letting my
concern come into my voice, "How you doing?"

She answered me exactly as she had the day before, with a fixed grin
and a perky "Fine."

At two-thirty she still hadn't shown up at rehearsal. I sent Lily Choi out to look for her, but she had vanished.

The rehearsal was rough. We were still doing the blocking we hadn't been able to do during the vacation rehearsals, still working on the high school scenes. The kids were bored and acting up, especially—as always—José, Keisha, and Tunisia. During the last half hour of the rehearsal, I gave everyone a break from blocking and let them do a line-through of the whole play. But I was frustrated. With all the goofing off and interruptions, we had hardly made any progress.

Monday, March 1

I came into school at ten in the morning to work independently with José and Tunisia. José was in great shape. He had his whole part memorized. The only section that still gave him trouble was the long poem—written by Arlene Salter—at the end of the play. He told me that he hadn't bothered to memorize it because he said he was just going to read it off of a paper. "No," I said, "you're just going to *pretend* to read it. After the first few lines you'll gradually let the paper down and speak the rest of it to the audience." José kept on asking me why he couldn't just read it, but it was clear that he understood perfectly well and would eventually come around.

When the session was done and we were getting ready to leave the writing room, José asked, "Am I gonna get to use a real gun?"

At first I thought he was joking, but then I saw from his expression that he was perfectly serious. "No, José, you're going to use one of my son's toys."

"Aw, c'mon! Can't I use a real gun? I know someone who can get one for you."

"Thanks, but that's all right."

JOSÉ HAD TO GO TO JOAN GOLD'S ROOM TO PICK UP HIS BACK-pack. It was Joan's prep period, so I went over to her desk to say hello. Without even raising her head to look at me, she said, "Xia's absent again," scoring another point in our long-standing debate about Xia's worthiness. I didn't take up the challenge, because I was in a hurry to see Tunisia.

I found her in her Spanish class. When I walked into the room she gave me a sullen stare and said, "I don't want to do it now." Then she looked away, not even giving me a chance to respond.

"Well, when *do* you want to rehearse?" I asked, addressing the back of her head.

Without looking around, she answered, "I don't know."

I put on my boss-teacher voice: "Come outside, Tunisia."

Head lowered and sulky, as if she were going off to prison, she followed me out into the hall. I asked her if she wanted to be in the play.

"I don't know." She didn't meet my eye.

"Well, *decide,* because I have to know if I can count on you. If you tell me now that you don't want to to be in the play—fine. You're the only one affected by your decision. But if you wait until the last minute, you could wreck the play for everybody." She didn't respond, so I asked her a second time if she wanted to be in the play and she said, "No."

"Okay. But I want you to think about it. I only want you in the play if you are enjoying it—which doesn't seem to be the case. But I want to give you time to change your mind. If you show up at the rehearsal this afternoon, I'll consider you in the play and I'll forget this conversation. If you don't come, well, that's it. You're out."

I was very upset when I left Tunisia. We seemed to be losing cast members by the handful. I was beginning to worry that my biggest problem was not getting enough rehearsal time but merely keeping the group together until opening night. I went straight down to the main office to call Xia, who had finally gotten a telephone. It seemed that if nothing else, the advent of her stepfather had provided her family with decided economic benefits.

The first piece of good news was simply that Xia answered the phone, which meant that she hadn't been cutting school. Then, when I asked if she was going to be able to make it to rehearsal, she answered, to my immense relief, with an unequivocal "Yeah."

"So, why aren't you here now?"

"My mom had a miscarriage on Saturday and I had to stay home to take care of her."

"Oh. I'm sorry. How's she doing?"

"Well, she lost a lot of blood. She had this big hemorrhage. And now she's all yellow and tired. And this morning, when she got out of bed, she fainted."

My wife had also hemorrhaged during the birth of our daughter, losing 60 percent of her blood. From Xia's description, it sounded as if her mother was in exactly the same condition. I gave Xia all the advice that our doctors had given us, and told her I would see her at three.

Feeling that now I had a potential point to score in the great debate with Joan Gold, I hurried back upstairs, hoping to catch her before the end of her prep period.

What I really wanted to do was not win our debate but end it. Joan had been one of my best friends and allies at the school. She had helped me through my first nervous year teaching the junior high and, through her advice, confidence, and stabilizing effect in the classroom, had played an important role in the success of all of my projects, including the Bensonhurst and Thomas Jefferson plays. I wouldn't have been half so surprised and troubled by her antagonism toward Xia had I not had such respect for her judgment. It was disconcerting that she and I could have such different impressions of the girl, and it was largely to put my mind at ease that I wanted to win her over to my side.

Joan was not in her room, but as I turned away from the door, I saw her coming down the hall.

On hearing my news about Xia, she protested, "But Steve, that's exactly my point! Her mother shouldn't be putting this burden on her. All I want is for Xia's family to realize that she *has* to come to school, that her education *matters*. They shouldn't be using her as a baby-sitter."

"But her mother fainted when she got out of bed this morning. She obviously can't take care of herself, and who else is going to take care of her?"

"This is always happening with Xia. You've seen my attendance book. She's never at school. Maybe this morning her mother really did need her, but that can't be true all the time. Look at Tunisia. Her mother died a couple of years ago and her father is all on his own—but does he act like Xia's mother? No. He makes his kids *work*. Every kid in that house knows they have to work."

What working had to do with Xia's mother's health problems was not clear. But the prep period was over, and I had to hurry home to take care of my daughter for a couple of hours until my wife could get back from her job; then I could return to school for the rehearsal.

I walked into the auditorium at exactly three o'clock, and, as she had promised, Xia was waiting for me on the stage.

Twenty minutes later—that is, twenty minutes late—Tunisia walked in the door with Keisha and Chantell. Despite the girls' lateness, I was very happy to see Tunisia and welcomed her back. She completely ignored me, however, which led me to wonder if she had come back not by her own free will but because she had been forced by her two friends.

The rehearsal went well. At last we finished blocking the high school scenes and went on to do the only other scene employing every member of the cast: the funeral. Since Celeste wasn't there to be the Minister, I asked Tunisia to fill in, but she refused. So I asked Hernan Rodriguez (who had a minor Cast Member part) to do it instead.

Before we could even start the scene, Xia asked, "How come Celeste is still in the play when she never comes to rehearsals?"

"Yeah," said Keisha. "We don't even know how good she is. She might embarrass us when we perform."

"Let's not be too hard on Celeste," I said. "She's good. We all know that. Besides she's had a pretty good reason for missing rehearsals."

I was astonished to hear Xia, of all people, reply: "She's been using what happened in her family too much. That's over now."

"The reason she's not here," I explained, "is that she has to take care of a third-grader after school."

Mayra said: "She's just using that baby-sitting job as an excuse to talk to Sasha."

I assumed that what Mayra meant was that Sasha was accompanying Celeste when she walked the third-grader home and took care of him. Only afterwards did it occur to me that she might have meant that Celeste no longer *had* the babysitting job.

The blocking of the funeral scene and final exit went smoothly. And I think everyone was pleased—with the exception of Tunisia, who was sulky and rude throughout the whole rehearsal. At one point, when I was explaining how I wanted each Cast Member to exit after finishing his or her speech, Tunisia shouted out: "Why do you keep talking so much? That's what slows everything down."

Turning to her, I said, "The reason I have to keep explaining the same things over and over again, Tunisia, is because people like you keep interrupting me." She didn't say another word after that, but she glowered at her feet for the remainder of the afternoon, adding a dissonant note to what otherwise had been a very good rehearsal.

That night I began to wonder if the kids in the cast didn't have a point. Maybe it was a bad idea for Celeste to have such important roles, given how little she was able to rehearse. In the four weeks since I had announced the parts, she had managed no more than half an hour of rehearsal with the whole cast. Also, during independent rehearsals I had been having with her, she had not been able to imbue the Minister's eulogy with any passion or pathos. In the end I decided to ease everyone's worries about Celeste's performance, including her own, by giving the Minister to someone else (maybe Shanequa Franklin—the Bensonhurst Chorus Leader—who had been hanging around rehearsals lately) and letting Celeste concentrate on her opening monologue and the Liquor Store Clerk.

Tuesday, March 2

In the morning Jessica and I rehearsed the three "boys" and Celeste in the robbery scene. We had planned to use the auditorium but came to school to find that the lower grades were having an assembly, so instead we did the scene in a large lobbylike area opening onto the back stairwell on the second floor. We had adequate room to perform there but were constantly interrupted by classes passing back and forth.

Despite such frustrations, the rehearsal went fairly well. Celeste gave the Clerk a comic edge that, frankly, the play sorely needed. Celeste's Clerk had seen it all before and had such an air of resignation during the robbery that she was able to joke with her assailants, asking them if they wanted "paper or plastic" to carry the money off. None of the other actors who had done this scene in Celeste's absence had ever managed to make this line work so naturally.

Once we had completed the robbery scene, we wanted to do a couple of other scenes which featured the "boys." While Jessica was setting the first of these up, I took Celeste down the hall for a talk.

I began by telling her what a great job she had done with the Liquor Store Clerk. Then I let her know about the concerns the other cast members had about her having been to so few rehearsals. (I didn't say anything about the baby-sitting because I didn't want to turn this into a confrontation.) Celeste seemed to take everything I said with complete alacrity. And when I asked her how she would feel about giving up the part of the Minister, she said, "That's fine. I never liked that part anyway."

It was done. Painless.

The second part of the rehearsal didn't go very well. José kept hamming up his speeches, and Keisha started to argue with him. Deciding this was a sign that they were getting tired, I said we had done enough for the day and sent everyone back to their classes.

All through the rehearsal, Tunisia had been hanging around watching. I knew that she had pretended to her teacher that she had to rehearse in order to get out of class, but I didn't call her on it: I was tired of fighting with her. After my conversation with Celeste, an idea popped into my head. Almost on impulse, I asked Tunisia to stay behind when the rest of the cast was leaving.

She got that sulky expression on her face and told me she had to go with Keisha. "Wait a minute," I said, as she started to move away. "I've got good news."

This stopped her. "What?"

Keisha was lingering a few steps away. I told her to go back to class because I wanted a private talk with her friend.

"Uh-oh!" She rolled her eyes and hurried off.

I turned to Tunisia. "You saw me talking to Celeste?"

Tunisia nodded cautiously.

"I was asking her if she would mind if I gave the part of the Minister to someone else. She said she didn't, so I was wondering if you would like to do it?"

Tunisia's whole face popped open with surprise. "Really?"

"Sure, if you want to do it. Do you?"

A tremor of worry crossed her brow: "I don't know."

"You don't have to if you don't want to. I was also thinking of asking Shanequa."

That did the trick. "All right," she said. "I'll do it."

We went straight off to the writing room, where she read the part over silently a couple of times. It was very short, and she almost had it memorized by the time she stood up to perform.

She hadn't gotten half a sentence out before I saw that she was ten times better at this part than Celeste. Her voice was deep and rich, and she spoke the lines in the mounting and falling cadences of an evangelical preacher.

When she had finished I clapped and told her that her performance was absolutely perfect, that I couldn't think of a thing to improve it. She was so excited that she actually hopped up and down, kicking her heels out sideways. I couldn't get over the transformation. Ten minutes before she had been this sulky recidivist convict, and now she was a gangly six-year-old on Christmas, all bounces and proud giggles.

"When I do this," she said, "I hear Martin Luther King talking in my head."

"Perfect! You couldn't hear a better person."

We did the piece over a few more times, until the repetition seemed to take some of the fire out of her performance. Then I let her go, telling her she was wonderful, she'd got the part.

The door closed behind her. I was alone in the writing room and I almost did a childish dance of my own. "You've had a breakthrough!" I told myself incredulously. "That's what you've had: you've had a breakthrough."

That afternoon at three o'clock, with my one-year-old daughter, Emma, on my hip, I met Xia, Arlene, and Mayra in the art room and spent a serene hour and a half listening to them gossip and helping them paint the play's only scenery: a row of gray school lockers, topped by a jumble of bright, ballooning graffiti gradually disappearing into a mist of black spray paint.

Wednesday, March 3

I came to school to work with the three mothers, only to find that Xia was absent again. Unable to face Joan, I stopped off at Rachel's office, where I heard that this time Xia had gone out to Queens because her grandmother was sick. "What we've got to get this family is a housekeeper," said Rachel.

"What we've got to get them is a live-in nurse!" I said.

Thursday, March 4

My second seventh-grade class was canceled because of a Walt Whitman Academy awards assembly. Not having anything else to do and figuring it would give me some insight into the quality of my students' work outside of my own classes, I accompanied Joan down to the auditorium and took a seat in the back row. Rachel was the MC, standing, microphone in hand, just in front of the stage and beside a table stacked with about fifty award certificates.

I was pleased to hear Rachel call out Mayra's name for awards in math and in leadership. Keisha and Arlene also got awards in math, and in most other subjects as well—which was no surprise; they were both extremely smart girls. I was also pleased to hear that, despite her feud with Joan, Xia was granted an award in language arts, as well as in art and leadership.

As is always the case, the awards assembly afforded a very clear picture not only of the students' academic accomplishments but of their social standing as well. When some students were called, the room was silent, apart from the normal rustle and murmur of perpetually restless adolescents. When Xia, Mayra, and Arlene were called, there was scattered clapping. But every time Rachel spoke Keisha's name, the whole room erupted in shouts and applause, which got louder with each successive occasion.

It was Celeste who started the booing, first when Arlene's name was called for the second time, and then whenever a relatively unpopular child's name was called, and finally, merely automatically, whenever anyone, even Keisha, was given an award.

Award assemblies are very delicate affairs at schools like the Walt Whitman Academy, where so many students have so little respect for academic excellence and even lower respect for themselves. Perhaps more than to recognize accomplishment, these assemblies are intended to bolster the students' always delicate self-esteem, which is why so many awards are given. The hope is that, just as a diploma from the Wizard of Oz instantly transformed the Scarecrow into a math whiz, the rise in self-confidence inspired by an award will result in genuine academic improvement during the remainder of the year—an improvement that will authenticate anything that might have been tenuous about the award in the first place.

When the audience goes along with the intended spirit of these assemblies—when the announcement of an award evokes cheers, even if only some of the time—the awards probably do help boost low student self-esteem. But when the audience goes against the intended spirit—when the awards are met by boos—then they can actually become destructive. The students feel blighted rather than rewarded, foolish rather than smart. And if the booing goes on long enough, if the people running the assembly cannot control the audience, then the assembly becomes worse than a farce. It becomes a confirmation of the secret malingering suspicion of everyone in the room, teachers as well as students, that the institution pretending to celebrate academic success is itself nothing more than a hollow failure.

One of the reasons Celeste was able to continue booing her class-mates for so long—joined only halfheartedly by a few other kids in the room—was that she was seated at the center of a long row where no teacher could reach her. Finally, one teacher grew so angry that he plunged down the row, stepping over students' knees and on their feet, grabbed Celeste by the arm, and dragged her out of the auditorium.

I watched this whole scene play out, hating to see Celeste in so much trouble but understanding the teacher's anger perfectly. Later, in the main office, I overheard Fran and Rachel talking about Celeste. Fran said, "I don't see that we have any choice. The newspaper delivery job is meant to be an honor. We just can't let her keep doing it." Rachel drew her breath to speak, but Fran cut her off. "I know Celeste has had a terrible time lately, but she's been getting away with murder in every single one of her classes since she came back—and now this! I'm as sorry for her as anybody, but we've got to show her that certain behavior just won't be tolerated."

Rachel sighed heavily: "I guess so."

"Listen," said Fran, "it's for her own good."

"I hope you're right."

I did too.

Friday, March 5

As soon as I came in for my regular T&W sessions with the two eighth-grade classes, Joan told me that Xia was absent for the third day in a row. She refrained from making any additional comment other than to cast me a half-inquisitive, half-reproving glance over the top of her glasses, which I pretended not to notice. My stance had become that Xia may have been a problem for Joan and for other teachers, but she had always come through for me, so I was not going to lose faith in her. But even so, I was worried.

After that day's rehearsal, we would have only three more before the first performance, which was less than a week away. I had no doubt that Xia would have her lines memorized and that her performance would be more than adequate, even if she didn't have another moment of rehearsal. But she had missed so much of the blocking! The best per-formance in the world would look ridiculous if the actor didn't know where she should be standing or how to move.

I was having similar worries about Celeste, who had a firm grasp on her own scene but not a clue as to what she should be doing during the rest of the play, when, since none of the cast ever left the stage, she would have to be a cross between a dancer and a piece of mobile scenery. During her class, I crouched down beside her desk.

"You coming to rehearsal this afternoon?" I asked.

Her perkiness and fixed grin were gone. She answered with a blank-eyed somnambulistic nod.

"What's up?" I said. "You okay?"

"Of course!"

"You sure you don't want to talk about it in the hall?"

Her answer was firm and loud: "No." She glanced at me for the first time, then looked away.

"Okay, Celeste. I just want to make sure that you're really coming this afternoon. Last week you told me you would, but you didn't show up."

"I'm coming," she said impatiently. "But I have to leave at ten minutes to three to pick up the kid I baby-sit for."

"You don't need ten minutes just to walk over to his classroom."

"Yes I do. His mother doesn't want him waiting around. They get out at five to three."

"All right. All right. But why don't you bring him back to the rehearsal? I'm sure he'd have fun watching us."

"Uh-uh! His mother wants me to bring him straight home."

"Okay. Not today. But listen, I want you to do me a favor. Ask his mother if he can come to the rehearsals on Monday and Tuesday. I'm going to make the final adjustments in the blocking for the whole play on those days, and you've missed all of it. You really need to come, so ask his mother. You can tell her that I'll have Erin or Siobhan take care of him while you're busy. She can even call me if she wants."

"All right," she said in exasperation.

"So you'll ask her?"

"All *right*, I said!"

"And you'll be in the auditorium at two-fifteen?"

No answer.

I scribbled my telephone number on a piece of paper for the third-grader's mother and went on to the next student.

After I had finished both classes, I went to the writing room, where Siobhan was working with Lily Choi and Julie Madera. Both girls had only Cast Member parts. Lily was Cast Member 8, both of whose speeches had been written by Xia. Lily had no trouble with her closing speech: "I think that everyone should integrate and try their best to fight violence with love." But she had terrible trouble with her opening one: "My cousin and some of his friends were playing around the house. One of his friends found a gun that was left in the house and thought it was a toy and shot my cousin in the chest. My cousin died in my aunt's bed."

She was trying to do the speech from memory and would get halfway through the first sentence, stop, then stamp on the floor and shake her lowered head, moaning about how she had messed up. She did this over and over again, never getting all the way to the end of that first sentence. I have no doubt that her trouble had something to do with her brother's death, since everything in Lily's life at this time was somehow affected by that terrible event. But she had had exactly the same problems when rehearsing her family play, in which her role could hardly have been more tame: a little girl spoiled by her grandmother. My sense was that Lily acted up like this primarily as a way of drawing attention to herself and perhaps giving herself an excuse in the event of failure. Siobhan was doing a wonderful job at keeping her patience, telling her after each aborted attempt: "That's all right, Lily. You'll do it. Just take a deep breath and try again."

After listening to this routine four or five times, I interrupted. "Lily, do you want to do this speech? You don't have to if you don't want to. You can just come on and be silent, or we can even slip you onstage later in the play." Cast Member 8's opening monologue was not particularly impressive, so I could make this suggestion without too much risk to the play, even though I didn't think she would take me up on it. "What do you think?"

Lily was silent a moment, then declared, "Of course I want to do it!"

"All right. Just read it through one time. You don't have to do it from memory." She performed the monologue perfectly, so I dismissed her, telling her we would work on it more at the rehearsal. She walked out with a reaffirmed commitment and a modest success. I thought that was the best way to leave things for the time being.

Julie had been heaving sighs and drumming her fingers on the desk all through Lily's rehearsal. Julie was skinny, with coffee brown skin and a head of Orphan Annie curls. She had done an excellent job as the daughter of Celeste's drunken artist father. I had given her the opening

Cast Member monologue—Cornell Vargas's piece about his father's murder—because I thought Julie would be able to put real feeling into it and because her little-girl manner would give it some extra poignancy.

Julie, however, was something of a prima donna. I don't think she had ever believed me when I told her I thought Cast Member 1's monologue was the single most important speech in the play. She thought that she should have been given one of the mother's parts and spent most of every rehearsal making it clear to me how insulted she was.

As Siobhan and I listened, Julie gave her monologue an adequate but passionless recitation. I knew that she could do much better. Deciding that her ego needed a little feeding, I told her what a good actress she was, that she had a rare gift for bringing out the emotional nuances of a piece, and that I wanted her to do the piece again, but this time try to feel everything the speaker would feel on reexperiencing the death of her father. "Okay," she sighed, and gave another lackluster performance.

The time had come to put on some pressure.

I said: "You're just not putting enough feeling into it, Julie. I know you can do better."

"I can't," she moaned.

"Why not?"

"Because I don't want to relive my past."

"But it's not your past."

"Yes it is. My father got shot too. He got shot three times in the chest."

Siobhan and I looked at one another across the top of Julie's head. Neither of us said a word for a moment.

Finally I managed: "I'm sorry to hear that . . . Did it happen recently?"

"No. I was just a baby—ten months old. It happened on a Friday and my parents were going to get married that Saturday. That's why I have my mother's name and not my father's. He was a cabdriver. I think he got shot while driving his cab. But he was in Boston. He used to travel a lot because his first wife lived in Boston and she wouldn't let him see the kids unless he brought money. So he was always driving his cab up to Boston. And one night he just got shot."

• • •

346 • Will My Name Be Shouted Out?

As I listened to Julie's story, I thought about a child in my eight-year-old son's private school class who had suffered a divorce. All of the parents of the other children gossiped to one another, saying, "Oh what a terrible thing to happen!" "The poor child!" "At his age especially!" And so forth. When our son came home from school describing the poor child's bad moods and misbehavior, my wife and I shook our heads knowingly and counseled tolerance and pity, saying, "You have to understand; he's having a hard time now." But such pain was almost nothing to the children at the Walt Whitman Academy. Virtually every one of them came from a broken home. And so many of them had suffered far worse losses and had far more frightening things done to them. Was it any wonder, then, that these children couldn't pay attention to their schoolwork and freaked out whenever any pressure was put on them?

That afternoon at the rehearsal, Tunisia was more tranquil than usual, but otherwise showed no other evidence of the breakthrough that had made me so happy.

Xia didn't show. And neither did Celeste.

José and Keisha acted up in their normal way, but I got more than normally angry with them.

Monday, March 8

I came to school worried that José and Keisha would be carrying grudges from Friday's rehearsal, but they were in great spirits and worked very well together. No fights. By the time they went back to their classes my mind was considerably eased about the two of them. I knew that they would not let me down. I was, however, no longer quite so sure about Xia, who, they had informed me, was still absent. I tried calling her at home, but there was no answer. I didn't have her grandmother's number with me at school.

At lunchtime I sought Celeste out in the cafeteria and found her sitting by herself at a table while her classmates waited in line to get their lunches. Like many girls in the junior high, Celeste was skipping lunch. Unlike most girls, however, Celeste hardly had to worry about her weight—a strong breeze would have blown her over—which made me wonder, as I sat down next to her on the bench, if, in addition to her other problems, she also had an eating disorder.

"Celeste," I asked, "did you talk to the mother of your third-grader about bringing him to rehearsal?"

"No." Her expression was tight lipped and blank. "I'm not baby-sitting for him."

"So you can come to rehearsal?"

"No. I have to go straight home from school."

"Oh, Celeste!" I felt a general plunge of spirits. "I told you this was a very important rehearsal. We're performing on Thursday. That's only three days away. And you haven't learned any of the blocking. Do you know your part?"

She shook her head.

"Celeste!" My spirits sank even lower. "How do you expect me to let you stay in the play?"

No response.

"I don't think I can keep you in. It's not fair to the other kids. They've been working so hard, and they say that you haven't been baby-sitting but just using that as an excuse to hang out with Sasha."

Celeste didn't deny the charge.

I really didn't want to kick her out of the play but saw that I had to keep to my standards or the scant discipline among the rest of the cast would fall apart. I decided to see how much the play mattered to Celeste. I said, "What do you want to do?"

"Not be in the play, I guess."

"Really? Is that *really* true?"

No response.

"I'll tell you what: you see what you can do to come to at least part of the rehearsal this afternoon. If you come, you're still in the play; if you don't, I'll give your parts to someone else."

This strategy had worked with Tunisia, but it didn't with Celeste.

At the rehearsal, the kids told me that she was outside "chillin'" with Sasha. They also said that she had told them I had kicked her out of the play. Even though I had partially decided to risk losing Celeste as a way of demonstrating my fairness and my seriousness about rehearsals to the rest of the cast, I could not bear to have them think that I had kicked her out. Instead I recited the conversation quoted above, making it clear that Celeste was out through her own choice.

Celeste's Cast Member 2 speech had been Cesaré Lopez's account of hearing about her sister's murder. This was one I hated to lose, but I thought it would only cause confusion if I asked one of the other actors to drop her Cast Member speech and learn this one. Celeste's other part, the Liquor Store Clerk, was indispensable. I originally wanted to offer it to Julie Madera, but she was absent, so I asked Lily Choi if she would do it. I knew that Lily's performance would be pathetic by comparison to Julie's and certainly to Celeste's, but I also knew from Siobhan that she really wanted a larger part in the play, so I decided to risk it.

Lily was silent and expressionless for a good ten seconds after I made the offer, then finally nodded, cracked a small smile, and said, "Okay." I sent her off with Fred Glover to work on the lines while I gathered the rest of the cast together to begin the rehearsal.

I had originally intended to make my final directorial changes—including blocking—on the first half of the play but decided to start with the second half, so that Lily could get a chance to do the robbery scene. No sooner did I explain this to the cast than Tunisia shouted out, "That don't make no sense!" And Keisha chimed in with, "Everybody knows you should start a play at the beginning!"

Before I could think up a suitably witty response to these remarks, the door at the rear of the auditorium clanked open and Xia entered carrying a plastic bag. The cast rushed from the stage to gather around her, and Fred and I followed.

Xia had brought clothing she intended to wear in the play: a long black skirt with a gold top and a snugly fitting black jacket. Everybody wanted Xia to put her outfit on, but I worried that changing would waste too much time, so I said that tomorrow would be a dress rehearsal and that everybody should wear his or her costume.

I hoped that Xia's return, which must have been nearly as much of a relief to her fellow actors as to me, would make for a smooth rehearsal—but instead it was our worst rehearsal yet. The kids were too nervous about the impending performance. Keisha and Tunisia kept up with their complaints and constant fits of temper. José was continually clowning: mimicking the walk of the other actors or making faces at them while they were in the middle of their monologues. Even Mayra, who had no lines in the second half of the play, kept putting her hands to her head and moaning, "I'm missing computer!" (Apparently the Computer Club, to which Mayra belonged, was being given instructions for some contest that day.)

Xia was my one consolation. Her performance was flawless. She had no trouble picking up the blocking. If not for her seriousness—and that of the other two mothers, Chantell and Arlene—the rehearsal might have been an infuriating washout.

While the kids were packing up their things to go home, I took Xia aside and said, "I'm really glad to see you here, Xia. But you know, you can't skip school and come to rehearsals."

"I didn't skip school. I was helping my grandmother."

"I know that. But the point is, if people find out that you come to rehearsal on days when you don't come to school, they may force me to drop you from the play."

She lowered her head: "I'm sorry."

"Just make sure you're at school every day until Friday, okay?"

She looked up at me, smiled, and ran off with Mayra.

The "people" I was talking about were, as I was sure Xia understood, only one person: Joan Gold. It seemed to me that she was angry enough at Xia to try to make some trouble. I hoped she wouldn't find out that Xia had come that afternoon—but she did.

Tuesday, March 9

Joan stopped me in the hallway first thing on my arrival at the school the following morning. "I hear you kicked Celeste out of the Drama Club yesterday."

Squirming yet again, I explained how I had done everything I could, but Celeste just wouldn't come to rehearsals.

"All I can say is that it's too bad, especially when you think of all the family troubles she's been having. At least she's been coming to school—unlike Xia. Xia's the one you ought to throw out of the play, and let Celeste stay."

Joan's every word evoked a pang from my conscience. I couldn't reply. Seeing my anguish, she patted me on the hand and said, "Don't worry about it, Steve. I know you're over a barrel."

After this exchange, I went down to the office to talk to Fran Kaplan about the final details of Thursday's performance. On the bench beside the mailboxes I found Lily, looking glum and very self-contained, though she had obviously been crying. She pretended not to notice me until I spoke. "Lily, what are you doing here?"

"I'm in trouble."

The notion of Lily in trouble was so outlandish that I almost thought she was joking. "What did you do?"

She didn't get a chance to answer before the school secretary shouted out: "She got in a fight. She knocked down another girl on the playground and was hitting her."

"Is this true?" I asked.

Lily only nodded. Just at that moment, Fran told me she had a minute to speak with me in her office. It was Lily's turn after me. As we passed each other in the doorway, I said a silent prayer that her punishment wouldn't include being forbidden to participate in the play.

We were to rehearse from one-thirty to three that afternoon because another group had reserved the auditorium for after school. I wanted to do a quick independent practice of the breakfast scene with Khalil and his mother before the rehearsal because I hadn't been satisfied with the way it had worked in the previous day's rehearsal. I found Anna and Xia in the cafeteria and brought them, with their lunches, up to the writing room.

The breakfast scene, which occurs on the morning Khalil has decided to shoot his friends, is a sort of dance of approach and retreat, recognition and denial between the mother and son. As we had blocked it at the previous rehearsal, the movements of each actor had been too static, with Alexandra standing throughout and Khalil mostly sitting. It had occurred to me that after exclaiming to her son that he wouldn't be late for school because it was only seven in the morning, Alexandra should become concerned and sit at the table with Khalil, who would then stand up, saying, "Look, I have to go to school now." Then, after she had told him that she cared for him and he sat back down, she would stand up, move away from him, then come back to stand behind him and place her hands on his shoulders, as he looks up at her and says, "Can I ask you something?"

Xia and Anna did the scene this way and it worked much better. Jessica came in while we were rehearsing and added some brilliant touches, including having Alexandra step away from her son when he asks, "Why is this world so cruel?" as if the question was too much for her to contemplate. Her withdrawal, coupled with her inability to answer Khalil's question, beautifully set up Khalil's sudden flight from the house saying, "I hate this world! I hate this life!"

Xia worked seriously and gave a moving, tender performance. But something was bothering her. Between her bouts of acting she made no jokes, cracked no smile. She just sat on the window ledge with that half-angry, shut-down expression of hers.

Sensing that yet another obstacle to the performance might be looming, I walked out with her while Anna remained behind to do additional work with Jessica.

"So how you doing?" I asked as we went down the dark steps from the writing room to the stage.

"All right." She heaved a sigh.

"You don't sound all right."

She stopped outside the stage door. "My dad got arrested last night."

"Your *dad*?" I asked, remembering that her father was in jail.

"My stepdad."

"Why? What happened?"

"My stepdad doesn't really know anybody in our new neighborhood. So sometimes he goes back to our old block, just to hang out with his friends. And that's what he was doing the other day when the police came to arrest some drug dealers down the block a little. And . . . well . . . after the police arrested those drug dealers, they took my stepdad along with them, just because he was on the same block." As she said this, Xia's fury at the injustice of it shook her voice.

"Have they let him out yet?" I asked.

"No. They're not going to let him out. He's going to jail."

This didn't make sense to me. "They can't hold him, Xia. He didn't do anything."

"Yes, they can. The thing is, he was already in jail for eleven years. He only just got out of jail nine months ago, and he was on parole, and he wasn't supposed to be associating with drug dealers—and he *wasn't!* But the cops don't care. To them the fact that he got arrested with drug dealers is the same thing as associating with them. He's going back to jail and he won't be out for years."

She said this with such assurance that I couldn't contradict her. "How's your mom doing?"

"She's upset."

Xia didn't seem to want to talk about this any longer, so I just told her—pathetic response as it may have been—that I hoped everything would work out.

I didn't know what to think about the arrest. It didn't seem so unlikely to me that an ex-con, whatever his parole restrictions, would get involved in the drug trade soon after getting out of jail. On the other hand, innocent black and Latino men got arrested all the time in New York. One thing I was pretty sure of, however, was that with the stepfather in jail, Xia and her family would not be able to sustain their new affluence for very long.

During that afternoon's rehearsal—the dress rehearsal—rather than merely work on the first half of the play, as I had originally planned, I decided to do a complete run-through. There were mistakes, mostly little ones that I let go with no more than a couple of words' comment. I didn't want to interrupt the play's momentum. On the contrary, I wanted the play to come to life. And as it did, haltingly, awkwardly—a bit like Frankenstein's monster—the cast and I began to sigh inwardly with relief. Now we could see how all the sweating over the blocking had paid off. Now we remembered why the play had seemed so exciting to us in the first place. When I called the cast together for a few words about the next day's rehearsal, there was an eager attentiveness in everyone's face—no moaning, no teasing. Everyone understood what I was telling them and why I was saying it. The process made sense. We were a team. It was one of those good moments that made all of the arduous ones seem worthwhile.

The only person who didn't seem to enjoy herself was Lily. She wouldn't say her lines loudly enough for anyone on the stage to hear, let alone the audience. And she kept messing them up. Siobhan would take her aside for extensive coaching and sympathy sessions, but they didn't seem to do any good. At one point, after doing the robbery scene, Lily sharply turned her back as Siobhan approached and flung her script over her shoulder. I was getting worried that she simply wasn't going to work out as the Clerk. I wanted to talk to her after rehearsal, but she left too soon. I told Mayra to study her parts.

Yet another potential threat to the play was Julie Madera's continued absence. Nobody knew where she was or when she would be back. I asked Shanequa, who had been hanging around as usual, if she would be interested in doing the opening monologue, and she accepted eagerly. Clearly she had been waiting for just such a request all along.

Wednesday, March 10

We were now only one day from the first performance—in front of the whole Walt Whitman Academy—of *Will My Name Be Shouted Out?* Just before starting our final rehearsal Wednesday morning, I took Lily aside.

"Listen, Lily," I said, "I saw that you were pretty upset yesterday. I can understand why this play would make you upset. I just want to say that you don't have to do it if you don't want to. You can be my assistant. And you can help with the props and anything else you want. Would you rather do that?"

"No."

"Do you want to be in the play, then?"

"I don't know."

"Listen, Lily, it's too late for 'I don't know's.' We have to know whether we can count on you. Tell me definitely: do you want to be in the play or not?"

"I don't know."

"Lily, that's not good enough. We can't have anyone in the play who doesn't really want to be. I'm going to ask you one more time and if you say 'I don't know,' it means 'no.' Do you want to be in the play?"

"Yes."

So we did the rehearsal, and Lily was fine. What a surprise!

We ran through the play twice. Siobhan and Jessica came back at three to do yet more work with Xia and Anna on the breakfast scene. Jessica reblocked it beautifully. Julie Madera still was absent, so Shanequa filled in for her and did a fine job. But when I got home Julie called me to say that she had been having stomach flu and would be coming on Thursday. She told me that Arlene had told her everything she needed to know about the blocking. I was dubious but said she could at least do the opening monologue.

I knew that Shanequa would be disappointed, but my first loyalty had to be to Julie, since she had been in the Drama Club all year, whereas Shanequa had only started hanging around with us again in the last couple of weeks. Also, I was a little annoyed with Shanequa, because that afternoon I had gotten an indication that she had begun plotting with Tunisia just as she had with Yolanda.

It had happened after Shanequa finished her first reading of Julie's monologue. Tunisia came up to me and said, "Shanequa should do my monologue."

"Why?" I asked. "You've been doing a fantastic job."

"I can't do it."

"Nonsense! You'll be wonderful. Besides, Shanequa's already got a monologue to practice."

That night I hardly slept. I woke up at two having thought of all sorts of last-minute changes and encouragements I had to make the following morning. Then, when I finally got back to sleep about three-thirty, Emma woke up and I had to give her a bottle. I got back to sleep again around five and was awake again at seven.

I Told You I Couldn't Do It

I ARRIVED BEFORE SCHOOL OPENED ON PERFORMANCE DAY TO SET up the scenery and props on the auditorium stage. The performance was to be at ten because we had to have the auditorium cleared by eleven, when the lower grades would come down to lunch and then flock to the auditorium to watch cartoons and music videos (as they always did when it was too cold or wet to go outside). By nine o'clock the whole cast, including Julie Madera, had assembled on the stage. I took it as a good sign that everyone had come of their own volition and hadn't had to be bribed or cajoled out of a classroom.

They were all avid-eyed, a bit breathless, very excited, but at the same time subdued, waiting for me to tell them what to do. As I watched them show off their costumes and make gentle fun of one another, I began to feel increasingly confident in the assertion with which I had reassured myself countless times over the past weeks, that however disorderly our rehearsals had been, when the time came to perform, the kids would pull through.

The aspect of the performance that worried me most was still the blocking. We had had to make so many changes, and some of the kids—Xia and Julie, in particular—had missed so many rehearsals, that I wasn't at all sure the play mightn't be ruined by actors bumping into one another or discovering themselves all alone in the wrong corner of the stage. I called the cast together and explained that we didn't have

355

time to go through the whole play before our performance, but that I wanted to do a "fast-forward" rehearsal, in which the actors would walk through the play at triple time, only speaking the cue lines.

Predictably, Keisha complained: "That's crazy! We're gonna get all confused." And Tunisia said: "We got to go get our costumes on!" But once the cast got the hang of doing the play at a pixilated pace, they all enjoyed it. José in particular had fun hurrying through his performance like a silent movie comic. There were a few mistakes, but on the whole the cast did well. And at the rehearsal's conclusion, I was greatly relieved. The cast went up to the writing room to get into their costumes. I gave the props and scenery a last check-over and drew the stage curtains.

SOON THE AUDITORIUM WAS LOUD WITH THE CHATTER OF THE sixth, seventh, and eighth grades—the whole Walt Whitman student body. I scanned the audience for Celeste and spotted her a few rows back from the front talking to two of her friends. I had been worried about how she would take being a part of the audience rather than onstage and was pleased to see her as animated and engaged with her friends as ever.

While the last of the students were being settled into their seats, I went backstage to remind the cast that it was perfectly normal to be nervous and to make mistakes. If anyone forgot a line, all he or she would have to do would be to stage-whisper, "Line!" and Jessica, who would be seated in the front row, would give it to them. (I had learned from the previous year's experience not to trust this crucial job to a student!) Siobhan and Fred would also be stationed in either wing of the stage to help kids with last-minute panics or confusions.

After making some introductory remarks to the assembled students and teachers, I took a seat in the audience myself and watched as the heavy ragged-bottomed curtain was pulled open in a series of jerks by Shanequa, to whom I had given the job of stage manager—opening the curtain being her only responsibility. Then I waited for José to walk to the middle of the stage and pull out the folded piece of composition paper from which he would pretend to read Ian Moore's poem.

I waited and waited.

After what seemed like minutes, the stage was still empty and I had heard nothing but Siobhan's exasperated hiss, "José!" some scuffling, and José's half-giggled whisper: "No! No! I can't!" Exchanging horrified glances with Jessica, I leapt from my seat to see what was the matter. I was already halfway to the stage when José shot from behind the curtain as if propelled by a shove. Pausing to give the audience a bemused smirk, he proceeded with complete self-possession to the center of the stage, pulled out the composition paper, and read Ian's poem perfectly.

I knew what was happening: José was signaling to his classmates that he wasn't so uncool as to take this play—which was, after all, a form of schoolwork—completely seriously. The same thing had happened with some of the actors last year when they had performed in front of their peers the week after their wonderful twentieth-anniversary performance. My hope was that, having signaled his coolness, José would now be able to settle in and do the play straight. If he, as the star, continued to pull such tricks, the play would be a fiasco.

One by one, after José had finished with Ian's poem, Julie, Mayra, Keisha, Arlene, and Anna walked from behind the curtains, performing their monologues as well as they ever had in rehearsal. Only Lily spoke her lines too softly to be heard, but she didn't stumble over any of them. I began to breathe easier and sank back into my seat . . .

. . . until Chantell appeared on the stage.

Chantell was performing Ricky Ortiz's monologue about playing Russian roulette. Her performance started out uncharacteristically weak. She gave the impression that she was reading from cue cards at the back of the auditorium rather than speaking from her heart. I was a bit disappointed but not concerned until she spoke the line, "Are you scared to die?" All at once she looked stricken, her eyes flickering as if she were searching for missing cue cards. Then she squeaked, clamped both her hands over her mouth, and ran off the stage. Again I heard Siobhan's voice, but Chantell wouldn't return to the stage. Tunisia walked out but didn't even get through the first sentence of her monologue before she duplicated Chantell's comic embarrassment and ran shrieking into the wings.

Once again Jessica and I exchanged horrified glances, but this time I remained pinned to my seat, paralyzed by the sense that a momentum was building up that I was powerless to affect and that, at any moment, would destroy the play.

The next speaker—thank goodness!—was Xia, who walked onto the stage with all the compelling gravity of a grieving mother, utterly un-fazed by the clowning of the two girls who had preceded her. She was as good as she ever had been. By the end of her monologue, all the play's intrinsic dignity and power had been restored, and Xia had once again proved herself to be as "smart and reliable" as I could ever wish her to be.

The play suffered no other major gaffs. Once Arlene had finished her first monologue as Ian's mother—also giving a very strong perfor-mance—Chantell had sufficiently recovered herself to do a passable Ethel Sinkler, though for some reason she pitched her voice higher than normal and swayed her head and shoulders back and forth as she spoke, as if she were a precocious six-year-old showing off by reciting a series of long memorized speeches.

Tunisia had no speaking parts until the end of the play, when she was the Minister. During the instant after her cue my temples prickled with anxiety, but she stepped forward confidently and eulogized the two murdered boys and their friend in a rich, rousing voice in which the cadences of Martin Luther King were distinctly audible. I was not only relieved but proud of her for having come back so well from her initial embarrassment.

WHEN JOSÉ, AFTER FINISHING HIS FINAL MONOLOGUE, SIGNALED the end of the play by looking up with an expectant grin, whoops, cheers, and applause filled the room, and Jessica and I slumped down in our chairs exhausted, musty with anxious sweat and genuinely grate-ful to the whole cast for having pulled back from the edge of disaster.

Once all the actors had taken their bows and descended from the stage, they were mobbed by their classmates, who praised and teased them in about equal parts. At one point I found myself standing beside Joan Gold, who complimented the play and then said, "It's a shame that a couple of the kids nearly spoiled it right at the beginning."

We talked a bit about how kids this age were always so embarrassed in front of their peers. Then I couldn't resist saying, "Did you notice that it was Xia who saved the day? If she hadn't come out and given such a strong performance, the whole play would have collapsed."

Joan understood my message and looked me straight in the eye: "Steve, I never said that Xia wasn't talented. She's a very bright girl. The problem is her family. They won't take her education seriously. And what am I supposed to do about that?"

This was a reconstruction of her original position, but one that met me halfway by lifting blame from Xia and placing it on her mother. It was meant as a sort of peace offering, which I accepted implicitly. Joan and I parted on good terms, our friendship restored.

As the crowd began to abate, I congratulated each cast member individually on her or his performance, making sure to let Xia and Arlene know that I thought they had saved the play.

As soon as I came near Tunisia, she barked out, "I told you I couldn't do that Cast Member speech!"

"Tunisia, I—"

"I told you I couldn't do it! Didn't I? But you wouldn't listen! I told you I would mess it up! Why didn't you let Shanequa do it?"

"Tunisia—"

"You should have let Shanequa do it!"

"Tunisia, I don't want to talk about that. I want to tell you what a good job you did on the Minister, but you won't even let me give you a compliment."

This remark clearly took Tunisia by surprise. She was silent a long while but then turned her back without saying a word and walked off. When it was time for the cast to head out to a local pizza parlor for a lunchtime cast party, she was nowhere to be found.

As we were getting ready to go I asked Mayra if she would go find Celeste and see if she wanted to come along. Overhearing this request, Siobhan stepped up and said, "I don't think that would be a good idea. I saw her run out of the auditorium in tears during the middle of the performance."

The following day I arrived about lunchtime to gather the cast together for our trip down to the newly established Teachers & Writers Collaborative Center for Imaginative Writing, where we would have an evening performance for the cast members' families and friends, as well as for members of the Collaborative and other guests. I had chosen to have the evening performance outside the school because I thought it would make the play seem more important to the kids—not just a school production but something closer to real theater. The reason I wanted to get the cast downtown so early was that none of them had even seen the center, let alone rehearsed there, and I wanted plenty of time to reblock the play to suit the new space.

I had hardly walked onto the third floor of the school when Arlene came up to me and said, "Tunisia's not coming!"

"What! Why not?"

"I don't know. She just said she's not going to do it."

I was annoyed by this news but not terribly concerned. I figured that Tunisia's never very robust self-esteem simply needed another dose of flattery before she would feel confident enough to go back onstage, especially after what I believed was a mostly voluntary screwup the day before.

As Arlene and I set off down the hall to find her, we met up with Keisha, who told us that Tunisia didn't want to do the play because no one from her family was coming and she wouldn't have anyone to take her home to the Bronx.

As soon as Tunisia saw me at the door of her classroom, she crossed her arms on her chest and said defiantly, "I'm *not* going!"

I gestured for her to come with me. Once we were out in the hall, I asked her why.

"Because I don't want to!"

"You must have a reason."

"I just don't want to. Why you keep asking me that? I just don't want to."

"Is it because no one from your family is coming? If you are worried about getting home, I can drive you myself—"

She cut me off. "No. That's not the problem! I just don't want to!"

At this point my annoyance began to escalate into anger. Tunisia had made me jump through so many hoops to keep her in the play, and I had just about lost all my patience.

"You realize what you are doing?" I asked. She just gazed at me blankly. "You're letting down all of your friends in the cast. You've got one of the most important of the opening monologues. And how're we going to do the play without a minister?"

"Shanequa can do it."

"No she can't. She's never even looked at the part. But that's beside the point. The point is that when you agreed to take the part, you were making a promise to me and to every member of the cast that you wouldn't let us down when it came time to perform. And now you're breaking that promise."

"I don't care. I'm not going."

I left it at that. I was tired of pushing her. When I spoke to Rachel later, she thought I should call Tunisia's father and get him to make her go along, but I wanted Tunisia to live with the consequences of her own decision.

I had only just sent Tunisia back into her classroom when Shanequa and Chantell stepped up to inform me that Shanequa was ready to do both of Tunisia's parts.

This was now very definitely beginning to seem like a plot—and for the second year in a row, no less. But unlike when Yolanda bowed out at the last minute, I didn't see any alternative.

I was all set to tell Shanequa to come along but realized that her parents hadn't signed a permission slip and so, technically, I couldn't take her out of the school. As I began to explain this point she said, "Bing!" and pulled a crumpled but signed permission slip out of her pocket—the one I had given to her on Wednesday when I thought she would have to take Julie's part. I had to call her parents to double-check, but she was in. Once again the play was back from the brink of disaster.

A minute later, however, I thought it had tumbled right over the edge.

The last cast member I had to pick up was José. When I went to get him from his classroom, he shrugged and said, "Sorry, Steve, can't do it."

Aghast, I asked him why not.

"Just can't do it!" He turned up both palms to indicate helplessness. "Family problems."

There was, of course, no Shanequa to take José's place. Not even Xia could learn his huge part in the few hours we had until the performance. And if she could, who would be able to handle her own substantial part?

The collapse of my spirits must have been visible on my face, because José's expression instantly converted from a harried frown to a delighted grin. He took a mock swing at me, said, "Hey, Steve, come on! I was kidding!" He took off down the hall and I ran after him. At the hall door I cornered him, but he ducked under my arm. "I'm not going to kill you now, Figueroa!" I shouted after him. "But as soon as you finish your last line in the play—then you better run!"

•   •   •

THE TEACHERS & WRITERS COLLABORATIVE CENTER FOR Imaginative Writing had opened only the previous year, just in time for the twenty-fifth anniversary celebration. The center itself was a long, elegant, book-lined room, with an open area at one end used for performances. A broad zigzag corridor, opening off the performance area, led to the postmodern/Victorian glass-walled offices of Teachers & Writers' director Nancy Shapiro and the other administrative and publishing staff. Daylight pouring through parallel walls of eight-foot-high windows filled the offices and corridor equally and cast fans of reflected brilliance all across the floor of the performance area.

"Wow!" said Mayra as Jessica and I herded the cast through the front door. "This is beautiful!"

José asked in a hushed voice, "This where we're going to do the play, Steve?"

The kids were all clearly impressed by the center, which made me happy, because it meant that they would be more proud to perform there and probably would take their rehearsal more seriously. Keisha, of course, couldn't resist making a few of her know-it-all remarks: "How we gonna put on a play here? There ain't no stage! I thought we were gonna do this in a theater!" But once we actually got around to rehearsing, she wasn't a problem. She listened, she was reasonable, and she did good work.

The incorrigible one was José. He kept saying his lines in crazy voices and intentionally goofing up scenes. He was, as always, very funny, but every time he messed up or caused someone else to mess up, we had to do the scene over again.

The kids, bored but also increasingly worried that they might make fools of themselves in front of their parents and a room full of strangers, began to get angry at him. Finally I had to give him a public bawling out in a louder and angrier voice than I had ever used in my four years of teaching: "You know what you are, José? You're a prima donna! Do you know what a prima donna is? A prima donna is an actor who doesn't care about his part or about anyone else in the play. He only wants to call attention to himself. He thinks he's a great actor, but he's not, because a real actor knows that he doesn't matter at all, that all that matters is his part and the play, and that he's only good to the degree that he helps make the play a success."

José was livid by the time I had finished talking, but from then on he did what he was supposed to do. And what is more, natural actor that he was, he used his fury to brilliant effect in his performance. During his postrobbery scene with Anna, he contemplated his gun as he talked, sometimes pointing it at his own chest for emphasis, sometimes at Anna. His manner was so authentically sinister that Anna started to laugh and cried out, "Don't do that!"

Jessica and I simultaneously leapt from our chairs to say: "No! Keep it! It's perfect!"

Keisha concurred: "I was getting scared just watching him."

That was the most exhausting rehearsal I had ever endured; it took at least twice as long as I had expected. When at last it was finished, Fred (who had arrived in the middle of the rehearsal) and Jessica took the cast downstairs to Teachers & Writers' vacant former offices to eat pizza, drink soda, and freak out for the hour before show time, while I put up the scenery, arranged the chairs, and helped set up the video equipment that would record the performance.

Periodically I went downstairs, each time finding Jessica and Fred standing in the same dazed helplessness beside the ravaged pizza boxes and drained soda bottles while our thespians hurtled, shrieked, leapt, and pounced on every side of them. Even Xia was red faced, sweaty, and all but inaccessible inside that netherworld of play euphoria—what my mother used to call being overexcited. I had never before quite understood why overexcitement had been such an undesirable condition to my mother, but as I dodged the rocketing children in that loud, sweat-humid room, I began to have strong doubts as to whether letting the kids vent their anxiety through continual frenetic activity had been such a good idea.

The last time I went down, I found José lying on the floor with his head in Jessica's lap and his hands over his face. Anna, it seemed, had hit him in the eye with a tennis ball. When I convinced him to take his hands away, I saw that his eye was perfectly clear although a small disk of skin around it was very faintly flushed. José, of course, was determined to play this injury for everything it was worth: "I'm gonna have a black eye for the play! I can't see! Everything is blurry. No, I mean it! Everything out of this eye is blurry!"

I told him he could lie on the floor for a while if he wanted to. But when I turned to the rest and said that it was time to get into their costumes, José was on his feet in an instant and I never heard another word about his eye.

Jessica, Fred, and I synchronized our watches. I told them to bring the cast up at quarter after seven and I would begin my opening remarks when I saw them in the hallway.

I RETURNED TO THE CENTER FOR IMAGINATIVE WRITING AND found that the seats were filling fast. By seven-fifteen every chair had been taken, and a dense crowd was standing at the back of the room and along the walls on either side.

My remarks were in essence identical to those with which I had introduced *On This Day a Poor Boy Died* almost a year earlier. I talked about the events that had inspired the play, the method of composition, and how long and hard the actors had worked. But when I assured the audience that they were about to witness an impressive job of acting by a talented group of seventh- and eighth-graders, I did so with none of the confidence that I had had the year before. This production had been fraught with too much turmoil; there had been too many setbacks, too many unpleasant surprises. But most of all, I had been humbled in the intervening year.

I had realized that, as successful as the earlier play might have been or as our current play might yet be, the problems that my students had to live with every minute of their lives were larger and more intractable than I had let myself recognize, and that those problems were especially pernicious because they did not remain problems of society or the economy, they did not stay out on the street, nor did they even remain matters of parents' or friends' weakness, cruelty, or fear; instead they ate straight into my students' hearts, wounding their dignity and hope, causing them to treat themselves as the world had treated them and often turning them into their own worst enemies.

As I spoke to the audience of parents, friends, colleagues, and strangers, I remembered the lonely fury in Tunisia's eyes and thought of her dead mother. I remembered Lily stamping the writing room floor in frustration at her inability to remember three sentences, and I thought of her brother, shot through the heart and head. I thought of Julie's father, shot three times in the chest on the eve of his wedding. And of Celeste in her apartment while her mad, drunken mother overturned the furniture and slapped the pictures from the walls. And of Xia taking care of her own drunken mother and being turned away, on her father's birthday, from the prison where he would spend the next twelve years. I thought of the stepfather who had briefly come into Xia's life and who was now also lost to prison. And of José and his cousin huddled over their Halloween candy while masked thieves pointed guns at them and rifled the apartment for drugs. And of Keisha's uncle firing a pistol in the hallway. And of Cornell's father being shot as they climbed the stairs, talking about a new pair of sneakers. And of Cesaré's sister, murdered by her husband. And of my many other students cowering in their beds, afraid of bullets flying through the window or the shouts, bangs, and smacks from the next room. I thought of the drunkenness, brutality, and fear that were so intimate to so many of these children that Keisha could insist that such things were merely normal.

Last year a part of me had believed the Hollywood finish to the Bensonhurst Project. As I had watched the cast members blinking and grinning in a storm of applause, I had allowed myself to imagine that I had helped give them a foundation of inspiration and strength that they might build on for the rest of their lives. At the start of this year, when Rachel told me about the Bensonhurst cast's rising grades, popularity, and aspirations, I had allowed myself to believe that this was confirmation that these young lives were indeed on an upward course. I didn't have grand fantasies. Maybe, for a moment or two, I had imagined a thank you at an Oscar ceremony. But mostly I had just hoped for a steady accretion of confidence that would help to build lives of ordinary decency and happiness. Never had I imagined that Ricky and Celeste would remain so convinced of their own mediocrity that they would not dare even attend the LaGuardia auditions. Never had I imagined that Xia, in innocence or self-deception, would simply turn her back on her best chance for the future. Never had I expected to see so many doors slam so soon on these talented young actors.

Celeste, overwhelmed by the chaos and brutality of her life, had become lost to me. Ricky, too, had moved out of my orbit, and I had no idea where he was headed. Xia, remarkably, remained steadfast, even when all the people who ought to have been her strongest supports were crumbling in the face of huge problems and their own inadequacy or were simply being taken away. As I addressed the audience of *Will*

My Name Be Shouted Out? I thought about how Xia's had been the most stunning success last year. And about how tonight, perhaps, she would have another triumph. But also, I wondered: How long could Xia endure the enormous forces that seemed arrayed against her? How many times could she lose the things she hoped for and needed most before she succumbed to the same despair as had taken Celeste?

As I spoke that night, I had no doubt of the talent of the actors waiting just outside the door or of the quality of the play they had helped to write, nor even did I question the validity of the work that Jessica, Fred, Erin, Siobhan, Daniel, Matt, Elizabeth, Jenifer, and I had done over the last two years. But I had acquired some of my students' sense of futility and fear. And I did share some of their belief that nothing could be counted on and that anything could go disastrously wrong at any minute.

I CONCLUDED MY TALK WITH A PREARRANGED CUE: "AND NOW I give you *Will My Name Be Shouted Out?*" I saw José hesitate in the doorway and Jessica lean over to whisper in his ear. I took my seat beside Siobhan—who was the prompter for this performance—glanced at her, and lifted my gaze pleadingly toward heaven. She gave me an anxious smile and we both turned our eyes forward as José moved through the audience to the performance area and began to unfold his piece of composition paper.

THE ASSERTION WITH WHICH I HAD COMFORTED MYSELF throughout the last weeks was now soundly substantiated: the kids didn't merely pull through, they surpassed themselves—just as had the previous year's cast.

José was wonderful—full of spunkiness and mischief but also solemn realism—especially when he was talking to the other characters. Keisha and Anna were both thoroughly convincing boys. Keisha's Tyrone was muted yet charismatic, sinister yet tragically helpless. Anna's Khalil was full of bluster and vulnerability, very much a street kid, if not remotely black. Arlene, whose performance had been so strong the day before, unaccountably kept forgetting lines in the middle of her monologues—though she never dropped out of character as she whispered, "Line," to

Siobhan—and in the end delivered a fine, moving performance. (Afterward I heard that she had been upset because her divorced parents, who were in the midst of a custody battle, were both in the audience.) Shanequa occasionally appeared to have to search for her lines but managed to turn her pauses into a credible mannerism of her characters—one that was particularly effective when she was the Minister. But it was Xia who, true to form, delivered the strongest performance of the evening. Her Alexandra was as full of compelling gravity as she had been the previous morning and became the tough, grieving soul of the play. When she pleaded with the Lord to "take" her troubled son, Khalil, the audience was so utterly quiet that her every intake of breath could be heard at the back of the room.

I recognized the cast's new seriousness almost as soon as they made their entrances, and thus was able to relax right away into the magic of their performances, and to rediscover the play's authenticity and drive, which I had all but lost track of, especially during the last couple of weeks of rehearsals. If anything, I felt the play was stronger and more moving than *On This Day a Poor Boy Died* (Matt Sharpe, who was in the audience, told me afterward that he had felt the same way). But it was the cast I was most impressed by—and proud of. With all of our frustrations and setbacks, they really had worked very hard, and in the end, by anyone's definition, they really had succeeded—and what is more, they knew it themselves.

My wife, who happened to be in the hallway comforting our daughter at the time, told me that when Hernan exited the performance area after completing his final monologue, he clenched his fists, did a little dance, and exclaimed, "Yes! I did it!" My wife also said that every cast member who followed him made similar expressions of exaltation and relief: gasping, jumping up and down, patting one another on the back, hugging. When I called the cast back onto the stage, as the room rang with applause, Keisha bowed, then thrust both fists up over her head Rocky-style; Chantell and Arlene kept doing embarrassed half curtsies; and all the cast wore delirious, cheek-bursting grins.

Even after the applause had died down and the audience had been invited to have refreshments in an adjoining room, the actors still couldn't leave the stage. They kept getting together and spontaneously reperforming their favorite scenes for friends and relatives who had come late, and just for the joy of reliving the performance. The robbery scene, in particular, must have been done four or five times.

Eventually the play yielded to another form of narrative art, as all the cast members and at least a dozen of their siblings, cousins, and friends, as well as my own son, Simon, sat in a circle and listened to Keisha's older brother tell ghost stories. Whenever Keisha's brother would come to a particularly scary part of a story, José would put his hands over his ears and call out, "Oh no! I can't stand it! Please don't tell anymore!" When José's hands weren't over his ears, one of them was stretched across the shoulders of Xia, who was sharing the same large easy chair with him, and the other was stroking the back of her hand, which rested on his thigh.

XIA AND JOSÉ WERE THE ONLY CAST MEMBERS WHO HAD HAD NO family or friends come to the performance. Xia's mother had explained to me on the telephone that she had intended to come, that she had even invited Xia's uncles and aunts to come with her—I could hear them chatting and laughing in the background—but that, as she put it, "I don't read too good, so I didn't know where to go." Xia's mother would have had to be a very bad reader indeed not to be able to make sense of the flyer with the T&W address and subway instructions that I had given to all the cast members to take home. And even if she couldn't read the flyer, why couldn't one of the aunts or uncles, who sounded like they were having such a wonderful time in the apartment, have read it for her? I was very annoyed with all of them but contented myself with telling Xia's mother that she should be proud of her daughter.

"Oh, I know," she said. "She's such a good, smart kid. I don't know where she gets it."

I drove Xia and José home with my family. Xia sat in José's lap in the backseat next to my children, Simon and Emma. Throughout the long drive, the kids—all except for Emma, who instantly fell asleep in her car seat—traded ghost stories and jokes. Simon was only eight, and though not at all a bad storyteller, he simply wasn't up to the level of his thirteen-year-old companions. But Xia and José listened to his stories, laughed at them, and never showed the least impatience. On his part, he listened with rapt attention to everything they said, clearly loving being admitted, at least temporarily, into the world of authentic teenagers. There was a lot of good feeling in that car, and it made me very happy.

In a way, that car ride was the fulfillment of some of the deepest desires that I had nourished during all my years of teaching. For the forty-five minutes that Xia and José were in my car with my family, it was almost possible for me to feel that they had become my children, that all the limits of class, race, history, and experience that separated us so unjustly had been melted into nothing by simple domestic affection.

Conclusion:
Changing the World

1

I ALWAYS COME CLOSE TO TEARS AT WALT WHITMAN GRADUATIONS. Half the time I feel ridiculous, for these ceremonies are nothing if not huge, maudlin clichés—an ordeal to participants and audience alike. But I also know that the graduations mark a deeply significant passage in the lives of my young students, that they are something like secular bar and bat mitzvahs. At the end of junior high these thirteen- and fourteen-year-olds, while perhaps not yet truly men and women, are nevertheless going out into a world full of adult-sized problems that, for the most part, they will have to deal with on their own.

I watch my students in their shiny blue-and-white gowns, with their mortarboards stuck like thumbtacks on top of their new hairdos, and I can't help but wonder: How many of them will be dead in ten years? How many will be broken down by drugs, by brutal marriages? Which of them will I meet on the sidewalk in stinking clothes, barefoot, palm extended? Whose picture will I see in the paper over a horror story about a child thrown out a window, a rape on a rooftop, a revenge killing in a social club?

I also wonder, of course, which of them will find happiness, love, a job that pays the bills without destroying the spirit. Half of them? Three-quarters? One-quarter? I really have no idea—which, I suppose, is part of the reason why their fate seems so insecure to me. But whatever the actual statistic, the odds against *all* of these very young men and women are much too high. For some of them they are overwhelming.

Everyone who speaks at these occasions feels the way I do. We are all afraid to let these children go. We are all afraid of the world they have grown up into. Rachel Suarez always makes the most beautiful speeches. She acknowledges everything that is dangerous and wrong in this world by speaking about what is good and beautiful. She helps the graduates see the best parts in themselves. She tells them that they will make mistakes in life but that she hopes those mistakes will always be on the side of compassion and enthusiasm and never on the side of anger or indifference. I am moved by her speeches because I know, as she does, that there is a degree of futility to her own compassion and enthusiasm for these students. But at the same time I believe that her dauntless emotional generosity, year after year, is heroic, beautiful, and just exactly what these kids and the world need so much more of.

I began this book by speaking about limits. Another reason why I am so moved at these ceremonies is that they bring home what is perhaps the most profound limit of all. I respond to so many of my students as if they were my own children. But of course they are not. Our relationship is temporary and superficial by definition. A momentary transcendence of the limits of our roles as teacher and students may be moving and influential on both sides (and paradoxically may embody the highest ideal of the relationship), but it must remain momentary. My students have to go on with the rest of their lives, and I have to go on to the next batch of inspiring, infuriating, and always terribly needy kids.

After Xia, Celeste, Ricky, Mayra, Isaac, Shanequa, José, Keisha, Chantell, and Tunisia had received their diplomas and filed out of the auditorium, I sought them each out in the deafening, hot, densely crowded cafeteria across from the auditorium—the very room where most of them had performed in *On This Day a Poor Boy Died*. This was probably the last time I would see any of them. I wanted somehow to make my good-bye an acknowledgment of the whole of our relationship—an impulse that probably would have been impossible to fulfill even under the most ideal of circumstances, but certainly not in the thick of sixty-six shouting, shoving, hugging, laughing, weeping new graduates and their families. "Congratulations . . . Good luck . . . Bye" was all I got to say to any of them.

José said, "Hey, Steve! Guess what? I'm gonna be in a movie. These casting people came here just after we finished the play. I tried out and I got the part!"

"Fabulous!" I said, patting him on the back, but he was swept away by a crowd of friends before I could get any more details.

Celeste gave me a long hug, and in the next second she gave the exact same hug to someone else.

I could tell that my students were touched that I had come to the graduation. But for that moment in the cafeteria at least, it was their friendships with one another that they cared about. Those were the relationships that had had the most profound effects on them. Those were the relationships that might really last or be most sorely missed. My presence was appreciated, but when it came down to the really serious business of the moment, I was little more than an interloper.

THE FOLLOWING YEAR—1993–94—WAS NO LESS EXCITING AND disturbing than the two I have described. Once again Daniel and I helped the Drama Club put on some plays. Once again the chief obstacles we had to overcome were the deep anger, insecurities, and troubled home lives of our actors. Once again there were dramatic fights at school and students who chose to use their writing folders as confessionals. Once again my seventh and eighth grades wrote a play that contained much writing that was brilliant and moving and much that was deeply depressing.

This last fact was especially troubling because that year I had attempted to follow through on the advice of Beth Rogovin, the library coordinator, by having my students write a play that I hoped would help them find "a way out" of their despair.

The idea was to imagine that the next Malcolm X (that is, the next leader of "the people") was a sixteen-year-old living somewhere in New York City, and then to tell the story of the crisis that transformed him from an ordinary teenager into a potential leader. My students had no trouble writing about the crisis—his girlfriend gets pregnant and he is shot by some "gangbangers"—but despite frequent discussions of the ways his personal problems were connected to larger social conditions, almost no students wrote about the moment when he recognized that connection or about his decision to help other people like himself.

One reason for the neglect of such transformative moments was, of course, that they were simply not as exciting as guns and sex. But another, far more distressing reason was that, for so many students, a decision to try to make the world better was just naive foolishness. As Arlene Salter put it:

> The worst problems right now are drugs & murder. We take it all so easily nowadays. Like it's an every day thing—which it is. this is a problem that cannot be solved (I don't think) by our generation. We are so violent that I don't think we have much hope. I think we will destroy ourselves if it goes on. People will end up hating each other. No love just hate. We have so many guns, drugs, knives, murders, rapes, hatred, crime, and this is not even the half of it . . . It is like we're in a tunnel of violence and we set off a bomb that blocked the only entrance out.

2

THE MOST IMPORTANT THING TO REMEMBER ABOUT THE experiences recounted in this book is that they are nothing special. They will be repeated in their general outline and even in many of their particulars again and again, not only in my career but in the careers of countless teachers all over this country. Every public school, especially those in working-class or poor districts, has its Celestes, Yvettes, Xias, and Rickys. All across the nation there are millions of students unable to concentrate because they are haunted by memories of brutality inflicted on them, on family members, or on friends. There are millions who worry about their jobless, drunken, or drug-addicted parents, or simply about the dangerous walk home. There are millions of children who come to school every day with swollen limbs, aching stomachs, or improper dosages of seizure medicine because their parents have poor health insurance or none at all. Every school in America is filled with students who are frustrated, afraid, furious, or just confused. Some of them boo their classmates at awards assemblies; some of them get into fights on the playground, pull knives on teachers, take drugs, or just put their heads down on the desk. Whatever they do, they damage both their own education and that of their classmates.

The inspiration for Teachers & Writers Collaborative came during a series of federally sponsored meetings in the mid-1960s about the "crisis in education." Despite countless other meetings since that time, despite the founding of scores of institutions and the publication of libraries of books all aimed at ending this crisis, it is still with us today and still feels as new and as desperate as ever. Somehow we haven't gone far enough or in the right direction in our quest to give American students the education and future they deserve.

For most of the past decade and a half, the federal government has primarily chosen to treat the crisis in education as if it were a simple matter of inadequate standards and Kafkaesque bureaucracy. This is safe politics. Nobody can deny that less red tape and more stringent and precise standards would help students and teachers alike. And in this necessarily budget-conscious era, targeting such problems has the additional advantage of having a low price tag; in theory, at least, cutting red tape should even save money.

What is wrong with such federal initiatives is that they completely fail to address the most severe problems in our schools. As frustrating as red tape may be and as much as standards may vary from locality to locality, it is not as if there are no teachers in American classrooms or as if those teachers don't know what they want their students to learn. If you ask any teacher—again, especially but not exclusively in working-class or poor school districts—what single factor most inhibits her from accomplishing her ideal educational goals, she will tell you that it is the relentless intrusion into the classroom of the social problems that the students suffer both out on the streets and in their own homes.

The simple truth is that the crisis in education is not taking place only, or even primarily, in the schools. It is also the AIDS crisis, the crisis of homelessness. It is child abuse, racial and ethnic animosity. It is the terrible inadequacy, especially for low-wage earners, of health insurance and child care. It is the drug trade, which rots the souls not only of individual addicts but of whole neighborhoods and which loads street corners with armed thugs who inspire terror in some children and awed respect in others. It is the ever wider proliferation of ever more lethal weapons. And perhaps more than anything else it is the 20 percent decline in the real value of the average American's salary since 1972, a decline that has been especially precipitous in our inner cities, where high-paying factory jobs have been replaced by low-paying and often part-time service sector work.

The public schools, along with the hospitals, are the main areas where middle-class Americans come into contact with the squalor and the pain endured by so many of their fellow citizens. These institutions are, in effect, messengers bearing grim tidings of the nation's economic health and of the consequences of social policy, tidings that, for the most part, the middle class has responded to by fleeing to the segregated safety of private schools and the suburbs. Lately, however, the response of choice, especially among politicians, has simply been to try to murder the messenger.

This past school year—1994–95—P.S. 227/Walt Whitman Academy's budget was slashed for the fourth year in a row. One result was that the school had only enough money to pay Teachers & Writers Collaborative for a forty-two day residency—a cut of nearly two thirds from the 1989–90 school year. The cut would have been far more substantial if not for the strong support of the school's administration and parents. Fran Kaplan and Rachel Suarez staged a sit-down strike in the Board of Education's district office, forcing the arts programs coordinator to give the school three-quarters of the money allocated for the twenty-one schools in the district. And the Parents' Association managed to raise additional money by setting up a lunchtime candy stand—compromising their children's teeth and waistlines so that T&W could be at the school seven days longer and stage another Drama Club production. But what will happen next year? If the budget cuts proposed by the federal and New York's city and state governments are enacted, all of the district's arts money may be gone, and no sit-down strike of any duration will be able to get it back.

Teachers & Writers itself may not survive. The Collaborative gets a large portion of its funding from the all-but-doomed National Endowment for the Arts, as well as from the endangered New York State Council for the Arts. If these organizations fold and the more than sixty schools—including P.S. 227/Walt Whitman—served by Teachers and Writers don't have enough money to pay for writer residencies, it is hard to imagine how T&W will be able to continue to operate.

Writer-in-the-schools programs are, of course, far from the most important initiatives being sacrificed. The funding of the Chapter One program, the main federal effort to enhance the education of economically disadvantaged children, was reduced by the Clinton administration in 1994. The Republican-controlled Congress has been moving to cut funds for special education programs that help physically, emotionally, and intellectually handicapped children, as well as funds for school lunch programs and for providing guidance counselors and social workers. And then, of course, huge cuts are also being proposed for programs outside of school: Aid to Families with Dependent Children, food stamps, Medicaid, Head Start, and—just at the point when all these other cuts guarantee a flood of children whose parents won't be able to take care of them—foster care and adoption programs.

3

LOOKING OUT ON THIS NATION'S PRESENT POLITICAL CLIMATE from the vantage point of the Walt Whitman Academy, it seems to me that one important reason for the present draconian shift in tax and social spending policies is that not enough people are practicing the skills I tried to teach my students, the skills of a good novelist or playwright.

I began teaching fiction and playwriting to my students at Walt Whitman Academy because I wanted them to have fun while learning to write. I also thought that by asking them to imagine the needs and viewpoints of other people and encouraging them to look beyond stereotypes, I would provide my students with skills that would be useful to them in every aspect of their private lives, from their business negotiations to their marriages. And finally, in a school where so many students seemed only to respect the Virtues of Strength, I thought that learning to understand what it would be like to be other people would, quite naturally, encourage the exercise of the Virtues of Compassion, in particular sympathy, solidarity, and tolerance.

In so much of public discussion today, there is a complete failure to look beyond the stereotypes of poverty and see the poor as human beings, who for all of their particular pain and neediness, are more like every other American than different. When the poor are mentioned in public debate, they are almost never real people—never, as I would say to my students, "fully developed characters"—but only the clichéd embodiments of prominent social problems: teenage moms, welfare cheats, muggers, crackheads, failures.

When the poor are not allowed to be real people, when they are defined only by the problems from which they suffer, it becomes all too easy to forget that these problems are not *"natural"* to them, that poor people don't *like* living in homes with busted locks and broken elevators, where bullets fly through the windows and rats scuttle across the kitchen

378 • Will My Name Be Shouted Out?

floor; that poor parents don't want to beat their children or see them grow up to become drug addicts, prostitutes, or thieves, or get gunned down on the sidewalk; that, if anything, the poor hate the ghetto more than the middle class and would never voluntarily stay there in order to receive the average national welfare payment of a mere $298 a month. The stereotypes of poverty also make it hard to remember that there are millions of people living in ghettos who are passionate believers in "family values" and "the work ethic," who hold down two and three jobs to keep their families off welfare and give their children a shot at college. Many of these people do manage to scramble up the steep slope into the middle class, but all too often they lose their footing along the way because they or their spouses get laid off by a "downsizing" corporation or develop serious illness for which they are not adequately insured, or suffer any of the dozens of other calamities that people with slender financial means are prey to in this country.

There is no question that the poor are far more vulnerable than more affluent Americans, but perhaps the most important fact that the stereotypes of poverty obscure is the degree to which the middle class and the poor suffer from the same problems. The economic forces that throw so many members of the middle class into cold sweats over geometrically expanding credit card bills or that have caused a whole generation of baby-boomers to blame themselves for not being able to achieve the economic security of their parents are the very same ones that mean that an unemployed steelworker and his family have to spend their nights sleeping in their car, or that a single mother with two kids and two years of college has no choice but to take a minimum-wage job at a fast food joint.

Our national failure to practice the skills of a good novelist or playwright not only denies the poor their humanity and drives wedges between people who have so much in common but also inspires social policy that will not work. It means that people fail to see that the poor don't need any additional incentive to escape their besieged neighborhoods and lives. It means that people don't see the absurdity of forcing women on welfare to work without providing them with safe, dependable child care they can afford. It means not understanding the basic decency of a mother who chooses to stay on public assistance rather than take a low-paying job and lose Medicaid coverage for her children. It means not understanding that most teenaged mothers don't have children because they are impulsive or irresponsible—or because they want to trade the agony of birth and the sacrifices of motherhood for a below-subsistence wage from the government—but because, like Yvette Santoro and Denise Sandoval, as many as two-thirds of them have been brutalized, abused, or abandoned by their mothers and fathers (often they have also been raped), and they are looking for love—for the one thing they can imagine having in their lives that might be pure and satisfying and good.

In the long run, however, the gravest danger of not exercising the skills of a novelist or playwright is that it makes it so hard for us to exercise the Virtues of Compassion. We are living at a very troubled moment in history—a time when most people outside of an ever smaller and ever richer elite are suffering economically; a time when social and technological change has proceeded more rapidly than many of us have been prepared for; a time of much confusion, much anxiety, and much anger. It is natural, in such an era, that many people should become enamored of the Virtues of Strength; that they should put their faith in strong leaders, tough policies, and tough love; and even that they should become fearful of weakness, whether it be the weakness of a bleeding heart or of that segment of society that suffers most from the problems that affect us all.

There is no question that our nation has many difficult decisions to make—decisions thrust upon it by economic circumstance and the shortsightedness of past leaders. But as we make those decisions, we cannot let our admiration for strength lead us to abandon the Virtues of Compassion. If we cut off a whole class of people from our sympathy or allow ourselves to take from the weak only because they are powerless to stop us, we will not end the crisis in the schools or make our streets safer; we will not breed healthier, happier children or more competent workers. What we will find instead is that the problems we might have contained will have grown to dreadful proportions, that we will have built a world where the strong might find prosperity and security but where the vast majority are condemned to live with the violence, fear, cynicism, and despair that my students are struggling so desperately to escape.

4

I RECEIVED TWO GREAT SHOCKS WHEN I FIRST BEGAN TO WORK in New York City's public schools. The first was the discovery of how little I knew about the lives of people I passed every day on the street. The second was the discovery of how little I knew about literature and writing.

The morning I arrived at P.S. 313 I was nervous about how well I would handle the students, but I was certain that I knew my subject and why I should teach it to fourth-, fifth-, and sixth-graders. Within five minutes of stepping in front of my first class, however, that certainty vanished. I couldn't think of a single thing that literature and writing—at least as I understood them—had to offer these frenzied, frightened, and sad children who had so many other much more pressing needs. I felt like a charlatan and a parasite.

I can't say that I have ever fully recovered from the shock of what I learned about my fellow New Yorkers, since it hits me anew every time I hear that a student has suffered from or witnessed some act of terrible cruelty. But I have learned to live with the shock and to do what I can for my students in my lessons and in our personal relationships. I have also learned to live with the limits of what I can do.

It has proven easier to get over the shocking irrelevance of literature in part because I saw almost immediately that, even if my students needed many things far more than they needed to write haiku or nonsense poems, they could still have fun in my class and be proud of what they had written. Nevertheless, it wasn't until I started the Bensonhurst Project that I was finally rid of the suspicion that there were better ways for my students and I to use our time.

The reason the Bensonhurst and Thomas Jefferson projects were so successful is that they allowed writing to do what I had always thought it should: help my students gain a deeper understanding of some of the most dangerous and troubling things in their lives so that they might be better able to rise above them. This would never have happened had I not rejected the standard writer-in-the-schools curriculum's emphasis on form over content—on the way writing works rather than on what it actually says. But that does not mean that I ever abandoned the standard curriculum. On the contrary, the success of the Bensonhurst and Thomas Jefferson projects only made many of the classic Teachers & Writers assignments more appealing to my students and to me.

It was a great relief, after a week or a month of contemplating bitter truths, to write a set of impossible instructions or a poem in which every line began with the word "underneath." And however much I may have believed that writing's most important purpose was to help my students build a better life, that process had to include taking time out to be dazzled by beauty and have a bit of fun. My work with the plays also made me much less hesitant about discussing personal or controversial issues that came up in student writing. In the past, out of discretion or fear of opening Pandora's box, I often glossed over moving or troubling passages in the students' work merely by saying "Isn't that beautiful?" But now, when appropriate, I often seize the difficult issues at the heart of such passages as an opportunity to gain the class's interest and to show how writing can unlock the world's secrets. I want my students to understand that writing is enriched by what it gives us from life, and that life is enriched by what is given to it by writing.

In the end, however, the main reason the Bensonhurst and Thomas Jefferson projects increased my respect for the standard curriculum is that they made me feel better about all types of literary activity. The most important lesson I learned helping my students write and perform those two plays was that literature is something much bigger than I had ever imagined, that it is not only the best writing or even only writing at all, that it is not only about life but is, itself, a part of life.

My students wrote. They listened to me read poems, stories, and excerpts from plays. They read aloud and listened to their own writing and the writing of their friends. They were saddened by the writing. They laughed at it. They were surprised. They talked about how and why it was moving, true, funny, scary, beautiful. They talked about the issues raised in the writing: about whether it was right to kill for self-protection, about whether it was practical to turn the other cheek, about how people lie to themselves and can be cruel to the ones they love. My students thought about what they read and what they wrote. I know because I saw it in their writing. Sometimes they thought *as* they wrote. Sometimes they enjoyed their writing and sometimes they hated it. They were taken by inspiration. They got writer's block. They worried that they were no good. They triumphed. They saw that they had done poorly, that they were telling lies, that they were plagiarizing. They did things they never thought they could do. They created works of art by working together. They made friends and enemies, had crushes, made fools of themselves, and earned one another's respect. When my student actors gave a play to their audiences, they were given back applause. They saw that adults were impressed by them, proud of them, angry at them. Their friends, too, were impressed, or envious, or indifferent—for indifference is also a part of the process. All of my students, the actors and the writers, gained memories that they will have for the rest of their lives. I did too.

This is literature—not just the reading and the writing, but the thinking, feeling, living, and remembering. This is how literature "matters" most, how it can shape individual lives and even change the world.

5

SHORTLY AFTER I FINISHED THE FIRST DRAFT OF THIS BOOK, THE movie in which José Figueroa had a starring role was released commercially. It was a serious film about drugs and violence in New York City but aimed to please popular audiences. For the most part it got respectful and positive reviews, some of which specifically praised José, who played the best friend of the main character.

The hairs on my arms stood up when I saw José on the screen. He was so present, so much the way he had been when we worked on the Thomas Jefferson play—the film was shot only weeks after his graduation. I could tell right away why he had been picked by the casting director. He was a natural. The character he played was not as intelligent as José, both more and less articulate, but so full of the same gruff pluck and wacky wile that I felt almost as if I had magically been granted a little extra time with him, as if the movie were a seance—which was one of the reasons why it was so horrible to watch his character get killed. I didn't see it, in fact. I had to cover my eyes.

As I left the theater, I felt proud. José had really been good up there on the screen. The first time he appeared the audience laughed at his goofy smirk—the same one he wore that day when he had to be shoved out onto the stage by Shanequa. In the lobby I heard people talking about his lines, saying, "I really liked it when that little kid said, 'I bust some dope moves.' He was funny!"

During the movie I had seen how José had been helped by professional direction. Only once had I caught him simply reciting his lines, as he had all too often for me. But it wasn't only the direction. José had genuine talent and charisma. I had seen it that day he auditioned for me, and I saw it again on the screen. He was an artist. And as depressing as that movie may have been, I walked out of the theater elated, as I always am when I experience true art.